HISTORICAL RECORDS

OF THE

24TH REGIMENT.

PRINTED AT THE
"BREMNER" PRINTING WORKS,
DEVONPORT.

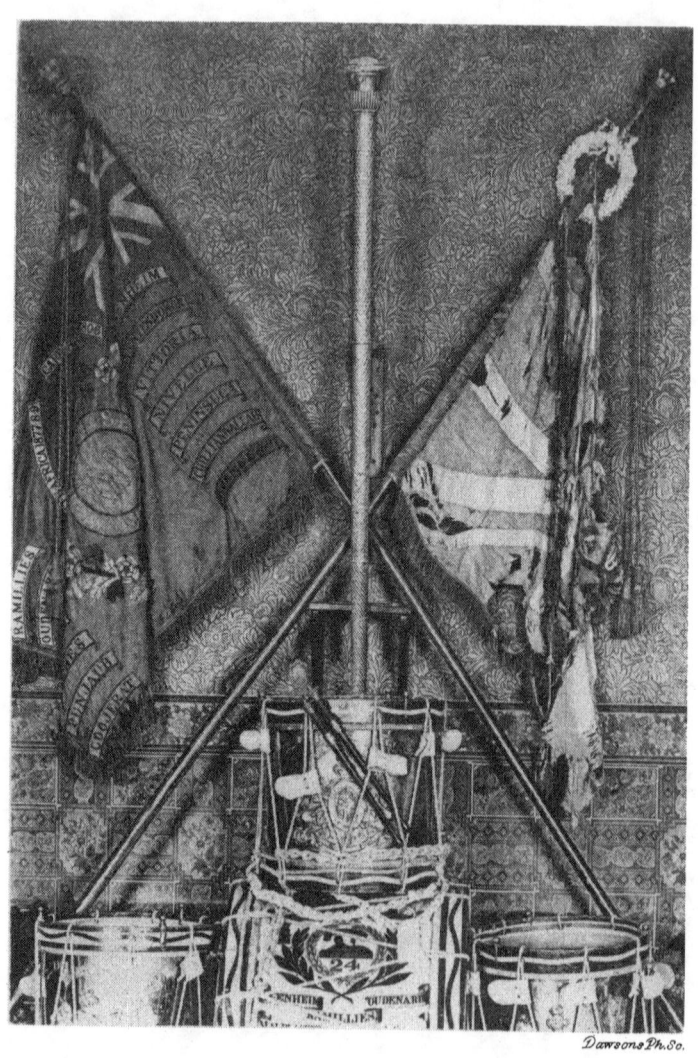

Colours presented to the 1st Batt. 24th Regiment in June 1866, and still carried by the Battalion.

HISTORICAL RECORDS

OF THE

24TH REGIMENT,

FROM ITS FORMATION, IN 1689.

Edited by

COLONEL GEORGE PATON, late Commanding 24th R.D.
COLONEL FARQUHAR GLENNIE, late Commanding 1/24th Regt.
COLONEL WILLIAM PENN SYMONS, Commanding 2/24th Regt.
LIEUT.-COLONEL H. B. MOFFAT, *Hon. Sec.*

The Naval & Military Press Ltd

Published by

The Naval & Military Press Ltd
Unit 10 Ridgewood Industrial Park,
Uckfield, East Sussex,
TN22 5QE England

Tel: +44 (0) 1825 749494
Fax: +44 (0) 1825 765701

www.naval-military-press.com
www.military-genealogy.com
www.militarymaproom.com

In reprinting in facsimile from the original, any imperfections are inevitably reproduced and the quality may fall short of modern type and cartographic standards.

PREFACE.

IN compliance with the wishes of the Officers serving in the Regiment, and of many of those who have left it, that the Historical Records of the Regiment should be published, Colonel G. Paton, Colonel F. Glennie, and Colonel W. P. Symons have undertaken to edit the work.

The Records now published have been compiled from the Orderly Room Books of the 1st and 2nd Battalions and Depôt; from Colonel Symons' MS. Historical Account of the Regiment (which includes the results of researches in the Public Record Offices in London and Dublin, at the British Museum and the United Service Institution), and from information kindly supplied by ex-Officers of the Regiment, whom the Editing Committee take this opportunity of thanking for their very interesting communications.

The Editing Committee are much indebted to Mr. H. Manners Chichester for his invaluable assistance in the compilation of the work. His labours, and those of Colonel Symons, have been rendered the more arduous by the loss of the Official Records in 1810, when they were thrown overboard during an action with French men-of-war.

The services of officers who have served in recent years have mainly been taken from *Hart's Army List*, and from the *Official Army List*.

The Editing Committee are much indebted to Mr. S. M. Milne, of Calverley House, Leeds, for the interesting chapter he has supplied on the Badges, Equipment, &c., of the Regiment, and for his kind assistance in various ways, especially in the preparation of the Illustrations of Costumes.

The Publisher of the book is Mr. A. H. Swiss, of Devonport, whose experience of Regimental Record work and painstaking interest in the success of the same, justify the hope that the book has been brought out in a form likely to please its readers.

GEORGE PATON, *Colonel.*
FARQUHAR GLENNIE, *Colonel.*
WILLIAM PENN SYMONS, *Colonel.*

October, 1892.

CONTENTS.

Year.		Page.
	CHAPTER I.	
1689-1702.	Raising of the Regiment	1
	Early Services	4
	Death of King William III.	17
	CHAPTER II.	
1702-1714.	Marlborough appointed Colonel	18
	The War of the Spanish succession—	
	Blenheim	21
	Ramillies	35
	Oudenarde	38
	Malplaquet	41
	Accession of the House of Brunswick	48
	CHAPTER III.	
1714-1750.	Ireland	49
	Vigo	52
	Carthagena	54
	Scotland	58
	CHAPTER IV.	
1751-1782.	Royal Clothing Warrant	62
	Defence of Minorca	63
	A second battalion formed, which becomes the 69th Foot	66
	Germany	67
	America	70

CONTENTS.

Year.		Page.

CHAPTER V.

1782-1800.	County title bestowed	75
	Home	76
	Canada and Nova Scotia	77
	Egypt	80
	Badge	83

CHAPTER VI.

1802-1824	Renewal of the War—the regiment formed in two battalions	85
	Services of the First Battalion	87
	Cape of Good Hope—Mozambique	90
	India	94

CHAPTER VII.

1804-1814.	The Royal Army of Reserve	99
	The regiment forms a second battalion	100
	Services in the Peninsula	102
	The battalion disbanded	132

CHAPTER VIII.

1824-1848.	At home—Peninsular honours	135
	Canada	137
	India—Limited Enlistment Act	148

CHAPTER IX.

1848 1850.	Punjaub campaign	149
	Chillianwallah	152
	Roll of the dead	164
	Goojerat	165
	Additional notes	166

CHAPTER X.

1850-1861.	Punjaub honours	171
	The Indian mutiny	174
	Another second battalion added	181
	Home	184

CONTENTS.

Year.		Page.
	CHAPTER XI.	
1858 1874.	Services of the First Battalion, 1862-1874	185
	Services of the Second Battalion, 1858-1874	190
	CHAPTER XII.	
1875-1878.	Services of the First Battalion : Griqualand	195
	Kaffir war of 1877-1878	197
	Proceeds to Natal	207
	Services of the Second Battalion	208
	Kaffir war of 1878	209
	Proceeds to Natal	219
	Services of the Mounted Infantry of the regiment	220
	CHAPTER XIII.	
1878-1879.	Services of the First and Second Battalions in the Zulu war	223
	Isandhlwana	229
	Rorke's Drift	245
	Roll of the killed	257
	Re-formation of the First Battalion, and services of both battalions to the end of the war	263
	CHAPTER XIV.	
1879-1881.	The Story of the Colours—Lieutenants Melvill and Coghill	268
	Services of both battalions to 1881	274
	CHAPTER XV.	
1881-1892.	The regiment named the South Wales Borderers— Services of the First Battalion	276
	Services of the Second Battalion	280
	CHAPTER XVI.	
1742-1873.	Notes on the Costume and Equipments, contributed by S. M. MILNE, Esq.	284

ILLUSTRATIONS.

The Photogravures are produced by the Typographic Etching Company. Those of the Colours and the two first Colonels of the Regiment are from photographs taken by Messrs. Wyrall, of Aldershot. Permission was kindly given to photograph the portraits of Sir Edward Dering and Colonel Daniel Dering, in the gallery at Surrenden.

The Coloured Plates and Woodcuts of Costumes are all from reliable sources, and every care has been taken to copy faithfully the work of the original artists.

FULL PAGE ILLUSTRATIONS.

	ARTIST.	
Colours presented to the First Battalion 24th Regiment in June, 1866	From a Photograph	Frontispiece.
Sir Edward Dering, 3rd Baronet of Surrenden, first Colonel of the 24th Regiment, 1689	After an Oil Painting	To face p. 2
Colonel Daniel Dering, 1691	After an Oil Painting	,, 6
John Churchill, Duke of Marlborough, Colonel of the 24th Regiment, 1702-1704	From an Engraving	,, 18
Grenadier, 1751	David Morier	
Officer, 1792	E. Dayes	
Officer, 1814	From Contemporary Evidences	
Private, 1840	From Contemporary Evidences	

ILLUSTRATIONS.

	ARTIST.	
Officer, 1850	From Contemporary Evidences	
Private, 1879	R. Simkin	
Major Gonville Bromhead, V.C.	From a Photograph	To face p. 250

ILLUSTRATIONS IN TEXT.

Regimental Seal	page	75
Chako Plate, 1856-68	,,	171
Chako Plate, 1868-80	,,	185
Glengarry Cap Badge, First Battalion, 1871-82	,,	195
Helmet Plate, 1879-81	,,	268
Wreath presented by Her Majesty The Queen, 1880	,,	270
Regimental Button	,,	275
Private, 1742	,,	284
Grenadier, 1768	,,	286
Officer, 1808	,,	290
Officer (Levee Dress), 1828	,,	296

Private, 1751.
(Grenadier Company.)

Officer. 1792.

Officer, 1814.

Private, 1840.

Officer, 1850.

Private. 1879.

APPENDIX.

A

	Page.
Victoria Cross Roll and services of the recipients	303
Note on Medals for Distinguished Service	307

B

a Biographical notices:
    (i) Officers - - - - - - - - 308
    (ii) Warrant officers - - - - - - - 340
b Succession of Colonels, 1689-1892 - - - - 341
c Succession of Lieutenant-Colonels commanding battalions, 1858-1892 - - - - - - - - - 342
d Rolls of Officers from the *Monthly Army List*, 1823, 1829, 1842, 1852, 1858, 1862, 1872, 1879, 1880, 1881, 1892 - 343

C

a Notes on the Colours - - - - - - - 363
b Regiment Call and old Regimental March - - - 370
Addenda:
    Note on Drum-Major's Staff - - - - - ⎫
                                                                                                   ⎬ 371
    Note on General Glyn's campaign - - - - ⎭

HISTORICAL RECORDS

OF THE

24TH REGIMENT.

CHAPTER I.

1689-1702.

Raising of the Regiment—Early Services—Death of King William III.

A STANDING Army in England dates from the days of the Restoration, although down to the year 1689 its existence was virtually unrecognized by the law of the Realm. It was set on foot by Charles II. as a small force for the king's guards and garrisons, and was enlarged by his brother, James II., during the troubles of 1685 and 1688. When King William III. and Queen Mary received the Crown (14th February, 168$^8_9$) it consisted of the Guards, horse and foot, together with the eleven oldest regiments of Cavalry and the twenty-one oldest regiments of Infantry now existing, all of which were paid out of the Civil list.*

But, notwithstanding the national dislike to a permanent army, expressed in the famous Declaration of Right, the political exigencies of the time speedily led to a further increase in the strength of the army and the passing of a law putting the force upon a more constitutional footing. On 21st March, 1689, after receiving the news that James II. had landed at Kingsale, at the head of a French army, the House of Commons resolved itself into a Committee of the whole House, to discuss the question of Irish Supply, and voted the money for a large increase in the number of regiments to carry on

---

* See Clode, *Military Forces of the Crown*, vol. i.; Simmons, on *Courts Martial;* Macaulay, *History of England,* vols. iv. and v.

B

the war. A week later the alarm caused by the Mutiny, stirred up by Jacobite emissaries, in two regiments under orders for Holland, led to the passing of the Mutiny Bill, giving legal sanction to the maintenance of a standing army with the consent of Parliament, and providing for the punishment of mutiny and desertion and other crimes mentioned, which previously were not legally punishable by military law in time of peace. The Mutiny Bill passed the House of Lords on 28th March, and on 3rd April, 1689, became law. With a few intermissions it has been renewed periodically ever since.

Meanwhile, steps had been taken for the raising of new regiments by noblemen and country gentlemen, whose political sympathies were well known. Among these was Sir Edward Dering, 3rd Baronet of Surrenden, near Ashford, in the county of Kent, the representative of an old Kentish family that had suffered much for its devotion to King Charles I. in the Civil War.* *(Appendix B.)*

Sir Edward Dering's commission as Colonel was dated 28th March, (old style) 1689, which has been adopted officially as the date of formation of his regiment, since known as the TWENTY-FOURTH REGIMENT OF FOOT.

Orders for the issue of arms to the new regiments had been given already, as appears by the following entry in the Records of the late Board of Ordnance :—†

" To the Duke ffrederick, Marechal de Schomberg, Master General
" of Our Ordnance.—Whereas Wee have ordered the several
" Regiments of ffoot mentioned in the list hereto annexed, to be
" forthwith raised for Our Service, Consisting of Thirteen Companys
" in each Regiment, of 60 Private Soldiers, 3 Sergeants, 3 Corporals,
" & 2 Drums, in each Company. Our Will and Pleasure is that, out
" of the Stores remaining in the Office of Our Ordnance you cause to
" be delivered to the Severall Colonells, or to such Person or Persons
" as shall be appointed by Them to receive the same, such Arms as
" have usually been delivered to other Regiments of ffoot, according

---

* Sir Edward Dering was known in his county by the sobriquet of the " Black Devil of Kent."

† *Ordnance Warrant Books*, vol. x., in Public Record Office, London.

Sir Edward Dering, 3rd Baronet, of Surrenden.
First Colonel of the Regiment (1689)

" to the numbers of Companys of Soldiers above mentioned. And
" for soe doing This, together with the usual Indents, shall be Your
" Warrant and Discharge.

" Given at Our Court at Whitehall, this 16th day of March 168$\frac{8}{9}$,*
" in the ffirst Year of our Reign.

" By His Majesty's Command,
" Shrewsbury."

Then follows the list of 14 new regiments :—

The Duke of Norfolk's	Lord Herbert of Cherbury's
The Marquis of Winchester's (2)	Lord Lovelace's
The Earl of Kingston's	Sir Henry Ingoldsby's
The Earl of Roscommon's	Sir Edward Dering's
The Earl of Drogheda's	Sir Thos. Gower's
Lord Viscount Castleton's	Colonel Thos. Erle's.
Lord Viscount Lisburn's	

The " usual arms " were heavy firelocks, throwing an ounce ball, and by some accounts provided with plug bayonets, which were issued to two-thirds of each company, the remaining third having pikes eighteen feet long. The customary formation was in six ranks, with the musketeers in the centre and the pikemen on the flanks of each company. Officers carried half-pikes ; sergeants, halberds ; all wore swords. The grenadiers had firelocks which they slung at their backs when not in use, swords, hatchets, and a pouch of hand grenades.

There is a yet earlier mention of a " Deering's Regiment " in the *War Office Marching Books*, dated 8th March, 1689. As the Military Records in Dublin do not go back beyond 1697, it is impossible to say for certain whether the order refers to some antecedent corps in Ireland, under the command of Daniel Dering *(Appendix B)*, whom the Kentish historian, Hasted, calls "a colonel in Ireland,"† or merely to certain Irish officers for whom employment

---

* The Official year then commenced on 25th March. See footnote, page 10.

† Great efforts were made about this time to find employment for dispossessed Irish Protestant officers. The *London Gazette*, 8th April, 1689, directs that such Protestant officers as have been disbanded in Ireland and lately quitted their commands and are not yet employed, do bring their names and certificates to the Commissary General of Musters, who is directed to make out lists of their names and commands, with a view to their being immediately received into His Majesty's Service.

had been found in raising men for Sir Edward Dering's prospective regiment. It is addressed to the Officer Commanding at Wells, Somersetshire, and runs thus :—

"Our Will & Pleasure is that ye cause some Officers of Colonel "Dering's Regiment of ffoot, lately come to England for making "recruits, to repair to the Quarters of Colonel Talmash's Regiment, at "Wells, and embark with them for Belfast, where they will receive "300 men of the recruits of the said Regiment, & that the others "repair with all Express to Bristol, to join Colonel ffoulke's "Regiment, & embark with it for Belfast, where they will receive 130 "recruits of the said Regiment for Colonel Dering's Regiment."

An order of the 22nd April, 1689, directs Sir Edward Dering's regiment of foot to march from Maidstone and Dartford to Worcester, Litchfield, Tamworth, and Ridgely. A subsequent order in June directs the regiment to enlarge its quarters to Walsall, and in July it appears to have been on Warwick and Coventry.

The month after, Sir Edward Dering's regiment formed part of the force of fifteen thousand men—horse, foot, and dragoons—including the fourteen newly raised regiments of foot, which were sent under King William's favorite general, Marshal Schomberg, to the aid of the Protestants in Ulster.

Story, one of the historians of the Irish War, who was an army chaplain and well informed regarding the military details of the Williamite forces,* includes Dering's among the regiments mustered at Belfast at the end of August, and afterwards in Schomberg's entrenched camp at Dundalk. The season was a very unhealthy one and among Schomberg's raw ill-found troops, in their low-lying camps, sickness was soon rife, and the mortality great.† One of the earliest victims was Sir Edward Dering, who died at the end of September.

---

* G. Story, *Impartial History of the War in Ireland*, London, 1693; and *Continuation of the Impartial History*.

† See Macaulay, *History of England*, vol. iii., pp. 425-30. A fact not mentioned by Macaulay and other writers is, that influenza had been epidemic just before, attended by an epidemic catarrh among horses, apparently resembling the modern "pink-eye," which wrought fell havoc in King James's forces, at Kildare.

Story writes of him that "he was much lamented by all who knew "him. He left a good fortune in England, to serve the King in this "expedition, as did three of his brothers, one of whom, Captain John "Deering, who died since at Tanderogee, was a very ingenious young "gentleman."* Story also says that when Schomberg withdrew his troops to higher grounds about Carlingford Bay, the Irish took the bodies of Sir Edward Dering and two other colonels who died in camp at Dundalk out of Lord Bellew's vault, under Dundalk Church, "and buried them nigh the church door, but the bodies "were not desecrated as was reported at the time."†

Sir Edward Dering was succeeded in the colonelcy of the regiment by his brother, Colonel Daniel Dering, under whose command it appears to have been some time quartered at Armagh.‡

The annexed extracts from Schomberg's General Orders for December, 1689, are worth giving, as illustrating the fashion of regimental routine two hundred years ago :—

"The captains or officers commanding companies to meet at at 2 of the "clock at the Guard-House each Tuesday to punish offenders & to "consider what may be for the good of the regiment, & that the Country "to have notice thereof, & it there be any complaints against the Soldiers "they be heard."

"The Soldiers to have strict orders to attend Divine Service every "Sunday, & that the Officers doe punish Swearing & other Vices as "directed by the Articles of War."

"The Soldiers that are to mount the Guard to be there by 6 of the "clock in the morning & to exercise till 11 of the clock, & that the "Chaplain be there to read Prayers before the Guard mounts."

"Every Captain to take heed of the General's Orders for regulating the "Foot & the Major General's for exercising & diligently observe the same."

"An Officer to visit twice a week the Sick & a serjeant twice a day & to "give the Chirurgeon & the Chaplain notice that they may repair to them "at once when needed."

1690-91.

On 14th June, 1690, King William landed at Carrickfergus, to assume the command of the Army in person; and on 1st July was

---

* Story, *Imperial History*, p. 29.   † *Ib.*, p. 36.   ‡ *Ib.*, p. 38.

fought the battle of the Boyne, followed by the flight of King James and the entry of William into Dublin. There is no evidence that Dering's regiment took any active part in the campaign. The regiment does not appear among those actually engaged at the Boyne and afterwards reviewed by King William at Finglass.

Colonel Daniel Dering died, and was succeeded in the colonelcy by Colonel Samuel Venner *(Appendix B)* from 1st June, 1691. Story refers to Venner's, late Dering's, regiment as still left in the North in June, 1691.* In July, Colonel Ramsey and Captain Kingsley, with one hundred men of Venner's, late Dering's, and some Militia, routed a party of horse and foot under old Sir Teague O'Regan, a noted Irish leader, near Sligo, and took some prisoners.† Lord Drogheda's and Venner's were sent to meet the artillery-train coming from Athlone when the Army was marching from Galway to Limerick.‡ Venner's regiment took part in the siege of Limerick in September, 1691, and, after Sarsfield's surrender of the place, marched into garrison in the town.§ The regiment was brought to England in December, 1691.

1692.

The *Marching Orders* for January this year contain an entry of an order sent to the postmaster at Cirencester, Gloucestershire, to deliver to Colonel Venner, directing him to march his regiment to Wells, Glastonbury, and Bridgwater, to be quartered and remain, ending with the injunction then customary, "and the Soldiers are to behave "civilly and pay their landlords."¶ A gap in the *Marching Books* renders it difficult to follow the movements of the regiment, but in May it appears to have been at Guildford and places adjacent, having probably been brought thither by the alarms of invasion, caused by the French massing troops and Militia on the coast of Normandy to divert attention from their designs on Namur. Narcissus Luttrell, in his *Relation of State Affairs*,‖ mentions that on 28th June, 1692,

---

* Story, *Continuation of Impartial History*, p. 110; also *Historic MSS. Commission: Rep.* iv., p. 322.   † *Ib.*, p. 176.   ‡ *Ib.*, p. 188.   § *Ib.*, pp. 204-63.
¶ *W.O. Marching Book*, vol. viii.
‖ Narcissus Luttrell, *Relation of State Affairs, 1671-1714*, Oxford, 1857. (Reprinted from original MSS. in All Souls Library, Cambridge.) Vol. ii.

Colonel Daniel Dering.
Died 1691.

Colonel Venner was tried at Whitehall by a General Court-martial, of which Brigadier-General Leveson was president, "on a general "complaint by his regiment," and that, "after a full hearing, he was "ordered to refund the money to the complainants." It appears that a sum of £6,000, accumulated arrears of pay, was then due to Venner on behalf of the regiment.*

All fears of invasion were dispelled by Admiral Russell's great victory over the French fleet off Cape Barfleur (La Hogue), on 19th May, 1692, which it was proposed to follow up with a grand expedition to the coast of France after the fleet had refitted. Fourteen regiments of foot, among which was Venner's, were encamped in readiness on Portsdown Hill. Luttrell† details the busy preparations making early in July. The troops were to have with them six month's provisions. A supply for four months more was to follow. They were to take sixty pieces of cannon and twenty mortars and an abundance of other munitions of war, including thirty thousand stand of spare small arms. A sum of £40,000 was sent down for current expenses, and each soldier received 20s. "by way of encouragement." On 26th July, 1692, all the troops were on board. What followed is briefly told by Macaulay :‡ "The transports sailed, and in a few hours "joined the naval armament in the neighbourhood of Portland. On "the 28th a general council of war was held. All the naval "commanders, with Russel at their head, declared that it would be "madness to carry the ships within range of the guns of St. Malo, "and that the town must be reduced to straits by land before the "men-of-war in the harbour could, with any chance of success, be "attacked from the sea. The military men declared with equal "unanimity that the land-forces could effect nothing against the town "without the co-operation of the fleet. It was then considered "whether it would be advisable to make a descent on Brest or "Rochford. Russel and the other flag-officers, among whom were "Rooke, Shovel, Van Almonde, and Evertson, pronounced that the "summer was too far spent for either enterprise. We must suppose

---

* *Treasury Papers*, vol. xxiii., p. 75. See also Appendix B, note 2.
† Luttrell, *Relation of State Affairs*, vol. ii., p. 516.
‡ Macaulay, *History of England*, vol. iv., p. 290.

"that an opinion in which so many distinguished admirals, English "and Dutch, concurred was in conformity with what were then the "established principles of the art of maritime war. But why all "these questions could not have been discussed a week earlier, why "fourteen thousand troops should have been shipped and sent to sea "before it had been considered what they were to do or whether they "could do anything, we may reasonably wonder. The armament "returned to St. Helens, to the disgust of the whole nation."

From St. Helen's, Venner's and other regiments—under Meinhardt Schomberg, Duke of Leinster, son of Marshal Schomberg—proceeded to the Downs, and thence to Ostend, where they landed at the end of September and encamped a little way from the town on the Nieuport road. Reinforced by a detachment from the Army in Flanders, they marched to Furnes, which the enemy evacuated on their approach. After throwing up some defences there, they marched to Dixmude, where they were employed in repairing the fortifications, and remained in garrison until December, when Venner's and some other regiments returned to Portsmouth.*

1693.

During this and the two following years the regiment appears to have been chiefly employed as marines, although not returned as a sea-service regiment.

In May, 1693, Venner's regiment, then at Portsmouth, was ordered to exchange its pikes for snaphances—short firelocks, suitable for boat-service—preparatory to embarkation. An Admiralty letter, dated 11th November, 1693, explains the distribution of Venner's and other regiments on board the fleet during the summer :†

COLONEL VENNER'S REGIMENT OF FOOT.

The Colonel's Company
,, Lieut.-Col.'s ,,   } . . 3 Cos. in the *Norfolk* . . Capt. Jones
Capt. Venner's‡ ,,
The Major's ,,   } . . 2 Cos. ,, *Royal William* . ,, Shewell
Capt. Mead's ,,

---

* D'Auvergne, *History of the Campaigns in Flanders*, vol. i.
† *Treasury Papers*, vol. xxiv.
‡ Captain Venner was presumably a son of the colonel. No further particulars of him have been obtained.

Capt. Stopes's Company	. . . .	in the *Boyne* . . .	Capt.	Good
,, Southwell's ,,	. . . . .	,, *Lennox* . . .	,,	Carr
,, Wray's ,,	. . . . .	,, *York*	,,	Killegrew
,, Oldfield's ,,	. . . . .	,, *Hampton Court* .	,,	Graydon
,, Kingsley's ,,	. . . . .	,, *Expedition* . .	,,	Dover
,, De Course's (De Courcy's?) Co. . .	,, *Royal Sovereign* .	,,	Whittaker
,, Tichbourne's Company	. . .	,, *Plymouth* . . .	,,	Lake
,, Studd's ,,	. . .	,, *Sterling Castle* .	,,	Saunders

The list has the following postscript, which is not attached to those of the other regiments: "*This regiment did duty in all respects as the "seamen.*"

So far as can be learned, the ships in which Venner's regiment was carried all belonged to the Main Fleet, or Channel Fleet as it would now be called, and their most important service appears to have been convoying the Mediterranean trade down Channel and past the Bay of Biscay. Captain Parker, of Ingoldsby's (18th Royal Irish,) another of the regiments embarked, describes the magnificent spectacle in the Channel on a bright June morning, with eighty English and Dutch war-ships in line of battle "ahead" and some four hundred and fifty sail of merchantmen—English, Dutch, Danes, Swedes, Flemings, and Hamburgers—under their convoy. " All the " sea, from the line of battle to our English coast, seemed as a floating " wood covered with canvas, and as the weather was very fair they " made a most glorious appearance."*

After proceeding to a distance of fifty leagues beyond Ushant, the admirals opened their sealed orders, and found that they had to return to the Channel, leaving Rooke with the Turkey convoy to complete the service. The latter were in the disastrous fight off Lagos. But, so far as can be ascertained, all the ships carrying companies of Venner's returned to the Channel, and were employed during the remainder of the year in cruising there and convoying the North Sea, and Baltic, and Irish trades.

1694.

A Board of General Officers, assembled at Gemblours Camp, in Flanders, this year, by order of King William, fixed the precedence

---

* Captain Robert Parker's *Memoirs*, Dublin, 1735.

of the regiments of the Army, which had been the source of many disputes. English regiments were directed to take seniority according to their dates of formation; Scotch and Irish from the dates on which they were first severally placed on the English Establishment.

It will be remembered that when King William came to the throne there were twenty-one regiments of foot already existing. These are now the twenty-one senior regiments of infantry, from the Royal Scots (late 1st Foot) to the Royal Scots Fusiliers (late 21st Foot). Of the fresh regiments added to the Army during King William's reign—and they were many—three of the fourteen first raised alone survive, taking rank respectively as 22nd, 23rd, and 24th in order of seniority. These are:

> The Duke of Norfolk's Regiment, raised 16th March, 1689,* (afterwards the 22nd Foot).
> The Lord Herbert of Cherbury's Regiment, raised 17th March, 1689, (afterwards the 23rd Royal Welsh Fusiliers).
> Sir Edward Dering's Regiment, raised 28th March, 1689, (afterwards the 24th Foot).

The strength of the regiment (24th) is shewn this year as consisting of thirteen companies, including one of grenadiers, with forty-four officers, one hundred and four non-commissioned officers, and seven hundred and eighty privates and drummers. Number of servants allowed, sixty-nine. Servants were at this time reckoned as supernumeraries and non-effectives. Some twenty years later an increase of pay was given to commissioned officers, and their servants discontinued, or included in the effectives.

Schemes for attacking the French coast were again brought into prominence. In May, 1694, Venner's regiment (24th) with others, including a battalion of detachments of the Foot Guards, were once

---

* The official year, down to 1751, was reckoned from 25th March. Consequently the seniority of the 22nd Foot and the Royal Welsh Fusiliers is shewn in the Army List as dating from 1688 or 168$\frac{8}{9}$, and that of the 24th Foot from 1689, although all three dates belong to the calendar year 1689.

To identify the 24th Foot during the frequent changes of colonels, the numerical rank is bracketed thus (24th) in the subsequent portion of this history, although the regiment probably did not actually acquire this seniority until after the reductions of the Peace of Ryswick, 1697.

more encamped on Portsdown Hill in readiness for embarkation. On 29th May the fleet put to sea, "to plunder the French seaports," the prints of the day record.* A council of war was held, and it was decided that the naval squadron, under Lord Berkeley, with the troops under Lieutenant-General Talmash on board, should proceed direct to attack Brest. The squadron parted from the fleet on 5th June, and on 7th June arrived off Brest. The gallant young Marquis of Carmarthen, who with Lord Cutts went in to reconnoitre Camaret Bay, reported the formidable character of the defences and the difficulties to be encountered; but Berkeley and Talmash appear to have made up their minds that the difficulties were overestimated, and a landing was ordered for the following day.

Carmarthen was sent in with six ships to engage the batteries, whilst a landing was effected by Talmash with seven hundred, or—by some accounts—nine hundred, troops put into lighter vessels for the purpose. They were met by a heavy cross-fire from the batteries, in the midst of which some of the boats got aground at a distance from the shore. A scene of wild confusion and carnage ensued. The troops that got on shore gallantly withstood repeated attacks, but were driven back on their boats, and got off with difficulty. The ships sent in to cover the landing were terribly mauled; the *Monk*, Carmarthen's ship, got out with the greatest difficulty; the *Teesep*, a Dutch man-of-war, was sunk with all her crew, save eight. General Talmash was wounded, mortally it proved; seven hundred officers and men (among whom was Colonel Venner) were reported killed and wounded on shore, and four hundred more on board the ships. Berkeley abandoned all further attempts on Brest, and with his shattered force was back at St. Helens on 15th June. The rest of the summer was passed by the fleet in harrying the French coast. They bombarded Dieppe; they knocked down part of Havre de Grace; they laid Gravelines in ruins. In an attack on Dunkirk they were worsted. What share the troops had in these rather inglorious proceedings is not recorded.

An order of 25th September, 1694, directs five companies of

---

* Burchett, *Naval Transactions*, 162-66; Macaulay, *History of England*, vol. iv.

Venner's regiment (24th) on landing from the fleet at Chatham to be quartered in the neighbourhood of Rochester and Strood, and further entries in the *Marching Books* show that in October the regiment was in country quarters in West Kent, with head-quarters at Maidstone, whence it removed into Essex and Suffolk, with head-quarters at Braintree and a detachment at Landguard Fort, and in November the same year was ordered to London.* The regiment, presumably, was in London at the time of the death and funeral of the Queen.

1695.

Narcissus Luttrell records that on Saturday, 9th March, this year, Colonel Samuel Venner was again tried by a General Court-martial, and "t'is thought he will be broke." Later he reports that "Venner's "regiment is given to Colonel Brudenell."† That Colonel Venner was deprived of his regiment is confirmed by the appointment of the Marquis de Puizar *(Appendix B)* as colonel, from 1st March, 1695.

On 9th March, 1695, Puizar's, late Venner's, regiment (24th) was ordered from quarters at Guildford, Reigate, and Croydon to Portsmouth; and on 25th March embarked with three other regiments, Stewart's (9th Foot) and Coote's and Brudenell's (afterwards disbanded), under Brigadier-General Wm. Stewart, as a reinforcement for the Mediterranean Fleet, which, under the command of Admiral Russel, was assisting the Spaniards against the French in Catalonia. The troops joined the fleet at Cadiz at the end of April. After going through the Straits‡ and executing various movements off Sardinia and elsewhere in concert with the Turkey convoy at Messina, the fleet appeared off Barcelona on 19th July, and Brigadier Stewart was directed by the Admiral to inform the Spanish commander that the troops (about three thousand men) could not be left longer on shore than six or seven days at a time, and to ask how they could best co-operate for the recovery of Palamos, which was held by the French as a base of operations against Barcelona. In concert with the

---

* *W.O. Marching Book*, vol. ix.
† Luttrell, *Relation of State Affairs*, vol. iv., p. 450.
‡ Gibraltar was not taken by the English until 1704.

Spaniards, the English regiments and some Dutch troops were put on shore near Palamos, and the town was "bombed;"* but on the receipt of tidings that a powerful French fleet was approaching, the troops were re-embarked, and the fleet sailed for the coast of Provence. There it encountered a succession of tempests that drove it back to the Straits, and eventually to Cadiz. On the arrival of Sir George Rooke from England with fresh ships, Admiral Russel returned home, taking with him the regiments under Brigadier Stewart.

Orders issued in November direct companies of the regiment landed at Havant, Gravesend, Faversham, and elsewhere, to march to London, where the regiment was quartered in the Tower.†

1696.

An order in February, 1696, directs a detachment of Puizar's regiment (24th), doing duty over naval stores at Greenwich, to rejoin at the Tower. This was the period of the assassination plot and invasion alarms, described in the fourth volume of Macaulay's *History of England*. Another order, dated 30th March, directs the regiment, on relief by a battalion of the 1st Guards (Grenadiers), which had been brought home from Flanders,‡ to march from the Tower of London into Gloucestershire and the adjacent districts. In the course of the summer the regiment had detachments at Cheltenham, Gloucester, Ludlow, Northbeach, Cirencester, Worcester, Hereford, Ross, and Monmouth. Orders directing the interchange of quarters by companies mention Lieutenant-Colonel William Tatton;§ Captains Tichborne, Lake, Harris, Pollexfen, and Vere (?) among the officers commanding companies; the others are not described by name. In November the regiment removed from quarters in Worcestershire and Herefordshire into Kent, where it had its head-quarters at Canterbury, with detachments all over the county

---

* Burchett, *Naval Transactions*, pp. 271-85.
† *W.O. Marching Book*, vol. ix. *Ib.*
‡ Hamilton, *History of Grenadier Guards*, vol. 406.
§ A memorial of Lieutenant-Colonel Tatton, in *Treasury Papers*, vol. xxxvii., 9, claims a sum of £410 19s. 9d. for personal losses when employed "in the Straits."

from Sandwich to Woolwich. The establishment of the regiment was the same as in 1694. The cost for the year was £16,145 3s. 4d.*

1697.

Puizar's regiment (24th) remained in its Kentish quarters until the end of May, 1697, when it was hurried off to Gravesend to embark in transports for Dutch Brabant. It landed at Ostend on 5th June, and was met by orders directing it to march to Brussels by way of Mechlin. It remained with the army in the entrenched camp at Cockelberg until the signing of the Peace of Ryswick, in October, when it returned to Portsmouth and was sent to Ireland.

1698-1700.

The Regiment was in Ireland during these years. A memorial of the Marquis de Puizar, dated 6th June, 1698,† shows the regiment as stationed in Ireland, and reduced to an establishment of forty men a company. The memorial states that when the regiment was sent from the Tower of London into Gloucester "to recruit and mend," all the worst men who had been at sea were discharged, and others had since been reduced. The memorial claims arrears of "sea-pay," at the rate of 6s. a week for each sergeant, 4s. 6d. a week for each drummer, and 3s. 6d. a week for each private, from 25th March to 31st October, 1695, for twelve sergeants, twelve drummers, and two hundred and sixty private men discharged.

1700-2.‡

On 1st March, 1701, Colonel William Seymour *(Appendix B)*, from a disbanded regiment of foot, was appointed colonel in the room of the

---

* The strength of the Army this year was eighty-seven thousand four hundred and forty of all ranks, whereof sixty-nine thousand three hundred and forty-two of all ranks were foot. See *Treasury Papers*, vol. xlii., p. 22.

† D'Auvergne, *History of the Campaigns in Flanders*, vol. ii., p. 77; *Treasury Papers*, vol. xlii.

‡ A change in the Calendar was made in the Low Counties in 1700, which may be noted here, as it explains the discrepancies in dates sometimes met with in contemporary accounts of the succeeding campaigns. The Gregorian, or "new," style, which had been in use in Germany, France, and other Continental countries, including the Roman Catholic Netherlands, since the 16th century, was

Marquis de Puizar, deceased, and the regiment for a brief period was known as Seymour's. The Peace of Ryswick, that turned so many of King William's veterans adrift in the world, proved little more than a truce. On 1st November, 1700, the King of Spain died, without issue, and Louis XIV., who claimed the crown on behalf of his grandson, in opposition to the Archduke Charles of Austria, sent troops into the Spanish Netherlands and detained the Dutch garrisons which held the frontier fortresses under a previous convention included in the Treaty of Ryswick. King William soon after despatched a British force, in which was Seymour's regiment (24th), from Ireland to Holland. The King's letter to the Lords Justices of Ireland is worth reproducing as a quaint example of Military correspondence and an introduction to an important chapter in the regimental story :—

"Most Reverend Father in God, Our Right Intirely Beloved
"Councillor, and Our Right Trusty and Right Well-Beloved Cousins
"& Councillors. We greet y° well.

"Whereas it is necessary for Our Service that the Regiments here-
"with mentioned be forthwith sent to Holland for the Succour of the
"States General of the United Provinces, to wit, Our Royal
"Regiment of Foot and Our Regiments commanded by Colonels
"Webb, Stewart, Sir Beville Granville, Jacobs, Emanuel How, Stanley,
"Brydges, Frederick Hamilton, Ingoldsby, and William Seymour.*
"Our Will and Pleasure is that y° give immediate orders for the
"march of those Regiments from their respective Quarters to our
"City of Cork, the Regiments of Colonel Stanley and Colonel

---

adopted in Holland and the rest of the Protestant Netherlands the day after Sunday, 18th February, 1700, being called Monday, 1st March, 1700. The new style was not adopted in England and English Official Records until 1752. Consequently, in the accounts of the ensuing campaigns, dates in England are given in the old style, and those of events on the Continent, as the dates of Marlborough's victories, in new style.

Royal Regiment (afterwards 1st Foot)
Colonel Webb's (afterwards 8th the King's)
,, Stewart's (afterwards 9th Foot)
,, Sir Beville Granville's (afterwards 10th Foot)
,, Jacob's (afterwards 13th Foot)

Colonel E. How's (afterwards 15th Foot)
,, Stanley's (afterwards 16th Foot)
,, Brydge's (afterwards 17th Foot)
,, Fred. Hamilton's (afterwards 18th Foot)
,, Ingoldsby's (afterwards 23rd Fusiliers)
,, Wm. Seymour's (afterwards 24th Foot).

"Ingoldsby excepted, which are to go to Belfast, where, upon the "arrival of the naval squadron—under Admiral Hopson—and other "ships appointed by Our Commissioners of the Admiralty, y° cause "the said Regiments to embark for Holland.

"Given at Our Court, at Kensington, this Sixteenth day of May, "in the Year One Thousand Seven Hundred and One, in the "Thirteenth of Our Reign.

"(Signed) By His Majesty's Command."

An entry in the *Marching Books*, dated 12th June, 1701, directs Brigadier-General Richard Ingoldsby to assume command of the regiments going from Ireland to Holland, to "take care of them on the voyage," and on arrival to report himself to the Prince of Nassau-Saarbruck.

The troops sailed from Cork on the 24th June, reached Helvoetsberys on the 8th July, and, proceeding thence by canal boats, arrived at Breda on 11th July.

On 7th September, 1701, King William concluded the triple alliance, since known as the "Grand Alliance," with the Emperor of Germany and the United Provinces of Holland, the principal object of which were to prevent the union of the Crowns of France and Spain and to secure the Spanish Netherlands as a frontier barrier for Holland. In company with Marlborough, who had been appointed English representative with the States General of the United Provinces, William set out to inspect the troops in Holland. On 20th September, 1701, a Breda letter relates,[*] "His Majesty reviewed the "twelve regiments of English foot, encamped about two miles from "this place. After passing along the line in front and rear, he saw "each battalion file off in single companies, and being well satisfied with "the good condition they were in, gave orders for their decamping "and returning to their respective quarters. After the review, His "Majesty was entertained by the Earl of Marlborough, at his Lord-"ship's quarters, near this place."

---

[*] Letter from Breda, in *London Gazette*, September, 1701. The two battalions of the Royals counted as two regiments.

Whilst the King was thus engaged, James II. of England died, at St. Germains, and Louis XIV. at once recognised his son (known in England as the Pretender) under the title of James III. This attempt to dictate a Sovereign to the English people touched profoundly that feeling of jealousy of foreign interference, than the strongest of English national sentiments, and aroused a storm of resentment. By dissolving Parliament when the excitement was at its height the King obtained a large majority pledged to support his policy in the war that now appeared inevitable, but which he was destined not to witness. On 8th February, 1702, King William died, and the Princess Anne reigned in his stead.

CHAPTER II.

1702-14.

Marlborough appointed Colonel—The War of the Spanish Succession (Blenheim, Ramillies, Oudenarde, Malplaquet)—Accession of the House of Brunswick.

1702.

ON 12th February, 1702,—three weeks before the death of King William—John Churchill, Earl of Marlborough, was appointed Colonel of the future 24th Foot, which thenceforth became Marlborough's regiment for the time being. Colonel William Seymour was transferred to the Queen's Marine Regiment, the future 4th King's Own Foot.* The great commander was then in the 53rd year of his age and the 36th of his military service, a lieutenant-general, and late colonel of a regiment of English foot, which had been disbanded on the Peace of Ryswick, in 1697.

Meanwhile, several accessions had been made to the Grand Alliance, the object of which, as before mentioned, was to prevent the prospective union of the Crowns of France and Spain, which would eventually place Spain and the Spanish Netherlands, much of Italy, Sicily, and last, but not least, the wealth of the Spanish Indies in the hands of France. Among the new adherents was the Elector of Bavaria, who joined on condition of the Emperor of Germany recognizing his title of King of Prussia, with which originated the powerful monarchy now presiding over a United Germany.†

---

* This regiment, and not the 24th, was Seymour's Regiment, which took part in the Cadiz Expedition.

† It may be useful to recall the fact that the German Empire at this period—the Holy Roman Empire, it was sometimes called—was ruled over by the Head of the House of Hapsburg, the present Imperial House of Austria, in which the Imperial dignity had become practically hereditary, although still nominally elective—the electors being the Archbishops of Mayence, Trèves, and Cologne, and the reigning princes or "Electors" of Saxony, Brandenburg, Hanover, Bavaria, and other German States. Of these, the Archbishop of Cologne and the Elector of Bavaria, who originally had joined the Grand Alliance, sided with France; the Elector of Saxony, having been made King of Poland, was too much occupied with his own affairs at first to interfere in Western Europe; the rest supported the Grand Alliance.

John Churchill, Duke of Marlborough.
Colonel of the Regiment. 1702-1704.

On 4th May, 1702, a solemn Proclamation in London of War against France and Spain, like Declarations being made the same day (15th May new style) at Vienna and at the Hague, opened the War of the Spanish Succession—a war that, in the words of an eminent historian, was prolonged for twelve years and carried on in various quarters—a war undertaken with justice and waged with moderation—a war pregnant with great actions and important results.* It was the era of Marlborough's Victories, in which Marlborough's regiment—the Twenty-fourth Foot of after years—bore no mean part.

When Marlborough arrived in Holland, in the summer of 1702, to assume command of the British, Dutch, and Confederated German troops, with the rank of captain-general, his regiment, with the rest of the British foot under Brigadier Ingoldsby, had already been some time in the field. They had assembled on 10th March at Rozendaal, on the road from Breda to Bergen op Zoom, where the news reached them of the Accession of Queen Anne. As England was not yet actually at war with France, it was decided that they should take part in the forthcoming campaign as part of a corps of Imperialists. On 16th April, 1702, the Prince of Nassau-Saarbruck laid siege to the important fortress of Kaiserwert, and Ingoldsby's battalions struck their tents and marched into the Duchy of Cleves, to join a corps of Dutch and Germans, under the Dutch commander, Athlone, with which they encamped at Cranenburg, on the Lower Rhine, to cover the siege. Marshall Boufflers, military adviser to the youthful Duke of Burgundy, the grandson of Louis XIV. and the nominal commander-in-chief of the French armies, made an attempt to seize Nimeguen; but was foiled by Athlone, after some sharp skirmishing in the neighbourhood of that place. Kaiserwert fell on 15th June, and when Marlborough collected his troops on the line of the Waal, near Nimeguen, shortly afterwards, he found himself at the head of a motley force of various nationalities amounting to sixty thousand men. At Draakenberg he reviewed seventy-six battalions of foot, one hundred and twenty-six squadrons of horse, and sixteen guns. The English foot was divided into three brigades, whereof that commanded by Brigadier Stanley

---

* Lord Mahon's (Earl Stanhope's) *History of the War of the Spanish Succession.*

consisted of a battalion of Orkney's (1st Royals), Granville's (10th Foot), Stanley's (16th Foot), and Marlborough's (24th Foot).

Restrained from bolder measures by the counsels of the Dutch field-deputies who accompanied him, Marlborough addressed himself to the reduction of the fortified places in the hands of the French. Venloo was taken in September; after which the fall of Ruremonde, Stevensvaart, Maesyck, and the castle of Worth, freed the Meuse up to Maestricht. Advancing swiftly and silently, Marlborough all but surprised Bouffler's army in the streets of Liège. Firing the suburb of St. Walburg, the French withdrew into the citadel and Chartreuse, to which siege was forthwith laid by Marlborough. Stanley's brigade, in which was Marlborough's regiment (24th Foot), were in the right attack on the citadel. The citadel was stormed on 23rd October, 1702; and although there is no express mention of the fact, there can be no doubt that the grenadiers of Marlborough's and of the other regiments of Stanley's brigade were in the storming column of twelve hundred English grenadiers spoken of by Marlborough as first in the breach, and to whose "extraordinary bravery" he bore emphatic witness.* In November the troops quitted the valley of Liège, and went into quarters for the winter in Holland. For his successes, Marlborough was made K.G., and received a dukedom.

1703.

When Marlborough assembled his forces in May, this year, at Maestricht, after Bonn had fallen to a corps of Dutch and German troops, Marlborough's regiment (24th) was brigaded with a battalion of Orkney's (1st Royals), Stewart's (9th Foot), and How's (15th Foot), under Brigadier-General Withers, in the division of Lieutenant-General Charles Churchill, Marlborough's brother.

The greater part of the year was spent in endeavours to bring on a general engagement, but the French, now under Villeroy, who had taken Tongres, but retired precipitately on Marlborough's approach, hung behind their lines, where Marlborough would have attacked them but for the reluctance of the Dutch generals and field deputies,

---

* *Marlborough Despatches*, vol. i., p. 70.

with whose counsels he was hampered. In a letter to the Dutch general, Opdam, dated 3rd July, 1703, Marlborough, whose care of his men was proverbial, refers to the sufferings of the troops in the incessant marches and counter-marches, made with the object of bringing the enemy to battle: "We have had a cruel march for the poor soldiers to-day, for the most part up to their knees in mud and water, and shall be obliged, I fear, to halt here to-morrow; but we shall continue the march to draw nearer to you, and await with impatience your views of the measures essential to our progress."* Operations were carried on against the fortified towns remaining in the hands of the French. Huy, a strong fortress on the Meuse, above Liège, was invested on the 16th and taken on 25th August. Limburg, in the Spanish Netherlands, was invested on the 10th and surrendered on 28th September. Spanish Guelderland having thus been freed from the French, and Holland relieved from immediate fear of invasion, the troops marched into winter quarters in Dutch Brabant.

1704.

Although in the preceding campaign the French had been compelled to retire from the line of the Rhine and Meuse, they had been more successful against the Imperial troops in Central Germany, and had formed a design of uniting the French and Bavarian armies in the Black Forest, marching direct on Vienna, and placing the Elector of Bavaria on the Imperial throne. Marlborough, who was instructed by the English Government to concert measures for the relief of the Empire, decided to lead the troops that could be spared from the defence of Holland, including sixteen thousand British, to the seat of war in Germany; but his design was kept a profound secret from all save the Imperialist leader, Prince Eugene of Savoy. The troops were reviewed at Maestricht on 11th May. Colonel Tatton, of Marlborough's regiment (24th), who was well acquainted with Germany, was selected as assistant to General Cadogan, Marlborough's quartermaster-general. Starting from Bedburg, near Juliers, 19th May, 1704, Marlborough commenced the famous march that ended in the

---

* *Marlborough Despatches,* Letter in French to Opdam.

victories of Schellenberg and Blenheim, and proved him the greatest commander of modern times. On reaching Bonn, the army proceeded along the left bank of the Rhine, "the stores and sick being sent up the river in boats, the men marching joyously along, quenching their thirst in Rhenish wines." The inhabitants were regularly paid for everything, and ample supplies were forthcoming. "We generally began our march," writes Parker, of the Royal Irish,* " about 3 o'clock in the morning, proceeded four or four-and-a-half leagues (fourteen to sixteen English miles) each day, and reached our ground about 9 o'clock. As we marched through the countries of our allies, commissioners were appointed to furnish us with all manner of necessaries for man and horse; these were brought to the ground before we arrived, and the soldiers had nothing to do but to boil their kettles, pitch their tents, and lie down to rest. Surely never was such a march carried out with more regularity and less fatigue to man or horse." The troops always halted on Sundays. Everywhere the smart, well-equipped appearance and fine bearing of the English attracted notice.†

At Coblentz, instead of turning up the Moselle towards Treves, as expected, Marlborough, to the surprise of all, and of none more than the French, crossed the Rhine by a bridge of boats and ascended the right bank as far as Cassel, opposite Mayence, where he arrived at the beginning of June. Hearing that the French under Marshal Tallard had crossed the Rhine at Brissac, and were on their march to the Danube, Marlborough pushed on with his cavalry, and having crossed the Neckar, met for the first time his future companion in victory, the Prince Eugene of Savoy, the Imperialist commander, in the neighbourhood of Mondelsheim, on 10th June. Three days later the Margrave or Hereditary Prince of Baden joined, and it was decided that Marlborough and the Prince of Baden, who was at the head of the confederate German troops, should exercise the command-in-chief

---

* Captain Parker's *Memoirs*.

† See Captain Parker's *Memoirs*. Also Captain Milner's *Compendious History of Marlborough's Campaigns*. Milner was a captain in the 1st Royals, in which he had been orderly-room clerk, as it would now be called. Both Parker and Milner served through this and the succeeding campaigns.

on alternate days; Prince Eugene having a separate and distinct command on the Rhine.

Advancing from Ulm towards the Danube, the Allies found themselves, on 1st July, 1704, in sight of a force of twelve thousand French and Bavarians entrenched on the heights of Schellenberg, with their right resting on the Danube and their left on the covered way of Donauwörth, an important fortress, the possession of which was desired preparatory to invading Bavaria. At noon the following day the troops had reached the foot of the heights, which were crowned by unfinished entrenchments, becoming every day more formidable. Marlborough turned his day of command to account by ordering an assault of the heights the same evening. At 6 p.m. on 2nd July, 1704, the attack began. Fifty grenadiers of the Guards, of whom only ten came back, led the way. The Guards, Orkney's (1st Royals), and Ingoldsby's (23rd Royal Welsh Fusiliers), formed the first line. A second line followed, of which Marlborough's regiment (24th Foot) was the right flank battalion. Thirty squadrons of horse supported them, with some battalions of Austrian grenadiers. Brigadier Fergusson led the first line; Count Horn and other generals bringing up the rest. Lieutenant-General Goor, of the Dutch Service, commanded the whole. The first discharge of musketry struck down Goor, and a temporary check was caused by the men mistaking a ravine they had to cross for the ditch of the entrenchment and throwing the fascines they carried into it. "The enemy then came out of their entrenchments," says a contemporary account, "with bayonets *in* their pieces, but they were quickly obliged to return there again."* The lines, however, were not yet won. Again and again the assailants were repulsed, until some Baden troops, on Marlborough's right, got into the entrenchments at a point that had been nearly denuded of troops. The defence slackened, and the British, pressing into the works, swept all before them. The Duke of Marlborough coming in with the first

---

* This statement, which is made in the *London Gazette* and other contemporary accounts, would suggest that what were called *plug* bayonets (*i.e.*, those inserted *in* the muzzle of the piece instead of fitting *over* it with rings or a socket hilt) were in use.

of the Horse, found the Foot pursuing the enemy, and ordered Brigadier Fergusson to keep them to their colours, "while he made a clear stage with the Horse alone."* Lord John Hay's Dragoons (Scots Greys), who had been dismounted to support the infantry, remounted their horses and joined in the pursuit.

Marlborough described the fight as "the warmest that has been known for many years." Sixteen pieces of cannon, thirteen colours and standards, and all the enemy's tents and baggage, were captured.

Lediard† and other writers show the casualties in Marlborough's regiment (24th Foot) as one captain (Powell), one sergeant, and twenty-eight "centinells" killed, and two lieutenants (Whalley and Gardiner) and forty-four "centinells" wounded. This is one of the very few instances during the campaigns in which any record of regimental losses has been preserved.

The immediate result of the victory was the possession of the fortress of Donauwörth. The Allies crossed the Danube, and a month was passed in marches and counter-marches and laying waste the Electoral lands with fire and sword. They penetrated as far as Augsburg, but it was found impracticable to attack the formidable entrenched camp which the Bavarians had formed there. They therefore retired a few stages, and the brave, but unmanageable, Prince of Baden was set to besiege Ingoldstadt. Hearing that Tallard had effected a junction with the remains of the Bavarian army, Prince Eugene, leaving a part of his army on the Rhine to watch Villeroy, marched with the rest to join Marlborough. Marlborough and Eugene effected a junction of their forces on 9th August, and on 12th a reconnaisance in force through the Pass of Dapf.heim, discovered the French and Bavarian armies in a strong position on the little plain lying between the Danube and Blenheim, or Blindheim, and the wooded heights to the north of it. On the morrow, 13th August, 1704, was won the famous victory of BLENHEIM.

The accounts recently printed by the Austrian War Office, which

---

* *London Gazette.*
† Lediard's *Life of Marlborough*, vol. i.

are, perhaps, the most complete yet published,* show that the strength of the opposing armies was as follows :—

Under Prince Eugene and the Duke of Marlborough: Imperialists, Prussians, Danes, Celle-Hanoverians, Hessians, Dutch, British. Foot. 64 battalions. Horse. 166 squadrons. Guns. 53.

French and Bavarian Armies - - 78 ,, 143 ,, 90.

The British troops, which included all that had marched into Germany with Marlborough, consisted of the following regiments :—

> HORSE.—Lumley's (1st Dragoon Guards), Wood's (2nd Dragoon Guards), Cadogan's (5th Dragoon Guards), Wyndham's (6th Dragoon Guards), Schomberg's (7th Dragoon Guards).
> DRAGOONS.—Royal Scots (Scots Greys), Royal Irish (5th Lancers).
> FOOT.—1st Guards (Grenadier Guards) one battalion, Orkney's (1st Royals) two battalions, Churchill's (3rd Buffs), Webb's (8th The King's), Lord North and Grey's (10th Foot), Brigadier How's (15th Foot), Earl of Derby's (16th Foot), Brigadier Hamilton's (18th Royal Irish), Brigadier Rowe's (21st Fusiliers), Lieutenant-General Ingoldsby's (23rd Royal Welsh Fusiliers), Duke of Marlborough's (24th Foot), Brigadier Ferguson's (26th Cameron's), Colonel Meredith's (37th Foot).
> ARTILLERY TRAIN.

The Allies advanced in nine columns, and formed in order of battle about 7 a.m. Lord Cutts was in command of the ninth column, on the far left, beside the Danube, consisting of the Guards, Orkney's (1st Royals), and Ingoldsby's (23rd Fusiliers), under Brigadier Fergusson; and North and Grey's (10th Foot), How's (15th Foot), Rowe's (21st Fusiliers), and Marlborough's (24th Foot), under Brigadier Rowe; together with a brigade of Hessians and some English Horse. To Cutts was assigned the task of attacking the entrenched village of Blenheim.

Marlborough delayed to allow the Imperialists under Prince Eugene to get into line on the right, and in the interval of waiting,

---

* *Feldzüge der Prinz Eugene von Savoye. Aus der K.K. Kreigs-Archivs.* Vienna, 1877.

divine service was performed by the chaplain at the head of each British regiment. Marlborough then rode down the line, and, with his customary humanity, pointed out personally to the surgeons the best points for collecting and tending the wounded. Bridges were also thrown over the Nebel, a little stream with steep banks and marshy bottom that interposed between the belligerent armies About noon, hearing that Prince Eugene was ready, Marlborough ordered Cutts to begin the attack. Cutts' troops went down to the stream, occupied two water-mills on its banks, under a fire of grape, and passed up the opposite side, Rowe's brigade leading. A volley of small arms at thirty paces struck down many officers and men; but not a shot was fired in return until Brigadier Rowe, who was leading on foot, struck the palisades of the village with his sword. A furious fight was soon raging around, the assailants striving in vain to tear down the palisades, firing and striking wildly between them with their clubbed muskets at the defenders, who kept up a ceaseless fire from within. In a few minutes the gallant Rowe was mortally wounded; the men fell thick and fast; and, with broken ranks, the brigade recoiled on the Hessian supports. The French Horse charged the right of the broken brigade, but were driven off by the English Cavalry, who, coming within the fire of the village, had themselves to retire. Ferguson, with the Guards, Orkney's, and the Welsh Fusiliers, renewed the attack; but without artillery to breach the palisades all efforts were in vain, and Marlborough, who had not previously been aware of the strength of the post, directed Cutts to retire under shelter of some rising ground. But Cutts' battalions held their ground, and kept the twenty-two French battalions occupying Blenheim engaged, while the battle was being decided elsewhere. After the French centre had been driven off the field in disorder, the veterans posted on Blenheim still held out, and the task in which Cutts had failed seemed no easy one for the whole army. Charles Churchill took post in rear of the village, with his right on the Danube; Orkney approached from the north side; Cutts, with Rowe's and Ferguson's brigades, reappeared on the side next the Nebel. For a time there was sharp fighting; but it was the interest of both sides to put an end to strife that might prove bloody to the victors, but must be fruitless to the vanquished. The French prepared to capitulate. Churchill would hear of nothing but unconditional surrender. "No resource remained; to resist was hopeless; to escape impossible With despair and indignation the troops submitted to their fate; and the Regiment of Navarre burned their colours and buried their arms that such trophies might not grace the triumph of an enemy. Twenty-four battalions and twelve squadrons surrendered themselves prisoners of war, and thus closed the mighty struggle of that eventful day"

In lead pencil, on a scrap of paper, written on horseback, Marlborough sent to his wife the first tidings of the victory :*—

"I have not time to say more than to beg you to present my humble "duty to the Queen, & to let Her Majesty know that Her Army has had a "Glorious Victory. M. Tallard & two other generals are in my coach; I "am following the rest. My aidecamp, Colonel Park, will give Her "Majesty an account of what has happened. I shall do so in a day or "two more at large.
"(Signed) MARLBOROUGH."

The trophies of the victory, which saved the German Empire and destroyed the power of France in Central Europe, consisted of one hundred guns, twenty-four mortars, one hundred and twenty-nine stand of colours of foot, one hundred and seventy-one standards of horse, seventeen pairs of kettle-drums, three thousand six hundred tents, etc., etc. The loss in men on the side of the enemy was also very great; the casualties, including prisoners of war and deserters, amounting to quite forty thousand men before the dispirited remains of the French army reached Strasburg.

The victorious troops bivouacked on the field of battle, forming a hollow square round the vast crowd of prisoners, and resting on their arms all night to guard them. On 16th August a solemn thanksgiving was held in the camp, and salvoes were fired in honour of the victory.

The following particulars of the total allied loss at Blenheim have

---

* The note was published in the *London Gazette* of 10th August, 1702 (old style). The battle was fought on 2nd August, old style, or 13th, new style.

lately been published by the Austrian War Office from statistics preserved in the Imperial Archives at Vienna* :—

Total Loss of Allies ...	4,635 killed,	7,676 wounded.
Whereof British ...	676 ,,	1,928 ,,

The most authentic account of the British casualties is that contained in the Treasury Records, from which the following is an extract:

ROLL OF SURVIVORS OF BLENHEIM.

From a list of recipients of the Queen's Bounty for the campaign in Germany, in 170⅔, contained in *Treasury Papers*, vol. xciii., paper 79.

COLONEL TATTON'S REGIMENT.

Colonel and Captain of a Company	Wm. Tatton	£75
Major and Captain of a Company	P. Mead	£51
Captain	Oldfield	£30
,, ...	Watkins, wounded . . .	£60
,, ...	Pollexfen, wounded . .	£60
,, ...	Lacoude, wounded . . .	£60
Lieutenant	Ray	£14
,, ...	Bright	£14
,, ...	Melery	£14
,, ...	Ramsay	£14
,, ...	Whitehall	£14
,, ...	Finch, wounded . . .	£28
,, ...	Albutton, wounded . . .	£28
,, ...	Walley, wounded . . .	£28
,, ...	Stapleton, wounded . .	£28
Ensign	Lancaster	£11
,, ...	Warren	£11
,, ...	Parr	£11
,, ...	Thomas	£11
,, ...	Ramsay	£11
,, ...	Gardner	£11
,, ...	Borkley	£11
,, ...	Bollard	£11
,, ...	Burton	£11
,, ...	Furnesse, wounded . .	£22
,, ...	Douglasse, wounded . .	£22
Chaplain	W. Maturin	
Adjutant	Davis	
Quarter-Master	Grophy	
Chirurgeon	Cormack	
Mate	Dobben	
32 Serjeants . . . . each		£2
15 Corporals . . . . ,,		30s.
442 Drummers and Privates . . . . ,,		20s.

Officers killed: Captains Tichborne, Powell, Fitzsimmons; Lieutenant J. Parrett. Died of Wounds: Captain Gardner. The total casualties among the non-commissioned officers and soldiers not given.

---

* *Feldzüge der Prinz Eugene*, vol. vi. The French loss is estimated in this work as between five thousand and six thousand killed and seven thousand to eight thousand wounded.

24TH REGIMENT.

Marlborough gave his share to increase the amount to be distributed. Wounded officers, as shewn above, received double. A special allowance, not shewn above, was made out of the Bounty to wounded non-commissioned officers and soldiers.

COMPASSIONATE ALLOWANCES PAID FROM THE BOUNTY:

To the Orphans of Captain Tichborne (3)	£60
To the Orphans of Lieutenant J. Parrett	£30
To Mrs. Gardner, widow	£60
To Mrs. Fitzsimmons, widow	£60

Comparison of the foregoing returns with a MS. preserved in the British Museum gives an idea of the strength of the regiment, as well as of its losses, in this particular campaign.

It appears from the MS. in question that the following non-commissioned officers and men of the regiment were "respited" during the year, that is to say, were disallowed on the muster-rolls until replaced by fresh effectives :—

	Serjeants.	Corporals.	"Centinells."
From the muster after the action at Schellenberg until the muster on 25th August, 1704.	1	2	28
From the muster after Blenheim until 25th October, the date of the first muster after arrival in Holland.	4	6	75

We have therefore:

	Officers.	Serjeants.	Corporals.	Drummers and Privates.
Survivors of Blenheim, as per Treasury Roll	31	32	15	442
Officers killed, as per Treasury Roll*	5			
Non-commissioned officers and men disallowed on the rolls, as per British Museum MS.		4	6	103
Duty strength on arrival before the Schellenberg	36	36	21	545

The duty strength of the regiment before the action at Schellenberg was therefore thirty-six officers and five hundred and eighty-two

---

* The *London Gazette* names two other officers of Marlborough's regiment as deceased during the campaign—Captains John Bayley and Vere.

non-commissioned officers and men, and its loss at Schellenberg and Blenheim, together, was five officers and one hundred and thirteen non-commissioned officers and men; besides wounded in the proportion of something like two to one to the killed.

The victory laid the whole of Bavaria at the feet of the conquerors, and as there was no other enemy in Germany, Marlborough decided to return to the Low Countries as soon as possible. He retraced his steps in three columns, at first following the route by which he had advanced. He crossed the Neckar at Lauffen on 2nd September, but instead of marching down the right bank of the Rhine, he turned to the left, crossed the Rhine at Spires, and advanced towards Villeroy's army. The war now resolved itself into a succession of sieges. The German troops laid siege to Landau, and the British encamped at Weissenburg, to cover the siege.

On 13th October, 1704, Brigadier Meredith, with a battalion of Orkney's (1st Royals), Hamilton's (18th Royal Irish), Ingoldsby's (23rd Royal Welsh Fusiliers), and Tatton's, late Marlborough's, (24th Foot), was ordered to march from the camp at Weissenburg towards Germersheim, there to embark on the Rhine for Holland. These, and five other battalions which had gone before in charge of French prisoners, were to replace ten battalions of Dutch foot ordered out of garrisons in Holland to march to the Moselle. Curiously enough, this is the only mention of Marlborough's regiment (24th Foot) in the published *Marlborough Despatches*.

On 25th August, 1704, Lieutenant-Colonel William Tatton was promoted to colonel of the regiment in the room of the Duke of Marlborough, K.G., who had been appointed colonel of the 1st Foot Guards (Grenadier Guards)* on 25th April† preceding Tatton, apparently, had been acting colonel for some time.‡

---

* See Successions of Colonels inserted in the older volumes of the *Annual Army List*.

† The *Historical Account of the Grenadier Guards* says 19th April.

‡ It may be noted that in the Blenheim year, a bill to legalize Impressment for the Land Service was introduced in the House of Lords, but was thrown out as unconstitutional in principle.

ROLL OF OFFICERS OF THE REGIMENT, 1704.

(From the earliest MS. Army List in the War Office.*)

COLONEL TATTON'S REGIMENT OF FOOT.

Colonel	William Tatton	
Lieutenant-Colonel	Patrick Mead	
Major	— Oldfield	
Captain	Samuel Freeman	December, 1691
,,	Thomas Pollexfen	20th March, 169¾
,,	Francis Jefferys	17th October, 1695
,,	George Watkins	
,,	— Lacoude	
,,		
,,		
Captain-Lieutenant		
Lieutenant	John Ray	
,,	— Finch	12th February, 170½
,,	Daniel Bright	
,,	— Albutton	
,,	— Gale	
,,	John Walley	18th October, 1695
,,	Abraham Stapleton	
,,	— West	
,,	— Whitehall	
,,	Francis Melery	18th October, 1695
,,	John Ramsay	
,,		
Ensign	— Lancaster	
,,	William Warren	
,,	— Parr	
,,	Timothy Thomas	18th October, 1695
,,	Ralph Ramsay	18th October, 1695
,,	— Furness	
,,	John Gardner	
,,	Daniel Deering	
,,	Henry Borkley	1st June, 1702
,,	Jo. Bollard	1st June, 1702
,,	John Douglas	7th August, 1695
,,	— Burton	
Chaplain	— Maturin	
Adjutant	— Davis	
Quarter-Master	— Grophy	
Chirurgeon	— Cormock	

---

* This is the earliest roll of the regiment that has been discovered, other than the Blenheim roll. It is contained in a small MS. book, which appears to have been commenced in 1704 and continued for about two years. The book is now in the War Office Library. The spelling of the names in these early records is very uncertain.

The publication of printed army lists "by authority" did not commence until many years later—the *Annual Army List* in 1754, the *Monthly Army List* during the Peninsular war.

1705.

Colonel Tatton appears to have returned to England on leave with the Duke of Marlborough after the arrival of the troops in Holland. Some letters from him to the Right Honble. R. Southwell, Secretary of State for Ireland, are preserved in the British Museum. In one, dated from the Smyrna Coffee House, St. James', in January of this year, he refers to Ensign Daniel Dering *(Appendix B)*, a young officer appointed before Blenheim was fought, who appears not to have joined. The regiment is very short of officers, he says, "which is very dangerous." If it is not convenient to Mr. Dering's friends that he should join at once, he hopes some other arrangement may be made. If Mr. Dering is otherwise provided for, he hopes "a good genteel young man may be chosen for his regiment." *

On 23rd January the colours and standard taken at Blenheim were carried in solemn state from the Tower of London to be laid up in Westminster Hall. The Standards of Horse were borne by dismounted Life Guardsmen; the Colours of the Foot by a party of one hundred and thirty-eight pikemen of the Foot Guards, all of whom marched past before the Queen in St. James' Park.† The incident is specially noticeable, as it is generally believed by the best authorities that the pike had by this time been discarded in the field, in the British as well as the French army. Puységur, who is supported by other French military writers, says the French discontinued the pike about 1703-4, and that the French infantry at Blenheim had muskets and "socket" bayonets—*i.e.*, bayonets fitting *over* the muzzle.‡

The earlier months of the year were spent by Marlborough in surmounting administrative difficulties. The French still held Flanders, and the greater part of Brabant, and it was proposed that two columns—one, under Marlborough, to move up the Moselle, the

---

* British Museum, Additional MS., 21, 494.
† Hamilton, *Grenadier Guards*, vol. i.
‡ Sibbald Scott, *History British Army*, vol. ii., p. 64. Puységur, *Art de la Guerre*, vol. i., p. 290.

other, under Prince Louis of Baden, to enter Lorraine—should carry the war into the enemy's country. The allies advanced, and took up a position between Perle and Ellendorf; but, hearing that Marshal Villeroy and the Elector of Bavaria were advancing on Liège, they marched back to the Meuse. As the enemy had not yet laid siege to Liège, Lord Orkney was sent forward with all the grenadiers of the army and one hundred men from each battalion, which caused the French to abandon their project and retire behind their lines.

These stupendous entrenchments—reaching from the Meuse to Antwerp, which had taken three years to construct—were forced, with little loss, by Marlborough's troops on the morning of 17th July, 1705, between Neerwinden and Helixem, under cover of a heavy fog, while the main body of the French army was assembled to oppose an expected attack at a point miles away. On this occasion, Tatton's regiment (24th Foot) was brigaded with Ingoldsby's (18th Royal Irish), Farrington's (29th Foot), and Temple's (afterwards disbanded). Other movements followed, but the French having taken up a strong position behind the Dyle, and the Dutch generals refusing to co-operate in forcing the passage of the river, Marlborough's plans were frustrated.

The following extracts from the journal of that worthy old Puritan, Major Blackader of the Cameronians, give some idea of the hard work involved in the campaign:—

> *May 20-24th, 1705.*—Marching every day . . . . Drawing near the enemy and in prospect of fighting.
>
> *June 5th.*—Getting account this day that we are to march back again just the same way as we came up.
>
> *June 21st.*—Crossing the Meuse. This day hath been a fatiguing, long march, continuing from three in the morning until eleven at night. A great many of the army fell by with weariness and some died, it being a scorching hot day.
>
> *July 16th.*—When I came home, I found that our regiment and the whole army had orders to march immediately. We guessed it was to attack the French lines; accordingly we marched at nine o'clock, and marched all night.
>
> *July 17th.*—We attacked the French lines this morning, and got in much easier and cheaper than we expected. The lines were partly forced and partly surprised, for the French had a part of their

army there, but not sufficient to make head against us, not knowing that we were to attack them at that place, for there was made a feint against them in another place, which made them draw their forces that way. Our Horse had some action with them, and beat them wherever they encountered them. Our Foot had nothing to do, for the enemy fled before they came up.

July 19th.—Resting this day over against the enemy. The town, (Louvain) between us is firing upon us, and some of the bullets coming in among our tents, but little harm done.

July 23rd.—I observe that all this campaign, that, in all the skirmishes between us and them, it appears we are masters of them, and could beat them as easy as a mastiff worries a cur dog; but, at the same time, I observe that we are, as it were, chained down, and cannot get them soundly beat. It is currently believed here, both at the time and now, it is the States and their generals that hinder us to fight and improve our advantages as we might.

August 7th.—This day there was a great preparation and all the appearances and dispositions for a battle. We were to attack the enemy—20 battalions of us—through the wood of Soignies. The action threatened to be a very bloody one, for they were well fortified and occupied a strong position at Waterloo. . . . . . If it had come to a battle, in all probability it had been one of the bloodiest most of us ever saw. . . . . . There was also a stratagem used, which, had it taken effect, would probably have decided the battle in our favour. There were twenty battalions— ours, Ferguson's, as one—and horse conform, that were to march through the wood, and post themselves quietly in the wood till we should hear the battle was fairly gained, then we were to come out and attack them in rear. Accordingly we marched at three in the morning and posted ourselves in the wood, and stayed there till three in the afternoon; General Churchill commanded us, but the Duke finding it impossible to attack them, as I said, we came off.

August 20th—We have been there six weeks, marching and countermarching, and seeking all occasions of coming on the enemy, yet our prospects have been blasted, and we have been kept as a lion in chains and cannot get out. There seems also to be a spirit of division sown among our generals, and as long as it continues I never expect we shall do great things. I confess I begin to turn more dull than when the prospects of death and danger were more frequent.

Early in November the British ended the campaign by marching back to quarters in Holland.

1706.

At two meetings of the general officers in the Great Room at the Horse Guards in February this year, the following proposals respecting the clothing to be provided for regiments of foot were agreed to:—

> *For the first year.*—A good cloth coat, well lined, which may serve for the waistcoat the second year; a pair of good thick kersey breeches; a pair of good strong stockings; a pair of good strong shoes; a good shirt and neckcloth; a good hat, well laced.
>
> *For the second year.*—A good cloth coat, well lined, as for the first year; a waistcoat made of the former year's coat; a pair of strong kersey new breeches; a pair of good strong stockings; a pair of good strong shoes; a good shirt and neckcloth; a good hat, well laced. That all the accoutrements: as swords, belts, patronashes, and drum-carriages be made good as they are wanted; that recruits be supplied with a new waistcoat, and one shirt and one neckcloth more than the old soldiers who have some linen in hand. That the sergeants and drums be clothed after the same manner, but everything of its better kind.

Early in May this year Marlborough's army assembled near Bilsen, between Maestricht and Brussels, and marched to meet Marshal Villeroy, who, "having received reinforcements and relying on his superiority," was moving on Judoigne.

On 23rd May, 1706, Villeroy and the Elector of Bavaria were found forming in order of battle, with their centre resting on the village of RAMILLIES, where Marlborough attacked and routed them.

All the plans of the battle in the British Museum, of which there are several—one especially, a highly elaborate one, dedicated to the Duke of Marlborough, and supposed to have been executed in 1707,— represent Tatton's regiment (24th Foot) in brigade with a battalion of Orkney's (1st Royals), North and Grey's (10th Foot), Ingoldsby's (18th Royal Irish), Farrington's (29th Foot), and Meredith's (37th Foot), under Brigadier Meredith, in the Dutch General Pallant's division; Meredith's brigade for the right of the second line. The other battalion of Orkney's was with the Guards in the first line.

The battle commenced with a feint by the British foot against the enemy's left, causing the latter to weaken his centre to support his left. Marlborough then assaulted the centre with the full weight of his cavalry, infantry, and guns, forcing it and carrying the village of Ramillies. Disorder began to appear in the enemy's ranks, and a renewal of the attack on the left carried all before it. The pursuit of the enemy was carried far into the night. All his cannon, many colours and standards, and a large number of officers and men were taken. The victory was as complete as that of Blenheim; the allied loss was but one quarter as great, while the immediate results were far more important. A magnificent army was annihilated; and so sudden and unforeseen was the success, that fortresses that had resisted powerful armies for months were given up without a struggle. When the magistrates of Antwerp delivered up the keys of their city to Cadogan, they declared that they had never been given up since they were presented to the Grand Duke of Parma, and then after a siege of twelve months. Ostend, which once withstood a three years' siege, surrendered a few hours after the batteries opened. On 26th July, General Salisch, with thirty-two battalions and six squadrons, laid siege to Menin, where Tatton's regiment (24th Foot) arrived as a reinforcement on 14th August. On 18th August the covered way and counterscarp were stormed, and on 22nd August the city surrendered. The allied loss at the siege was two thousand six hundred killed and wounded.

The fall of Ath in September was the last event of this astonishing campaign, which resulted in the acquisition of nearly the whole of the Spanish Netherlands. This, with the command of the vast system of water-ways, made a new opening for communication with England, by Ostend. The troops then went into quarters at Brussels, Ghent, and Louvain.

1707.

In May, this year, the army assembled near Brussels, and Marlborough's regiment (24th Foot) was brigaded with the second battalion of Orkney's (1st Royals), Webb's (8th The King's), Ingoldsby's (18th Royal Irish), and Temple's (afterwards disbanded), under Brigadier-General Sir Richard Temple, afterwards Viscount

Cobham. The campaign passed without any event of special importance, and the troops returned to winter quarters.

In the course of the year the Duke of Marlborough inspected the various regiments of the army in their respective quarters, and saw them practised in volley-firing by platoons. In the camp at Meldart, where four battalions were thus exercised, Milner* tells us that the signals were given by a staff-officer – Colonel Blakeney,—who stood on a pontoon opposite the centre of the line and waved a colour, the signal being repeated by a tap of the drum in each battalion; each battalion had its drum-major and a drum posted in front of its centre.

This was the year of the union of Scotland and England. Scotland was thenceforward designated in official documents as North Britain; and England and Wales, South Britain.

The Union Flag, as displayed before the union with Ireland—*i.e.*, without the red Irish saltire—became the principal colour of the British foot. Previously the English foot had carried a white flag with the red cross of St. George, and the Scotch a blue flag with the white cross of St. Andrew, as their principal colours.

1708.

On 9th March, 1708, Brigadier-General Gilbert Primrose *(Appendix B)* exchanged the regimental majority of the 1st Foot Guards (Grenadiers) for the colonelcy of Tatton's regiment (24th Foot) with Brigadier-General William Tatton, and Tatton's regiment became thenceforward known as Primrose's.

An Act of Parliament passed this year, in accordance with the recommendation of a Board of General Officers, allotted the counties of Essex, Suffolk, Norfolk, and Cambridge as recruiting grounds for Primrose's (24th Foot) regiment and certain others.

Information having been received that the French king was fitting out a huge armament at Dunkirk for a descent on Scotland, with the view of placing the Pretender on the British throne, Admiral Sir George Byng was despatched to watch the enemy's movements, while

---

* Milner's *Compendious History of Marlborough's Campaigns*, p. 199.

a naval squadron, under Admiral Baker, was sent to Ostend to bring over ten British regiments as a reinforcement.

On 26th March, 1708, a battalion of the Guards, one battalion of Orkney's (1st Royals), Argyll's (3rd Buffs), Webb's (8th The King's), North and Grey's (10th Foot), Hertford's (15th Foot), Godfrey's (16th Foot), Ingoldsby's (18th Royal Irish), De Lalo's (21st Fusiliers), Sabine's (23rd Fusiliers), and Primrose's (24th Foot) embarked at Ostend, and on 1st April arrived at Tynemouth. The French fleet, with the Pretender on board, was dispersed in a storm, and the project was abandoned. After suffering much discomfort and privation when windbound off the mouth of the Tyne and on the return voyage, the troops relanded at Ostend on 30th April, and Primrose's (24th Foot) and the other battalions from Ghent returned to that city.

In May, Marlborough again assembled his army in the neighbourhood of Brussels. His efforts were at this time directed to save the fortress of Oudenarde, which, by its position, afforded a connecting link in the defence of Flanders and Brabant. Oudenarde was invested on 9th July, and the French commanders—the Duke of Burgundy and Marshal Vendôme—designed to occupy the strong position at Lessines, to cover the siege. In this they were foiled by Marlborough, who by a forced march reached Lessines before them, and disconcerted their plans. The French then moved in the direction of Gavre, where they had prepared bridges for passing the Scheldt. With a view of meeting the enemy in the march, and bringing on a general engagement, Cadogan was sent forward at dawn on 11th July to bridge the river near Oudenarde for the army to pass. Later on the same day Marlborough obtained the famous victory of OUDENARDE over an army far outnumbering his own, in cavalry, infantry, and guns.

The French were driven from the field with great slaughter and in utter confusion, while the loss on the side of the allies was less than at Ramillies. The enclosed and broken nature of the ground and the approach of night, for the battle became general late in the afternoon and was continued after dark, restricted the fighting pretty much to the infantry. The British contingent of seven regiments of cavalry and seventeen battalions of infantry had only fifty killed and one hundred and thirty wounded.

24TH REGIMENT.

The following list of British regiments engaged in the Battle of Oudenarde, 11th July, 1708, is given in Boyer's *Annals of Queen Anne*:—

Squadrons.

3 Royal (North?) British Dragoons	[2 D.]	}	With 4 Spanish squadrons. Stair.
3 Royal Irish	„	[5 L.]	
3 Lumley ...	... [1 D.G.]	}	with 3 squadrons Spanish. Kellum
2 Palmer ...	... [6 D.G.]		
2 Cadogan ...	... [5 D.G.]		
2 Wood ...	... [3 D.G.]	}	Sibourg.
2 Schomberg ...	... [7 D.G.]		

Battalions.

1 Evans	[Disb.]	with 3 batts. of Germans.	Evans.
1 Brit. Guards ...	[G.G.]	}	Temple.
1 Roy. Brit. ...	[1 F.]		
1 Temple	[Disb.]		
1 How	[15 F.]		
1 Roy. Brit. ...	[1 F.]	}	North.
1 Lalo	[21 F.]		
1 Preston	[26 F.]		
1 North	[10 F.]		
1 Argyle	[3 F.]	}	Primrose.
1 Primrose	[24 F.]		
1 Godfrey	[16 F.]		
1 Webb	[8 F.]	}	Sabin.
1 Sabin's Fusiliers ...	[23 F.]		
1 Meredith	[37 F.]		
1 Ingoldsby ...	[18 F.]		

The second battalion of Guards (composed of the 1st Guards and Coldstreams) does not appear in the list.

The opportune arrival of Prince Eugene with fresh Imperialist troops enabled Marlborough to follow up his great victory at Oudenarde with the siege of the fortress at Lille, the defences of which were so strong and extensive, and the garrison of fifteen thousand men under Marshal Boufflers so well provided, that the French at first regarded Marlborough's movement against it as a feint to cover some more feasible project than an attempt on the famous masterpiece of Vauban.

On 13th August, 1708, Lille was invested by Prince Eugene with his own troops and a large reinforcement from those under Marlborough. The trenches were opened on 22nd, and the siege operations were pushed on vigorously; but the defence was so resolute that the progress of the besiegers was slow, and their loss heavy. On the night of 7th September, the counterscarp at one of the points of attack was taken, but only with the sacrifice of one thousand men. On 23rd, a tenaille was stormed by four hundred British grenadiers under Major Blackader of the Cameronians (26th Foot), and the lodgment on the counterscarp was extended. The expenditure of ammunition and stores had been so great that the besiegers were anxiously looking for the arrival of a large convoy from Ostend, and when these supplies arrived, the attacks were carried on with renewed energy. At last the garrison, greatly reduced in numbers and weakened by privations, were unable to defend such extensive works, and capitulated, but only for the town, on 23rd October. The besiegers, who had lost about twelve thousand men already, were glad to accept this measure of success, and allowed the garrison, still under their veteran governor, Marshal Boufflers, to retire into the citadel, there to prolong a desperate defence, which lasted to 9th December.

In three plans of the siege, Cadogan's Horse (5th Dragoon Guards), Godfrey's (16th Foot), Ingoldsby's (18th Foot), Lalo's (21st Foot), Sabine's (23rd Foot), and Primrose's (24th Foot), are plainly shewn; and this evidence is confirmed by a letter from Sir Richard Temple, from which it is clear that up to 10th September five British battalions only had been engaged in the siege, and that those five had then lost five hundred men. There is no doubt that several other British regiments were employed, for different periods, during the siege of the city, and the subsequent siege of the citadel; and that the grenadier companies and other detachments were sent from the covering army to take part in various assaults.

After the fall of Lille, Ghent was captured and Bruges delivered up to the allies. The troops then again went into winter quarters.

1709.

The army did not take the field this year until the beginning of June. The first event of importance was the siege of Tournay, which occupied the months of July and August. At the siege, Primrose's regiment (24th Foot) formed part of the covering army.

On the very day that the citadel of Tournay surrendered, 31st August, 1709, Marlborough, leaving a small garrison there, marched with part of his army to besiege Mons. The French were led to believe that Douay was his object, and so the opportunity of reinforcing the garrison of Mons was lost. But as soon as they found out their mistake, they too marched towards Mons, and the hostile armies came in sight of each other on the morning of 9th September. The French took up strong positions near the village of Malplaquet and began to entrench themselves. Marlborough proposed to attack them at once, but even his friend Eugene preferred waiting for the arrival of some more troops from Tournay. The attack was therefore postponed till 11th September, and the French took advantage of the delay to further strengthen their position, so that their camp "resembled a fortified citadel;" and the battle in which Marlborough drove them from it, known as the Battle of MALPLAQUET (or Blaregnies), was the most sanguinary he ever fought, and not the most successful. The opposing forces amounted to about one hundred and twenty thousand men on each side. At the first dawn of light on the eventful 11th September, 1709, Brigadier-General De Lalo's brigade, consisting of Webb's (8th The King's), De Lalo's (21st Fusiliers), and Primrose's (24th Foot), assembled under arms. Ingoldsby's (18th Royal Irish) belonged to the brigade, but did not arrive in time to take part in the line. As was customary, prayers were read by one of the chaplains, and when the thick fog which concealed the armies from one another cleared off, the troops moved forward to attack the triple line of entrenchments, thickly studded with cannon and bristling with bayonets. The attack was commenced by two brigades on the right, under Schulenburg and Lottum. De Lalo's brigade was detached to the assistance of the latter, who was unable to make head against the French brigade du Roi posted in the entrenchments skirting the road of Taisnieres, where there was much desperate fighting among the trees, with ever varying success. Eventually the French left was driven back. The Prince of Orange had meanwhile failed against the enemy's right, and Marlborough forbade further movement until a general advance had been made by the centre, under Orkney. The latter, with the Guards, the Royals, Argyll's (Buffs), Webb's (8th The King's), Godfrey's (16th Foot), Ingoldsby's (18th Royal Irish), De Lalo's (21st Fusiliers), Primrose's (24th Foot), Dalrymple's (Cameronians), Evans's (afterwards disbanded), and two foreign brigades swept all before them, carrying one entrenchment after another, overthrowing the Bavarian Grenadiers and Cologne Guards, but suffering very heavily in so doing. At last Boufflers, finding his left had already retired, gave orders for a general retreat.

Musketry fire played a very important part in the engagement. Parker, of the Royal Irish, says that the French muskets threw a ball of twenty-four to the pound; the English, sixteen to the pound. These weights are about the same as were used by the French and English respectively in the Peninsula, a century later. He also says that the French fired by alternate ranks of the whole line; the English, volleys by successive platoons, and that both the weight of missile and the moral effect produced by the mode of fire were in favour of the English.* There was, of course, no aiming in those days, but it has been suggested that the clumsy top-heaviness of the pieces made the men fire low.

The loss of the French at Malplaquet has been generally estimated at twelve thousand men, while that of the allies has been variously stated at thirteen thousand five hundred to twenty thousand. It is probable that the total number of killed and wounded on the side of the latter did not exceed sixteen thousand. A letter to Mr. de Cardonnel, and a return accompanying it, copies of which are annexed, are curious and interesting.†

---

* Captain Parker's *Memoirs*, p. 139.
† War Office Report on Regimental Honours.

Copy of a Letter from Mr. Cardonnel.

"Sir,   "Camp a Havré the 26th Sept., 1709.

"We have no letters from your side to acknowledge, but we expect
"with impatience an account of Mr. Graham's reception with the con-
"firmation of our victory. You have enclosed a computation of what it
"cost us among our foot only. You will find it a very large one, but I hope
"it will lessen when they come to give their lists upon oath. *That of the
"horse is not yet perfected.* 'Tis generally allowed there was more men
"killed and wounded in this battle on both sides, than in those of Blenheim,
"Ramilies, and Audenarde put together.

"I send you likewise a relation of the action by a French officer of note.
"'Tis approved of here as a very just and reasonable account. You will
"please to lay both these papers before Mr. Secretary. *I hope we shall be
"wiser than to make our loss public, as they have done theirs in Holland.*

              "I am, truly yours,
                 "A. de CARDONNEL.
"Mr. Tilson."

Copied from original attached to Mr. Cardonnel's letter of September 26th, 1709.

Liste de la perte de l'Infantérie des Hauts Alliés, tant tués que blessés a la Bataille de Tasniéres, l'onzième Septembre, 1709.

		Colonels.		Lieut.-Colonels.		Majors.		Capitaines.		Subalternes.		Total d'Officiers.		Bas Officiers et Communes.		Total des Mortes et Blessés.
	Battaillons.	Morts.	Blessés.	Morts.	Blessés.	Morts.	Blessés.	Morts.	Blessés.	Morts.	Blessés.	Morts.	Blessés.	Morts.	Blessés.	
L'Armée de son Altesse Mons. le Prince de Savoy.																
Impériaux	7	..	3	1	1	..	..	2	6	4	11	7	21	183	307	518
Danois	8	1	1	1	2	..	2	5	9	8	42	15	56	519	694	1,284
Saxons	7	1	1	1	2	..	2	3	6	7	22	12	33	184	477	706
Palatins	7	..	..	..	2	1	2	1	9	1	7	3	20	83	253	359
Hollandois	12	2	..	..	2	1	1	2	7	23	16	44	28	70	683	818	1,599
Hessois	6	..	2	..	1	1	1	1	12	5	20	7	36	128	356	527
Wirtemberg	3	..	..	..	1	..	..	1	2	11	15	12	18	120	272	422
	50	4	7	5	10	3	9	20	67	52	161	84	254	1,900	3,177	5,415
L'Armée de son Altesse Mons. le Prince et Duc de Marlborough.																
Anglois	..	4	2	4	3	..	3	13	26	13	*61	34	95	541	1,186	1,856
Prussiens	18	2	4	1	1	1	6	2	17	9	33	15	*61	294	833	1,203
Hanoveriens	12	..	1	1	2	..	4	2	12	10	44	13	63	285	1,056	1,417
Hollandois	30	6	6	5	11	5	14	42	116	85	242	143	389	2,238	5,692	8,462
Somme	..	16	20	16	27	9	36	79	238	169	*541	289	862	5,258	11,944	18,353

* Three evident clerical errors have been corrected. With these exceptions, the figures are as in the original.

There appear to be no other return extant. A roll of British officers killed at Taisnieres (Malplaquet) is published in the *London Gazette*, No. 4,595, but does not include the name of any of Primrose's regiment (24th Foot).

After Malplaquet, Primrose's formed part of the covering army at the siege of Mons, and on the fall of that fortress went into quarters for the winter.

LIST OF BRITISH INFANTRY AT MALPLAQUET.

From Boyer's "Annals of Queen Anne."

2nd batt. Guards.	Lalo's	[21 F.]
Lord Orkney's 1st batt. ... [1 F.]	Sabine's	[23 F.]
,, ,, 2nd ,, ... [1 F.]	Primrose's ...	[24 F.]
Argyle's ... ... [3 F.]	Preston's ...	[26 F.]
Webb's ... ... [8 F]	Orrery's ...	[Disbanded.]
North's ... ... [10 F.]	Temple's ...	{ [Afterwards Newton's. Disbanded.]
How's ... ... [15 F.]		
Godfrey's ... ... [16 F.]	Evans's ...	[Disbanded.]
Ingoldsby's ... ... [18 F.]	Meredith's ...	[37 F.]
Erle's ... ... [19 F.]	'Pendergrass's'	[Disbanded.]

Erle's [19 F.] appears in this list only, and is not said to have had any officers killed or wounded.

The differences in the numbers of British battalions in this and other actions, as given by several writers, may be accounted for by some Scotch regiments in the Dutch service being included in some lists and omitted in others.

List of British regiments at Malplaquet, from a Dutch plan in the British Museum, bearing the imprint 'Gravenhage (Hague):

Squadrons.			Battalions—*continued.*		
3 Stair's dragoons	..	[2 D.]	1 Northengray		[10 F. North and Grey's.]
2 Ross drag. ...	..	[5 L.]	1 Royal	..	[1 F.]
2 Lumley	..	[1 D.G.]	1 Sabine	..	[23 F.]
2 Cadogan	..	[5 D.G.]	1 Orrery	..	[Disbanded.]
2 Schomberg ..	..	[7 D.G.]	1 Argile	..	[3 F.]
1 Palmer	..	[6 D.G.]	1 Temple	..	[Disbanded.]
2 Wood	.	[3 D.G.]	1 Evans	..	[Disbanded.]
			1 Godfrey		[16 F.]
Battalions.			1 Web	..	[8 F.]
Preston	..	[26 F.]	1 Primrose	..	[24 F.]
Pendegras	..	[Disbanded.]	1 Lallo	..	[21 F.]
2 Gard Brit. ...	..	[G.G. and C.G.]	1 Ingoldsby	..	[18 F.]
1 Royal	..	[1 F.]	1 Tullibardine's (late Argyle's).		
1 Me-edith	..	[37 F.]	1 Hebron.		

Erle's [19 F.] does not appear in this list of twenty battalions, which is the number said to have been engaged. Howe's [15 F.] also does not appear.

24TH REGIMENT. 45

REGIMENTAL ROLL OF OFFICERS, BY COMPANIES, IN 1809.

From a MS. in War Office Library.

BRIGADIER PRIMEROSE'S (? Primrose) Regiment.

CAPTAINS, &c.	LIEUTENANTS.	ENSIGNS.
Brig. Wm. Tatton, Col., 25 : 8 : 1704. Gilbert Primerose, 9 : 3 : 1707/8.	Capt. & Lieut. Wm. Fflanner, 18 : 6 : 1705. Jno. Burton, 24 : 4 : 1708.	Chas. Fowler, 24 : 12 : 1807. Saml. Crich, 10 : 4 : 1708.
Patk. Meade, Col., p. bvt. 1 : 1 : 1705/6. Lt.-Col., 25 : 8 : 1704.	7ohn Parr, 25 : 3 : 1705.	Mich. Swift, 25 : 3 : 1705.
Thos. Oldfield, Lt.-Col., p. bvt. 1 : 1 : 1705/6. Major, 25 : 8 : 1704.	Timothy Thomas, 25 : 8 : 1704.	Danl. Durel, 25 : 8 : 1704.
Fra. Jeffreys, Major, p. bvt., 1 : 1 : 1706/7. Captain.	Swift Philley, 15 : 3 : 1704-5. Simon Roach, 24 : 4 : 1708.	John Gray, 21 : 3 : 1704/5 Thomas Tempest, 8 : 6 : 1709.
John La Coude.	Abrabm. Stapleton. Ralph Ramsey, 15 : 8 : 1704.	Granadiers.
Sir Robt. Rich, 25 : 8 : 1704. Charles Midford, 9 : 3 : 1707/8.	Fra. Mahoy.	Simon Roach, 25 : 1 : 1706/7. Edmd. Roach, 24 : 4 : 1708.
Jirmin Duce, 18 : 3 : 1706/7.	John Burton, 25 : 8 : 1704. Ralph Bagnal, 24 : 4 : 1708. Christopher Ganey, 8 : 6 : 1709.	Cha. Leman, 20 : 5 : 1705.
Benjn. Drake, 25 : 8 : 1704.	John Ray, 25 : 4 : 1703. Henry Berkely, 24 : 10 : 1708.	Wm. Bonfoy, 1 : 9 : 1706.
Thomas Albutton, 18 : 6 : 1705.	Peter Carnac, 25 : 3 : 1705.	John Bellard, 1 : 6 : 1702/3.
Thos. Pollexfer, Major, p. bvt. 1 : 1 : 1705/6. Captain.	James Maxwell, 23 : 12 : 1705.	Samuel Ffurnis, 27 : 2 : 1702/3.
Maurice Zulestein, 25 : 8 : 1704. Alex. Abercromby, 16 : 3 : 1708/9	John Douglas, 25 : 8 : 1704.	Wm. Baker, 24 : 4 : 1707. John Gordon, 1 : 3 : 1708/9.
Verney Lloyd, 26 : 8 : 1704.	Peter Groffy, Capt., p. bvt., 1 : 7 : 1706. Lieut., 25 : 10 : 1704.	Henry Berkely, 1 : 7 : 1702. Cha. Douglas, 24 : 2 : 1708/9.
Phillip Bragg, 25 : 8 : 1704.	Saml. Blackwell, 24 : 12 : 1707.	John Gardiner.

STAFF OFFICERS.

James Maxwell, Adjutant, 25 : 3 : 1705.
Henry Berkly, 24 : 2 : 1707/8.
James Maxwell, 24 : 10 : 1708.

Peter Groffey, Quarter-Master, 1 : 5 : 1704.
Peter Maturin, Chaplain.
Peter Carnac, Chirurgeon.

1710.

The great event of this year was the siege of the important fortress of Douai, which Marlborough invested with a large force on 23rd April, 1710. Trenches were opened on 4th May. The town was very strongly fortified and resolutely defended, but after fifty days of open trenches, was compelled to surrender on 27th June. The success was dearly bought. The Allies had eight thousand and seven killed and wounded, in numbers exceeding the strength of the garrison. Eight British regiments of Foot took part in the siege, viz.: Erle's (19th Foot), Mordaunt's (21st Fusiliers), Sabine's (23rd Fusiliers), Primrose's (24th Foot), Preston's (26th Cameronians), Hans Hamilton's (34th Foot), and Sutton's and Honeywood's—afterwards disbanded. They had five hundred and sixty-four killed, and one thousand three hundred and thirty-nine wounded. Lediard gives the loss in Primrose's (24th Foot) during the siege of Douai, as one captain, six sergeants, and twenty-nine privates killed, and two captains, seven subalterns, six sergeants, and one hundred and forty-two privates wounded.

After the fall of Douai, the siege of Bethune was commenced in August. As the French army avoided a general engagement by keeping behind a series of entrenchments, the allies laid siege to St. Venant and Aire. The first-named fortress surrendered on 30th September, but Aire held out until 9th November, 1710. The besieging force of forty battalions of Foot had one thousand, nine hundred and twenty killed, and four thousand, eight hundred and forty-two wounded. There appears to have been a vast amount of sickness as well.

An old plan of the siege, now in the British Museum, shews Primrose's Regiment (24th Foot) amongst those present at the siege of Aire, the other regiments of British foot being Webb's (8th The King's), Godfrey's (16th Foot), and Macartney's, Murray's and Collier's—afterwards disbanded.

An Act of Parliament passed in this year enabled Justices of the Peace to impress vagrants and others having no known means of subsistence for service in the Land Forces. Men so impressed were not to be under five feet five inches in height, and had to serve for five years; they were not sworn in. The measure is said by no means to have improved the character of many regiments.

1711-12.

Before the opening of the campaign of 1711, the French had prepared a formidable line of entrenchments, covering the positions of their armies near the French frontier, and vauntingly styled by Marshal Villars, "Marlborough's *Ne plus ultra.*" By a series of masterly movements, Marlborough succeeded in forcing these lines at Arleiux, on 5th August, 1711, and laid siege to Bouchain, a fortified town on the Scheldt, in Hainault, which surrendered on 13th September, 1711. The fall of Bouchain ended that long career of victory, which, for the number, importance, and uniformity of its successes, has no equal in modern history.

Marlborough was recalled from the command of the Allied Armies on political grounds. On 27th October, 1711, he quitted the army, and was replaced by his rival, Ormond.

Under the Duke of Ormond, the army again took the field in 1712; but after the fall of Quesnoy, a suspension of hostilities was agreed to, which lasted until the peace. Of the movements of Primrose's regiment (24th Foot) during the campaigns of 1711-12 there are no details. When Ormond's troops separated from the Imperialists under the Prince Eugene, on 16th July, 1712, the regiment was in quarters at Ghent, with a strength of six hundred and forty-seven of all ranks.*

1713-14.

In May, 1713, peace was proclaimed in London, the preliminaries having been signed at Utrecht on 11th April, 1713, (31st March, old style). By the peace of Utrecht, as it was called, Gibraltar, Nova

---

* Milner's *Compendious History*, last page.

Scotia, and other dependencies were ceded to Great Britain. The troops—excepting two regiments at Ghent and the garrison of Dunkirk—were at once withdrawn from the Low Countries, and sweeping reductions followed.

Primrose's regiment (24th Foot) went to Ireland, where it was stationed when Queen Anne died, on 1st August, 1714, and the House of Brunswick peacefully succeeded to the British throne in the person of King George I.

CHAPTER III.

1714-50.

Ireland—Vigo—Carthagena—Scotland.

1714-16.

PRIMROSE'S regiment (24th Foot) was on the Irish Establishment at this period.

A Royal Warrant, dated 30th June, 1713, had fixed the establishment of regiments of foot in Ireland as follows:—one colonel, one lieutenant-colonel, one major, ten captains, eleven lieutenants, nine ensigns, one chaplain, one adjutant and quartermaster, one surgeon, one mate, twenty sergeants, twenty corporals, ten drummers, and three hundred and twenty privates.

The *Marching Orders and Lycences*, now among the Irish Public Records in Dublin, contain a *lycence*, *(i.e.*, leave out of the Kingdom) to Major-General Primrose for three months, from 14th May, 1714; also, a "Humble Memorial" from the same, dated Dublin Castle, 18th January, 1715, praying the Lords Justices to have the Muster-Master General "cheques" (check) standing against certain officers and men of his regiment removed. Checks thus placed against the names of all absentees were removed on their rejoining, by special authority, after each quarterly muster.

Primrose's regiment, which appears to have been at Galway early in the year, was ordered to march to Dublin in two divisions, starting 2nd and 3rd May, 1715.*

On 1st June, commissions, under the new royal sign-manual, were issued to all officers actually serving. The annexed list shows the officers of the regiment whose commissions were thus renewed:—

---

* The march from Galway to Dublin was made in ten days, including a Sunday halt.

COMMISSIONS ISSUED TO MAJOR-GENERAL GILBERT PRIMROSE'S
REGIMENT OF FOOT, 1ST JUNE, 1715.

(From *Home Office Records, Military Entry Book*, vol. xi., f. 73.)

*Gilbert Primrose	to be colonel and captain of a company	
*Patrick Meade	„ lieutenant-colonel and captain of a company	
*Thomas Pollexfen	„ major and captain of a company	
Charles Millwood	„ captain of a company	
Richard Harwood	„ „ „ „	
*Philip Bragg	„ „ „ „	
Benjamin Drake	„ „ „ „	
Venny Lloyd	„ „ „ „	
Gilbert Primrose	„ „ „ „	*(Appendix B)*
*Thomas Albritton	„ „ Grenadiers	
*John Douglass	„ captain-lieutenant	
*John Parr	„ lieutenant	
*John Billord	„ „	
*Timothy Thomas	„ „	
James Maxwell	„ „	
*John Gardiner	„ „	
*Henry Barkley	„ „	
Julius Cæsar Parks	„ „	
Christopher Gearey	„ „	
*Samuel Furniss	„ „ Grenadiers, 1st lieutenant	
Michael Swift	„ „ „ 2nd lieutenant	
Samuel Needham	„ ensign	
— Warren	„ „	
John Gordon	„ „	
Wm. Congrave	„ „	
James Gabriel Maturne	„ „	
— Widrington	„ „	
Ralph Lisle	„ „	
John Scott	„ „	
Chas. Milson	„ „	
*Peter Maturin	„ Chaplain	
James Maxwell	„ Adjutant	
Samuel Mungan	„ Chirurgeon	

---

* Those marked (*) were survivors of Blenheim. Major-General Gilbert Primrose and Captain—afterwards General—Philip Bragg, from whom the 28th Foot derived its *sobriquet* of "Old Braggs," served in the 1st Guards during the earlier campaigns.

About this time the Hanoverian "White Horse" badge was conferred by King George I. upon various regiments. How these regiments were selected is unknown regimentally, and enquiries at the Heralds College have elicited no information on the subject. It is, however, a regimental tradition that the 24th Foot should have been numbered among those bearing the badge on their colours and appointments.

Entries in the Irish Military Records render it not improbable that Primrose's (24th Foot) was one of the regiments sent over from Ireland to Scotland for awhile during the rising of 1715, which, if correct, may throw some light on the tradition in question. No express record of the circumstance can be found.

In May, 1716, the regiment moved in three divisions from Dublin to Wexford.*

1717-18.

In March, 1717, Primrose's regiment, then distributed in detachments in the South of Ireland, was ordered to Drogheda, but was detained at Kilkenny *en route*, "in order to their embarkation for Great Britain, should there be occasion."† In July, 1717, the regiment appears to have been at Galway—an order of 9th July directs four companies to march from Galway to Waterford.

On 10th September, 1717, Colonel Thomas Howard *(Appendix B)* was appointed colonel of the regiment, *vice* Gilbert Primrose. From Colonel Howard the regiment derived its *sobriquet* of "Howard's Greens," which very probably came into use twenty years later, when Colonel Howard was transferred to the Buffs, to distinguish his old regiment from the Buffs—then called "Howard's." When Colonel Honble. Charles—afterwards Sir Charles—Howard was appointed to the 19th Foot in 1738, the last regiment became known as the "Green Howards" in contradistinction to the old "Howard's Greens," or 24th.

---

* See *Irish Marching Orders and Lycences*, 1716. Among the numerous march routes herein entered is one for a company of Primrose's regiment, from Cork to Bantry in three days. The distance is about fifty-seven miles, *i.e.*, nineteen English miles a day.

† *Marching Orders and Lycences*, April, 1717.

1719.

The assistance given by the Spanish Court to the Stuart cause led to the organisation of an expedition this year, the destination of which was understood to be a descent on the coast of Spain. The troops, consisting of a brigade of guards and some line regiments, were collected in the Isle of Wight, under command of Richard Temple—Viscount Cobham. Howard's (24th Foot), which had lately moved from Limerick to detachments at Kilkenny, Castlecomer, Longford, etc., was brought over with three other regiments from Ireland to join the force.* The fleet, with four thousand troops on board, left St. Helens for Corunna; but, finding that place well defended, coasted along to Vigo, where Cobham landed with the grenadier companies on the evening of 29th September. Next day the rest of the troops were put on shore, and advancing under a harmless fire from some peasants encamped at Bocas. Shots were fired from the fleet into the city, which surrendered; the garrison under Don Gonzales de Soto retiring to the citadel. On 5th October the village of Rondadella was burned, and the Governor offered to capitulate. Colonel—afterwards Lord—Ligonier was sent in with terms; but as it was contrary to the Spanish military code to surrender before a battery had been erected against the place, some guns were landed for that purpose, and next day De Soto capitulated. The English Guards occupied the gates, and the Spaniards marched out, taking only their private property with them. Cobham then brought his troops into the city, as the rains had rendered the camp very uncomfortable. On 12th October, Major-General Wade sailed up the river with one thousand men, took possession of Ponte Vedra, and brought back some guns and other trophies. Taking with them the guns and stores

---

* According to the *Irish Marching Orders and Lycences*, 1719, the Muster-Master-General's checks on Colonel Howard's regiment (24th), which in the ordinary course would have been removed at the end of the quarter, were removed on 17th August, 1719, which probably was the date of the regiment leaving Ireland. See also *London Gazette*, 1719. The regiment was in Ireland again in December-January, 1719-20, as leave is recorded to Lieutenant Congreve to be absent " on extraordinary occasions " in Great Britain. (*Lycences*, January, 1720.)

24TH REGIMENT.   53

left by the expedition of 1702, the British then re-embarked and returned to Portsmouth. Howard's (24th) went back to Ireland.

1720-24.

The volume of *Irish Marching Orders and Lycences* from June, 1720, to June, 1724, is missing from the Record Office, so that the movements of the regiment during that period cannot be followed.

The undermentioned officers and men of the regiment were absent, recruiting in Great Britain, in November, 1724: Captain John Parr, Captain Christopher Gearey; Sergeant Joseph Wallis and Drummer David Collins of Brevet-Colonel Pollexfen's company, Sergeant Henry McGill and Corporal Patrick Vaughan of Captain Parr's company, Corporal Barnaby Muckleroy and Centinell Stephen Phillips of Captain Gearey's company, Corporal Benjamin Carpenter and Drummer Thos. Slenty of Captain Albritton's company, Sergeant John Dobbs of Colonel Drake's company, Sergeant Joseph Norris of Captain Maxwell's company, and Corporal William Fagon of Captain Harwood's company.

A volume of *Miscellaneous Military Papers relating to Ireland*,* preserved in the British Museum, shews that in 1725 Colonel Thomas Howard's regiment (Benjamin Drake, lieutenant-colonel; Gilbert Primrose, major) had one company at Bray, three at Wicklow, two at Arklow, and two at Wexford. The regiment was "in very good order, but weak through desertion;" in 1726 the same regiment and

---

* British Museum Add. MS. 23,636. The miscellaneous orders contained in this volume shew, *inter alia*, that regiments in Ireland were ordered to have their firelocks fitted with steel rammers instead of wooden ones as early as 1724: that the duty mounted daily in Dublin at that period consisted of one captain, four subalterns, ten sergeants, twelve corporals, five drummers, and one hundred and seventy-five privates: that it was expressly enjoined that "no officer presume to mount any guard except in red or blew cloaths:" that recruiting parties were to be sent to England every November (no Irish were enlisted, a subject on which Archbishop Boulter remonstrated with the Lords Justices a year or two later) and were to return in April, so that the recruits might change quarters with their regiments in May: no regiment was to remain longer than two years in any place without express permission, and quarters were to be changed, so that regiments should be in their new quarters and the men in possession of their new clothing on 28th May (the King's Birthday).

officers had seven companies at Waterford and two at Duncamin Fort "in very good order, but very weak, wanting seventy-four to complete."

In May, 1727, Colonel Howard's (24th Foot) and five other battalions embarked for England,* presumably to join the force of ten thousand men, under Lord Stair, held in readiness to proceed to Holland, to aid the Dutch against the Austrians. The troops were not sent, and Howard's regiment returned to Ireland in September of the same year.

The regiment remained in Ireland, in various quarters, from 1726 to 1734, when, on landing at Bristol, it was marched to Woburn, Luton, and places adjacent, to be quartered and remain.† An order of 1735 removed it to Abingden and adjacent places, whence claimants for pension—presumably including the last regimental survivors of Marlborough's campaigns—were ordered to Chelsea, to appear before the Board.‡ Later in the same year, the regiment was reduced to the Irish Establishment, and went back, *via* Bristol, to Ireland, where it remained in various quarters during the next four years. The *English Marching Books* of the latter period contain occasional mention of parties of the regiment sent over from Ireland in quest of deserters.

1737-39.

On 27th January, 1737, Major-General Thos. Wentworth *(Appendix B)* was appointed colonel, *vice* Thos. Howard, transferred to the Buffs.

In June, 1739, Wentworth's regiment (24th Foot) was ordered, on landing at Chester from Ireland, to send four companies to Manchester, three to Lancaster, and three to Preston, and a later order directs the regiment "to be aiding and abetting the Civil Magistrates in suppressing the riotous weavers and other disorderly persons."

1740-41.

Fresh disputes with Spain, arising out of the right of maritime search claimed by the latter, and the cruelties alleged to be perpe-

---

* The *London Gazette*, 31st May, 1727, notifies the embarkation of these regiments, and directs that men who may have deserted from them in Ireland, and re-enlisted in other corps, are *not* to be claimed or molested.

† *W. O. Marching Book*, 1734-35.   ‡ *Ib.*

trated on British seamen, resulted in another rupture with Spain. Porto Bello was taken by Admiral Vernon, and an expedition was planned against Carthagena. This city, the present San Juan de Carthagena, on the Caribbean Sea, the capital of the United States of Columbia, was in those days a place of note—the residence of the Spanish Captain General of the Indies, and one of the seats of the Inquisition.

Wentworth's regiment (24th), Lieutenant-Colonel Theophilus Sandford commanding, with Hector Hammond as major, was sent from Liverpool to Birmingham, and from Birmingham, *via* Southampton, to the Isle of Wight, to encamp until further orders. Towards the end of October, 1740, Harrison's (15th Foot), Wentworth's (24th Foot)—each raised to one thousand rank and file, part of Cholmondeley's (34th Foot), the six new marine regiments (disbanded in 1748), and a train of artillery, the whole under command of Lieutenant-General Lord Cathcart, embarked and sailed with Admiral Ogle for the West Indies. They encountered a terrific storm in the Bay of Biscay, but arrived in Jamaica in January, 1741, in time to prevent a hostile descent on that island. They had in the meantime suffered irreparable loss by the death on the voyage of Lord Cathcart, who was succeeded by Major-General Wentworth, an officer much less fitted to cope with the difficulties of the situation, which were many and vexatious.

Reinforced at Jamaica by four new regiments of American Provincial (marines) and one thousand slave pioneers, the expedition arrived off Carthagena early in March, 1741. Boca Chica, as the harbour is called, was defended by several outlying forts, which it was necessary to reduce before the fleet could enter. A landing was therefore effected, and on 9th March ground was broken against Fort Louis. The siege-works were carried on by the negro pioneers, assisted by the white troops. But the negroes were difficult to manage, and would not work at all under fire. The brunt of the work thus fell on the white troops, among whom sickness was soon rife, owing to the great heat and the malarious surroundings. The engineers asked for assistance from the fleet. The admiral refused to give it. Meanwhile, the troops, who seem to have behaved admirably, toiled on amidst ever-increasing sickness and privation.

A battery, formed of casks filled with sand, opened fire with thirty mortars and cohorns on 13th March. The principal battery of twenty-four-pounders began that day, opened on 22nd March; on 25th March Fort Louis was stormed; the boom across the mouth of the harbour was destroyed, and the fleet entered. The unseemly differences between the naval and military authorities were then renewed with increased acrimony. The admiral declared that Fort St. Lazar, the citadel of Carthagena, could be stormed without assistance from the fleet. The general maintained that this could not be done, and complained bitterly of the whole work of the expedition being thrown on his toil-worn, fever-stricken troops. At last, stung by the admiral's sarcasms, Wentworth ordered a night attack by escalade on Fort St. Lazar. One thousand two hundred men, under Major-General John Guise, were told off for the duty. Owing to some mistake, they found themselves at daybreak, on 9th April, opposite the wrong face of the fort, and after an attempted assault, maintained with great gallantry for some time, were beaten off with a loss of six hundred killed and wounded. The periodical rains had by this time set in, deluging the country and drenching the troops. The enterprise was accordingly abandoned, and on 16th April, 1741, the troops re-embarked. Many died on board the fleet from local distempers.* The troops were subsequently landed at the eastern end of Cuba, and employed in some operations against the Spaniards at San Jago de Cuba until November, 1741, when they returned to Jamaica. The regiment lost in the expedition: Lieutenant-Colonel Theophilus Sandford; Major Hector Hammond; Captain Christopher Gearey; Lieutenants Stanley, Jones, Whitwell, Parr, and Pemberton; Ensigns Holt and Wingfield. Of the one thousand originally embarked, only two hundred and nineteen non-commissioned officers and men survived.

---

* Dr. Dalrymple, one of the physicians of the army, is said to have cured many of the most desperate cases of remittent fever by wrapping the patients in blankets wetted with warm decoctions, which threw them into a profuse perspiration, and so carried off the disease, thus anticipating a mode of treatment advocated as something modern in the nineteenth century.—Surgeon-Major Gore, in *Colburn's United Service Magazine*, May, 1878.

1742-45.

Orders were sent to Portsmouth and Plymouth in December, 1742, directing Wentworth's regiment (24th Foot) on landing from the West Indies, to march to Reading. From Reading it appears to have proceeded, early in 1743, to Wolverhampton, where it was quartered when the news arrived of the victory at Dettingen (14th June, 1743), and during the rest of the year. In February, 1744, it marched from Wolverhampton to St. Albans, thence to Barnet, afterwards to the Tower of London, then to Exeter, Falmouth, and later to Plymouth.

Early in the year, Lord Stair, then commanding the forces in South Britain (England and Wales), sent a circular to commanding officers of regiments, asking in what counties they would prefer to recruit.

A General Order, dated 6th April, 1744,* followed, by which certain recruiting districts were assigned to regiments in England, determined, it would appear by answers received to the circulars, and directing that officers and non-commissioned officers be forthwith sent into such districts to receive such able-bodied men and volunteers and such pressed men as should be turned over to them by the Commissioners appointed by the late Act of Parliament for the more speedy and effectual Recruiting of His Majesty's Land Forces and Marines.†

Devonshire, Somersetshire, and Cornwall formed the recruiting district of Wentworth's (24th) regiment.

Another General Order of 29th April, 1744,‡ directs that "every "Volunteer and Man Impressed by the Commissioners, if he is able- "bodied and fit for His Majesty's Service, shall be received, even if he "is under five feet five inches :

"The officer is not to receive any man who is not able-bodied, by

---

* British Museum Add. MS., 20,005. *Lord Stair's Order Book*, 1744-45.

† This was a renewal of the Act referred to on page 47. Voluntary enlistment for life had been the rule after the peace of 1713.

‡ *Ib.*

"being too old or too young, or having any manifest infirmity, or being "too small in stature:

"The officer is to divide his recruits into three classes according to "height: 1—The tallest men; 2—Men for regiments in Flanders; "3—Men for marching regiments."

On 22nd January, 1745, Major-General Daniel Houghton was appointed colonel, *vice* Thos. Wentworth, deceased.

An order in March, 1745, to Houghton's (24th) regiment, still at Plymouth,* directs it to send a guard to Totnes, to take charge of the impressed men for Major-General Phillips (40th Foot), in Newfoundland, who had saved themselves by jumping on the rocks when the *Tyger*, transport, went ashore at Berry Head, and "when they have sufficiently recovered from their wounds and bruises to conduct them back to Plymouth."

The Marching Books of this date also contain an entry relative to the apprehension of Naval deserters, promising every soldier who shall apprehend an impressed seaman at a distance of more than two miles from Plymouth a reward of twenty shillings, and six-pence a day subsistence-money to be allowed for each deserter until handed over.

Later in the year (1745) the regiment had its head-quarters at Plymouth and five companies at Bristol.

1746-47.

In January, 1746, when the country was full of Jacobite alarms and the Rebel Army had just recrossed the Border, Houghton's (24th) regiment was ordered from Plymouth to Newbury and Reading, and thence, in March, to the Tower of London. Soon afterwards it was ordered to embark at Gravesend for North Britain. A General Order, dated Inverness, 6th May, 1746, includes the regiment in nineteen then in Scotland, and as at the time of the battle of Culloden (15th April, 1746,) there were only fifteen regiments in the country, it would appear that Houghton's must have arrived in the interim.

An order of H R.H. the Duke of Cumberland, dated Inverness,

---

* *W. O. Marching Book*, under date.

27th May, 1746, directs the regiment to march to Fort William, to relieve the 6th Foot.

Detachments of the regiment under Captain Millar were sent on board the sloops *Furnace* and *Terror*, in June, 1746, to make descents on the West Coast of Scotland. In one of these expeditions they got tidings of the rebel Lord Lovat, and after a three days' search found him wrapped in a blanket and hidden in a hollow tree on a small island in Invernesshire.* A poor old fellow, seventy-nine years of age and well nigh bedridden, he was nevertheless regarded at the time as a most important prisoner, as the precautions taken to guard "that old fox" on his way to London sufficiently testify. He arrived in London 27th June, 1746, and was executed on Tower Hill on 9th April, 1747. The mask worn by the executioner and the block on which he was beheaded are still preserved in the White Tower of the Tower of London.

A party of the regiment appears to have been in the neighbourhood of London, billeted at Hampstead and Highgate, during the Jacobite trials; but whether they were connected therewith, or on some regimental errand, is not certain.

In July, 1746, the regiment was at Fort William, in Major-General Blakeney's district, which extended from Fort William to Speymouth.†

An order of H.R.H. the Duke of Cumberland, at this period, directs that no recruits be enlisted under five feet five inches, nor under seventeen or over thirty years of age.‡

During the years 1746-47, Houghton's regiment (24th Foot) was chiefly employed in road-making, and constructed the well-known road from Arrochar up the Pass of Glencroe, near the top of which is a stone seat inscribed :—

REST AND BE THANKFUL.

THIS ROAD WAS MADE BY SOLDIERS OF THE 24TH REGIMENT IN 1746.

LORD ANCRAM, COLONEL.

---

* The story is related in Walter Scott's *Tales of a Grandfather*. Additional details will be found in Chambers' *History of the Rebellion of 1745*, and in Dr. Doran's *London in Jacobite Days*.

† Maclachlan's *Order Book of William Duke of Cumberland*.   ‡ *Ib.*

The date would suggest that the stone was put up later, as Lord Ancram was not colonel until 1747. The *Ordnance Gazetteer of Scotland* says the original stone has been replaced by another.* The site has found a place in Wordsworth's verse, and the road, traditionally, is one of those celebrated by an enthusiastic officer in the well-known couplet :—

"Had you seen these roads before they were made,
You'd fall on your knees and bless 'Giniral' Wade."

On 5th December, 1747, William, Earl of Ancram, was appointed colonel, in the room of Major-General Daniel Houghton, deceased. The regiment thenceforward became known as Lord Ancram's, but a few years later, whilst this nobleman was still in command, the practice of distinguishing regiments by their colonels' names fell into disuse.

1748-50.

During the years 1748-49 the regiment remained in Scotland.

An order addressed to the commanding officer of Lord Ancram's regiment (24th) at Newcastle-on-Tyne in June, 1750, directs that "it being reported that the keelmen at Newcastle-on-Tyne and places "adjacent have left their work in a body and are preventing loaden

---

* The following is the account given in the *Ordnance Gazetteer*: Glencroe, an alpine glen of Lochgoilhead parish, in the north of Cowal district, Argylshire, is flanked by Ben Arthur, the Brack and Ben Donich, and traversed by the impetuous Croe Water, and the road from Loch Lomond to Inverary, by way of Arrochar and Glenkinglas. The rocks consist almost entirely of mica slate, shining like silver, beautifully undulated, and in many parts imbedded in quartz. Large masses, fallen from the mountain, lie strewn on the bottom of the glen; others of every shape jut from the mountain's side, and seem every moment ready to fall; and torrents descend the cliffs and declivities in every diversity of rush and leap, making innumerable waterfalls. The road was formed by one of the regiments under General Wade immediately after the Rebellion of 1745. It descends a mile and a half in precipitous zig-zag, and though proceeding then at an easier gradient, is everywhere difficult and fatiguing. A stone bench, inscribed "Rest and be thankful," is placed at the summit, and superseded a plainer one placed on the spot by the makers of the road. It has been sung by Wordsworth :

"Doubling and doubling, with laborious walk,
Who that at length has reached the wished-for height,
This brief, the simple wayside call can slight,
Rest and not be thankful?"

"keels from coming down the river, you are to be aiding and abetting "the civil magistrates in the suppression of these disorders, but *not* to "repel force with force unless absolutely necessary and thereunto "required by the civil magistrates."

A curious illustration of the fact that the tactics of modern strikes are not as novel in their inception as is sometimes asserted, and likewise of the increasing reluctance to appeal to the military power, which can be traced in the Order Books from the time of the passing of the Riot Act in the reign of George I.

Ancram's (24th) regiment was stationed at Canterbury, Chatham, and Chichester later in the year.

CHAPTER IV.

1751-82.

Royal Clothing Warrant—Defence of Minorca—A Second Battalion formed, which becomes the 69th Foot—Germany—America.

1751.

ON 1st July, 1751, a Royal Warrant was issued regulating the standards, colours, etc. of horse and foot. According to a schedule accompanying this Warrant, the 24th Foot had *willow-green* facings; it was distinguished from the two other regiments wearing similar facings, the 36th and 39th Foot, by having the red coats lined and turned back with *white* instead of the colour of the facings. The white lining appears to have been altered to green soon afterwards. No mention is made in the Warrant of any regimental badge or device.

About this time it became customary to designate regiments by their NUMBERS instead of by their COLONELS' NAMES as theretofore, although the practice did not find general acceptance for some years.

1752.

By the Act 24, Geo. II., c. 23, of this year, the "new style" was adopted in the calendar. The day after Wednesday, 2nd September, was called Thursday, 14th September, 1752. From that day the modern, or new style, was used in dating all official documents in England, Ireland, and the British dependencies, as it had previously been in Scotland and on the Continent.

1753-55.

The 24th Regiment was stationed in the island of Minorca.

1756.

On 8th February, 1756, the Honble. Edward Cornwallis *(Appendix B)* was appointed colonel in the room of Lord Ancram, transferred to the 11th Dragoons.

Disputes had arisen between Great Britain and France relative to

24TH REGIMENT.

aggressions in North America, but there had been no actual declaration of hostilities when the news arrived of active preparations in progress at Toulon, it was supposed with a view to an attack upon Minorca. The garrison of the island consisted of the 4th King's Own, 23rd Royal Welsh Fusiliers, 24th and 34th regiments—in all, under two thousand four hundred and sixty duty men. General, afterwards Lord, Blakeney was in command.* The French armament, under Marshal the Duke de Richeleiu, left Toulon on 13th April, 1756, and appeared off Cittadella on 18th April. In a few days the French were masters of the island, with the exception of the Castle of St. Philip, a strong fortress, much out of repair, into which the garrison was withdrawn. The French opened their batteries against it on 8th May; but, finding them too distant, pushed forward a body of troops, which on 12th May occupied the town of St. Philip and commenced erecting batteries under cover of the houses, within two hundred yards of defences. The siege that followed was as hardly contested as any that British troops have been called upon to endure.

In consequence of this attack upon Minorca, war was declared against France on 18th May, 1756, commencing the conflict which lasted till 1763, and is known as the seven years' war.

Exposed to the fire of sixty-two guns, twenty-one mortars, and four howitzers, besides an incessant fire of small arms from the houses close around, the little garrison held out gallantly for many days. On 19th June their hopes were raised by the appearance in the offing of the fleet under Admiral Byng, with the expected relief. On 27th June, the *fiftieth* day after the batteries opened, Marshal de Richelieu decided that the time had come for the assault. At 10 o'clock the same night, attacks were delivered by French columns at several points simultaneously. They were met with stubborn determination, and again and again the assailants were repulsed with much slaughter. But, strong in numbers, the French returned to the

---

* See Cannon's *Historical Records*, 4th, 23rd, and 34th regiments. Much interesting information respecting the state of the defences at the siege will be found in General Whitworth Porter's *History of the Royal Engineers*, vol. i.

breaches, and ultimately succeeded in effecting lodgments in the Queen's Redoubt, and the Argyle and Anstruther batteries (which last blew up with three companies of French grenadiers). The conflict continued from 10 p.m. till 4 a.m, when the French commander beat a parley for the removal of the wounded and the burial of the dead. The French took advantage of this cessation of arms to strengthen their lodgments. Their success is said to have cost them two thousand men killed and wounded, whilst the loss of the defenders did not exceed forty-seven. A Council of War having decided that the garrison could not withstand another assault, and there being no prospects of succour, terms of capitulation were proposed and accepted, and two days later, on 29th June, 1756, the remains of the heroic little garrison marched out of the place.

In chivalrous testimony to the "noble and vigorous defence made by the English," the Marshal de Richeleiu, in answer to Art. 2 of the Capitulation, decreed to the outgoing troops "all the honours of "war they can possibly enjoy under the circumstances: drums "beating, colours flying, firelocks at the shoulder, twenty rounds of "ball-ammunition in each pouch, gun-matches lighted," etc., etc., in token of "the veneration every military person should feel for such "action."*

The marching-out strength of the 24th was one lieutenant-colonel, one major, seven captains, thirteen subalterns, one chaplain, one adjutant, one surgeon, twenty-three sergeants, twenty-seven corporals, sixteen drummers, and six hundred and five privates. During the siege it lost six killed and sixty-one wounded. The small proportion of casualties compared with the French loss (estimated at five thousand), is explained by the immense extent of bomb-proof cover (subterranean) in the castle.

By the terms of the Capitulation, the late garrison was carried to Gibraltar, whence the 24th subsequently returned to England, and, landing at Portsmouth, marched to Nottingham and Derby to recruit.†

---

* See *London Gazette*, 20-24th July, 1756, in which the text of the Capitulation is given in full.

† *W.O. Marching Book* under date.

ROLL OF OFFICERS OF THE TWO BATTALIONS OF THE 24TH REGIMENT OF FOOT.

From *Annual Army List*, 1758.

Rank	Name	Date	Year
Colonel	Edward Cornwallis M.G., 12 February, 1757.)	8 Feb.,	1752
Lt.-Col.	Wm. Rufane	27 Feb.,	1751
Major	Wm. Godfrey	4 March,	1751
,,	Wm. Preston	26 Aug.,	1756
Capt.	*Edward Martin	7 May,	1744
,	Jas. Goring	1 June,	1746
,,	Joseph Darby	22 Feb.,	1747
,,	Henry Goddard	29 April,	1754
,,	Robt. Preston	26 June,	1754
,,	John Johnstone (27 April, 1756.)	25 Aug.,	1756
,,	John Berkenhunt	26 Aug.,	1756
,,	Aaron Clayton	27 Aug.,	1756
,,	Rich. Edwards	28 Aug.,	1756
,,	*Benjamin Bromhead	29 Aug.,	1756
,,	Wm. Momresson	30 Aug.,	1756
,,	Peter Boileau	31 Aug.,	1756
,,	*Geo. Monk Martin	2 Sept.,	1756
,,	Jas. Macrae	3 Sept.,	1756
,,	Thos. Cook	4 Sept.,	1756
Capt.-Lieut.	John Hill	9 March,	1757
Lieut.	*Ralph Haughton	26 June,	1754
,,	Robt. Carr	31 March,	1756
,,	John Hy. Bastide	14 April,	1756
,,	Robt. Sutton	18 May,	1756
,,	Robt. Johnstone (2 January, 1756.)	25 Aug.,	1756
,,	C. Kellond Courtney (3 January, 1756.)	26 Aug.,	1756
,,	Thos. Gladwin (27 April, 1756.)	27 Aug.,	1756
,,	Loftus Cathcart (14 July, 1756.)	28 Aug.,	1756
,,	Hans Cleland	29 Aug.,	1756
,,	Thos. Blunt	30 Aug.,	1756
,,	Ralph Walsh	31 Aug.,	1756
,,	Geo. Thompson	1 Sept.,	1756
,,	Leonard Ord	2 Sept.,	1756
,,	Wm. Agnew	3 Sept.,	1756
,,	John Ross	4 Sept.,	1756
,,	Chas. Tarrant	5 Sept.,	1756
,,	Wm. Boodger	6 Sept.,	1756
Lieut.	*Valentine Green	7 Sept.,	1756
,,	*Abraham Scott	8 Sept.,	1756
,,	Samuel Hughes	9 March,	1756
,,	Wm. Skinner	21 Sept.,	1756
,,	— Don	22 Sept.,	1756
,,	Courtland Schuyler	22 Sept.,	1756
,,	*Philip Baggs	25 Sept.,	1756
,,	*Jas. Patterson	26 Sept.,	1756
,,	*John Bover Benson	27 Sept.,	1756
,,	*John Jessor	28 Sept.,	1756
,,	*Thos. Horton	29 Sept.,	1756
,,	Jas. Ashe	30 Sept.,	1756
,,	John Travers	1 Oct.,	1756
,,	Ed. Kidley	2 Oct.,	1756
,,	*John Bromhead	3 Oct.,	1756
,,	John Tydd	4 Oct.,	1757
,,	John Tate	5 Oct.,	1757
,,	*Edm. Stafford	6 Oct.,	1757
,,	*Hy. Caldwell	7 Oct.,	1757
Ensign	— Brooke	31 Aug.,	1756
,,	*Joseph Lovell	9 March,	1757
,,	Thos. Goddard	24 Sept.,	1757
,,	Wm. Hunter	25 Sept.,	1757
,,	Jas. Verchild	26 Sept.,	1757
,,	Goodin Dehany	27 Sept.,	1757
,,	Patrick Agnew	28 Sept.,	1757
,,	Ramsden Appleyard	29 Sept.,	1757
,,	Peter Margaret	30 Sept.,	1757
,,	Andrew Jamaison	2 Oct.,	1757
,,	Arthur Albert	3 Oct.,	1757
,,	Thos. Bell	4 Oct.,	1757
,,	*— Jones	5 Oct.,	1757
,,	John Wall	6 Oct.,	1757
Chaplain	Benjamin Span	19 Feb.,	1754
Adjut.	Samuel Hughes	20 Dec.,	1756
,,	John Hill	25 Aug.,	1756
Qr.-Mr.	Robert Carr	11 Feb.,	1756
,,	Ralph Haughton	25 Aug.,	1756
Surgeon	Ed. Gee	19 Sept.,	1746
,,	— Morrison	24 Sept.,	1757
,,	Ag. Calcraft.		

N.B.—Those marked (*) are shown as promoted in the 69th Foot, in its first appearance in the Army List, viz.: *Annual Army List*, 1759.

1757-58.

The Regiment in Two Battalions.

After its return home, the 24th, in common with some other foot regiments, was augmented to twenty companies, and formed in two battalions.

In May, 1757, the 1st battalion moved to Loughborough, Market Harborough, and Melton Mowbray; the 2nd battalion (ten companies) to Leicester. In July, both battalions were at Amersham camp; and afterwards, the 1st in the Isle of Wight, the 2nd in Dorchester camp. A French descent on the South Coast was then regarded as imminent. In September, 1757, the 2nd battalion, seven hundred strong, served in the Rochfort expedition under Sir John Mordaunt. On its return it was placed at the disposal of the Admiralty for duty on board the fleet. The War Office *Marching Books* refer also to the transfer, in November this year, of a company 24th to the 79th Foot, then raising at Chelmsford, under the command of Colonel, afterwards Lieutenant-General, Sir Wm. Draper: "The company 24th Regiment drafted for "the regiment raising under your command to be quartered till "further orders at Ingatestone."*

On 23rd April, 1758, the 2nd battalion 24th, which appears to have been still employed under the Admiralty, was, like other second battalions of the same standing, formed in a separate corps. It was made the 69TH REGIMENT OF FOOT.

1758.

The Regiment a Single Battalion again.

In April, 1758, the 24th was in the Isle of Wight, and moved to Portsmouth. On 1st of June it sailed with the expedition to the coast of France, under command of Chas. Spencer (2nd) Duke of Marlborough. The troops, seventeen thousand men, landed in the

---

* The 79th Regiment left England in 1758, and served with great distinction in the Carnatic, and afterwards captured Manilla. It was disbanded after the peace of 1763. According to the *Annual Army List* no 24th officers were transferred with the company.

Bay of Cancale and marched to St. Malo. Finding that place too strong for a *coup de main*, they marched back and re-embarked, the rear-guard, which was closely pressed by the French, suffering some loss. After returning to the Isle of Wight, the expedition proceeded to Cherbourg, where preparations were made for a descent, but a gale sprang up and played havoc among the transports, and supplies ran short, so the expedition, having done nothing, returned once more to the Isle of Wight, where the troops were disembarked. Later in the year, the regiment was at Ipswich, where "the men at Dover arrived from the French coast" were directed to join.

1759.

During this year—the year of the victories of Minden and Quebec—the regiment was broken up in detachments in Essex and Suffolk.

1760-63.

In May, 1760, the British troops under the Marquis of Granby, serving with the Allied Army under Prince Ferdinand of Brunswick, which was employed in defending the Electorate of Hanover whilst Frederick of Prussia was warring with the French and Austrians, received a considerable reinforcement. The detachments of the 24th were called in to head-quarters at Chelmsford, and the regiment embarked for Germany with the 5th, 8th, 11th, 24th, 33rd, and 50th, "Six of our best regiments," wrote the Duke of Newcastle to Granby.*

On 1st July, 1760, the 24th fought at Corbach (misspelt Corbake in some accounts), where it had eight men reported missing in the retreat. Lord Granby spoke in high terms of the conduct of "Cornwallis's." On 31st July, the same year, at Warburg, where Prince Ferdinand routed the French, taking ten guns and one thousand five hundred prisoners, the 24th was in General Waldegrave's brigade of Lord Granby's corps, and had Captain Carr and one non-commissioned officer and three privates killed, and Lieutenant Ord and twenty-one privates wounded, and three privates missing. It was engaged in many other affairs during the year with Lord Granby's

---

* *Historic MSS. Commission: Rep. on Rutland MSS.*

corps, which had its head-quarters at Corvery, near Hoxter, for the winter.

On 25th October, 1760, George II. died, and was succeeded by his grandson, George III.

In February, 1761, the 24th, with other British regiments, to whom the post of honour appears to have always been assigned, marched through the deep snow into Hesse Cassel, and took part in various operations which drove the French back on the Fulda and afterwards upon Frankfort-on-Maine, with the destruction of all the magazines and stores they had collected for the forthcoming campaign. The armies, however, ultimately resumed their former positions, and in July, Prince Ferdinand, with his ninety-five thousand allied troops, found himself menaced by two French armies of the aggregate strength of one hundred and sixty thousand men, under the Duke De Broglie and Marshal Soubise. They effected a junction at Soest, and on 15th July, 1761, De Broglie attacked Granby's corps at Fellinghausen, but, owing to what Prince Ferdinand called the "indescribable bravery" *(unbeschreibender tapferkeit)* of the British, failed to dislodge them. This was followed on the morrow by an attack of the whole French army, which, after five hours' firing, was compelled to retreat in what ended in a flight towards the Rhine. In this engagement the 24th had Lieutenant-Colonel Cook, commanding, two non-commissioned officers and eighteen rank and file killed, and Lieutenant Verchild, eight non-commissioned officers and forty-two rank and file wounded, and twenty-seven rank and file missing. The regiment was in various other operations with Lord Granby's corps, including the passage of the Dymel, when he drove the French back into their camp at Cassel.

In 1762, among other affairs, the regiment was with Lord Granby when he cut off the French rear-guard on 24th June. On this occasion the Grenadiers de France, the Grenadiers Royale, and other French *corps d'elite*, laid down their arms at Wilhelmstahl to the 5th Foot, which thence acquired the privilege of wearing grenadier caps, long before its conversion into a fusilier corps. The despatch makes no mention of the 24th Foot, but it appears in the record of service of General Thomas Scott, *(Appendix B)* who died in 1842, and was an ensign in the 24th at the time, that he was wounded, carrying the King's Colour of the regiment on the occasion.

The 24th was also engaged at the defence of the Fulda, during the siege of Cassel, in the same year. Picquets of various regiments, numbering four hundred and twenty men, under command of Major Home, 25th Edinburgh Regiment,* had been thrown across the Fulda, to occupy the further bank. The river was so swollen that the men had to join hands in fording it. They remained in a very critical position all night. On the following morning they received an attack from two thousand French, whom they held at bay until the 24th got over in support and the French were driven off.

It should be observed that during the campaigns of 1760-61-62, the Grenadier company of the 24th, like those of other British foot, was attached to one of the two Grenadier battalions, which with the Highland regiments, formed the advanced guard of the army, and were repeatedly engaged with the enemy on the above and many other occasions. Their conspicuous gallantry was recorded again and again, but their casualties were included in the aggregate of the flank battalion to which they belonged, and cannot now be traced regimentally.

Peace was concluded in 1763, ending the Seven Years' War. The 24th Regiment then proceeded from Germany to Gibraltar.

1763-68.

The regiment was stationed at Gibraltar during this period. A return of the last-named year shows the regiment with thirty-two officers, forty-seven non-commissioned officers, and four hundred and fourteen privates fit for duty and fourty-four sick.

A notice in the *London Gazette*, dated War Office, 10th January, 1767, contains the following announcement: "Whereas many mistakes and "inconveniences have arisen from the want of an authentic publication of "the Commissions granted to Officers in His Majesty's Army, notice is "hereby given that the said Commissions shall, for the future, be regularly "published in the *London Gazette*."

---

* Afterwards Governor Home, who was murdered by the insurgent Blacks in Grenada in 1796.—See *Historical Record* 25th K.O. Borderers.

1769-76.

The 24th Regiment returned from Gibraltar to Ireland in 1769, and was stationed there until after the outbreak of the war in America. Lieutenant-Colonel Simon Fraser *(Appendix B)*, a very talented and distinguished officer (not to be confounded with Simon Fraser, Master of Lovat), was first and principal aide-de-camp to the lord lieutenant, Lord Townshend, and in 1771 was appointed quartermaster-general in Ireland in the room of Colonel Gisborne. The light company was formed at this period.

On 14th January, 1776, Major-General William Taylor *(Appendix B)* was appointed colonel in the room of the Honble. Edward Cornwallis, deceased. In April, 1776, the regiment embarked at Cork, with other reinforcements, for Canada, and on 1st June landed at Quebec, which had been besieged during the winter by an American army, but just withdrawn. Colonel Simon Fraser joined at Quebec and assumed command of the regiment, which took the field at once. It was engaged in the affair at Three Rivers, 8th January, 1776, when it had some men wounded. The Americans retreated, leaving General Thomas, a number of officers, and four hundred men prisoners in the hands of the loyalists. Colonel Simon Fraser was appointed to command a brigade consisting of the 24th Regiment (Major Robert Grant commanding) and a grenadier and light battalion. Subsequently, the regiment proceeded to St. Johns, and prepared vessels and bateaux for embarkation on Lake Champlain. In these it crossed, with the rest of the army, to Crown Point, which was abandoned on the British approach. The Americans having thus been driven out of Canada, the troops went into winter quarters. During the winter— a very severe one—Fraser's brigade was stationed on the south side of the St. Lawrence. Lieutenant Thomas Scott, 24th regiment, who had been much employed in scouting duties with small parties of Canadians and Indians, was one of the officers selected by the commander-in-chief, Sir Guy Carleton, to reside in the Indian villages during the winter, to prevent the enemy tampering with the tribes. Lieutenant Scott resided at the Lake of Two Mountains, whence he brought with him one hundred of the best warriors, with whom he was upon a variety of active and severe service in the ensuing spring.

1777-82.

After various minor operations in the spring, the 24th Regiment took the field with Lieutenant-General Burgoyne's army (about seven thousand men), in June, 1777, which was to penetrate to Albany by way of the lower lakes.

At Hubberton, on 7th July, 1777, the American army was overtaken by Fraser's brigade, which formed the "advanced corps," and a smart action took place, in which the 24th had Major Robt. Grant, commanding, and a number of men killed, and Captain Maisters, Lieutenant Poor, Ensign Meredith and a great number wounded. The exact number of casualties is not known. One thousand two hundred of the enemy, with a full proportion of officers, were taken prisoners.

The army moved along the Hudson River, and on 19th September, 1777, at a place called Freeman's Farm, otherwise Still Water, again attacked the Americans, and forced them to retreat. Major Agnew, who had succeeded Major Grant in command of the regiment, Captains Blake and Fergusson and Ensign Doyle were wounded, and many men killed and wounded. Captain the Honble. Stephen Digby Strangways* then assumed command of the regiment.

---

* This officer, a son of the first Earl of Ilchester, appears in his previous commissions under the name of Digby. The following letter, relating to him, minuted in the *Calendar of Home Office Papers*, of 1771, shews that the 24th, under Colonel Fraser, was considered a desirable regiment. The lord lieutenant (Lord Townshend) writes to Lord Rochdale, (Home Office,) "humbly hoping" that Captain the Honble. Stephen Digby, brother to Lord Digby and senior captain of the 24th, may have the majority rendered vacant in the 58th by the promotion of Colonel—afterwards General—John Burgoyne in another corps, and that His Excellency's son, "who is serving without pay as a cornet in the 4th Dragoons," may have the vacant company in the 24th. But, His Excellency is "most desirous that it should "be understood that his solicitude is chiefly on account of Captain Digby, who is "a meritorious officer and a relative of the late Lady Townshend." He retired as lieutenant-colonel, half-pay, 76th Foot, in 1783, and died at an advanced age in 1836.

ROLL OF OFFICERS OF THE 24TH REGIMENT OF FOOT.

(Annual Army List, corrected to March, 1777.)

Colonel	Wm. Taylor	15th Jan., 1776	M.G., 29th Sept.
Lieut.-Col.	Simon Fraser	14th July, 1768	
Major	Robt. Grant	5th March, 1775	
Captain	Wm. Agnew	20th May, 1767	
,,	Hon. Stephen Digby Strangways	17th April, 1769	
,,	Rich. Master	14th March, 1771	
,,	And. Jamaison	26th Sept., 1772	
,,	Henry Pilmer	28th March, 1775	
,,	John Blake	7th July, 1775	
,,	Jas. Verchild	14th Nov., 1775	
,,	Wm. Ferguson	3rd Feb., 1776	
,,	John Jones	2nd March, 1776	
Capt.-Lieut.	Geo. Coote	2nd March, 1776	
Lieutenant	Thos. Scott	7th June, 1765	
,,	Rich. Bucraft	13th Feb., 1766	
,,	Robert Pennington	10th Feb., 1770	13th Feb., 1762
,,	Wm. Campbell	26th Sept., 1772	
,,	Chas. Williams	16th July, 1774	
,,	Thos. Bibby	28th Jan., 1775	
,,	Chas. Erle	28th March, 1775	
,,	Geo. Cotter	7th July, 1775	
,,	Robt. Stiel	14th Nov., 1775	
,,	Ed. St. Eloy	3rd Feb., 1776	
,,	Boyle Spencer	1st March, 1776	21st March, 1759
,,	Chas. Johnson	2nd March, 1776	
,,	Thos. Reed	3rd March, 1776	
Ensign	Wm. Doyle	16th July, 1774	
,,	John Ferguson	31st August, 1774	
,,	Minchin Hobart	28th Jan., 1775	
,,	Jas. Power	28th March, 1775	
,,	Quin John Freeman	7th July, 1775	
,,	Wm. Fuller	3rd Feb., 1776	
,,	John Kyrwood	1st March, 1776	
,,	Rich. Stowe	2nd March, 1776	
,,	Nicholas Foster	3rd March, 1776	
,,	Hy. Pringle	4th March, 1776	
Chaplain	T. Towezin Church	21st Dec., 1775	
Adjutant	Robt. Pennington	1st May, 1775	
Qr.-Mr.	John Ferguson	6rh April, 1776	
Surgeon	Samuel Sone	30th April, 1771.	

On 7th October, 1777, the American army, which, having been strongly reinforced, had assumed the offensive, attacked Burgoyne in the same ground. In the action—sometimes known as of Behmus Heights—a quick movement of the 24th light company saved the left of Burgoyne's force when retreating to the camp.* Brigadier Simon Fraser was struck by a rifle-ball, and died of his wound the following morning, to the profound regret of the whole army.† Much resentment was aroused at the time by the Americans—in ignorance of the nature of the proceedings—opening fire on the funeral party.‡ Captain Jones and Ensign Foster were wounded in the same engagement. Burgoyne now retired to Saratoga, where on 11th October, the 24th were again engaged, and had Honble. Stephen Digby Strangways wounded and thirty men killed and wounded.

On 17th October, 1777, the army under Lieutenant-General John Burgoyne being completely surrounded, without supplies or prospect of relief, capitulated to the American General Gates. The terms of convention were as follows:—

The Troops under General Burgoyne, to the number of five thousand seven hundred and ninety, to march out of their camp, with the Honours of War, to the verge of the river, where the arms and artillery are to be left, the arms to be piled by word of command of their own officers. All officers to retain their carriages and best horses, and to be permitted to wear their side arms. The troops to proceed to Massachusetts Bay, and to be quartered in or as near as may be to Boston, under their own officers, until transports arrive to convey them to England, on condition of never serving again in North America during the present contest.

Owing to disputes as to the treatment of prisoners etc. the provisions of the capitulation were never carried out, and the troops remained prisoners until the peace.

---

* Hume and Smollett, *History of England*, vol. iii.

† A fact, that speaks more than pages of panegyric, is that, years afterwards, a considerable sum was repaid to Colonel Fraser's family, by order of the House of Commons. It had been paid by him, out of his own pocket, for shoes for the men of his brigade.

‡ A painting of the incident, which has often been engraved, is now at **Farraline House, Stratherrick, Invernesshire.**

Under Lieutenant-Colonel Lord Balcarres *(Appendix B)*, who was promoted to Colonel Fraser's vacancy, from the 53rd regiment, 8th October, 1777, the 24th proceeded from Saratoga to Boston, and thence to Bunker's Hill. Lord Balcarres and Major Agnew went home on parole, and most of the officers followed in succession, either by exchange or on parole. From Bunker's Hill the regiment was marched into Virginia, and thence from place to place until the peace, when it numbered less than one hundred men, who returned to England to join the head-quarters—such as they were—at Alresford, Hants.

The position of the prisoners in America in regard to the Mutiny Act must have been highly anomalous, and desertions must have been numerous to account for the diminution of numbers. The muster-rolls of the regiment for this period—if ever rendered—are now lost. What was the fate of the Colours is unknown. No mention can be found of them, and it can only be presumed that they were brought home at last.

CHAPTER V.

1782-1802.

County Title bestowed—Home—Canada and Nova Scotia—Egypt—Badge.

1782.

ON 31st August, 1782, a Royal Warrant was issued conferring COUNTY TITLES on all regiments of foot not already possessed of some special designation in addition to their number. Such regiments were enjoined, in the interests of recruiting, to cultivate a connection with the localities after which they named. The 24th Foot was directed to style itself the 24TH (OR 2ND WARWICKSHIRE) REGIMENT OF FOOT, and to have a detachment for recruiting at Tamworth.* It retained the county title for just one hundred years.

Inspection of the Regimental *Muster Rolls* and War Office *Marching Books* of this period suggest a hopeless condition of the recruiting market; and more particularly does this seem to have been the case just after the introduction of county titles. The practice of enlisting for short periods (three years, or the continuance of the war) which had been revived a few years previously, had ceased, and long-service recruits were not to be got. The depot companies, represented by about a dozen men each, were kept incessantly on the move, in the vain hope of filling up their ranks. Two companies of the 24th thus appear successively at Tamworth and at Old Windsor, then back again at Tamworth and Coventry, from whence one company was sent to Lymington, Hants.

---

* The 6th Foot became the 6th (or 1st Warwickshire) Regiment of Foot at the same time, and had its recruiting company at Warwick.

1783.

On 21st February, 1783, Lieutenant-Colonel Richard England *(Appendix B)* was appointed lieutenant-colonel of the regiment. The parties of 24th (presumably recruiting) in the New Forest, were collected at Poole, and sent first to Winchester, and then, in May, to Hilsea Barracks, whence, in June, they marched to Alton and Alresford.

In July, the service companies, one hundred men in all, returned from America. An order of 21st July directs the soldiers of the 9th and 24th regiments, on landing from the *Adamantine* transport, to join their respective corps. The 24th men were all discharged on joining. Another order, of 21st August, addressed to "The officer "Commanding the 24th Regiment at Alresford," directs that "You "will cause the effective men of your regiment, under a subaltern, to "march to Winchester, there to assist in guarding prisoners of war, and "to be augmented to 1 capt., 2 subalterns, and 50 men, *whenever the* "*Regiment shall be in a position to supply them.*" Alresford, it may be observed, is in the centre of Hampshire. The regiment moved from thence to Dover Castle, in October, and on 31st December, 1783, was ordered to march from Dover and Rochester to Berwick-on-Tweed, there to await instructions from the officer commanding the forces in North Britain.

1784-88.

In 1784 the regiment was quartered in Edinburgh Castle. In 1785 it embarked at Glasgow for Drogheda, and was quartered at Belfast and other places in the North of Ireland. In 1786 it was at Galway; in 1787-88 in Dublin.

1789-92.

In April, 1789, the 24th Regiment, Lieutenant-Colonel Richard England commanding, embarked for Canada. It landed at Quebec, where it was stationed until December, 1791, when it moved to Montreal. In 1791, Canada was divided into the two provinces of Upper Canada (now Ontario) and Lower Canada (now Quebec). The 24th remained at Montreal until May, 1792, when the monthly return shows the regiment, consisting of eighteen officers, four staff, nineteen sergeants, ten drummers, and three hundred and seventy-five rank and file, Lieutenant-Colonel Rich. England commanding, on the march to Detroit. Detroit, at the far extremity of Lake Erie, was then a remote settlement in the backwoods, which a few years before had been the scene of some bloodshed between rival bands of traders contending for the monopoly of the Far West. Colonel England was one of the first landholders in this part of Canada, North-West.

1793-1800.

In this remote region—where but a few scattered clearings had as yet broken the solitude of the forest—the regiment—with its headquarters and five and a half companies at Detroit, three and a half companies at the Miami Rapids, and one and a half companies at Michilimackenaw—was, at the beginning of February, 1793, when a decree of the French National Convention against the King of Great Britain opened the long war of 1793-1815. It remained at Detroit until the fall of 1796. The Indians at this time were exceedingly troublesome, and the troops at the outposts had constantly to interfere for the protection of American, as well as Canadian, settlers.* Ever since the conclusion of the War of Independence, in 1783, chronic feuds had existed between the United States frontier settlers and certain Indian tribes who refused to "bury the hatchet," and were alleged by the Americans to rely upon British support. In 1791 a United States army, under Major-General Sinclair, had been routed and massacred close to the Miami villages. In 1793, Major-General Anthony Wayne, United States Army, was despatched with another force to act against the Indians, and, as the post which the 24th detachment had fortified at Miami was claimed as American territory, Wayne was instructed by Secretary Knox that "in the "course of your operations, should it become necessary to dislodge "the party at the Rapids of the Miami, you are hereby authorised to "do so in the name of the President of the United States"† Wayne

---

* See Cannon's *Historical Record* 5th Fusiliers.
† H. N. Moore's *Life of Anthony Wayne* (Philadelphia, 1847) p. 87.

defeated the Indians in a pitched battle near the Rapids, after which, his biographer states, "the fort was carefully reconnoitred within "pistol-shot distance, not, perhaps, without a latent wish that such "provocation would be given as would justify to the whole world its "capture."* But, Major William Campbell, 24th regiment, who was in command at Miami, was too wary and experienced a soldier to be drawn in this way. He remonstrated with General Wayne for making so near an approach to the post, and warned him against any act of hostility, as there was no war between Great Britain and the United States. Wayne replied that he had by right expelled an Indian enemy from United States territory, but that the British had committed an act of hostility by reoccupying a post admittedly on American soil. Campbell rejoined that, having been placed in command there by superior authority, he could not give up the post without orders, at the same time expressing a friendly hope that the question would be settled amicably elsewhere. The question was eventually settled by the Treaty of 1795, Detroit and the outposts being recognized as American territory, and the garrisons withdrawn.

On 13th November, 1793, Major-General Richard Whyte *(Appendix B)* was appointed colonel, *vice* Taylor, deceased. On 10th August, 1794, the thanks of the Legislative Council of Upper Canada were voted to Major William Campbell, 24th regiment, "for his temperate "and dignified forbearance and otherwise meritorious conduct during "his command at Miami in the preceding year."† On its return from Detroit the regiment was stationed at Montreal. The depôt at this time appears to have been at Chatham, and a number of officers employed in England recruiting. Lieutenant John Bromhead of the regiment (afterwards Lieutenant-Colonel Bromhead, C.B., 77th Foot), was deputy assistant adjutant-general in Canada. In 1797 the regiment removed to Quebec, where the corporals and privates of the 5th Foot were transferred to it in a body, the officers and sergeants of

---

* H. N. Moore's *Life of Anthony Wayne* (Philadelphia, 1847) p. 197.
† *Annual Register*, 1795. Major Campbell was promoted to a lieutenant-colonelcy, and died in 1797.

that regiment going home to recruit it.* The 24th remained at Quebec until November, 1799, when the uneasiness prevailing at Halifax, Nova Scotia, caused it to be sent thither as a reinforcement. Major Charles Erle was at this time in command. At the conclusion of the Maroon War in Jamaica, in 1795, some six hundred Maroons had been deported from Jamaica, and settled in the neighbourhood of Halifax.† At first they seemed to do well; but in a year or two want and discontent began to show amongst them, and it was found necessary to place them under guard at Port Pleasant. Much anxiety was caused about the same time by the frequent mysterious attempts to fire the naval yard at Halifax. After the arrival of the 24th at Halifax it was decided to ship off the main body of Maroons to Sierra Leone, which had been ceded by the native chiefs to the British Government some years before, and was proposed for a negro settlement under the auspices of Messrs. Clarkson, W. Wilberforce, and other leading advocates of the abolition of slavery. Accordingly, in August, 1800, a body of three hundred and fifty Maroons was sent on board H.M.S. *Asia*, under guard of a detachment of the 24th, commanded by Lieutenant Lionel Smith *(Appendix B)*, who had been employed on the staff in Nova Scotia, with Lieutenant H. D. Tolley.‡

---

* The late Colonel Landmann, R.E., in the first series of his *Recollections* (London, 1852,) gives a good deal of gossip about the 24th at Quebec. The garrison, when Landmann was there in 1798-99, consisted of the 24th, 26th Cameronians, and Canadian Volunteers. The 24th was stationed in what was known as the Jesuits' Barracks, which the Jesuit fathers had been allowed to retain when Quebec was taken forty years before, upon the condition that no further additions should be made to their numbers. In 1798, a solitary old Jesuit survived, who lived in a corner of the 24th barracks. Landmann tells a number of anecdotes of Colonel England, whose gigantic stature acquired for him the *sobriquet* of "Great Britain," and who was a noted *bon vivant*.

† When the Spaniards were dispossessed of Jamaica in Cromwell's day, their slaves betook themselves to the mountains, and, reinforced by runaways from time to time, became very troublesome neighbours. A Maroon rebellion was put down in 1795 by Lord Balcarres (a former lieutenant-colonel, 24th), who was then in command of the troops. About six hundred Maroons were deported, with their own consent, to Nova Scotia, and of these, three hundred and fifty were transferred to Sierra Leone, in October, 1800, at a cost to the British Government of £5,903 10s. 9d.

‡ Afterwards Major-General Henry Tolley, C.B., many years lieutenant-colonel commanding 16th (Bedfordshire) Regiment. Died 25th December, 1837.

of the regiment, as second in command, for conveyance to Sierra Leone.

On 22nd September, 1800, the rest of the regiment embarked at Halifax for home, under command of Major Charles Erle, and on arriving at Portsmouth occupied Hilsea Barracks. In December the regiment marched to Exeter. Early in December the detachment, serving as marines on board H.M.S. *Asia*, returned from Sierra Leone, under command of Lieutenant H. D. Tolley. Lieutenant Lionel Smith remained to conclude the arrangements at Sierra Leone and Goree, and on his return was promoted in the 85th Regiment. A captain's detachment also joined head-quarters from Lynn, where it had been stationed as a depôt.

1801.

The Act of Union, taking effect from 1st January, 1801, necessitated a change in the blazon of the Union Flag, which was forthwith introduced in the colours and standards of the army. *(See Appendix C.)*

The regiment remained at Exeter and Tiverton up to June, 1801.

THE CAMPAIGN IN EGYPT IN 1801.

Before pursuing the narrative further, it may be well here to recall briefly the course of events in a part of the world whither the regiment was soon to proceed.

On 8th March, 1801, a British expeditionary force, collected chiefly from Minorca and Malta, under the command of Lieutenant-General Sir Ralph Abercromby, K.B., landed in Egypt, in Aboukir Bay—the scene of Nelson's victory of the Nile two years before. At the time of the landing, the French armies that had overrun Egypt were concentrated at Alexandria and Cairo. Some fighting followed, and on 21st March, 1801, the French were defeated in a great battle before Alexandria, in which Abercromby fell. General—afterwards Lord—Hutchinson, Abercromby's successor, after some delay, moved up the Nile towards Cairo with the double purpose of separating the two French armies, so as to be able to deal with them in succession, and of effecting a junction with the Indian contingent, known to be on its way up the Red Sea, under General Baird. Cairo capitulated on 27th June, 1801. The other army remained in Alexandria, blockaded by a small British force under General Coote.

When the news of Abercromby's victory of 21st March reached home, additional troops were at once ordered to Egypt. The 24th Regiment, Lieutenant-Colonel John Randall Forster commanding, then in Exeter barracks, was directed to march to Plymouth Dock (Devonport), where, on 4th June, 1801, it embarked with other reinforcements—including the 22nd Light Dragoons, some drafts of the Foot Guards, the 25th, 26th Cameronians, and the Swiss Regiment of Watteville, then just taken into the British service. They reached Alexandria at the beginning of July. A return, dated 9th July, 1801, shows the 24th with two battalions of the 20th and the Ancient Irish Volunteers,* forming the sixth brigade, commanded by Brevet-Colonel Blake, 24th regiment, with Lieutenant John Chatterton, 24th, as his brigade-major.

An officer present with the army thus describes its condition at this time :—†

"Owing to the difficulty in procuring specie, no pay was issued to the "army, and, except when officers made advances to the men out of their "own pockets, which was done at a great loss, as over twenty per cent. "was lost on the exchange, the soldiers had not wherewithal to purchase "the necessaries of life. Living entirely on their rations in a country "abounding with every luxury, and particularly the musk and water "melons, so grateful in hot climates, they could not command a melon or "a bunch of grapes for want of money, and yet not a murmur was heard. "Everything was paid for as scrupulously as in Leadenhall or Covent "Garden market, and, with the thoughtless generosity of their character, "the British always raised every market by offering more than was asked."

On his return from Cairo, General Hutchinson decided to push on the siege of Alexandria with vigour, and on 17th August, General Coote, with the Guards and two brigades of the line, crossed Lake Mareotis in boats to attack the city from the western side. Some sharp fighting ensued, particularly at the capture of Fort Marabout

---

* A corps of Irish Fencibles formed out of the Irish Militia in 1798. As in other Fencible regiments of that period, the men had engaged for limited service, and not to go out of Europe. At Minorca they volunteered to go on to Egypt, and thenceforward were known as the Ancient Irish Volunteers.

† The late Major-General D. Stewart of Garth, who was present as a captain, 42nd Highlanders. See his *Sketches of the Scottish Highlanders*, vol. i.

by the 54th Regiment. On 24th August, General Brent Spencer followed with Blake's brigade and some Turks and Mamelukes to reinforce Coote; but on the following day the French proposed a three days' truce, and on 1st September, 1801, the city surrendered. Next day, amid the thunder of salutes from sea and shore, the British grenadiers took possession of the gates, and the Cross and Crescent flags were hoisted side by side above the walls. A return of the army, dated 15th September, 1801, shows the 24th in camp on the west side of the city without the walls, in brigade with the 26th Cameronians and two battalions 54th, under Major-General Lord Cavan. The regiment appears to have been very sickly during its stay in Egypt.*

The deaths of the undermentioned officers are recorded :—

Captain Edward Francis	died 30th August, 1801
Lieutenant T. E. Boyfield	,, 2nd September, 1801
Lieutenant Taylor	,, 21st August, 1801
Ensign Wm. Ball	,, 1st September, 1801.

Of the rest, Colonel Blake was acting as brigadier-general, so that the regiment was commanded by Lieutenant-Colonel John Randall Forster throughout the campaign. Lieutenant-Colonel Doyle was absent, D.A.G. in Canada. Captain O'Brien and Captain-Lieutenant Bellingham were absent (the latter without leave) in Canada. Captain Short (the former adjutant) and Lieutenant Wemyss were on leave when the regiment was ordered to Egypt, and, not rejoining, were returned absent without leave. Lieutenants Thos. Watkin Forster, Richard England, and Wm. Redding were left in charge of

---

* The monthly return, dated 1st August, shows twenty-eight officers present, and forty sergeants, thirteen drummers, and four hundred and forty-five rank and file fit for duty and ninety-five sick, and records one death. In that of 1st September, twenty-seven officers are present, and forty sergeants, fourteen drummers, and four hundred and two rank and file fit for duty, with one hundred and twenty-six sick—including two men wounded. The deaths of one officer and ten men are recorded. In the return of 1st October, twenty-five officers are shewn as present, forty sergeants, fourteen drummers, and one hundred and seventy-four rank and file fit for duty, and three hundred and forty-two sick. Two officers and twenty men died during the preceding month. The return of 1st November shows twenty-six officers present, forty sergeants, fourteen drummers, and two hundred and twelve rank and file fit for duty, and two hundred and sixty-four sick, and records seventeen deaths and one desertion. The regiment is said to have suffered severely from ophthalmia.

sick and baggage at Plymouth Dock. Lieutenant Tudor was absent as aide-de-camp to General Hunter, in Canada. Lieutenant Stisted, and Ensigns Collis and Galway were recruiting at home during the campaign. Volunteers A. Blake and Price served with the regiment through the campaign.

The regiment left Egypt at the end of October, 1801, for Malta, when the gold medals presented by the Sultan of Turkey to the British officers were distributed by Lord Hutchinson. The medals were of large size for general and field officers, and smaller for captains and subalterns, and were to be worn with an orange (terracotta) ribbon. The medal is figured in Carter's *Medals of the British Army*, (London, 1861).

1802.

On 27th March, 1802, peace was signed at Amiens, and the 24th and other regiments returned home. The 24th proceeded from Malta to Portsmouth, and was quartered at Hilsea Barracks.

Soon after its return home, the Horse Guards circular, given below, was sent to all the regiments engaged in the Egyptian campaign, authorizing the wearing of a badge, consisting of the figure of "THE SPHYNX," superscribed "EGYPT," which in after years became the regimental badge of the 24th (or 2nd Warwickshire) Regiment. The circumstances of the badge not being inserted in the *Army List* until January, 1813, appears to have given rise to a belief that it was granted at a later date than that of the circular.

"Horse Guards,
"6th July, 1802.

"SIR.—I have the Honor to inform you that His Majesty has been "graciously pleased to grant permission to the several regiments of His "army which served during the late campaign in Egypt, to assume and "wear on their colours a badge, as a distinguished mark of His Majesty's "Royal approbation, and as a lasting memorial of the glory acquired to "His Majesty's arms by the zeal, discipline, and intrepedity of His troops "in that arduous and important campaign.

"H.R.H. the Commander-in-Chief has directed me to make this "communication to you in order that the regiment under your command "may avail itself of the honor thus conferred by His Majesty; and I am "commanded at the same time to apprize you that a pattern of the badge "approved by His Majesty is lodged at the office of the Comptrollers of "Army Accounts, there to be had recourse to as circumstances may require.

"I am Sir, &c.,
"(Signed) H. CALVERT, A.G."

84   HISTORICAL RECORDS.

ROLL OF OFFICERS OF THE 24TH (2ND WARWICKSHIRE) REGIMENT OF FOOT.

Corrected to January, 1801.   From the *Annual Army List* for 1801.

Colonel	Rich. Whyte	13th November, 1793	Lt.-Genl., 26th Jan., 1797
Lieutenant-Colonel	John Blake	23rd March, 1797	Colonel, 1st Jan., 1798
,,	John Randall Forster	5th December, 1799	
Major	Chas. Erle	2nd September, 1795	Lt.-Col., 1st Jan., 1798
,,	Wm. Kelly	5th April, 1799	
Captain	Wm. Doyle	31st July, 1787	Lt.-Col., 22nd July, 1797
,,	Chas. Wm. Short	9th July, 1794	
,,	Edmund Henn	3rd September, 1795	
,,	Ed. Jas. O'Brien	28th October, 1795	
,,	Thos. Chamberlain	25th April, 1797	
,,	John Bromhead	31st October, 1799	
,,	Robt. Whyte	7th November, 1799	
,,	Ed. Francis	23rd May, 1800	
,,	Hy. Andrews	28th August, 1800	
Captain-Lieut.	Allan Bellingham	3rd May, 1799	
Lieutenant	Andrew Foster	9th April, 1794	
,,	Francis Wemyss	9th July, 1794	
,,	Thos. Watkin Forster	2nd February, 1795	
,,	Lionel Smith	28th October, 1795	
,,	Wm. Robison	25th May, 1796—(Robinson in the *Army List*.	
,,	Henry White	26th May, 1796	Robison in later lists.)
,,	Rich. England	28th May, 1796	
,,	Thos. Farrer	8th June, 1796	
,,	Wm. Langworthy	23rd June, 1796	
,,	Thos. Ware	24th June 1796	
,,	Oliver Mills	25th June, 1796	
,,	Henry Dunbar Tolley	25th April, 1797	8th September, 1795
,,	Chas. Hughes	11th May, 1797	
,,	Fred. Crofton	1st June, 1797	
,,	John Evans	7th June, 1797	
,,	Wm. Redding	20th March, 1799	Lieut., 9th October, 1797
,,	Danl. Baby	10th May, 1799	
,,	T. Hughes Jas. Williams	7th November, 1799	
,,	Rich. Adams	8th November, 1800	
,,	Thos. Acklom	11th January, 1800	Lieut., 21st Nov., 1799
,,	Wm. Tudor	23rd January, 1800	
,,	Thos. Edlyne Boyfield	17th September, 1800	
Ensign	Henry Collis	19th December, 1799—(Colls in the *Army List*.	
,,	Thos. Minster	11th January, 1800	Collis in later lists.)
,,	Denis Daly	28th August, 1800	
,,	John Chatterton	17th September, 1800	
,,	Chas. Grant	18th September, 1800	
,,	Fred. Netterville	26th September, 1800	
,,	John Galway		
,,	Francis John Fuller		
Paymaster	Rich. Morse Payne	2nd September, 1799	
Adjutant	Andrew Foster	{ 13th December, 1797 { Lieut., 9th April, 1794	
Quarter-Master	Peter Greenwood	5th October, 1795	
Surgeon	John Irwin		

Lieutenants Mills and Redding appear to have been recruiting at Coventry and Warwick at the beginning of the year.

N.B.—Major-General Daniel Baby, Major-General Denis Daly, Lieutenant-Colonel Chas. Hughes retired full-pay 24th Foot, and Major Fred. Crofton, late 22nd Foot—all subalterns in the 24th in Egypt—and Captain and Quartermaster James Murray, half-pay, 24th—in the ranks in Egypt—survived to receive the War Medal with Clasp for "Egypt," under G.O., 1st June, 1847.

CHAPTER VI.

1802-24.

Renewal of the War—The Regiment formed in Two Battalions—Services of the First Battalion—Cape of Good Hope—Mozambique—India.

1802-4.

IN June, 1802, the regiment, under command of Major Kelly, marched from Hilsea Barracks to Liverpool, where, in December, Lieutenant-Colonel the Honble. Godfrey Macdonald *(Appendix B)* joined and assumed command, *vice* Lieutenant-Colonel John Randall Forster, who retired from the Service.

On 18th May, 1803, the short truce afforded by the Peace of Amiens came to an end, and war was again declared against France. The regiment was at the time on the march from Liverpool to Ipswich, where it arrived in June. During the invasion alarms of the next two years, the regiment was stationed in the eastern counties, and nowhere was the danger more constantly present. In August, 1803, the regiment was reviewed on Bromswell Heath, with the 30th, 53rd, and 69th regiments, by H.R.H. the Duke of York. On 17th September, 1803, Sergeant-Major John Ward,* who had been regimental sergeant-major in Egypt, was appointed adjutant, *vice* Andrew Foster, who resigned the adjutancy only. In November, 1803, the regiment moved to Norwich, and in August, 1804, from Norwich to Woodbridge Barracks, Suffolk, when an order for the formation of a second battalion was received. *(See chapter vii.)*

---

* Retired as captain, half-pay, 24th Foot in 1816.

ROLL OF OFFICERS OF THE TWO BATTALIONS 24TH (2ND WARWICKSHIRE) REGIMENT OF FOOT.

Corrected to January, 1805. From the *Annual Army List*, 1805.

Rank	Name	Date	Year
Colonel	Rich. Whyte (Genl., 29 April, 1802)	13 Nov.,	1793
Lt.-Col.	Hon. Godfrey Macdonald	28 April,	1802
,,	Randolph Marriott	1 Sept.,	1804
Major	Wm. Kelly	5 April,	1799
,,	Chas. Hicks (Major, 25 Sept., 1803)	1 Aug.,	1804
,,	Thos. Chamberlain	1 Aug.,	1804
,,	Sam. Taylor Popham (Major, 1 Sept., 1804)	1 Aug.,	1804
Captain	John Bromhead	31 Oct.,	1800
,,	Henry Andrews	28 Aug.,	1800
,,	Chas. Crigan (Capt., 25 Jan., 1798)	4 Jan.,	1801
,,	Thos. Watkin Forster	16 July,	1802
,,	Wm. Bowyer	23 Feb.,	1803
,,	Andrew Foster	25 May,	1803
,,	Wm. Robison	25 June,	1803
,,	Arthur Blake	7 April,	1804
,,	Jas. Torre	2 Aug.,	1804
,,	Henry White	3 Aug.,	1804
,,	Thos. Andrew Green	4 Aug.,	1804
,,	Wm. Langworthy	5 Aug.,	1804
,,	Oliver Mills	6 Aug.,	1804
,,	Ludovick Stewart	27 Aug.,	1804
,,	Chas. Hughes	28 Aug.,	1804
,,	Thos. Craig	26 Oct.,	1804
Lieut.	John Evans	7 June,	1797
,,	Danl. Baby	10 May,	1799
,,	Rich. Adams	8 Nov.,	1799
,,	Wm. Tudor	22 Jan.,	1800
,,	Jas. Lepper	24 March,	1803
,,	Rich. Gubbins (Lieut., 25 Jan., 1803)	26 May,	1803
Lieut.	Thos. Malkin	1 Oct.,	1803
,,	Gasper Erck	7 April,	1804
,,	Wm. Hedderwick	3 Aug.,	1804
,,	John Clarke	5 Aug.,	1804
,,	T. G. Coote	6 Aug.,	1804
,,	Chas. Hy. Taylers	7 Aug.,	1804
,,	Thos. Ending	7 Sept.,	1804
,,	Chas. Robinson	8 Sept.,	1804
,,	— Ingram	10 Nov.,	1804
Ensign	John Ward (Adjutant)	17 Sept.,	1803
,,	Benj. Adams	1 Oct.,	1803
,,	John Brown	3 Dec.,	1803
,,	Thos. Andrews	23 June,	1804
,,	Wm. Abraham Le Mesurier	6 July,	1804
,,	Rich. Broad Wade (Ens., 24 Nov., 1802)	13 Aug.,	1804
,,	Joseph Ferris	15 Aug.,	1804
,,	John Jas. Gridley	25 Aug.,	1804
,,	Cromwell Doolan	26 Aug.,	1804
,,	John Blake	1 Sept.,	1804
,,	John Read Vincent	14 Sept.,	1804
,,	Wm. Arg. Lyon	5 Oct.,	1804
,,	N. F. Drumgoole	1 Nov.,	1804
,,	Wm. Brooks	8 Nov.,	1804
Paymaster	Rich. Morse Payne	2 Sept,	1797
Adjutant	John Ward (Ensign, ditto)	17 Sept.,	1803
Qr.-Mr.	John Mansell		
,	Thos. Maling	23 Nov.,	1804
Surgeon	Jonathan Featherstone	31 Dec.,	1803
Asst. Surg.	— Mann	17 March,	1803
,,	Wm. Dyason	24 March,	1803

SERVICES OF THE FIRST BATTALION.

1805-6.

Early in 1805 a French naval squadron escaped from Rochfort, attacked Dominica and pillaged Montserrat and St. Kitts. A few weeks later the Toulon fleet, under Admiral Villeneuve, eluded the vigilance of Nelson, passed the Straits of Gibraltar, released the Spanish fleet at Cadiz, and sailed in company with it to the westward. The gravest apprehensions were thus aroused for the safety of the British West India Islands, particularly Jamaica, and a force of twenty thousand men was at once ordered to assemble at Cork, under Lieutenant-General Sir Eyre Coote, K.B., to proceed thither as reinforcements. The 1st battalion 24th Foot, five hundred strong, Lieutenant-Colonel Honble. Godfrey Macdonald commanding, marched from Woodbridge to Portsmouth in April, and on 5th May, 1805, embarked for Cork to join the expeditionary force.

The return of Villeneuve, anticipating Nelson's pursuit, rendered the expedition unnecessary, and it was subsequently decided to despatch six thousand of the troops, under the command of Lieutenant-General Sir David Baird, K.B., K.C., to attempt the recapture of the colony of the Cape of Good Hope, which had been seized by the British in 1795 but given up to the Batavian Republic at the peace of Amiens.

The troops, including the 1st battalion 24th, sailed from Cork 27th September, 1805, and, after long delay, refitting and purchasing horses at San Salvador (Bahia), Brazil, arrived off Table Bay on 4th January, 1806.*

The original intention was to disembark at once, for which purpose the 24th Regiment was detached under convoy to make a demon-

---

* An interesting narrative of the voyage out, and a valuable memoir on the Cape in 1806, will be found in the *Life of General Sir Robert Thomas Wilson*, (Lond., 1861,) vol. i. Sir Robert was an intimate friend of Colonel Godfrey Macdonald.

stration towards Camps Bay. The wind failed, and by the time the
fleet got to the anchorage the day was too far spent to admit of any
attempt at landing. Next day, Brigadier-General Beresford, with the
first brigade, attempted a landing in Lospard's Bay, which had to be
abandoned owing to the heavy surf. Brigadier-General Beresford
was then detached with the cavalry and 38th Foot to Saldanha Bay,
a magnificent bay and anchorage ninety miles north of Cape Town.
On 7th January, 1806, the surf having abated, a landing was effected
by the rest of the troops near Blauw Berg, and on 8th January,
General Baird advanced towards Cape Town with the 24th, 59th, 71st,
72nd, 83rd, and 93rd regiments, amounting to four thousand and
sixty-six men, supported by two howitzers and six light field guns.
On ascending the Blauw Berg, the Batavian army, amounting to five
thousand men, with twenty-three guns, was observed drawn up in two
lines, with the apparent intention of turning the British right flank.
The troops were at once formed in two columns, whereof the left,
consisting of the Highland brigade, under Brigadier-General Ronald
Ferguson, advanced along the main road with great steadiness under a
heavy fire of round and grape shot and musketry, and eventually, by a
charge with the bayonet, broke down all opposition and drove the
enemy off with a loss of seven hundred men and three guns. The
right column, consisting of the 24th, 59th, and 83rd regiments, under
Colonel Joseph Baird, 83rd Foot, from its position, was not much
engaged; but the 24th grenadiers were successful in dislodging a
considerable force of horse and riflemen hovering on the British right
flank. The service was attended by the loss of Captain Andrew
Foster—a very gallant and promising officer who had been regimental
adjutant in Egypt—and three grenadiers killed, sixteen wounded, and
three missing. The subsequent advance on Cape Town was much
impeded by the nature of the country—a deep, arid sand almost
entirely covered with thick brushwood, which offered a serious obstacle
to the movement of the troops. On 9th January, while the troops
were in a position south of Salt River, awaiting the landing of the
battering train, a flag of truce arrived from the Commandant of Cape
Town, soliciting forty-eight hours' delay for the purpose of arranging
a capitulation. General Baird required the surrender of the outworks,

as a preliminary, within six hours, and thirty-six hours to prepare the articles of capitulation. The conditions were accepted, and the 59th Regiment took possession of Fort Knokke—a field-work on the right of the road leading from Wynberg into Cape Town. On the evening of the same day the terms were ratified, and the troops took possession of Cape Town.

Return of the killed, wounded, and missing of the forces, under the command of Major-General Sir David Baird, in the action of the 8th January, 1806, at Blauw Berg, Cape of Good Hope.

Regiments.		Killed.					Wounded.						Missing.
		Field Officers.	Captains.	Subalterns.	Sergeants.	Drummers.	Rank and File.	Field Officers.	Captains.	Subalterns.	Sergeants.	Drummers.	Rank and File.	Rank and File.
First brigade, commanded by Brigadier-General Beresford.	24th Regt.	..	1	..	..	..	3	..	..	..	..	1	15	2
	59th ,,	..	..	..	..	..	1	..	1	..	..	..	5	1
	83rd ,,	..	..	..	..	..	..	..	..	..	2	..	2	0
Second, or Highland brigade, commanded by Brigadier-General Ferguson.	71st ,,	..	..	..	..	..	5	1	..	..	2	..	64	1
	72nd ,,	..	..	..	..	..	2	1	..	1	2	1	33	1
	93rd ,,	..	..	..	..	..	2	1	..	4	1	1	51	..
Marine battalion		..	..	..	..	..	1	..	..	..	..	..	..	..
Total		..	1	..	..	..	14	3	1	5	7	3	170	8

(Signed) W. H. TROTTER, Major, 83rd Regiment,
Acting Deputy Adjutant General.

Eighteen years afterwards, on 14th July, 1824, a notification was received, dated Horse Guards, 8th July, 1824, stating that His Majesty had been pleased to approve of the 24th Regiment bearing upon its colours and appointments the words: "CAPE OF GOOD HOPE," in commemoration of the distinguished conduct of the regiment at the capture of that colony, 8th January, 1806.

1807-9.

Early in 1807, Lieutenant-Colonel Kelly assumed command in the room of the Honble. Godfrey Macdonald, who returned home and exchanged to the Grenadier Guards with Lieutenant-Colonel Geo. Duncan Drummond. *(Appendix B.)*

On 19th July, 1807, Lieutenant-General Sir David Baird, K.B., K.C., was transferred from the 54th to the colonelcy of the 24th Foot, *vice* Whyte, deceased. In September, 1808, Lieutenant-Colonel Randolph Marriott joined at Cape Town, with a draft of twelve officers and three hundred and forty men from the 2nd battalion, and assumed command.

During the above period the regiment was stationed at Cape Town. Major William Robison was deputy-quartermaster-general in the Cape Colony.

1810.

On 10th June, 1810, the regiment embarked at Cape Town in the Honble. Company's ships *Ceylon, Astell, Windham, William Pitt,* and *Euphrates,* and sailed for India. The last named struck on a rock soon after and put back to Cape Town. The *William Pitt* lost company and also put back. The rest proceeded up the Mozambique Channel, and on 3rd July, 1810, when in sight of the island of Mayotta, near Johanna, on the northern coast of Madagascar, fell in with and were engaged by a French squadron, consisting of two large frigates—the *Bellone* and *Minerve*, carrying fifty guns each—and a corvette—the *Victor*, of twenty guns.

After a gallant fight, for upwards of five hours, the *Ceylon* and *Windham* were captured, with four companies, including the flanks and head-quarters. During the action the 24th Regiment had nine men killed and Lieutenant-Colonel Marriott and forty-three men wounded. The colours and all the regimental books and records were thrown overboard to escape capture. As no copies of these documents existed their loss was simply irreparable. The whole of the prisoners, except a few recaptured in the *Windham*, were landed in the Mauritius in August, and there remained until the capture of the island by the British on the 3rd December following.

Extract from the log book of the *Astell,* giving an account of the action of the 3rd July, 1810, between the Honble. Company's ships—*Ceylon,* Captain Meriton, commodore ; *Windham,* Captain Stewart ; *Astell,* Captain Robert Hay—and two French frigates and a corvette :

At daylight three strange sail in sight, bearing N.E., close hauled on the larboard tack ; beat to quarters, and cleared ship for action.

9 o'clock. Signal made from commodore that the strangers were enemies.

11 o'clock. Commodore telegraphed that as we could not get away, we had better go under easy sail, and bring them to action before night.

At 2.30 the larger of the frigates and the corvette on our weather quarter, distant about half a mile. The frigate fired her lee bow gun, hoisted French colours, and immediately opened her fire upon us, which we returned, and commenced a close action. The commodore and *Windham,* ahead of us, firing upon her at the same time.

About 3 o'clock the corvette came into action, bore up under our stern, raked us, and took her station on our lee quarter. Returned her fire with our after larboard guns.

At 3.30 the corvette bore up to get without reach of our shot, we still continuing closely engaged, and the corvette firing. The commodore and *Windham* still ahead, the former engaged, and the latter firing as her guns would bear.

At 3.45 red ensign shot away and gaff brought down ; hoisted blue colours at the mizen topgallant mast-head.

About 4 o'clock Captain Hay was brought off the quarter deck, severely wounded in the left thigh.

At 4.15, the commodore dropped between us and the enemy, and kept up a spirited fire, and backed the main top-sail to get clear of her, and then renewed the action. The frigate then made sail and shot ahead, firing into the *Ceylon* and *Windham* as she passed, but directing most of her fire at the latter. After engaging the *Windham* for a short time and getting a little ahead of her, the frigate was right athwart our bows. Bore up with intention to board her, but could not effect it, she having too much way on. When she was about half a ship's length from us, we poured a broadside, and commenced a spirited and well-directed fire, and with our musketry fore and aft, completely cleared her upper deck and silenced her. She then hauled her wind on the larboard tack, engaging the *Ceylon* and *Windham* as she passed. When astern of the *Ceylon* she tacked, and whilst in stays her main and mizen topmasts went over the side. On seeing this, we hove all aback, with the intention of making a second attempt to board ; but the commodore and *Windham* drawing ahead, as we thought with a view of diverting the attention of the frigate that had not as yet been in action, we filled again to get into our station, went ahead of the commodore, and gave him three cheers, which he returned. Backed, and got into our station astern, and made all ready to renew the action with the frigate. She, however, instead of going to the assistance of her consort, made sail, and we being the sternmost ship, about 6 o'clock, brought us to close action, pouring in a very heavy fire of round and grape, and also from swivels and musketry in her tops, which we returned, and continued closely engaged. The commodore and *Windham*, a little ahead, kept up a heavy fire on the enemy as they could get their guns to bear. The corvette, now on our starboard quarter, kept up a cross fire on us.

About 7 o'clock, the frigate shot ahead of us, and we ceased our fire. When she was abreast of the *Ceylon*, that ship, after engaging her a short time, closely bore up, with the intention as we thought of boarding her. We hove up to support her; but observing that the *Ceylon* passed under the frigate's stern without firing, luffed up under his lee quarter and asked what were his intentions. They replied that they had struck to the frigate, that Captain Meriton and his first officer were killed, and that the ship was so completely disabled that to continue the contest longer would be sacrificing life to no purpose. The frigate was then a short gunshot on our starboard bow, and the *Windham* a mile astern.

Our ship being completely crippled in masts, yards, rigging, and sails, many guns rendered useless from the long-continued action, and the ship making three feet of water per hour, and there being no prospect of support from the *Windham*—she being so far astern—at 7.30 we put our helm up and stood to the westward. The frigate on perceiving this, again opened a tremendous fire on us, which we returned as long as we were in gunshot; then ceased firing, and stood to the northward and westward.

At near 8 o'clock the enemy in chase, and gaining on us, we got the ship in as great a state of readiness to defend her to the last extremity as circumstances would allow.

At 8.30 found that we were gaining. Employed in making all sail possible in the distressed state of the ship. At 12 o'clock, midnight, the enemy was out of sight.

The *Astell* anchored in Madras Roads on 1st August, 1810, and the detachment 24th Foot, consisting of Major Thomas Watkin Forster, commanding; Captains Hy. White, Thos. Craig and Rich. Gubbins;*

---

* This officer, the late Lieutenant-Colonel Richard Gubbins, C.B., was soon afterwards selected by the Duke of York for transfer to the 85th, when that regiment was reorganised in 1813. He commanded the 85th at New Orleans. His brother is believed to have been the donor of a very quaint and much-prized silver snuff-box, now in possession of the 1st battalion's mess.

and about three hundred rank and file, disembarked on 3rd instant and marched into the fort, "to there remain until ships were ready to take them on to Calcutta."

The following General Order was issued on their landing :—
"The Commander-in-Chief desires to offer his best thanks to Major "Forster, the officers, the non-commissioned officers, and soldiers belonging "to His Majesty's 24th Foot, on board the Honble. Company's ship "*Astell*, for their highly gallant and meritorious conduct during an action "of several hours in which it was engaged with a French squadron of very "superior force. His Excellency will have great satisfaction in transmitting "to England a report of their honourable conduct, to be laid before the "King.

"(Signed)   W. GRANT, Adjutant-General."

On board the *Ceylon* were Colonel Marriott; Captains Blake and Hughes; Lieutenants Blake, Ferris, Kelly, Doolan, Brocksbank, and Grindly; and Mr. Featherstone, surgeon; the head-quarters, flank companies, and three hundred men. On board the *Windham* were Lieutenants Parsonage and Wetherall and one hundred men. The *Ceylon* had four seamen, one lascar, and two soldiers killed; her captain, chief mate, seven seamen, one lascar, one lieutenant-colonel, and ten soldiers of the 24th regiment wounded. The *Windham:* one seaman, three soldiers, two lascars killed; seven soldiers, two lascars, three of her officers, and six of the crew wounded. The *Astell:* four seamen and four soldiers killed; her captain, fifth mate, nine seamen, one lascar, five cadets, and twenty soldiers wounded. Aggregate loss, twenty killed and seventy-six wounded. The colours of the *Astell* were three times shot away.

The East India Company settled a pension of £460 a year on Captain Hay, and presented £2,000 to the officers and crew of the *Astell* " as a mark of approbation for their distinguished bravery."

As before stated, the Island of Mauritius (Isle of France) surrendered to British Expeditionary Force on 3rd December, 1810, when the prisoners were released.

The above particulars are taken chiefly from James's *Naval History*, vol iv.

In Brenton's *Naval History of Great Britain* it is recorded : " The *Astell* was nobly defended by the detachment of the 24th Regiment. They went heart and hand with the captain and crew of the ship."

1811-13.

In January, 1811, the head-quarters and four companies of the regiment which had been prisoners of war, embarked at Port Louis under command of Lieutenant-Colonel Randolph Marriott, and landed at Calcutta in February, where the rest of the battalion joined from Madras and Cape Town. Major William Robison volunteered with the expedition to Java, where he served with much distinction on the quarter-master-general's staff. In 1813 the battalion remained at Fort William. A king's birthday brevet (4th June, 1813) raised Colonel Randolph Marriott to the rank of major-general, when Lieutenant-Colonel Charles Hicks assumed command.

1814-15.

Major White took over command in 1814. In July the battalion proceeded by divisions to Dinapur, where Lieutenant-Colonel Chamberlain assumed command.

On 24th November, 1814, the 24th Regiment was again reduced to a single battalion, by the disbanding of the second battalion. *(See chapter vii.)*

On 26th November, 1814, the service companies left Dinapur to take the field in the first Nepaul War. Active measures having been decided upon to determine the long-standing disputes between the Indian Government and the Nepaulese respecting territory seized and held by the latter, the Governor-General, the Earl of Moira (afterwards Marquis of Hastings) had directed the assembling of an army of four divisions, to make simultaneous attacks on as many points of the long line of Ghoorkha conquests as soon as the rains had subsided sufficiently to allow of an advance for the purpose. The total force sent into the field was seventeen thousand men, with sixty-eight guns. The first division, about four thousand Bengal native infantry, under Major-General Sir David Ochterlony, H.E.I.C.S., was to attack the western extremity of the Ghoorkha frontier. The second division, composed of H.M. 53rd Foot and native troops under Major-General Robert Rollo Gillespie, was to occupy the Deyrah Doon, a valley above the first range of hills, and attack the important Ghoorkha fortress of Jytak. The third division, under Major-General John Sullivan Wood, consisting of H.M. 17th Foot and native cavalry and infantry, was to march through the long-disputed Bhatnal and Sheoraj districts to Palpa. The fourth division, under Major-General Marley, consisting of H.M. 24th Foot and six thousand native troops, was to march direct to the Ghoorkha capital, Khatmandu.

Desultory operations had been some time in progress, when the fall of Major-General Gillespie, in an unsuccessful attempt on Kalanga, led Ochterlony to suspend operations at the opposite extremity of the line until he received reinforcements. It must be remembered that the mountainous countries forming the lower steps of the Himalayan ranges, destined at no remote period to be peaceful and familiar haunts of the Anglo-Indian population, had up to that time remained unvisited by Europeans, and their fastnesses were then explored for the first time for purposes of war.* Kalanga was afterwards taken; but Major-General Martindall, H.E.I.C.S., who succeeded John Sullivan Wood, failed against Jytak. Lord Moira's chief reliance had been upon the division that was marching straight to Khatmandu. It started from Dinapur 26th November, 1814.

After wasting some time in "a mischievous indecision," Major-General Marley, influenced probably by the unqualified disapproval of his proceedings expressed by Lord Moira, left his camp before daybreak one morning in February, 1815, without notifying his intention to the troops or providing for carrying on the command.† Colonel Dick then succeeded to the command of the division, until replaced by Major-General George Wood at the end of the month. But the latter officer, like his predecessors, was possessed by a spirit of caution and procrastination, and entertained the same views of the overwhelming difficulties confronting any offensive movements. He pleaded the advanced state of the season as an excuse for confining his operations to the plains. A march to Janakpur, on the Tirhoot frontier, showed that the Ghoorkhas had entirely abandoned the lowlands. After some tedious and harrassing marches, and the

---

* Mill, *History of India*, vol. viii., p. 41.   † *Ib.*, p. 50.

destruction of several stockades, the army was broken up, and distributed along the border-line from the Gandak to the Kusi. The 24th went into temporary cantonments at Amowa, in May, 1815, and there remained until November.

1815-18.

Negotiations between the Ghoorkhas and the Indian Government began in May, 1815, and were protracted through the rainy season; but, in the end, hostilities were resumed.

On 24th November, 1815, the troops under Major-General Sir David Ochterlony, who had been appointed to the chief command, again moved towards Nepaul, commencing what is known as the Second Nepaul War. Three days before starting, Colonel Kelly, C.B., arrived with ten officers and two hundred and eighty-eight men, most of them from the disbanded Second Battalion, and assumed command of the 24th.

The army was formed in four brigades, of which the first brigade, Colonel Wm. Kelly, C.B., 24th regiment, commanding, consisted of H.M. 24th Foot, the 1st battalion 18th Bengal Native Infantry, detachments of the 2nd battalion of the same regiment, and the Champara Light Infantry. It took the field in February, 1816, and, having been detached to the right, arrived on 27th February near the enemy's fort of Hariharpore. Early in the morning of 1st March, a force under Lieutenant-Colonel O'Halloran, H.E.I.C.S., was sent forward to occupy a height in front of the fort. The enemy kept up a smart fire of guns and small-arms until some field pieces were brought to bear upon them, with such effect that at 3 p.m. their fire was silenced. The 24th had four men killed and Brevet-Major Chas. Hughes, Captain Smith, Lieutenant O'Leary and twenty-seven men wounded on the occasion. Next day the regiment marched into the fort which had been abandoned during the night.

On 6th March, 1816, peace was concluded with the Rajah of Nepaul, and the regiment returned to Amowa, whence it marched, on 5th July, to Dinapur, arriving there on 18th July.

On 27th July, 1816, the grenadier and light companies of the regiment, under Brevet-Major Hughes, proceeded to Allahabad, and formed part of a flank battalion which made the campaigns of 1817-18, against the Pindarrees, with the grand army under His Excellency, the Marquis of Hastings (Lord Moira).

On 4th October, 1817, the rest of the regiment marched to the South West Frontier, and on 6th November arrived at Ontaru, where it formed part of the force under Brigadier-General Poole.

On 11th March, 1818, the regiment returned from Ontaru to Dinapur, where the flank companies rejoined. Major White was promoted to lieutenant-colonel, *vice* Chamberlain.

On 18th April a notification was received, dated Horse Guards, 6th August, 1817, stating that H.R.H. the Prince Regent had been pleased, in the name, and on the behalf, of His Majesty, to approve of the 24th Regiment being permitted to bear on its colours and appointments, in addition to any other badges which may have heretofore been granted to the regiment, the words: "TALAVERA, FUENTES D'ONOR, PYRENEES, ORTHES," in commemoration of the distinguished services of the late 2nd battalion of that regiment at Talavera on 27th-28th July, 1809; at Fuentes d'Onor, 8th May, 1811; in the Pyrenees in the month of July, 1813; and at Orthes, in the month of February, 1814.

Brevet-Major Hughes succeeded Major White in command in November this year, and in December was replaced by Major Green. On 15th December, 1818, the regiment marched to Ghazipur, arriving on 24th December.

1819-23.

Major Craig joined in January, 1819, and assumed command, and in October was succeeded by Lieutenant-Colonel Robison. On 12th November, 1819, it removed to Cawnpore, where it arrived on 12th December and remained for the next two years.

During this period news was received of the death of King George III. on 29th January, 1820, and the accession of George IV.

On 15th November, 1821, the regiment marched to Nagpur, where it arrived 23rd January, 1822. The march of five hundred and seventy-seven miles across country was performed at the rate of eight miles a day, allowing for halts.

H

In March, 1822, orders were received from Calcutta for the regiment to be held in readiness to embark for home. Men preferring to remain in the country were to be allowed to volunteer to other corps. On 8th-10th October, four hundred and eighty-three men volunteered to remain in India.

Major Craig had by this time succeeded Colonel Robison, C.B., in the command. The latter distinguished officer died at sea on 2nd May, 1823, within two days' sail of home.

On 23rd November, 1822, the regiment started from Nagpur for Bombay, a distance of five hundred and thirty-three miles, which it performed at the rate of eight and a half miles a day, arriving at Bombay 29th January, 1823.

On 10th February, 1823, the first division of the regiment, under Brevet-Major Baby, embarked in the *George the Fourth*, transport; and on 14th the head-quarters division, under Major Craig, consisting of seven officers, seventeen sergeants, eleven drummers, and one hundred and forty-eight privates, embarked in the *Charlotte*. The head-quarters arrived at Portsmouth, 2nd July, and marched into Haslar barracks. The two companies, under Brevet-Major Baby, landed at Gravesend on 11th July and marched to Chatham, where eleven men were invalided; the rest proceeded to Portsmouth. At an inspection of the regiment by Major-General Sir James Lyon, K.C.B., commanding the Portsmouth district, on 22nd July, 1823, eleven sergeants, one drummer, and eighty-six men were invalided. So that by volunteering and invaliding, the regiment lost five hundred and ninety-two men in nine months.

In July, 1823, the regiment marched to Fareham barracks, Portsmouth, where six officers and one hundred and eighty-five men joined from the depôt. On 6th November, 1823, Colonel Edward Fleming *(Appendix B)* exchanged to the command of the regiment, from half-pay, 53rd Foot, with Colonel Popham.

In February, 1824, a new set of accoutrements was ordered for the regiment by its colonel, General Sir David Baird, Baronet, G.C.B., K.C., and the patterns of the breastplates, buttons, and lace were altered.

CHAPTER VII.
1804-14.

The Royal Army of Reserve—The Regiment forms a Second Battalion—Services in the Peninsula—The Battalion Disbanded.

THE difficulties experienced in obtaining a sufficient supply of recruits during the preceding war period, and the opposition that had been offered to the practice of volunteering from the embodied Militia, then a recent innovation,* led to the passing of an act entitled the "Additional Forces Act," which took effect from 1st July, 1803, a few weeks after the renewal of the war with France. The objects of the act, as set forth in the preamble, were the "Establishing and Maintaining of a Permanent Additional Force for "the Defence of the Realm, and for augumenting His Majesty's Forces and gradually reducing the Militia." The permanent force was to be called the "Royal Army of Reserve," and the men were to be raised by ballot. The arrangements—the nearest approach to conscription ever made in this country—were as follows:—

The three kingdoms, of which the first census had been taken in 1801, were to be divided into districts capable of furnishing three thousand men fit to bear arms. With certain exceptions, all males within these districts between the ages of sixteen and forty-six, and not less than five feet two inches in height, were to be registered in their respective parishes for enrolment by ballot for home service only. To each district was to be assigned a line regiment, which was to raise a second battalion, *for home-service only*, from men ballotted for the reserve, the remainder of the ballotted men being formed into local battalions of reserve which were fully officered from the regular army, and were to be called up for a certain number of days' training every year. The enrolment by ballot was for five years' home service.

---

* During the period 1798-1800 second battalions had been added to a number of line regiments, which were formed of volunteers from the Militia, who engaged for three years only and not to go out of Europe. A meeting of lord-lieutenants of counties and militia commanding officers, held in London, 24th June, 1799, resolved unanimously, "That volunteering from the Militia when embodied was destructive to the force and degrading to all engaged in it."—*Ann. Reg.*, 1799.

Substitutes were allowed, for which a sum of £30, but afterwards £70 to £100, was paid, towards which the Government gave a guinea, the parish being accountable for the rest. Substitutes were liable for home service for five years or until the end of the war. The full quota of reserve men to be raised in the United Kingdom was forty-nine thousand eight hundred and eighty.

Nineteen line regiments were directed forthwith to form home service second battalions from men enrolled in the reserve, and were soon filled, but the 24th were not among the number.

1804.

On 1st May, 1804, the total number of men actually enrolled in all classes of the reserve in the United Kingdom was forty five thousand four hundred and ninety-two (about four thousand short of the full quota). Of these, two thousand eight hundred and seventy-three were ballotted men, and forty-one thousand one hundred and ninety-eight substitutes.

Enrolled men were allowed to engage for unlimited service, and of the total number actually effective in the above total, twelve thousand and seven had engaged for unlimited service, and twenty-five thousand one hundred and twenty-nine for limited (*i.e.*, home service) only.

On 29th June, 1804, another Additional Forces Act directed the formation of second battalions from the army of reserve by thirty-seven other line regiments—among the number being the 6th (1st Warwickshire) and the 24th (2nd Warwickshire) regiments of foot. The former was directed to form its new battalion at Liverpool, from men enrolled in the County Palatine; the latter was assigned to its county town—Warwick.

Warwickshire, with a population, according to the census of 1801, of two hundred and eight thousand one hundred and ninety inhabitants, whereof ninety-nine thousand nine hundred and forty-three were males,* had on 1st May, 1804, forty-nine thousand seven hundred and

---

* In 1801, the year of the first census ever taken, England and Wales had 9,156,171 inhabitants, of which Warwickshire had 208,190. In 1881, the year in which the connection of the regiment with the county ceased, England and Wales had 25,974,489; Warwickshire, 737,339.

nineteen persons registered under the Reserve Act. Of these, thirty-five thousand six hundred and fifty-three were registered as liable to ballot, in different (age) classes of the reserve; eleven thousand six hundred and twenty-four were members of accepted volunteer corps; two hundred and thirteen were actually serving in the army, marines or sea fencibles; two hundred and fifty-eight were exempt as clergy, medical men, teachers, and constables; two thousand nine hundred and sixty-two were exempt on account of infirmity; and nine were registered out of the county.

At Warwick, in September this year, the Peninsular SECOND BATTALION OF THE 24TH FOOT—second of the three second battalions the regiment has had—was formed by Lieutenant-Colonel Randolph Marriott from the 11th Battalion of the Reserve, assisted by a few officers and men of the regiment. Quartermaster-Sergeant Thomas Maling, of the regiment (afterwards Brevet-Lieutenant-Colonel Thos. Maling, 2nd West India Regiment) was appointed quartermaster, and soon after became adjutant of the new battalion. Quartermaster-Sergeant Robert Belcher, of the regiment, then succeeded to the quartermastership.*

1805-7.

The Royal Army of Reserve proved a failure—it never had a fair trial its advocates said. Anyhow, in 1805, the men actually serving in it were turned over to garrison battalions or were discharged, and the newly-born second battalions of line regiments were left to keep up their strength as best they might by older-fashioned methods of recruiting. A system of volunteering from the embodied militia was legalised; and in 1806, short service enlistment was introduced, men for the infantry engaging for seven years, without pension, with permission to re-engage for a second period of seven years, or fourteen years in all, with conditional pension, and for a third period, or twenty-one years in all, with life pension, an arrangement that continued in force throughout the Peninsular War and for some time after.

---

* This officer, who was quartermaster throughout the Peninsular campaigns, died as quartermaster, half-pay, late 5th Royal Veteran Battalion, **24th January, 1837.**

The 2nd battalion 24th for some time could not muster two hundred men.* Like other new battalions of the time, it was kept continually on the move, apparently with the notion of assisting recruiting. In January, 1805, it went to Birmingham; in February, to Coventry; in June, to Stratford-on-Avon; in August, to Chelmsford; thence, in November, to Colchester; and in January, 1806, back to Chelmsford. In November, 1806, it went to Dunstable; in December, to Warwick; in July, 1807, again to Stratford-on-Avon; and in September, back to Chelmsford, where it remained until April, 1808.

1808.

The 2nd battalion 24th marched from Chelmsford to Tilbury, and there embarked for Guernsey, under the command of Lieutenant-Colonel George Duncan Drummond, who succeeded Lieutenant-Colonel Randolph Marriott when the latter proceeded to the Cape to assume command of the 1st battalion.

1809.

In April, 1809, the 2nd battalion 24th embarked at Guernsey for Portugal, landing at Lisbon on 28th of April. On 1st May it marched from Lisbon to Santarem, halting about ten days at that place, and thence proceeding to Cordegas.

On 23rd May, 1809, Sergeant-Major Robert Top† was promoted to the adjutancy, *vice* Maling, who resigned the adjutancy only.‡

[Except where otherwise stated, the rest of this chapter is copied from a MS. book in possession of the regiment—the only record of the Peninsular Second Battalion known to be in existence.]

---

* Sir Willoughby Gordon, in *Military Transactions* Appendix, shows the 2nd battalion 24th as mustering:—

1st June, 1805	..	144 rank and file	..	288	wanting to complete.
,, 1806	..	187 ,,	..	213	,,
,, 1807	..	165 ,,	..	401	,,
,, 1808	..	400 ,,	..	480	,,

† This officer died of Guadiana fever in 1812.

‡ A monthly return, dated Cordegas, 25th May, 1809, the only return of the regiment for that year that can be found in the Public Record Office, shows the strength of the battalion, exclusive of officers, as follows:—

```
    39 sergeants  . . . . .  16 unlimited service, 23 limited service.
    22 drummers   . . . . .  12      ,,      10      ,,
   778 corporals and privates - 157  ,,      617     ,,       ,,
     3 boys  . . . . . . .  Unlimited service.
     1 boy   . . . . . . .  Limited service.
```

At Cordegas the battalion was joined by the 27th, 31st, and 45th regiments, composing a brigade under Major-General Mackenzie, which formed a Corps of Observation to watch the movements of General Sebastiani, who was posted at the bridge of Alcantra. The brigade was reviewed in June at Castillo Branco by Sir Arthur Wellesley. It then marched to Plasencia, where it was reinforced by the 87th and 88th regiments, some German hussars, and part of the 14th and 16th Light Dragoons, with a brigade of artillery.

MARCH TO BATTLE OF TALAVERA.—In July the brigade marched for Talavera, forming the advanced guard of the army, halted at Oropesa, and again resumed the march to Talavera. On the 22nd it came in sight of the enemy, who retreated; on the 23rd crossed the Alberché, and on the 24th marched to Cazalegos. On the 26th the brigade took up a position some distance in front of Cazalegos to cover the retreat of the Spanish army under Cuesta, which was flying in the greatest disorder back to Talavera. General Mackenzie's brigade afterwards returned towards the Alberché and re-crossed that river on the 27th after a most severe march.

The brigade halted in a very thick wood; the picquets were told off and ordered to pile arms. The 24th Regiment was at this time on the right of the brigade. It was observed that the other regiments of the brigade were piling arms and taking off their packs and accoutrements, the order having been passed along from the left. The 24th did the same. Shortly afterwards an order came to cut down wood and bushes, and it was generally understood that the brigade was to bivouac for the night. The officers collected in small groups near their companies to discuss the numerous and extraordinary reports in circulation relative to the situation of the army, it being well known that there was a French army of near fifty thousand men on the same ground with the British army and another French army, forty thousand strong, under Soult, cutting off the retreat by Plasencia. These facts came from too good sources to be discredited, and therefore created an extraordinary degree of excitement. The men dispersed among the trees, and were chopping off the boughs when the alarm sounded; but before the men could get on their packs and accoutrements the French light troops were in the wood. The picquets fortunately had not taken off their packs, and therefore had time to run to the front and join some of the 60th, who were keeping up a running fire and skirmishing with the advanced troops of the enemy. The brigade retired out of the woods, and formed regularly on the plain between it and the position at Talavera. The 24th had its three right companies moved towards a large building called Casa Salinas, opposite to which a French column was observed coming out of the woods.

Sir Arthur Wellesley was on this spot with some cavalry, and on seeing the three companies of the 24th approaching Casa Salinas, he ordered them back to the brigade, and they were saluted with a smart discharge of grape shot from the French guns on their return.

The brigade retreated across the plain, and took up its position that night in the second line, in rear of the centre of the British line.*

The brigade of Guards formed the first line, and close to them stood General Campbell's division, which formed the right of the line. The Spanish army was close on the right of the English army.

The battalion was at this time suffering much from dysentery, scarcity of provisions, and the heat of the weather. When it arrived on the ground at night-fall the men were completely exhausted, from hunger, thirst, and fatigue. It was expected that rations would be issued out that night, but officers and men were sorely disappointed.

There had been no regular issue for three days, and the officers were as badly off as the privates. The baggage was sent to Orepeza. One private servant, however, arrived from the baggage, and brought the ill-news that the regimental baggage had been plundered by the Spanish army, which was running away in the most shameful disorder. This report turned out but too true, and some of the

---

* As the brigade of Guards was but a short distance in front, some of the officers came across to the battalion. One of their ensigns, young Edward Methuen Irby, of the 3rd Guards, came to ascertain if his brother, Captain the Honble. Henry Edward Irby, of the 24th, had escaped the perils of the day. The two gallant and affectionate brothers had only just time to exchange a few words and shake hands for the *last time;* as when the 24th was covering the retreat of the Guards after their gallant charge the following day, the first object which caught the eye of Captain Irby was the dead body of his brother.

officers lost all their private and company money, the companies' books, and even their baggage animals. The women of the regiments who are generally the first to arrive with their small supplies of provisions, were also plundered by the Spanish runaways. The men lay down with their arms under their great coats, to keep them from the heavy dew that was falling.

On 28th July, 1809, the battle of Talavera commenced by a sudden and tremendous burst of artillery, followed by a close roar of small arms, on the left of the British army. The attack was begun by the enemy soon after daylight.

As soon as the small arms had come into play on the left, the fire from the French artillery was evidently changed in direction, and against the centre and right of the British. The men fell fast from shot and shell. The brigade was therefore ordered to lie down, and then the round shot did little damage, but the shells annoyed the men much. The firing ceased on both sides about 9 o'clock, and was not renewed until 1 o'clock. During this interval the wounded from both sides were removed from the field. The time was now come for the 24th Regiment to share in the honour and glory of the day.

The action recommenced by the enemy making a most determined and gallant attack on the right of the British line. General Campbell's division was hard pressed by this tremendous attack. General Mackenzie's brigade (or part of it) was ordered to support General Campbell's division, and, the distance being short, the 24th was soon formed in line on the left of that division, and opened an independent fire on a French column, which was in the act of deploying into line. This column was so cut up that it soon retired. The battalion continued in this position for some time, when it was ordered to cease firing. Soon after this a staff-officer came up with orders for the battalion to support the guards and return to its former ground. The battalion was faced to the left, and moved off in as quick a run as the men were capable of. It did not move over the same ground, but ran along in the direction of the front line. The left had only just come upon the right of the brigade of guards, when the latter charged the enemy, and the 24th instantly took up the ground vacated by the Coldstreamers, wheeled back by companies, to allow the retreating Coldstreamers to pass through, and then formed line and opened a steady fire, which soon checked the advance of the French line that was following up the Coldstreamers. The fire of round shot, grape, and musketry had in the short space of half-an-hour almost annihilated the battalion, and when the Coldstreamers returned to their former ground, the 24th had only one rank to show front, and even in that there were long gaps.

All the field officers, except Major Chamberlain, who took command of the brigade when General Mackenzie was killed, were at this time wounded, and the following officers killed or wounded—killed: Captain Evans. Wounded: Lieutenant-Colonel Drummond, Major Popham, Major Aylmer, Captain Collis, Lieutenant Grant, Lieutenant Vardy, Ensign Johnstone, Ensign Skeene, Ensign Jessiman. Total killed and wounded on the 27th and 28th July, three hundred and fifty-five rank and file. Strength of the battalion on the 27th, seven hundred and ten rank and file.

Some months after the battle of Talavera the London papers containing the despatch appeared. The officers of the 24th regiment were very much disappointed to see that the whole of the credit of supporting the Guards when they charged was given exclusively to the 48th Regiment.

The officer commanding the regiment accordingly remonstrated, and soon after a letter was received from Lord Wellington, in substance, "that there was no report made to him on the subject, owing to the death of General Mackenzie." Lord Wellington further said that he was aware of the mistake, and felt convinced that the 24th deserved an equal share of praise.

This letter was sent home for publication, and was lost in the *Marlborough* Packet. The letter never appeared in print, and thus the 24th Regiment have been omitted in every succeeding history as one of the regiments that particularly distinguished itself at Talavera.

His Grace the Duke of Wellington, in recommending the regiments distinguished at Talavera for that badge, included the 24th.

There was one circumstance which created some mistakes in this action, and that was the different colours of the facings of the men. One half of them had on their militia clothing, and it was not easy for staff officers in the hurry of the action to distinguish the number of the regiment.

The 24th Regiment had received a reinforcement of between three and four hundred men just before the advance to Talavera; most of them had light-coloured facings, and as the 24th had green facings, the officers of the regiment could only distinguish the new recruits from men of other corps by looking at their breast-plates.*

At the same time that the 24th Regiment supported the Coldstreams, the 48th Regiment supported the 3rd Foot Guards.

Nearly one half of the 24th were killed and wounded in supporting the Guards. Some of the men who were severely wounded while the battalion was moving in double-quick time from the left of General Campbell's division to the right of the guards, were burnt to death by the flames from the long, dry, grass, set on fire by the shells. The men who went out to try and save their unfortunate comrades were forced back, with their clothes burnt and their pouches blown up on their backs.

When the action was over the wounded were collected and sent off towards the town of Talavera. There were not fifty men left with the colours when the fatigue parties were sent off with the wounded.

The 2nd battalion won the badge for TALAVERA, now worn by the regiment.

The battalion remained on the same ground until the 3rd August, when the army marched for the bridge of Arzabispo.

The officers named below, left severely wounded at Talavera, were taken prisoners (and sent to France as soon as sufficiently recovered) when the Spanish army abandoned the position. The British army had then marched to encounter Soult, who was marching on Plasencia with an army forty thousand strong:—Major Popham, Captain Collis, Lieutenant Grant, Lieutenant Skeene, and Ensign Jessiman.

The fate of the young officer last named was as singular as it was unfortunate. He was left behind at Talavera severely wounded, and,

---

* These men were from the Tipperary, Westmeath, Northampton, Warwick, and other militia regiments, wearing yellow or other light facings.

when able, he attempted to make his escape, but failed to do so, though some other British officers succeeded at the same time. Some time afterwards, however, he managed to escape from Madrid, and joined a party of guerillas. Before he could rejoin the British army, he unfortunately was taken prisoner again, and having been found acting with the brigands (as the French termed the guerillas), he was not considered to be a prisoner of war. Some English soldiers who escaped said that an officer of the 24th Regiment was brought in with some Spaniards, and all of them were shot at Madrid. There can be no doubt this was Ensign Jessiman, and he was struck off the strength of the battalion by an order from the Horse Guards.*

The battalion suffered much from dysentry on the march from Talavera to Truxillo, and from thence to the encampment on the Guadiana. The weather was intensely hot, generally upwards of one hundred degrees Fahrenheit in the shade; and the troops were much harrassed by dragging artillery up some of the mountain passes.

The battalion halted a few days at Truxillo, and were joined by a few men from Plasencia who were left sick on the advance to Talavera. They reported that Soult's advanced guard had driven them out of Plasencia. When the battalion arrived on the banks of the Guadiana they were formed into a brigade with the 2nd battalions of the 42nd and 83rd regiments. The 83rd soon after marched to Lisbon, and they were replaced in the brigade by the 1st battalion 61st Regiment. General Cameron succeeded to the command of the brigade after General Mackenzie was killed. On General Cameron quitting the army, about the end of the year, Colonel the Honble. E. Stopford, of the guards, took over the command.

The battalion suffered so much from contagious fever on the banks of the Guadiana that it became quite a skeleton, and could not parade one hundred duty men when it left the encampment, and marched into winter quarters at Arroyo de St. Savan.

Adjutant Top died of this fever. He was succeeded as adjutant

---

* Ensign Jessiman had joined the 24th some months before from the Aberdeenshire Militia, in which he was a lieutenant.

by Sergeant-Major Hugh Fleming, from the 3rd Foot Guards.* Captain Straubenzie was sent to Lisbon very much debilitated from the same fever, and after lingering there some months he also died. It was not uncommon to see eight or ten graves dug in one day for the battalion.

An order was received from the Horse Guards about this time to strike off the strength of the battalion all the men who were returned as prisoners of war and missing. The battalion mustered near a thousand strong when it left Portugal in the month of May, and before the end of the year had lost about six hundred rank and file. It was therefore quite ineffective for many months.

In December the army broke up from its cantonments on the Guadiana, and entered Portugal by the route of Elvas.

1810.

The battalion crossed the Tagus at Villa Velha, and marched with the first division to the north-east of Portugal, by the route of Castillo Branco.

In February the head-quarters of the division were at Vizen, Colonel Stopford's brigade at Mongualdi and the neighbouring villages. The 24th were quartered at Mongualdi, where they remained till March, when they marched to Cortico, and remained there until July.

BATTLE OF BUSACO.—At this period the battalion was in a very efficient state, as a detachment had arrived from England, and the sick men left behind on the advance to Talavera had rejoined. When the army retired, in September, to Busaco, the battalion mustered about five hundred men.

The battle of Busaco was fought on the 27th September, 1810. The first division had only their light companies engaged in this action, so the 24th Regiment had not much to do in it. The light company was, however, very smartly engaged, and Captain Meacham, who commanded it, was very severely wounded. Some men were killed and a good many wounded.

---

* Afterwards Lieutenant, half-pay 7th Royal Veteran Battalion, and Military Knight of Windsor.

During the retreat to the lines before Lisbon, the battalion, in common with the others of the brigade, was in its turn employed in covering the retreat. The rear guard had a skirmish near Sobral on 10th October, and another sharp affair of picquets on the 14th, which everyone thought was a prelude to a general action, as the two armies were facing each other—the English in an admirable position.

Very heavy rains set in at this time, and the picquet duties were very severe, owing to the dreadful state of the roads and the absence of shelter.

The picquets of both armies were in the habit of conversing while the two armies remained inactive. The French officers were at these times highly pleased at getting English newspapers. They offered money in exchange, which of course was refused.

The disappointment was very great when the French army broke up and retired to Thomar and the Santarem, on 14th November. The English followed on the 15th, and the first division pursued the retreating enemy nearly to Santarem. This division was composed of the Brigade of Guards, the Brigade of Germans, and the "Brigade of the Line" (sometimes called the "Scotch Brigade," as there were two regiments with kilts in it, the 42nd and 79th, with the 24th). Major-General Nightingale commanded the "Brigade of the Line." It was halted at the end of a causeway one thousand eight hundred paces long, and was told off in regiments to carry this causeway and bridge at the point of the bayonet. The 24th Regiment, being on the right, was to lead.

This demonstration, however, turned out to be only a reconnaisance, and the battalion, next morning, marched to Cartaxo.

1811.

The campaign of 1811 opened on 5th March, with the memorable retreat of the French army from Santarem and Thomar, and its immediate pursuit by the English army. Major-General Nightingale's "Brigade of the Line" was ordered to follow up General Regnier's division of the enemy, which retreated by the mountain road of the Estrella to Espinhal.

The enemy's rear guard was soon overtaken, and then the 24th was, with little intermission, engaged in one of the most active pursuits of a flying enemy that is recorded in the annals of British warfare; presenting on the part of the French the most disastrous scenes, and on the part of the British the most brilliant successes. The French troops did not make a stand until 14th March, at Espinhal. On this day the battalion, moving along a mountain pathway, got on the left flank of the enemy and had some sharp fighting. The next day the battalion was hotly engaged, when the enemy retired across the Alva, and blew up the bridge. On the 16th the brigade halted. On the night of the 17th, the "Brigade of the Line" was detached to ford the river Alva, near Pombiero, and succeeded in crossing at daybreak unobserved by the enemy.

Two divisions followed immediately, and the left flank of the enemy was turned. The position of the French was one of the strongest in Portugal, had they properly defended the ford of Pombiero. It is believed that they were not aware of this ford. The consequence was that they were surprised, and of course totally defeated, with the loss of all their artillery, baggage, stores and provisions, and they were actually obliged to fly for their lives, and carried off only what they had on their backs. They fancied themselves so secure in this position of Ponte-de-Murcellan, that they sent out strong foraging parties, which did not return until late at night.

As they returned they were permitted by our picquets to enter their former camp, when they were not a little surprised to find themselves prisoners. The battalion came in for a good supply of different articles on this fortunate occasion.

The battalion was most actively employed on these five last days; principally acting on the flank of the enemy as light infantry.

On the 19th the army halted, having outmarched the supplies. On the 26th, the enemy moved towards Guarda, from which place they were driven on the 29th.

On this night the brigade made a forced march to cut off the enemy at Sabugal. Reynier's corps at Sabugal was nearly surrounded by three divisions of the English army. Owing to the very heavy rains, he escaped, but with great loss.

The retreat of the French army from Santarem to Spain was

marked by the immense number of baggage animals of all descriptions that lay littered along the different routes, with their panniers and pack saddles destroyed. The roads were also strewn with dead men, and every small village was crowded with their wounded. They collected together enough in each house to defend themselves against the Portuguese, from whom they could expect no mercy, after the horrid atrocities they had committed on the unfortunate inhabitants on their advance into Portugal the year previous.

On 1st May the British army began to assemble at Fuentes d'Onor.

Major-General Nightingale's brigade was posted in rear of the village of Fuentes d'Onor during the three days' attack on this position.

The light companies of the 24th, 42nd, and 79th, under command of Major Dick, of the 42nd, (with other troops) occupied the village.

The village was taken and re-taken three times on the evening of 3rd May The light companies at length, supported by the whole brigade, retained possession of it.

The 4th May was spent by both armies in manœuvring, with the result that the British left rested on Fuentes d'Onor, in a position at right angles to their former lines.

On the 5th the light companies only remained in Fuentes d'Onor, and nobly defended that important post. The remainder of the brigade, at first hard pressed, made a good stand behind some stone walls.

The 60th Riflemen were also hard pressed, and driven in on the 24th, who about this time were ordered to change front by throwing back their right wing, and to occupy a stone wall; but a heavy column of the enemy got possession of this wall first, and opened a flanking fire on the battalion, which was now quite exposed.

At this stage of the action Major Chamberlain, who commanded the battalion, was placed in a most perilous situation. He had gone to the front, and when the riflemen were driven back, his horse refused to leap the wall.

Some of the men threw down stones, and made a gap—just as the French skirmishers gained the spot—by which Major Chamberlain saved himself and his horse, and regained the battalion.

Fresh troops now came up to the support of the 24th, and the column of the enemy retired, exposed to a heavy fire of musketry and grape.

In this sharp affair, Lieutenant Ireland was killed, and Captain Andrews wounded and taken prisoner. He was taken to France, and kept there during the remainder of the war.

Parties were sent to bury the dead of both armies. Upwards of four hundred dead French infantry were brought out of the village, and it is believed that they removed an immense number more from the environs on their own side.

Colonel Kelly arrived from England on the evening of the 5th, but did not take command until the next day.

After the battle of Fuentes d'Onor, and the pursuit of the French from Santarem, the battalion was reduced to three hundred men. It took up its quarters on the 8th at a village in Spain near Aldea-de-Ponte.

Colonel Geo. Duncan Drummond, who was severely wounded at Talavera, went home, and, having recovered from his wound, returned to Portugal in the beginning of 1811, and received the command of a brigade of the light division, which he held during the campaign and until he died of a fever (produced by the irritation of his wound) in August. Never was there an officer of the 24th regiment more regretted by his brother officers.

1812.

The battalion moved in the beginning of January to the siege of Cuidad Rodrigo.

SIEGE OF CUIDAD RODRIGO.—" The weather was excessively cold, and as there was no camp equipage with the army, nor cover near the town, it was regulated that the troops should remain cantoned in the nearest villages, and that the duties of the siege should be taken by the light, first, and third divisions alternately, each remaining twenty-four hours on the ground to furnish the guards of the trenches and the working parties. The division coming on duty to march from its cantonments so as to arrive on the ground by mid-day."*

---

* Jones's *Journal of Sieges*, 2 ed., vol. i., pp. 210 *et seq.*

The light division commenced by taking the outwork on 8th January. On the 9th the third division was in the trenches, on the 10th the first division, on the 11th the light division, on the 12th the third division, on the 13th the first division.

REPULSE OF THE SORTIE.—Between 10 a.m. and 11 a.m. on 14th January the battering train was brought into the batteries. The French garrison made a sortie with about five hundred men at the moment of the relief of the divisions. A bad custom had prevailed of allowing the guard of the trenches and the working parties to withdraw from the trenches as soon as the relieving division was seen approaching, so that the works were left unguarded for some time during each relief, which the enemy could observe from the steeple of the cathedral, where they always had an officer on the look-out. The enemy succeeded in throwing down the gabions placed in advance of the first parallel during the preceding night, and would have pushed into the trenches, and probably spiked the guns, had they not been repulsed by a working party of the 24th, under Lieutenant Stack of that regiment, which was still in the trenches after most of the other working parties had left. The 24th lost one sergeant and two rank and file killed, and fifteen rank and file wounded. On the approach of some troops of the first division, under Lieutenant-General Graham, the French retired into the town. Had the guns been spiked, the siege must have been abandoned. The repulse of the sortie, especially by so small a force, when the reliefs were too far distant to render assistance, was therefore a very important incident in the siege.

Cuidad Rodrigo was stormed by the third and light divisions (the divisions next for duty) on 19th January, 1812.

MARCH FROM CUIDAD RODRIGO TO BADAJOZ.—Early in February, 1812, the first division marched to the south of Portugal to cover the siege of Badajoz. The battalion halted for a few days at Abrantes to receive their new clothing, which had arrived from England. The old clothing was actually in rags, and patched with so many colours that the red was scarcely distinguishable. A supply of necessaries was issued at the same time.

About the beginning of March the battalion joined the division in front of Badajoz and marched to Almendralejo, to watch the advance guard of the French under Soult, at Seville.

On 4th April, Soult advanced from Seville, with twenty-five thousand men, to raise the siege of Badajoz, and about the same time Marmont entered the north of Portugal with an army for the same purpose. The battalion being in advance, retired this day from Almendralejo and marched for Albuhera.

Sir Thomas Graham formed his corps on the old position of Albuhera and prepared to give Soult a warm reception. The advanced guard of the French took post in the wood opposite the English. In the night the picquets of the 24th Regiment were employed in trying the depth of the river all along their front. The night was dark, and in some places the French sentries did not see what was going on; in others, our officers and men were fired at while in the water, at only a few yards distance.

It was fully expected that there would be a sharp action next day. During the night the enemy threw up a number of rockets. These proved to be answering signals from the garrison at Badajoz, and so accurate was their information that, on 6th April, when Badajoz surrendered, Soult retired from Albuhera.

Thus the hopes of a general action fell to the ground.

Soon after the fall of Badajoz the division made a rapid march towards Castillo Branco, at which place Marmont's advanced guard had arrived from the north. Marmont, however, hearing of the fall of Badajoz, retreated to Salamanca. The division continued its march unmolested to the north, traversing the same country that it marched over in February. It took up its former quarters in the neighbourhood of Fuente Guiraldo, where it remained till the beginning of June, when the army advanced to Salamanca.

ADVANCE TO SALAMANCA.—The battalion commenced its march for Salamanca on 13th June, 1812.

The enemy evacuated Salamanca on 16th, but left garrisons in three very strong forts, called St. Cajetana, La Mercea, and St. Vincente. The battalion crossed the river Tormes and encamped on the heights of St. Christoval, about two miles in front of Salamanca, on the 17th. On 18th June, an officer and twenty men of the 24th

Regiment were sent into Salamanca to act as sappers with the sixth division, which was selected to besiege the forts.

Marmont's army returned on the 21st, and drew up in line along the low grounds, in front of the whole British army, which occupied the heights of St. Christoval.

On 22nd June, Marmont took possession of a commanding height on the right, but was driven from it immediately afterwards. The right wing of the 24th was detached, and took part in this affair.

On the 23rd there was much manœuvring by both armies.

On the 24th, Marmont succeeded in passing part of his army over the river, but the first and seventh divisions drove him back again the next day.

On the 26th, a fresh supply of ammunition having arrived for the great guns employed in the siege of the forts, a breach was made in the principal fort, and all three were taken by assault by the sixth division, and were blown up the next day.

Marmont retired across the Douro, followed by the British army. The 24th encamped at Nava on the 29th.

On 2nd July an advance was made to Medenia del Campo, where the 24th had some skirmishing with the enemy's rear guard.

The 24th remained near the delightful town of Medenia del Campo until the 16th, when it marched towards the river Gueraña—The officers of the regiment were at a gay ball on the night of the 15th, when a sudden order arrived to fall in and march off. This town is celebrated for its beautiful girls and Roman ruins.

The French army, having by this time received large reinforcements, crossed the Douro, and attempted to regain Salamanca. From the 16th to the 22nd July both armies were engaged in executing the most brilliant manœuvres, with varied success.

On 18th July, the fourth, fifth, and light divisions were engaged at Castrejon.

On the 19th, Marmont moved to his right. The British army took a parallel direction. General Cole's division had a sharp affair this day.

On the 20th, both armies continued to move along the ranges of hills towards Salamanca. There was only a small stream between them, and the skirmishers in the hollows could be seen by both armies actively engaged, while the cannon balls kept occasionally whizzing over their heads. The main bodies moved along till night, frequently within half cannon shot of each other, and expecting every moment that a change of ground would bring on a general action. A more brilliant military display than this was never witnessed, *where both armies did not engage.*

On the 21st most of the British army gained the heights of St. Christoval, close to Salamanca, and the same evening crossed the Tormes and rested on the left bank of that river.

This night (the one before the battle of Salamanca) the troops were deluged with rain. The thunder and lightning frightened some of the horses, which broke loose, and, galloping amongst the men, created much confusion, as it was imagined that the French cavalry had got in amongst them.

THE BATTLE OF SALAMANCA.—On the 22nd, the first division moved before daylight, and took possession of one of the largest of the hills, called "The Arapiles." The French, at the same time, occupied the "Lesser Arapiles." The left of the British army was immediately opposed to the right of the enemy, which rested on the "Arapiles."

The first division, to which the 24th Regiment belonged, did not come into action till near evening, when it advanced to the attack of the lesser, or French, "Arapiles." The enemy, having been beaten at all other points, were soon driven from this position, with the loss of the guns that they had on the top of it.

The first and light divisions continued the pursuit of the enemy until midnight.

The second battalion won the badge for SALAMANCA.

ADVANCE TO VALLADOLID AND MADRID FROM SALAMANCA.—On the night of the battle of Salamanca, the battalion took a number of prisoners during the pursuit to the fords on the river Tormes, where the battalion rested till daylight.

On the 23rd the battalion crossed the river and continued the pursuit of the enemy. The rear guard was soon overtaken. The French dragoons most shamefully deserted their infantry, which was most gallantly charged by the English and German cavalry. The first and light divisions coming up at the same time, three strong battalions of French infantry laid down their arms and surrendered. During the rest of this day the two divisions were in close pursuit of the main body, and towards nightfall drove the enemy past Peneranda.

On the 24th the battalion continued the pursuit.

On the 25th the enemy's rear guard halted for a short time at Arevala, but the first and light divisions soon drove them across the river.

On the 26th the enemy retreated towards Valladolid, and on the 27th crossed the Douro, closely pursued.

On the 28th the brigade halted near Olmedo, on the bank of the river Adaja; the cavalry in front.

On the 29th the enemy were in great strength on the left bank of the Douro. The first and light divisions crossed the rivers Eresma and Cega, and at night the enemy abandoned Valladolid, leaving behind them seventeen pieces of cannon, a large quantity of shot and shell, their hospital, and near one thousand men who were wounded during their retreat from Salamanca.

On the 30th the enemy retreated in the direction of Burgos, and this day the 24th Regiment, which formed the advance guard, crossed the Douro and entered the city of Valladolid. They were met by thousands of well-dressed people, who seemed rejoiced to see the British. The officers of the regiment got a good supply of comforts for themselves and their men at Valladolid.

MARCH FROM VALLADOLID TO MADRID.—On 1st August the British army was divided into two parts. General Clinton continued the pursuit of Marmont's army towards Burgos, while Lord Wellington pursued the remainder of the French army towards Madrid. The 24th accompanied the latter force.

Joseph Bonaparte was at Segovia with a large army; on Lord Wellington's approach he retreated to Madrid.

On the 12th the English army entered Madrid unopposed, and were very well received. The walls of the houses were hung with silken flags, and at night the city was brilliantly illuminated.

The enemy left a garrison of two thousand five hundred men in Fort Retiro; it was immediately invested, and surrendered the next day without firing a shot. Amongst the spoils were one hundred and eighty-nine brass cannon, twenty thousand stands of arms, and the eagles of the 15th and 1st French regiments. The 24th had one captain, three subalterns, and one hundred men warned to join the storming parties for the assault of the Retiro, just as it surrendered.

While the 24th Regiment remained at Madrid, it bivouacked in the royal gardens. Some grand bullfights and other fêtes were given by the Municipality to the Marquis of Wellington, and all the British officers were invited to attend. The houses of the principal people were lighted up every night, and splendid balls given in them.

MARCH FROM MADRID TO BURGOS OF THE FIRST, FIFTH, SIXTH, AND SEVENTH DIVISIONS.—Towards the end of August the first division, to which the 24th still belonged, marched for the Escurial, where it halted for a few days. The officers of the 24th regiment occupied the royal apartments of this once magnificent palace; the French, however, had left it in a very dirty and dilapidated state.

On 1st September the above-named divisions retraced their steps to Valladolid, which the French had regained whilst the British army was at Madrid.

On the 6th the French were driven from the heights in front of the town into Valladolid.

On the 7th they again evacuated Valladolid, and retreated rapidly until the 16th, closely pursued by the British army. The picquets had some sharp skirmishing on this day, in which the 24th were engaged. On the 17th the French retired to Burgos. On the 18th the battalion was engaged with the enemy's rear guard and picquets, on the road to Burgos. Colonel Sterling, of the 42nd regiment, took command of the brigade about this time. On the 19th the first division and General Pack's brigade of Portuguese crossed the river Arlanzon, below the town of Burgos. The battalion had some sharp skirmishing in crossing the river, and, as soon as the whole of the brigade had got over, they drove in the enemy's outposts, and, supported by the Portuguese, took the hill of St. Michael's, with the exception of the Horn Work. Towards evening the battalion paraded one hundred men and the light company, to storm the Horn Work at nightfall.

SIEGE OF BURGOS.—At the commencement of the siege, the battalion could only parade some two hundred and fifty men for duty.

FIRST ASSAULT OF BURGOS.—On 19th September, at nightfall, a Portuguese battalion and the 42nd Regiment were formed to escalade the front of the Horn Work; at the same time, the light companies of Colonel Sterling's brigade, and one hundred men each from the 24th and 79th regiments, under the command of Major the Honble. E. C. Cocks, of the 79th Regiment, were directed to escalade the rear of the Horn Work. The best accounts of the capture of this outwork, and the prominent features of the siege of Burgos, are in Colonel Jones's journal and Lord Wellington's despatches.

Colonel Jones's account of the assault on the Horn Work :—

"The firing party, on being put in motion, opened its fire, although one "hundred and twenty yards from the work, and continued to advance firing "to the edge of the ditch, by which time such numbers of them had been "killed and wounded that the rest dispersed. The Portuguese troops, for "the attack of the left demi-bastion, were preceded by a party of "Highlanders, under Lieutenant Pitts. The Royal Engineers carried the "scaling ladders, which they reared against the escarpe, and mounted "without opposition; but the troops could not be prevailed on to enter the "ditch. The attack on the right demi-bastion was equally unsuccessful. "During this time, Major Cocks led his party to the gorge of the work, "losing in advancing nearly one half of the men that he had with him from "the fire of the castle. The attention of the garrison of the Horn Work "being fully occupied by the attack in front, they neglected the defence of "the gorge, and the scaling ladders being placed against the palisades, the "work was entered at this point with but little opposition. Major Cocks "then divided his small party, posting one half on the ramparts, to ensure "the entry of the co-operating force in front, and the other half he formed "across the gateway, with a view to making the garrison prisoners. From "the weight of their superior numbers, however, they literally ran over our "small party, and escaped into the castle."

The battalion lost in this affair five rank and file killed, and sixteen wounded.

SECOND ASSAULT OF BURGOS.—The 20th, 21st, 22nd, and 23rd September were passed in carrying on the approaches to the place.

On the morning of the 23rd an attempt was made to carry the exterior line, but it failed, in consequence of the detachment of Portuguese, from the sixth division, not performing its allotted part. Major Lawrie, of the 79th, who commanded, after acting in the most gallant manner, was killed, and Captain Frazer, of the Guards, wounded.

On the night of the 25th, Lieutenant Walton, of the 24th regiment, was killed, at the moment he, with his covering party, was leaving the trenches to return to the camp, after having been twelve hours in the trenches.

The workmen now commenced mining the outer wall, and they suffered much from the enemy, who, having constructed long wooden troughs, placed them on the top of the wall, just over the entrance to the works, and rolled shells over their embrasures into the trenches.

On the 27th a second mine was commenced.

THIRD ASSAULT OF BURGOS.—On the night of the 28th the first mine was sprung, and made a breach. The storming party was selected from the sixth division. A few men of the advanced party gained the top of the breach, but the supporters having missed their way, the stormers were driven out of the breach, and the attack failed.

On 1st October two out of the three eighteen-pounders with which the siege was carried on became disabled, and from this period it became a musketry siege. Marksmen were placed at a distance of one hundred yards to fire into the embrasures during the day. These men, in some places, were posted before daylight, and could not be withdrawn till nightfall. Heavy rain set in, and the trenches became filled with water. Men and officers suffered much.

FOURTH ASSAULT OF BURGOS.—Storming of the exterior line by the 2nd battalion 24th Regiment on October 4th.

Extract from Lord Wellington's despatch, dated Villa-de-Tora, 5th October, 1812:—

"The fire from this battery improved the breach first made, and the "explosion of the mine, at five o'clock yesterday evening, effected a second "breach. Both were immediately stormed by the 2nd battalion 24th

"Regiment, under command of Captain Hedderwick. I had ordered them "into the trenches for that purpose, and our troops were established "within the exterior line of the works of the castle of Burgos.

"The conduct of the 24th Regiment was highly praiseworthy, and "Captain Hedderwick and Lieutenants Holmes and Fraser, who led the "storming parties, particularly distinguished themselves."

[Captain Hedderwick,* who commanded the battalion, received a brevet-majority; Lieutenants Holmes† and Fraser,‡ who led the wings, received companies respectively in the 8th West India Regiment and 1st Ceylon Light Infantry; Sergeant-Major William Fry, a distinguished soldier of the 95th Rifles, and Volunteer H. Wigmore, 5th Foot, were appointed to the vacant ensigncies.]

The above extract proves that Lord Wellington was not disappointed in the confidence which he placed in the 24th Regiment. The battalion could not parade more than one hundred and ninety-eight rank and file to storm the two breaches, though every man that could pull a trigger, including band, drummers, batmen, and servants, volunteered to go to the storm. One half of the battalion had been in the trenches and mines during the preceding night, and had not been long in camp when the order arrived for the battalion to fall in and march to the trenches. The men had not time to get their dinners, and not a soldier was left in camp, which, with the dinners, was left in charge of the women.

---

* This officer, who had been a subaltern in the 44th before joining the 24th, retired from the Service at the end of the war.

† Joined the 24th from lieutenant and adjutant 6th garrison battalion. He never joined the 8th West India Regiment, into which he was promoted, but remained with the Peninsular army as brigade-major of General Barnes's brigade. He afterwards served with the 78th Highlanders, and on the staff in North Holland, and in the Waterloo campaign. He died a lieutenant-colonel, half-pay, and deputy inspector-general of the Irish constabulary, in 1840. See *Colburn's United Service Magazine*, 1840, p. 240.

‡ Afterwards the celebrated General John Fraser, of Ceylon, many years quartermaster-general in that island. He originally joined the 24th in 1809, from lieutenant Royal East Middlesex Militia. He died a lieutenant-general, and colonel 37th Regiment, at Kandy, where he had large estates, 29th May, 1862. Some particulars of him will be found in Major John Skinner's *Fifty Years in Ceylon* (London, 1891).

The battalion was marched into the trenches, where they were told off into two storming parties, one hundred and forty men for the main breach and sixty men for the breach expected to be made by the second mine. Lieutenant Holmes volunteered to lead the advanced party at the main breach, followed by Captain Coote and fifty men. Lieutenant Fraser, in like manner, was appointed to lead the other advanced party, followed up by Captain Lepper and the remainder of his party at the mine.

These arrangements being made, the parties were lodged in parallels, within fifty yards of the place.

About 4 o'clock Lord Fitzroy Somerset was sent by Lord Wellington into the parallel with the final instructions for the storm.

Lord Wellington arrived on the hill about 4 o'clock p.m. to witness the storming. When the explosion took place, and the dust occasioned by the mine had subsided, the storming parties were first seen about half-way up the breaches, and, on the enemy being driven back from the main breach, Lord Wellington exclaimed, "Well done Twenty-Fourth."

The novelty of two breaches to be stormed by daylight created such curiosity in some, and anxiety in others, that, long before the time arrived, the hill in front of Burgos was crowded with officers and men from the besieging army. A number of officers had also come in from the advanced posts to witness so unusual an occurrence as the storming of a place by daylight.

Precisely at 5 p.m. Lieutenant-Colonel Jones, of the Engineers, who had made the arrangements for the assault, stood up at the entrance of the gallery and made the signal for exploding the mine. Colonel Jones exposed himself too much, and was severely wounded.

About one minute after the signal was made, the mine exploded, and in an instant both the storming parties stood up and ran to the breaches.

The party next the mine was almost covered with the clay and stones from the breach, and many of the men were severely injured by the falling stones.

The party got possession of this breach before the enemy recovered from the panic occasioned by the mine blowing up a great number of their men.

The party at the main breach was not so fortunate, as they had a greater distance to run to the breach, exposed all the time to a heavy fire. The enemy at this point did not suffer from the effects of the mine, and they made a very determined resistance. After expending their fire, they presented a formidable array of bayonets at the top of the breach.

The main body had by this time got about half-way up the breach, when Captain Hedderwick and the rest of the officers gave three cheers, upon which the whole party dashed in amongst the defenders of the breach, some of whom stood most gallantly.

A French sergeant made a rush at Captain Coote, but this officer fortunately caught the pike in his hand, and while struggling with the sergeant he received a shot through the shoulders, and fell down the breach. After the enemy were driven from the top of the breach, an officer, with a few men, attempted to make a stand behind a retrenchment cut inside the breach. They were instantly driven from it and pursued to their second line.

The battalion having got possession of the exterior line, were exposed to a tremendous fire from the second line. This, however, had been foreseen, and the parties, according to orders previously received, lodged themselves, some behind two large piles of shot and the rest behind a small building.

The battalion remained in these situations until nightfall, and then being relieved they returned to camp. Their losses during the day were one sergeant and eleven rank and file killed, Captain Coote, Lieutenant Stack, six sergeants, two drummers, and forty-eight rank and file wounded.

The camp was crowded with officers the day after the storming, coming to congratulate the officers of the 24th. This storming was considered one of the most extraordinary sights witnessed on the Peninsula.

Assistant-Surgeon Elkington, who had been left at Talavera with the wounded, returned from France, and it fell to his lot again to be left at Burgos in charge of the hospital. He was told by the French officers that they fully expected the exterior line would be stormed some night, but they were completely taken by surprise when the storming took place by daylight, and that they were looking with astonishment at the crowd collected on the hill when the mine was sprung.*

At 5 o'clock on the evening of 5th October the garrison made a sortie with three hundred men, and carried off a number of tools.

On the 6th and 7th, fresh mines were commenced under the second line. The weather excessively wet.

The French made another desperate sortie on the 8th, at 2 a.m., destroyed the works, and carried off the tools a second time. The 24th lost this night two rank and file killed and six wounded. Major the Honble. E. C. Cocks, of the 79th regiment, who commanded in

---

* "The *third* assault on the Castle of Burgos is a striking instance of the disadvantage of night attacks. Though close to the breach, the storming party, with the exception of five individuals, went to the wrong place on the springing of the mine, and did not find the breach made by it. But the next assault, the *fourth*, was so well arranged and executed, that it may be taken as a model for such operations. Instead of mixed detachments from different corps being taken, one entire battalion, the 2nd battalion 24th Regiment, was ordered on this duty, and Lieutenant-Colonel Jones, R.E., was sent by the Earl of Wellington to post them. . . . A wing of the battalion was posted opposite each breach, in close column of companies, as nearly as they could so form, and under cover, very close to the enemy. It was in daylight. There was a proper firing party well posted. When the mine sprung opposite the right wing of the battalion, which was to open a breach for its entrance, throwing up the earth as usual to a great height in the air, this half-battalion did not even wait for its fall, but marched forward amid the falling clumps, and in a few moments was in possession of the breach. The left wing moved forward as gallantly as the right, opening as they ascended the slope from close to about quarter distance column, and entered the breach a compact irresistible body. On the alarm, the defenders rose from behind a retired parapet, which they had formed in rear of the breach they were to defend. Their front rank appeared to be armed with spears, one of which Lieutenant Fraser, the brave leader of this wing, was seen to wrest from an opponent and then leap into the midst of the enemy, immediately followed by all his men. The names of Hedderwick (who commanded the battalion) and of Fraser and Holmes (who led the wings) have been deservedly recorded in the histories of the operation."— Sir Wm. Reid, R.E., on the "Assaults on the Castle of Burgos," in *Papers on Subjects Connected with the Corps of Royal Engineers.*

the trenches, was killed in successfully repulsing the sortie. Lord Wellington, and all the officers of the division, attended Major Cocks' funeral. He was buried close to Burgos, and the French ceased firing when they observed the funeral procession.

From the 9th to the 16th we fired red hot shot at the fortified convent, without effect. Continued mining and draining the trenches, whilst firing parties kept the enemy from the walls. The enemy erected a cavalier for riflemen to command the works.

Nine men were killed on the 17th, in the sap, by the fire from the cavalier. An attempt was made to blow up the cavalier, but it failed. The 24th lost in this attempt four rank and file killed, and three wounded.

A small breach was made in the second line, which was carried by a detachment of the German Legion, whilst a party of the Guards escaladed the line at the same time.

These detachments were, however, driven back before they could be supported.

On the 21st, the enemy having advanced on Burgos with a relieving army of thirty thousand men, preparations were made to raise the siege.

In consequence of some mistake, the brigade, with the exception of the 24th Regiment, marched to the front and joined the covering army. The battalion was left in the trenches for the last two days, and did not evacuate them until 5 a.m. on the 22nd, and not until the whole army had gained a day's march to the rear.

The garrison could not have been aware of the retreat, as they never molested the rear guard.

The retreat from Burgos commenced in floods of rain, the 24th Regiment forming part of the rear guard.

The River Carrion, near Duenas, was crossed on the 24th. The 1st battalion Grenadier Guards joined the division.

The army halted on the 25th. The picquets of the battalion had some sharp skirmishing at the Carrion, and some men taken prisoners.

On the 26th, marched to Cabacon, and crossed the Pisuerga.

The French army followed on the 27th, and formed in line on the opposite bank of the river. The 24th had to undergo a severe cannonade, but did not suffer, as the men were well under cover.

Halted in the same position on the 28th.

On the 29th, made a very rapid march, and crossed the Douro to Rueda. The army here took up a very strong position, whilst the enemy held the opposite bank of the Douro.

Remained in this position until the 6th November, and then marched towards Salamanca. The marches were long, and part of the country was so covered with water from the incessant rains, that no road could be discerned, and the battalion marched up to their knees in water. The men were at this time very badly off for clothing, and particularly shoes. The country was very flat, and scarcely a tree was to be seen. The men were therefore obliged to pull houses down for fuel, and if any of the wood was left after cooking, it was cut up, and each man carried a piece on his shoulder.

Sir Rowland Hill's corps formed a junction with Lord Wellington.

Lord Wellington's part of the army remained on the heights of St. Christoval, in front of Salamanca, until the 14th.

On this day the battalion crossed the Tormes.

It marched, on the 15th, to Aldea Tejada, to defend the passage of the Zanquera.

The greater part of the British army crossed the Zanquera on the 16th, and encamped on the Vamusca.

On the 17th the army continued its retreat to Portugal.

Sir Edward Paget was this day taken prisoner.

The army crossed the Aguada on the 19th, and went into winter quarters in Portugal.

The 24th Regiment joined the seventh division under the command of Earl Dalhousie, and formed part of the third brigade under Major-General Barnes.

1813.

In May, 1813, the army again took the field, and entering Spain, the enemy retreated to Vittoria, where an engagement took place on 21st June, which ended in their total defeat, with the loss of all their ordnance stores and baggage, together with the carriage &c. of Joseph Bonaparte.

The battalion obtained the badge for VITTORIA.

After the battle, the division continued the pursuit of the enemy towards the Pyrenees.

The battalion, however, had no opportunity of coming into close contact with the enemy until 25th July, when Major-General Barnes' brigade was ordered to support Sir Rowland Hill's division at the pass of Maya, where two brigades of that division were so long in action that they were obliged to give way.

Lord Wellington, in his despatch of the 1st August, says :—

"The brunt of the action fell upon the two brigades commanded by "Major-General Pringle and Major-General Walker, both in the second "division, under command of Lieutenant-General the Honble. Wm. "Stewart. These troops were at first obliged to give way, but having been "supported by Major-General Barnes' brigade, of the seventh division, they "regained that part of their post which was the key of the whole."

On the 30th, the division drove the enemy from the heights of Sorauren, which turned the enemy's flank, and forced them from their position.

Lord Wellington, in his despatch, says :—

"All these operations obliged the enemy to abandon a position which is "one of the strongest and most difficult of access that I have yet seen "occupied by troops. In their retreat from this position the enemy lost a "number of prisoners. The attack made by the Earl of Dalhousie was "admirably conducted."

The battalion was engaged in attacking the pass of Dona Maria on the 31st, which was gained, notwithstanding the vigorous resistance of the enemy and the strength of their position. The attack was made in a thick fog.

On 1st August, the battalion continued in pursuit of the enemy in the valley of the Bidassoa. Many prisoners were taken, and much baggage.

The battalion was engaged on the 2nd in one of the most dashing affairs that occurred during the war, when the brigade commanded by Major-General Barnes carried the heights of Eschalar, although defended by two divisions of the enemy. The brigade consisted of the 6th, 24th, and 58th, forming the Third Provisional Battalion of the Line, and the 82nd regiment.

Their conduct in that brilliant affair cannot be better or more truly described than by quoting the following despatch of Lord Wellington, dated Legaca, 4th August, 1813:—

"Major-General Barnes' brigade was formed for the attack, and advanced,
"before the fourth and light divisions could co-operate with them, with a
"regularity and gallantry which I have seldom seen equalled, and actually
"drove two divisions of the enemy, notwithstanding the resistance opposed
"to them, from those formidable heights. It is impossible that I can extol
"too highly the conduct of Major-General Barnes and these brave troops,
"which was the admiration of all who were witnesses of it."

During this action the 24th Regiment had Colonel Kelly, Captain Lepper, Captain Brickall, and Adjutant Fleming wounded, and a number of men killed and wounded.

The 2nd battalion obtained the badge for the battles of the PYRENEES.

After these actions the battalion remained in camp in the Pyrenees until 6th November.

On 10th November the battalion was engaged in the attack of the fortified heights and redoubts near Varra, and in the passage of the Nivelle, when the British army drove the enemy from all their strong positions. In these actions Captain Brickall and Ensign Marsh were wounded, and several men killed and wounded.

The 2nd battalion obtained the badge for the battle of the NIVELLE.

The rains having set in with great violence, the army went into cantonments about the middle of November. The 24th were quartered at St. Pè.

On 9th December the army again took the field, and drove the French across the Nive, when the 24th went into quarters at Ustarits.

1814.

In the beginning of the year a reinforcement of four subalterns and one hundred rank and file joined the battalion from England.

K

While the battalion was in the neighbourhood of Bayonne, the picquets were every night sent close to the enemy's lines, and the men posted on the bank of the river were ordered to fire on all boats, for the purpose of preventing supplies from being taken into Bayonne.

During these days the officers on picquet were in the habit of walking on the high embankments of the river, close to the walls. The French officers, accompanied by well-dressed ladies, were also in the habit of coming out of the town to view the English army. On these occasions, mutual compliments used to pass, the French officers taking off their caps and the ladies waving their handkerchiefs, and the English returned the compliments. On one of these occasions a French sentry, taking advantage of the absence of the French officers, fired at two of the officers of the 24th. The French officers hearing the shot, returned to the sentry, and immediately sent him in, a prisoner, under an escort.

At first the battalion occupied a few houses close to the walls. The garrison soon became jealous of these posts, and sent round shot through the houses. The picquets were then ordered not to show themselves during the day, and the battalion was then enabled to keep possession of the houses, a great boon.

On 20th February the army commenced operations.

The seventh division was now commanded by Major-General Walker, and the third brigade by Lieutenant-Colonel Gardiner, of the 6th regiment.

The battalion having marched with the seventh division towards Orthes, they arrived on 23rd February opposite the fortified posts at Hastingues and Oyergave, on the left bank of the Gave-de-Pau. These fortified posts were attacked, and the enemy driven within their tete de pont, at Peyrehorade.

On the 25th the division marched towards the Gave, whence the enemy retreated to Orthes, and on the 26th it crossed the Gave-de-Pau, and marched along the high road to Orthes, on the enemy's right.

BATTLE OF ORTHES.—On the 27th the enemy was posted in a strong position, their right on the heights near the village of St. Boes and their left on the town of Orthes.

The battalion came into action with the seventh division, attacking the heights of St. Boes, and advanced in line against the enemy, well covered by some companies of the Brunswick corps while descending one hill, crossing a valley, and ascending the hill on which the enemy was posted.

The enemy's artillery kept up a sharp fire on the battalion, well replied to by the English guns, until the brigade had got close to the top of the hill occupied by the enemy. The brigade reserved its fire until it got quite close to, in some places only thirty yards from, the enemy, when, having halted and fired a few rounds, it charged, and drove the enemy pell mell from the crest of the hill at the point of the bayonet.

The battalion occupied and remained on this hill until the French had been beaten at all other points, and then, joining in the pursuit about 4 p.m., drove the enemy that night to Soult-de-Navales, where the battle ended.

In this action the regiment lost many men, and Captains Le Mesurier and Ingram were wounded, and Lieutenant Stack was obliged to have his left arm amputated.

The 2nd battalion obtained the badge for ORTHES.

After this battle the regiment marched to Monte Marson, and thence to Bordeaux, which place it entered with the Duc d'Angouleme on 12th March, amid the acclamations of the people, who all mounted the white cockade.

On the 24th March the brigade crossed the Garonne, and remained in the neighbourhood of St. André-de-Culsue until peace was proclaimed in April.

The regiment returned to Bordeaux for a short time, in May, when the four companies of the 58th Regiment joined the 1st battalion of that regiment from Alicant.

The four companies of the 24th, which had been linked with those of the 58th, then marched to Pauillac, where they remained until June, when they embarked on board the *Bedford*, seventy-four guns, with the 68th Regiment, and landed at Cove, from whence they marched to Fermoy, and then through Cork to Bandon, where they remained until the middle of August, and then embarked at Cove for England.

Having been detained by contrary winds, they landed at Ramsgate in the beginning of October, and on the 24th of that month were disbanded by Major-General Sir Denis Pack.

The 2nd battalion obtained the badge for the PENINSULA.

Summary of the services in the Peninsula of the 2nd battalion 24th Regiment. Embodied in 1804, and disbanded in 1814, it existed only ten years. During this period it served in six brilliant campaigns under His Grace the Duke of Wellington, and earned the following badges for distinguished conduct, viz. :

Talavera - - - - -	27th and 28th July, 1809
Fuentes-de-Honor - - -	3rd and 5th May, 1811
Salamanca - - - - -	22nd July, 1812
Vittoria - - - - -	21st June, 1813
Pyrenees - - From 25th July to	2nd August, 1813
Nivelle - - - - -	10th November, 1813
Orthes - - - - -	27th February, 1814
Peninsula -	For the campaigns of 1809-10-11-12-13 and 14

The following remarks will also still further illustrate the active career of the battalion, and also explain the disadvantages under which it laboured.

In 1805 the 1st battalion was ordered to embark in the expedition for the capture of the Cape of Good Hope. It took with it the best and stoutest men of the 2nd battalion.

In 1808, again, the 2nd battalion were deprived of their most effective soldiers by Lieutenant-Colonel Marriott, who picked out three hundred and forty men to accompany him to the Cape, to join the 1st battalion, leaving, in fact, with the 2nd battalion nothing but boys and worn-out old men.

Being thus drained, it could not be considered a very serviceable regiment when it embarked the following year for the Peninsula.

Soon after its arrival in Portugal, a draft of very fine (but too young) men was received from the militia, but there was no time to have them drilled, as the army was already on the advance to Talavera.

At this period the battalion was about one thousand strong on paper, but sickness and other casualties reduced them to eight hundred on parade.

The following is a pretty correct statement of its losses in the first campaign.

	Rank & file.
Died of dysentry, fatigue, and lost by other causes, on the advance to Talavera, about	100
Killed and wounded in the battle of Talavera	355
Died of fever and ague on the banks of the Guardiana, about	100
Invalided and sent home after this campaign	50
Total struck off the Muster Rolls in 1809 ...	605

In addition to the above actual loss, many of the men in the different hospitals died in the course of a few months afterwards.

The battalion being thus reduced to a skeleton, and not having been fortunate in getting recruits, became one of the weakest regiments in the Peninsula during the next five campaigns. This was a very great disadvantage to the battalion, and it was in consequence only once selected for a particularly dashing service, viz., the storming of the two breaches at Burgos.

The strongest battalions were always selected on particular occasions, such as forcing the strongest points of a position or any other special service in an action, and they accordingly had a decided advantage over weak battalions.

The 24th Regiment was, however, exceedingly fortunate in having even the opportunities they had of distinguishing themselves, and obtaining such praise in the despatches, very particularly at Burgos and Eschalar.

The 24th took its share in all the campaigns on the Peninsula from 1809 to 1814, but owing to its weak state, after the first campaign, the lists of killed and wounded afterwards appear small by those of regiments of five times their strength. The 24th was not, however, the only battalion alike situated, as there were a number of 2nd battalions reduced to skeletons. Those that were so fortunate as to have their 1st battalions at home, were replaced by them.

The 2nd battalions of the 24th, 31st, 53rd, 58th, and 66th, and the 2nd Queen's, were broken up after the retreat from Burgos, and formed into three provisional battalions, which highly distinguished themselves in the two following campaigns.

ROLL OF OFFICERS OF THE TWO BATTALIONS 24TH (2ND WARWICKSHIRE) REGIMENT OF FOOT, IN OCTOBER, 1814,

The date of Disbandment of the Second Battalion of 1805-14.

From the *Monthly Army List*, November, 1814.

COLONEL—
Sir David Baird, K.B., K.C., G. 10 July, 1807

LIEUTENANT-COLONELS—
Randolph Marriott, M.G. - 18 Sept., 1804
2. Wm. Kelly, C. - - 22 Feb., 1810
1. Chas. Hicks - - 3 Oct., 1811
1. T. Chamberlain - - 11 June, 1813

MAJORS—
Sam. Taylor Popham - 14 Sept., 1801
2. T. Watkin Forster - 22 Feb., 1810
W. Robison - - - 3 Oct., 1811
1. Hy. White - - 4 June, 1813

CAPTAINS—
1. T. C. Green, M. - - 4 Aug., 1804
Ludovick Stewart, M. - 27 Aug., 1804
1. Chas. Hughes, M. - 28 Aug., 1804
1. Thos. Craig, M. - - 26 Oct., 1804
1. John Cathcart Meacham 28 Nov., 1808
2. Wm. Hedderwick -
2. Chas. Collis - - 31 Oct., 1805
2. Dan. Babey - - 6 Aug., 1806
2. Thos. Andrews - 7 April, 1808
2. Wm. Tudor - - 21 June, 1809
2. Jas. Lepper, M. - -
1. Thos. Martin - -
T. G. Coote - - - 22 Feb., 1810
2. W. A. Le Mesurier - 15 March, 1810
2. J. A. Ingram - - 3 Oct., 1811
2. Jas. Brickell - - 5 Jan., 1805
1. J. Ward - - - 22 Oct., 1812
2. J. Soden - - 20 March, 1808
C. Dinnehy - - - 6 May, 1813
1. J. Gridley - - 21 June, 1814

LIEUTENANTS—
1. E. G. Smith - - 8 Aug., 1805
1. John Blake - - 22 Aug., 1805
1. — Crome - - 18 Jan., 1806
1. Ponsonby Kelly - 27 Nov., 1806
1. John Ewing - - 28 May, 1807
1. Thos. Maling - - 23 Aug., 1807
1. Rob. Watson - - 22 Aug., 1807
1. Dav. Warburton - 13 Feb., 1808
1. Alex. N. Findlater - 18 Feb., 1808
1. Chas. Aug. Stuart - 18 Feb., 1808
2. Geo. Stack - - 4 Dec., 1806
Wm. Snodgrass - - 10 March, 1808
2. Thos. Allen - - 29 Sept., 1808
1. Joseph Brooksbank - 22 June, 1809
2. Geo. L'Estrange - 19 July, 1809
2. John Rope - - 20 July, 1809
1. John Harris - - 21 July, 1809
2. Fran. Gray - - 22 July, 1809
1. Rob. Robison - - 23 July, 1809
2. — Nokes - - 22 Feb., 1810

LIEUTENANTS, *continued*—
1. Thos. Barker Bainbrigge 3 May, 1810
2. Chas. Fred. Barton - 30 May, 1811
2. Mich. Hunt - - 8 Aug., 1811
1. Alex. Cameron - - 3 Oct., 1811
2. Chas. Jago - - 23 Jan., 1812
2. Geo. Erratt - - 2 April, 1812
2. Geo. Sunbolf - - 14 Sept., 1812
Geo. Ed. Quinten - -
2. Dunc. Rose - - 17 Dec., 1812
1. Wm. D'Acre - - 25 Feb., 1813
2. Edwin Pell - - 23 March, 1813
2. Hugh Fleming, Adjt. - 26 March, 1813
2. Jas. Millard - - 6 May, 1813
Rob. James - - 2 Dec., 1813
Christ. Hodge, P. - - 20 Jan., 1814
Arthur O'Leary - - 25 Jan., 1814
2. Geo. Arthur Bowdler - 22 Sept., 1814
John McGregor - - 26 June, 1814

ENSIGNS—
2. Alex. Child - - 16 Dec. 1811
2. Arthur Gray - - 11 July, 1811
1. Rob. Campbell - - 3 Oct., 1811
1. Rob. Marsh - - 31 Oct., 1811
2. Geo. Hewson - - 2 April, 1812
Ed. Thos. Smith - - 9 April, 1812
Wm. Mellis - - - 7 June, 1812
2. Hy. Wigmore - - 15 Oct., 1812
1. Thos. Kennedy - - 30 Oct., 1812
A. Backhouse - - 10 Dec., 1812
1. Peter Dore - - 8 April, 1813
1. Ed. Thos. Smith - - 9 April, 1813
1. Thos. Town - - 22 July, 1813
1. John Spooner - - 25 Dec., 1813
2. W. G. Gregory - -
Jas. Galbraith - - 23 June, 1814
John Carysfort Proby - 1 Sept., 1814

PAYMASTERS—
R. M. Payne - - 2 Sept., 1799
2. Isaac Buxton - - 6 Feb., 1800

ADJUTANTS—
2. N. Fleming - - 11 Jan., 1810
1. R. Watson - - 28 Oct., 1812

QUARTERMASTERS—
2. R. Belcher - - 1 Aug., 1803
2. C. Darlsing - - 24 Oct., 1811

SURGEONS—
1. Jonathan Featherstone - 31 Dec., 1803
2. John Heriott - - 16 April, 1811

ASSISTANT SURGEONS—
D. Kearney - - 11 March, 1813
2. John Fawcett - - 11 March, 1813
2. J. O. Burne - - 11 March, 1813

Agent—Macdonald.

CHAPTER VIII.

1824-48.

At Home—Peninsular Honours—Canada—India—Limited Enlistment Act.

1824-25.

IN 1824 the regiment proceeded from Portsmouth to Plymouth by sea, and occupied quarters in the Granby Barracks, Devonport. Notifications, dated as hereunder, were received, stating that His Majesty had been graciously pleased to approve of the 24th Regiment bearing on its colours and appointments the following distinctions, in addition to any already granted, in commemoration of the distinguished conduct of the late 2nd battalion of the regiment on these occasions: NIVELLE (authority dated 7th August, 1824), SALAMANCA, VITTORIA (authority dated 8th October, 1824), PENINSULA (for distinguished conduct from 1809, to July, 1814 (authority dated 4th March, 1825).

On 21st March, 1825, new colours, bearing these honours—the colours afterwards carried at Chillianwallah—were presented to the regiment.

In September, 1825, the regiment embarked for Ireland, landed at Kingstown, and proceeded to Kilkenny, sending detachments to Athy and Carlow.

1826-28.

In 1826 the regiment was collected in Limerick; in 1827 it was at Athlone; in 1828, in Dublin.

The regiment embarked at Dublin, 10th May, 1829, on board the *William Fawcett* and *Innisfail*, steam vessels. On arrival at Liverpool, six companies, with the head-quarters, marched for Manchester, two for Bolton, and two for Bury, at which stations they arrived on the 13th. One company detached from head-quarters to Middleton on the 18th.

On 20th May the following letter was received :—

"Adjutant-General's Office,
"Dublin, 16th May, 1829.
"Sir,
"In Lieutenant-General Sir John Byng's report to the Adjutant-"General of the Forces, of the embarkation of the 24th Regiment from "this command, the Lieutenant-General felt it incumbent upon him to bear "testimony to the order and regularity with which it was conducted, and by "his direction I have the honor now to transmit to you the enclosed extract "of a letter which he has had the satisfaction of receiving from Lieutenant-"General Sir Herbert Taylor in reply.

"I have, &c.,
"(Signed) J. GARDINER, D.A.G.
"Lieutenant-Colonel Fleming, Commanding 24th Regiment."

Extract of a letter from the Adjutant General of the Forces, addressed to Lieutenant-General Sir John Byng, dated Horse Guards, 14th May, 1829.

"I have laid your letter of the 11th instant before Lord Hill, who "orders me to express to you the satisfaction with which he received your "report of the exemplary and excellent state of order and discipline in "which the 24th Regiment embarked at Dublin for Liverpool. His Lord-"ship considers the circumstance highly creditable to the Officers and "Soldiers of the Corps."

On 13th July, a letter was received directing the Service companies to hold themselves in readiness to proceed to Canada.

The Service companies, leaving the Reserve companies at Manchester, embarked in canal boats on the 23rd July, and arrived at Paddington on the 27th, and marched to Woolwich on the 28th.

On 28th July the following letter was received :—

"Horse Guards,
"27th July, 1829.
"Sir,
"I have the honor to acquaint you that Lord Hill foregoes his "intended inspection of the 24th Regiment on its arrival in London, it

"appearing that its clothing has been packed up for embarkation, and the "reports of the state of the regiment which have lately been made by "Lieut.-General Sir John Byng and Major-General Sir Henry Bouverie, "having satisfied his Lordship that it is in high order in all respects.

"I have, &c.,
"(Signed) H. TAYLOR, A.G.
"Colonel Fleming, 24th Regiment."

The Service companies, under command of Lieutenant-Colonel Edward Fleming, embarked in the transports *Countess Harcourt*, *Kaisir*, and *Silvia* on 30th July, and sailed 1st August, 1829. They landed at Montreal 9th and 10th October, having left a corporal and four privates at William Henry.

On 18th August, 1829, the veteran colonel of the regiment, General Right Honble. Sir David Baird, Bart., G.C.B., K.C., died, and was succeeded by Major-General Sir Jas. Lyon, C.B., G.C.H., *(Appendix)* whose appointment was dated 7th September, 1829.

Sundry changes in the army took place about this time. The practice of enlisting men at option for "limited" (seven years), or "unlimited" service, which had been in force during the Peninsular war and after, was abolished by a Horse Guards order, dated 18th April, 1829. From that time, until the introduction of "short service" (10 years), in 1848, all recruits were enlisted for unlimited service, with claim to pension after 21 years.

The use of pikes by sergeants was discontinued, the pike being replaced by a short smooth-bore musket, called a "fusil," which was carried until the introduction of the Enfield rifle during the Crimean war.

The use of silver lace was restricted to militia and yeomanry corps. The 24th officers accordingly adopted gold lace and buttons in place of the silver formerly worn in the regiment.*

---

* A memorandum, accidentally found in a box in the orderly room of the 1st battalion of the regiment, on 10th May, 1887, appears to refer to a drum-major's staff made for the regiment at this time. It was made in 1829, all the officers of the 24th regiment subscribing to it. It was manufactured in Birmingham, and is of wood, covered with silver. Colonel Fleming was colonel at the time. So runs the note. The 80th Regiment is believed to have a similar staff.

1830.

The 24th Regiment moved in two divisions from Montreal to Quebec on 29th April and 3rd May.

[The MS. Records of the 24th Regiment of Foot forwarded to the Adjutant-General's Office, Horse Guards, by Lieutenant-Colonel Fleming, as stated below, here abruptly ends. The whole of the information it affords has been embodied in the preceding pages of this history.]

On 26th June, 1830, His Majesty King George IV. died, and was succeeded by H.R.H. the Duke of Clarence, as King William IV. The depôt of the 24th was stationed at Carlisle during this year.

1831-32.

In accordance with instructions received from the Adjutant-General, the Records of the regiment were sent to the Horse Guards, with the subjoined letter, and a rough copy of the MS. is now in the orderly room, 1st battalion South Wales Borderers.

"Quebec, 2nd April, 1831.
"Sir,
"I have the honor to forward the records of the 1st and 2nd "battalions of the 24th Regiment, and regret that they are not so com-"plete, or 1st battalion to so remote a date as I could wish, from the "circumstance of the books having been lost when the regiment was "taken on its passage from the Cape of Good Hope to India, in 1810.

"I have the honor to be, Sir,
"Your most obedient humble Servant,
"(Signed) EDWARD FLEMING,
"Lieutenant-Colonel commanding 24th Regiment."
"The Adjutant-General of the Forces, &c., &c.,
"Horse Guards, London."

In 1832 the flank companies, under Captain Henry Divé Townshend, went from Quebec to Montreal. Three other companies of the regiment wintered at Montreal in 1832-33.

1833-35.

On 1st March, 1833, Lieutenant-Colonel Francis Skelly Tidy, C.B., a distinguished veteran, who had commanded the old 3rd battalion 14th Foot at Waterloo, exchanged with Colonel E. Fleming, from Inspecting Field Officer of the Glasgow Recruiting District, to the command of the 24th. The head-quarters, under Major Charles Hughes, arrived at Montreal from Quebec during the summer. The depôt was at Newcastle-on-Tyne.

In 1834, the 24th, Lieutenant-Colonel Tidy, C.B., in command, was at Montreal. The depôt went to Ireland.*

In 1835 the regiment removed from Montreal to Kingston, where, on 9th October, Colonel Tidy died, to the sincere regret of his regiment and of the Canadians, whose respect and confidence he had won in a marked degree. A monument was erected at Kingston to his memory by the officers and men of the regiment.

1836-39.

Under Lieutenant-Colonel Charles Hughes, who succeeded to Colonel Tidy's vacancy, the regiment remained at Kingston until 10th May, 1837, when the head-quarters removed to Toronto, three companies, under Major H. D. Townshend, remaining at Kingston. The depôt went from Ireland to Portsmouth the same year.

Whilst the head-quarters were at Toronto, intelligence was received of the death of King William IV., on 20th June, 1837, and the accession of Her Majesty Queen Victoria.

Political agitation had been for some time rife in Lower Canada, and so menacing was the aspect of affairs there in the fall of the

---

* Asiatic cholera crossed the Atlantic in 1832, and made much havoc among the civil populations of Montreal and Quebec. It reappeared in 1834. The troops at Montreal were encamped on the island of St. Helens, and all communication with the city cut off. Only one death occurred at St. Helens, although a detachment at La Prairie, on the opposite bank, suffered severely. See "Report on Mortality among the Troops in North America." *Parl. Papers*, 1839, vol. xvi.

year 1837, that the Commander of the Forces, Sir John Colborne, afterwards Lord Seaton, deemed it expedient to reinforce the province with the 24th Regiment from Upper Canada. With the consent of the Lieutenant-Governor, Sir Francis Bond Head, the regiment was accordingly withdrawn by detachments from Kingston and Toronto at the end of October, and eventually arrived at Montreal on 18th November, 1837, having left two companies under Major H. D. Townshend at Carillon, on the Ottawa, and a subaltern's party at Bytown. This regiment was brigaded with the 2nd battalion Royals and the 32nd and 83rd regiments, and the men were furnished with mocassins and blanket clothing for the winter campaign, which had already begun with an attack by the insurgents on some volunteer cavalry escorting prisoners.

As the rebels were understood to be collecting in force at St. Denis and St. Charles, villages on the banks of the Richelieu or Sorel river, it was decided to make a combined movement against them with the Royals, under Colonel Wetherall, moving from Chambly, and a small force of three hundred men from Sorel. The latter, consisting of the flank companies 24th, under Colonel Hughes, the light company 32nd, and a six-pounder gun, R.A., under Colonel the Honble. Chas. Gore, C.B., D.Q.M.G., sailed on 22nd November, 1837, from Montreal to Sorel, and, being there joined by a company 66th, marched the same evening for St. Denis, twenty miles distant. The night was cold and wet, and so dark that barrack lanterns had to be used. The road was knee-deep in mud. After a twelve hours' march, the troops found the insurgents posted in a fortified stone building (a distillery), with a well-flanked barricade blocking the road. They were at once attacked; but the gun could make no impression on the defences, although a round shot passing through one of the windows, struck down twelve rebels at once. After some hours' sharp firing, the troops, dead-beaten, with their clothes freezing to their backs, were drawn off, and returned to Sorel, leaving behind them some of their wounded, and the gun, fast frozen in the mud. The loss was twenty killed and wounded, whereof the 24th companies had two killed and seven wounded. The detachment returned from Sorel to Montreal next day.* At St. Charles, Colonel Wetherall was more successful, and the rebels were driven out at the point of the bayonet, with some loss.

On 30th November the light company 24th, under Captain Maitland, again started with a stronger force, under Colonel Gore. Failing to break the ice of the Richelieu with a steamboat, they landed, crossed on the ice to St. Ours, and marched to St. Denis, which had been abandoned the night before. They then scoured the villages and recovered the wounded men and the six-pounder gun. It returned, through St. John's, to Montreal on 11th December. The same day the head-quarters of the regiment, which had been escorting arms to Harryville for the Loyal Volunteers, returned to Montreal, and remained there for the protection of the city during the absence of Sir John Colborne, who started with fifteen thousand troops, on 13th December, to disperse the insurgents collected in the country of the Lake of Two Mountains, to the north-westward of Montreal. These had their head-quarters in the villages of St. Eustachè and St. Běnoit, the latter situate in a tract of country known as Grand Brulé.

On 14th December the two companies of the 24th under Major H. D. Townshend, at the Carrillon Rapids, marched to Grand Brulé to co-operate with Sir John Colborne's force.

On the 15th the rebels were driven out of St. Eustachè, with heavy loss; and next day the greater part of those left laid down their arms at Grand Brulé. Major Townshend's party returned to Carrillon. Captain John Harris' company, with the two from Carrillon, was employed in dispersing rebels on the frontier of the Upper Province; and on 21st December one company from Carrillon and one from Montreal were sent to Chippewa, opposite Navy Island, just above Niagara Falls. The island was occupied by a body of insurgents and American "sympathisers," from Buffalo and other frontier towns. The rest of the regiment arrived at Chippewa, from Montreal, on 10th January, 1838, and Colonel Hughes assumed command of the troops

---

* Lieutenant Weir, 32nd, who was sent after Colonel Gore with despatches, missed his way in leaving Sorel, and was barbarously murdered by the St. Denis insurgents.

(regulars, militia, and volunteers) amounting to two thousand five hundred men. As an attack on the island was considered unadvisable, it was shelled for three days, and then evacuated. Major Townshend, with Captain Marsh's company from Carrillon, was despatched to Toronto, and thence to Amherstburg, where he assumed command of the troops and rendered important services on Lake Erie ; Captain Marsh's company returning on 11th April to Toronto, whither the 24th head-quarters had gone from Chippewa. In June, 1838, the head-quarters and three companies 24th again entered the Upper Province, and three companies were actively employed under Major Townshend on the Niagara frontier, where the rebels had again collected. The troops suffered very severely from the heat, having only the blanket clothing they had worn on leaving Montreal, in January. These companies regained head-quarters 11th August, 1838, and the regiment was once more collected at Montreal, and received new clothing and accoutrements.

Captain John Harris, who had been in command of the regiment before Navy Island, received the local rank of major from 10th July, 1838, and Major H. D. Townshend, who had the local rank of lieutenant-colonel, received a brevet lieutenant-colonelcy in recognition of his services.

On 4th November, 1838, news reached Montreal that a patrol of the 7th Hussars had been fired on near La Prairie. Two companies 24th, under Captain Marsh, were at once sent across the river, and were joined next day by the rest of the regiment which had been under arms all night. Under command of Lieutenant-Colonel Hughes, the regiment marched to St. Pièvres, and on 9th November to L'Acadie, where it joined a force under Sir John Colborne, and on 11th November entered Napierville, the chosen head-quarters of the insurgents, which was found to have been abandoned a few hours before. Some days later the regiment returned to Montreal.

The following statistics of the strength and mortality* of the Service companies of the regiment during the first seven years of its

---

* " Report on Mortality of the Army in North America." *Parl. Papers*, **1839**, vol. xvi.

service in Canada are taken from a paper laid before Parliament in 1839. Similar statistics appear not to have been compiled for the succeeding years.

YEARS.	AGES.										TOTAL.	
	under 18		18-25		25-33		33-40		40-50			
	Strength.	Deaths.	Strength.	Deaths.	Strength.	Deaths.	Strength.	Deaths.	Strength.	Deaths.	Strength.	Deaths.
1830	8	...	322	8	211	2	5	...	3	2	549	10
1831	8	...	282	6	192	4	5	...	3	...	490	10
1832	5	...	228	8	275	16	12	...	4	...	524	24
1st January, 1833, to 31st March, 1834 ...	4	...	133	1	322	7	27	1	4	...	490	9
1st April, 1834, to 31st March, 1835	1	...	81	2	322	12	30	2	5	...	439	17
1st April, 1835, to 31st March, 1836	5	...	99	5	301	10	43	3	3	...	451	18
1st April, 1836, to 31st March, 1837	5	...	96	1	276	5	50	4	4	...	431	10

The depôt, under Major G. F. Stack, K.H., remained in the Portsmouth command during the year.*

1839-41.

The regiment remained at Montreal until May, 1840, when it proceeded in two divisions: the first, under Lieutenant-Colonel

---

* *Naval and Military Gazette*, 19th May, 1838. 24th Depôt.—The officers of this depôt have presented to George and Ann Beechey a silver teapot, value fifteen guineas, bearing the following inscription : " To George and Ann Beechey, from " the officers or the depôt 24th Regiment, as a token of approbation of their " faithful services while in charge of the depôt mess, during the period of nine " years." George Beechey served twenty-eight years in the 24th, and was discharged to out-pension, with the rank of sergeant, August, 1837.

Hughes; the second, under Major Stack, K.H., to Kingstown.*

In February, 1840, the depôt, under Major Charles Hastings Doyle, removed from Portsmouth to Cork, and later to Fermoy, giving detachments to Kilkenny, Carlow, etc. In 1841 it removed from Kilkenny to Pigeon House Fort, Dublin, whence it returned to Portsmouth, to await the arrival of the regiment.†

In January the Service companies received orders to return to England. Leaving behind one hundred and ninety-two volunteers for regiments in Canada, the Service companies embarked at Quebec in the transport *Prince Regent* on 16th June, after a service of twelve years in Canada. They arrived at Plymouth on 26th and 28th July, 1841, and were quartered at Devonport. The depôt, which was quartered on Maker Heights, was consolidated with the Service companies on 1st August.

On 17th August Lieutenant-Colonel Thomas Hughes retired on full pay, after an uninterrupted service in the regiment of forty-six years. He was succeeded by Lieutenant-Colonel Townshend. On Colonel Hughes's departure, the following letters were left to be recorded.

"Devonport, 31st August, 1841.

"My dear Colonel,

"I enclose a letter from Lieutenant-General Jackson, com-
"manding in Canada, which I received after the embarkation of the
"regiment at Quebec. I beg you will be so kind as to communicate to
"the officers, non-commissioned officers, and men, the high opinion of them
"therein expressed, and which he authorized me to make known to them,
"but which circumstances prevented my doing. At the same time, may I
"assure them through you, of my deep regret at leaving a corps in which I
"have served 46 continuous years, and that I shall ever carry with me the

---

* Canadian papers of December, 1840, speak in terms of high praise of the conduct of Sergeant Roberts, 24th Foot, who was with an escort on board the *Comet* schooner, in a great storm off Cape Rowan, and rendered valuable aid to the shipping. The *Norfolk Observer*, (Canadian paper) says: "It is a duty we owe to the sergeant of the 24th, to say that it is generally believed that the safety of the ships and cargoes is due *solely* to his vigilant and manly conduct."

† Glasgow, where Colonel E. Fleming was still inspecting field officer, was a favourite recruiting ground of the 24th at this period.

"most lively interest for the honor of the regiment, and the most affection-
"ate good wishes for the welfare and happiness of every individual
"belonging to it.

"Believe me,
"My dear Colonel,
"Most truly yours,
"C. HUGHES.

"Lieutenant-Colonel Townshend, commanding 24th Regiment."

EXTRACT FROM SIR R. JACKSON'S LETTER.

"I cannot let you go from Quebec without a line to say how well
"satisfied I have been in every respect with the 24th Regiment since I
"have been in Canada. No regiment here is more entitled to commend-
"ation, and I shall not fail to mention my opinion in the proper quarter.
"Remember me to the officers, and tell the non-commissioned officers
"and men how well pleased I am with them, and their very creditable
"conduct under your difficulties in coming down from Kingston, and their
"soldier-like march and appearance in Montreal afterwards.

"R. P. JACKSON, Lieutenant-General.

"Lieutenant-Colonel Hughes."

1842.

In 1842 the regiment was stationed at Devonport.* The papers of the day speak of the band, at this time, as "the finest in the Service."

---

* A few years ago the following interesting letter from Lieutenant-Colonel G. Lloyd Williams, a Chillianwallah veteran who joined the regiment about this time, was received by Colonel J. F. Caldwell, then commanding 2nd battalion South Wales Borderers.

"Kandy, 9th December, 1885.

Dear Colonel Caldwell,
    Circumstances oblige me to be much away from home, and your letter arrived during one of my absences. My address, during these, changes so often, that letters are not forwarded. This will, I trust, plead my excuse for the delay in replying.

Though some eleven years in the 24th, I am like the knife-grinder—I have no story to tell. A curious case of promotion or two is all I know. A Lieutenant Harris, who was of sufficient standing, was sent recruiting, and enlisted a man of the name of Riley, who worked his way to colour-serjeant and bought his discharge; set up in business, failed, re-enlisted, worked his way up, got his commission. Eventually, Harris and Riley were made brevet-majors in the same Gazette.

A man named Searle enlisted whilst we were in Devonport, in 1842, I think.

Percussion arms (smooth-bore muzzle-loading muskets), calibre, 0·753; length of barrel, thirty-nine inches; weight, nine lbs. twelve oz., were introduced this year in place of the flint-lock musket.

1843.

The regiment embarked at Devonport for Glasgow in April. Major-General the Honble. Henry Murray, commanding at Devonport, published a highly complimentary district order on conduct of regiment during stay in garrison, and on embarkation, recording "the " satisfaction he has derived from the manner in which the regiment " carried on the duties of the service, and its efficiency as a corps, " which it will carry with it to whatever service it may be called."

A copy of the following letter was also received:—

"Horse Guards,
"12th April, 1843.
"Sir,
"I have had the honor to lay before the Commander-in-Chief " your letter of the 10th inst., and am directed to acquaint you that His " Grace is much satisfied with your report of the good conduct of the 24th " Regiment, on its embarkation at Devonport for North Britain.

"I have &c., &c.,
"JOHN MACDONALD, A.G.

"Major-General
"The Honble. Henry Murray,
"Devonport."

By good conduct he got so near his commission that when we embarked in 1846, in Cork, he was kept back, as his commission was daily expected. I just missed my majority by one above me putting in his name for purchase. I should have had to serve seventeen years before I should have again had a chance.

I believe I am the most wounded man alive—23 wounds: grape shot, musket ball, and sabre cuts. Though past sixty, I can enjoy a good day's tramp through paddy fields. I have walked all over Ceylon, and if anyone wants information, I think I can supply it, whether sporting or agricultural. Ceylon is a cheap country compared to India, and I wonder more do not come across to see our beautiful island. A grand field for antiquarianly inclined enthusiasts, a seat of civilisation when our progenitors were going about in woad. I'll back the present race of natives to outlie all the world. A very large proportion talk English.

Regretting my inability to add anything of an interesting nature to the Regimental Records,

I remain, very faithfully yours,
GEO. LLOYD WILLIAMS."

A letter was also received from Lieutenant-General R. Ellice, the colonel of the regiment, dated Florence, May 19th, 1843, addressed to Lieutenant-Colonel Townshend, saying that General Murray had written him "a most complimentary communication on the admirable "conduct of the regiment for the whole period it remained under his "command."

In October, this year, the regiment proceeded from Glasgow to Dublin.

1844-46.

The regiment, under command of Lieutenant-Colonel Townshend, was quartered in Dublin until September, 1844, when it moved to Kilkenny, giving detachments to various stations. In May, 1845, the regiment removed to Limerick, detaching companies to various out-stations.

In December-January, 1845-46, the regiment was assembled at Cork, where it was augmented to the Indian establishment, Major Stoyte obtaining the second lieutenant-colonelcy and Captain H. W. Harris the majority. On 28th April, Lieutenant-Colonel Townshend exchanged to half-pay, unattached, with Colonel Brooke *(Appendix B)*. After detaching a depôt company, consisting of Captain Daniel Riley,* Lieutenants F. Spring and F. C. Skurray, six sergeants, five corporals, two drummers, and forty-seven privates to join the provisional battalion at Chatham, the regiment embarked at Cork for Bengal, on the dates and on board the freight-ships specified below :—

> *Eclipse.*—6th May, 1846. Major H. W. Harris, commanding; Captains C. Lee, R. W. Fraser; Lieutenants L. H. Bazalgette, G. Lloyd Williams, C. M. Drew; Ensign W. Phillips; Assistant-Surgeon Hanbury.
>
> *Aurora.*—6th May, 1846. Major Howell Paynter, commanding; Captains C. H. Ellice, E. Wodehouse; Lieutenants J. Stainforth, J. S. Payne, Honble. R. Handcock; Ensign W. D. H. Baillie.
>
> *Lahore.*—7th May, 1846. Captain John Harris, commanding; Captain

---

* This officer, whose singular story is referred to in the previous foot-note, retired on full pay as captain and brevet-major, 8th April, 1848. He became brevet lieutenant-colonel in 1854, and died long afterwards.

C. R. Harris; Lieutenants G. F. Berry, W. F. Barclay, W. Selby; Ensign O. B. Payne; Assistant-Surgeon W. Furlong.

Coromandel.—7th May, 1846. Lieutenant-Colonel R. Brookes, commanding; Captain E. J. Fleming; Lieutenants J. H. Lutman, J. B. Thelwall, Jas. Daubeny; Ensigns H. C. B. Collis, E. S. Bull; Assistant-Surgeon J. Donald.

Poictiers.—With head-quarters, 8th May, 1846. Lieutenant-Colonel John Stoyte, commanding; Captains A. G. Blachford, W. G. Browne; Lieutenants J. S. Shore, G. Phillips; Ensigns J. A. Woodgate, T. M. Greensill; Paymaster G. A. Ferrier; Adjutant W. Hartshorn; Quarter-Master J. Price; Surgeon G. K. Pitcairn.

and arrived at Calcutta in 1846, as follows:

Poictiers, 28th August; *Lahore*, 7th September; *Aurora*, 9th September; *Eclipse*, 11th September; *Coromandel*, 29th September. The last named being one hundred and forty-five days on the passage.

1846-47.

After a few weeks at Dum Dum, the regiment proceeded to Ghazeepur; and on 16th January, 1847, marched, under command of Lieutenant-Colonel Richard Stoyte, from Ghazeepur to Agra, arriving there on 5th March. In April, Colonel Stoyte exchanged to the 17th Foot, with Colonel Pennycuick, C.B.K.H. In 1847 the Limited Enlistment Act (10-11 Vic., c. 37) came into force, which enacted that, after the passing thereof, no one should be enlisted to serve Her Majesty, or in the European forces of the East India Company, for a longer period than *ten* years in the Infantry and *twelve* years in the Cavalry and Ordnance Corps, to be reckoned from the day on which the recruit had been attested, should he have stated himself to be eighteen years of age; or, if not, from the day when he should complete eighteen years according to the attestation.

The Medal and Annuity for Meritorious Service was established by Royal Warrant, dated 24th May, 1847. One of the first recipients was Colour-Sergeant William Delany, 24th regiment.*

---

* According to Capt. Tancred's *Historical Record of Medals* (London, 1891), the medal issued to this non-commissioned officer is now in the collection of medals belonging to Captain Fowler, of Scarborough. It bears the date "1847." All other early specimens known, bear the date 1848. War medals were granted to the survivors of certain actions in the campaigns of 1793-1825, by order of Her Majesty, and of the Honble. East India Company, dated 1st July, 1847.

CHAPTER IX.

1848-50.

Punjaub Campaign—Chillianwallah—Roll of the Dead—Goojerat—After—Additional Notes.

1848.

THE wide-spread of defection in the Punjaub, following upon the assassinations and revolt at Mooltan in April this year, and the subsequent failure of the first siege, aroused the authorities at Calcutta to prompt and decisive action. " Unwarned " by precedent, untaught by experience, the Sikh nation have declared " for war," Lord Dalhousie told the assembled officers at Barrackpore, on his departure for the frontier, " and, on my word, sirs, they shall " have it with a vengeance ! "*

Troops were ordered to assemble at Ferozepore, to co-operate with the Mooltan force, as the " Army of the Punjaub," under the personal command of the commander-in-chief, Lord Gough. After some weeks of eager expectancy, the 24th, described as " a fine body of young soldiers," was ordered to the front. On 3rd October, 1848, the regiment, numbering twenty-seven officers (subsequently increased by ten from leave of absence) and one thousand and seventy-one non-commissioned officers and men, started from Agra, and, by forced march, *via* Delhi, halting one day only on the road, reached Ferozepore on 4th November.

On arrival, the regiment was brigaded with two regiments of Bengal Native Infantry, as the sixth brigade, under command of Colonel John Pennycuick, C.B., K.H., 24th regiment, with Captain C. R. Harris, 24th, as brigade-major. The sixth brigade subsequently became the fifth, on the breaking up of a native brigade. It formed part of the third division, which was commanded by Major-General Sir Joseph Thackwell, K.C.B., K.H., and afterwards by Brigadier-General Colin Campbell, 98th regiment—in later years Lord Clyde.

---

* Trotter's *India, under Victoria*, vol. i.

The regiment marched with its division from Ferozepore on 8th November, 1848, and on the road to Lahore lost a subaltern—Lieutenant Arthur Edward Frere, a younger brother of (the late) Rt. Honble. Sir Bartle Frere—and several men by sickness. Between Ferozepore and Lahore the grenadier company (Captain R. W. Travers; Lieutenant J. B. Thelwall) and the light company (Captain W. G. Brown; Lieutenants Sweton Grant, G. F. Berry, and G. Phillips) were employed as escort to the field battery attached to the brigade, which moved a day's march ahead of its brigade.*

The division reached Ramnuggar on 22nd November, the day of the cavalry fight there, in which the 14th Light Dragoons suffered so severely. It encamped on the left bank of the Chenab, opposite a large force of Sikhs on the far side. There, guarded by outlying picquets and videttes, the division remained the rest of the month, parades and inspections being the order of the day. On 1st December the larger part of the division was directed to march in silence at midnight, taking one day's cooked rations, leaving its tents standing and lights burning, with the object of crossing a ford four miles away, and so turning the Sikh flank, whilst their front was still menaced by the rest of the army. The supposed ford proved impracticable, and, after a long and weary detour, the infantry of the division crossed the river in country boats, near Wuzeerabad, about 8 o'clock the same night, the cavalry fording lower down. On the morrow the division moved along the right bank in the direction of the Sikh position opposite Ramnuggar.

---

* Two regimental pets may here find passing record. One, a small spaniel, called "Twopence," the inseparable companion of the men of the light company, by whom he had been taught to render various services—fetching lights for their pipes, and the like, "Twopence" fell ill on the march, when the men of his company took turns in carrying him, till his little life had fled. The other, a noble specimen of black buck, yclept "Billy," marched with the regiment from Agra, and charged at its head at Chillianwallah. Whether the Sikhs believed him to be a sacred animal is uncertain; but "Billy" came out of the conflict unscathed, and might have lived for years to wear the medal with which he was provided, but for his developing a most unfortunate spirit of pugnacity. After attacking and putting to flight a newly arrived draft from England, he was ordered to be destroyed, to the deep regret of his human comrades of the rank and file. For officers he never had the slightest respect.

On 3rd December occurred the combat of Sadoolapore. A strong force of Sikhs came out to oppose the further advance of Thackwell's division and to cover the retrograde movement of the rest of their troops. In the artillery combat which ensued, and lasted several hours, the 24th were most of the time lying down under fire.* The regiment had Colour-Sergeant James Collins and Private J. Murtle killed and four men wounded, of whom Colour-Sergeant Wm. Young and Private James Bibb died of their wounds. Major Henry Harris, commanding the regiment, had his horse killed under him. The division bivouacked on the ground for the night, during which the Sikhs retired, and in the morning again advanced. The wells, where the Sikhs had been, were found to be very foul, from powder thrown into them and other causes. The division had not moved very far when a pillar of smoke was seen to arise, followed by a loud and heavy report. This was the blowing up of the powder magazine in the Sikh camp. Shortly afterwards, the rest of the army, left behind at Ramnuggar, came up with the division, and the passage of the Chenab having thus been completed, the army advanced, and encamped at Heylah on 8th December, 1848. There it remained over the new year. Colonel Brookes joined at this time, and assumed command of the regiment.†

---

* General Sir Henry Norman, in a letter to Colonel Symons, when these records were in course of compilation, wrote: "Although my regiment was not in the same brigade with the 24th, we were encamped close to them after Sadoolapore for three weeks. They had not been long in India, and were smart, and composed of fine men. In marching from Ramnuggar to Wuzeerabad, preparatory to Sadoolapore, my regiment followed the 24th in column of route. During the march we were generally in a column of companies, and as adjutant I was often with the commanding officer at the head of our regiment; so I had the opportunity of counting the files of the rear (or light) company of the 24th, and noted down then that they had forty-nine files in the ranks. All my life I have been in the habit of counting the files when I see troops, but I never before, or since, have seen companies fall in so strong; and as we had left our camps standing with camp guards and men to look after the tents and baggage, you may imagine how strong the regiment was. It was a splendid looking corps, but a few weeks later could only turn out six weak companies."

† Colonel Brookes, who, although junior to Colonel Pennycuick in service and army rank, was senior to him in the regiment, had been on leave in England. He was married at Hove Church, Brighton, 24th June, 1848, and did not re-embark for India until November, 1848.

1849-50.

BATTLE OF CHILLIANWALLAH.—On 9th January, 1849, the Army of the Punjaub, under command of Lord Gough, moved from the camp, Heylah, into the jungle, in the direction of Jung, in quest of the Sikhs, who were supposed to be somewhere in the neighbourhood of the river Jhelum. They were eventually found in a commanding position at Russool, on a low range of hills near the river, with an entrenched picquet on a mound by the village of Chillianwallah, in the wooded plain, a couple of miles in advance. The Sikh force, comprising all the best surviving troops of the old Khalsa army, numbered about twenty-three thousand men,* with a powerful artillery, and was under command of the Sirdar Shere Singh.

On 13th January, 1849, the third division, now commanded by Brigadier-General Colin Campbell, C.B., 98th regiment, and consisting of two brigades, viz: the fifth brigade, under Brigadier John Pennycuick, C.B., K.H., 24th regiment, composed of H.M. 24th, and the 25th and 45th regiments Bengal Native Infantry, and the seventh brigade, under Brigadier Hoggan, 61st regiment, composed of H.M. 61st, with the 36th and 46th regiments Bengal Native Infantry, with No. 5 light field battery and half of No. 10 light field battery attached, formed the infantry of the left wing of the army, on the march from Dingee towards Russool.† The light company 24th, which with some artillery had formed the main picquet, miles in front of the main body, the night before, rejoined its regiment before the army came up with the Sikh outpost on the mound. The intention was that the mound should be stormed by the 24th. The regiment loaded,‡ and Brigadier-General Colin

---

* This is the estimate given by Colonel Malleson *(Decisive Battles of India)*, on the authority of Cunningham. The official estimates at the time are stated to have been far too high.

† *Memorandum of the part taken by the Third division, in the Battle of Chillianwallah.* By Colonel Sir Colin Campbell, K.C.B. (London, 1851.)

‡ Stress is laid on this point, from personal observation, by the late General Sir Edward Haythorne, then Major Haythorne, 98th regiment, A.D.C. to Brigadier-General Campbell, in a letter in *Colburn's United Service Magazine*,

Campbell made a stirring address, relating to the deeds of the 24th in the Peninsula. "He told us," writes an officer who was present,* "how on one occasion, when some corps, of which the 24th was one, "were ordered to carry a position at the point of the bayonet, it was "the only corps that obeyed the order, doing its part without firing a "shot." The Sikh post on the mound was found to be abandoned, a few dead being left in it, who had been killed by the English shells. Under the personal orders of the commander-in-chief, the division then formed in line to the left of the village of Chillianwallah (with reference to the front), arms were piled by the tired troops, and camp colour men were called for, to mark out the camp. It was believed that nothing more would be done that night, the enemy being only visible from the top of a tree.

The annoying fire opened by the Sikh artillery on the British camp, however, provoked the commander-in-chief to change his plans, and shortly afterwards, Major Tucker, D.A.G., conveyed orders to Brigadier-General Colin Campbell to attack the Sikh position without delay. These orders were repeated twice directly afterwards by two other staff officers.† The day was already on the decline, and it was not thought well to delay any offensive measures. It was arranged between Brigadier-General Colin Campbell and Brigadier Pennycuick, commanding the fifth or right brigade of the division, that as the British left appeared to be much outflanked by the Sikh right, Campbell should remain with the left or Hoggan's brigade, the nature of the ground rendering it utterly impracticable that any commander could superintend the attack of more than one brigade. It would seem, from the statement of the late Major-General Blachford, that in parting from Pennycuick's brigade, Colin Campbell repeated his injunction,

---

April, 1851, written to refute the statement made in that journal and other military papers, that at the subsequent assault on the Sikh position, the 24th was taken into the jungle without artillery or skirmishers, and with its arms unloaded. Lawrence Archer maintains that the line *did* enter the jungle unloaded. See *Punjaub Commentaries*, p. 59.)

* MS. Notes by Major-General de Berry.
† *Memorandum* by Sir Colin Campbell, K.C.B.

"Now, let it be said that the 24th carried the guns with the bayonet, "without firing a shot."* This was about 3 p.m. With Mowatt's field battery between them, and three guns, under Lieutenant Robertson, on the extreme left, and companies of skirmishers extended in front, the two brigades then advanced by the left at a given signal, and after clearing about two hundred yards, entered a dense jungle, which precluded the possibility of seeing a hundred yards in any direction. On emerging with Hoggan's brigade into comparatively open ground at the end of half-a-mile, Colin Campbell first became aware that not only was his division not supported by eighteen horse-artillery guns, under Colonel Brind, as the commander-in-chief had promised it should be, but that *the divisional guns had been withdrawn, without his knowledge or consent,* by some staff officer, whose name remains unrecorded. The advance of the entire division was thus unsupported by artillery, it being the only one so treated. Meanwhile, Pennycuick's brigade, consisting of the 24th Regiment, covered by its grenadier company under Captain Travers, extended as skirmishers, with the 25th Bengal Infantry on its right and the 45th Bengal Infantry on its left, was pitted against the Sikh centre, the exact position of which was not known, although it could be clearly seen whence the round shot came that poured into the ranks with increasing fury. It had originally been intended that the attack on the centre should be simultaneous with those of Hoggan's brigade on the left and Mountain's brigade on the right, but this was frustrated by the impetuosity of the 24th, who began to charge when they were still twelve hundred yards away from the guns, thereby outstripping the native corps on their flanks, and imperceptibly inclining towards the right at the same time, so that the right of the regiment was engaged before the left was up. Within

---

* In a private letter to Colonel Symons, dated Cromer, Norfolk, 9th February, 1880, General Blachford wrote: "I remember the words used by Sir Colin Campbell in his address to the regiment, just before its advance on the enemy's position in the jungle at Chillianwallah. He said: 'Let it be said that the 24th carried the position and guns at the point of the bayonet, without firing a shot.' Sir Colin said to me after the battle, 'I am sorry I said it. It would have been better to have sent in a volley or two before storming the guns.'"

fifteen minutes from the start, the struggling line emerged into a small opening, broken by pools and scattered trees, at the far side of which was the Sikh battery, occupying a small natural berme. A moment's pause, a headlong rush, and the guns were won, and the men busy spiking them, some having been provided with jagged nails for the purpose. But the Sikhs returned to the conflict, and after furious fighting, friends and foes in one tangled mass around the captured guns, the shattered remains of the 24th were forced back into the jungle.

"It is impossible," wrote the future Sir Colin, "for any troops to "have surpassed H.M. 24th Foot in the gallantry displayed in the "assault. This single regiment actually broke the enemy's line, and "took the large number of guns in their front, the commanding "officers of the brigade and regiment, together with numerous "subordinate officers, dying at the captured guns. Finding itself "surrounded, and the leaders having been killed, half the regiment "being *hors de combat*, a ruinous retreat became inevitable. While "retreating, it met the Native Infantry, which then turned also. "In a very difficult country, where sight is so much obstructed, it "might be wrong to impute blame to the native regiments; but, while "sparing censure on them, it would be in the highest degree "culpable not to mark, with the utmost precision, the circumstances "in which a gallant regiment found itself, after a devotion to duty "which has rarely been equalled, and never surpassed."*

In retiring, several groups of men rallied in the jungle, but it was thought best to get back into the open ground. Lieutenant Lawrence Archer and Colour-Sergeant Eastall rallied the remains of No. 7 company in the village of Chillianwallah. They were joined by men of other companies, and by Ensign Hinde, Lieutenant Clark, Ensign Baillie, Lieutenants Mackechnie, Drew, and Lutman, and again advanced in line by order of Colonel, now Sir Edward, Lugard, the adjutant-general of the Queen's troops, who rode away to the front before them.† Captain Blachford, with a party of men, joined during

---

* *Memorandum* by Sir Colin Campbell, K.C.B., pp. 13-14.
† Lawrence Archer, *Punjaub Commentaries.*

the advance,* and also many more collected by Lieutenant Berry, who, though wounded, had remained on the field. The regiment advanced to the support of Hoggan's and Mountain's brigades, but the Sikhs by this time were in full retreat towards Russool, having abandoned the guns they had fought so hard to save. The latter were brought into the British camp at the close of the action. The blowing up of some tumbrils at this time attracted the notice of the Sikhs, who sent a few parting shots at the men, disturbing them at their work. The 24th was thus the first and last regiment under fire on that memorable day. By this time it was dusk, and rain was falling fast. The 24th was ordered back into the open ground, where, without food or shelter, it passed the night, which was starless, cold, and wet, with frequent alarms.

The regimental loss was exceedingly heavy. One-half of the men and two-thirds of the officers were killed or wounded. Brigadier Pennycuick, a grey-haired veteran of many Indian campaigns, was shot through the heart during the advance. His son, the junior ensign, a stripling fresh from Sandhurst, was shot dead over his father's body. Lieutenant-Colonel Brookes, Captains Travers and Shore, and other officers fell at the muzzles of the Sikh guns. Major Howell Paynter's horse bolted with him out of fire, but not before the rider had received a shot through the lungs that ultimately proved fatal. Major Henry Harris, a tall portly old officer, whose horse had been shot under him, was seen by Lawrence Archer as the men were falling back, in a state of great exhaustion. He is believed to have been cut down by a Sikh sowar who had previously. ridden at Archer.

There were some remarkable escapes. Lieutenant, now Major-

---

* Colonel Macpherson, who had been himself severely wounded, writes: "When the regiment had been repulsed, and was retiring towards the village, I remarked Blachford, one of our mounted officers, whose bridle reins, strange to say, had been cut and the withers of his horse scooped by a round shot. He was rallying the men, who were in some confusion, and under circumstances of great disadvantage was exhibiting such perfect coolness, combined with such soldierly qualities, that I ever afterwards held in the highest esteem him, to whom I had—with youthful levity—sometimes taken exception on account of his deep religious bearing."—Colonel Macpherson, *Rambling Reminiscences.*

General, Lutman dashingly spiked a hot gun with his own hands. He came out of the conflict untouched. Lieutenant Williams had the fastening of his sword-belt struck by a ball, which, in sporting phrase, "knocked the wind out of him," just before reaching the guns. He fell into a bush, and the Sikh horsemen, swooping by, cut at and prodded him, inflicting on him twenty-three wounds with sword and lance. His skull was fractured, and his left hand sliced off at the wrist, a loss of which he only became aware when attempting to wipe away the blood fast streaming into his eyes from the fresh sword-cuts. Thanks to a vigorous constitution he speedily recovered from his injuries, and is still living.* Thelwall, the lieutenant of the grenadier company—afterwards the late Major-General Thelwall, C.B.—had also a fortunate escape. He was regimental orderly officer, and mounted for the day. His horse was killed under him, and he himself severely wounded in the thigh. Not long before, he had parted with a favourite horse to Captain C. R. Harris, the major of brigade. After that officer was killed, the horse, wandering riderless in the jungle, recognised and came up to its old master, and was the means of carrying him out of danger.† In wading through the sea of jungle in the attack on the Sikh position, the men were often completely lost to view, but the Colours, which were uncased, served as a sure mark to the enemy's gunners, and the officers carrying them—Lieutenant Phillips and Ensign Collis, the latter the son of an old Peninsular officer of the regiment—as well as all the sergeants of the colour-party, were killed.‡

The Queen's Colour was never found. It was supposed that when the bearer was shot it dropped into a pool through which the Colour-party struggled. According to one account the staff was broken, and the colour was rescued by Private Martin Connolly, of the regiment, who wrapped it round his body, but he was subsequently killed. It seems certain that it never came into the hands of the enemy, or

---

* Colonel Macpherson, *Rambling Recollections*.
† Lawrence Archer, *Punjaub Commentaries*.
‡ Although the native regiments on the flanks of the 24th never reached the guns, their losses were heavy. They both lost their colours, five in all, one being a honorary colour granted for distinguished conduct in the field in by-gone days.

Shere Singh would assuredly have shewn it to his prisoner, Lieutenant Bowie.* The reasonable supposition is that it was looted for the sake of the embroidery by our own camp followers, who were very busy that night. The officers offered a large reward for its recovery, but without success.

The Regimental Colour (now in Warwick Church) was brought in by No. 841, Private Richard Perry, an old soldier, who for this distinguished service was promoted to corporal 30th June, 1849, and sergeant 1st July, 1850, and soon afterwards was discharged at Chatham, on completing a service of twenty-one years one hundred and thirty-three days, with a pension of two shillings and sixpence a day, an annuity of £20, and a good conduct medal. (See also p. 184.)

A small portion of colour-belt, with clasp, taken from the body of Ensign Collis before burial, was presented to his family.

On the morrow of the battle the bodies of the thirteen officers and of Sergeant-Major Coffee were brought in by a patrol and reverently laid in the officers' mess tent until evening, when they received burial on the mound before spoken of, near the village of Chillianwallah, upon which now stands an obelisk to the memory of the slain.† An attempt was made to bring in the bodies of the non-commissioned officers and men, but this was found impracticable. The melancholy duty of collecting and interring the bodies of the rest of the dead on the field ot battle was therefore performed by the flank companies on the following day, the Sikhs, who came down in a threatening manner, looking on from a distance the while.

Annexed is the report of the officer commanding the regiment to the assistant-adjutant-general, after the battle: also, a letter from

---

* Lieutenant Bowie, Bengal Artillery, who had been taken at Peshawur, was still a prisoner of war in the hands of the Sikhs. After the battle of Chillianwallah he was allowed to visit the British camp for a day, on parole. He then said that Shere Singh had shewn him, with much pride, the guns captured from us, but he *never saw or heard of the 24th colour.*—Colonel Macpherson's *Rambling Recollections.*

† The site of the battle has been identified by the Indian antiquary, Cunningham, as that of the victory of Alexander the Great over Porus, King of the Central Punjaub. It is known to this day by the country people as Katalghur, "the house of slaughter."

Lieutenant-Colonel M. Smith, together with the names of those who fell, as they appear on the regimental monument in the grounds of Chelsea Hospital:

"Camp, Chillianwallah,
"15th January, 1849.
"Sir,
"In obedience to your orders of yesterday, I have now the honour "to report for the information of General Campbell, commanding the 3rd "Division of the Army, the following facts in regard to the part taken "by H.M. 24th Regiment in the engagement with the enemy on the after-"noon of the 13th inst.

"In the details of the several occurrences I shall have to confine "myself, 1st, To what passed under my own eye and observation; 2nd, To "facts affirmed to men by their respective officers and companies, several "of the non-commissioned officers, and also by soldiers of well-known "character in the regiment.

"1st. I beg leave to state H.M. 24th Regiment, with two native regi-"ments, the 25th on the right and the 45th on the left, composed the 5th "brigade, ordered to attack and take the position of the enemy in their "front. The order was given for the attack to be in line, and the left "battalion was to be the directing one.

"I was mounted, and acted as a supernumerary field officer in the rear. "In consequence of the thick jungle and bush, whole sections of com-"panies were constantly obliged to be doubling and filing in rear, so that "it was very difficult to keep the line in anything like order.

"On coming within range of the enemy's guns, an exceedingly heavy "fire was opened on the regiment, from round and grape shot. The "regiment continued to advance most steadily.

"My horse was soon after struck by a round shot on the withers, which "also cut my bridle, and obliged me to dismount. I had scarcely done so "when I heard a cheer, and on looking towards the regiment, saw Colonel "Brookes in front of the colours waving his sword over his head. The "regiment came to the double.

"Some minutes elapsed before I succeeded in quieting my horse to "allow me to remount. The regiment was not then in sight, but I "dashed off in the direction I thought it had taken, but after going a few "hundred yards, I met the 45th N.I., upon which I turned to the other "direction, and after some time I fell in with a part of H.M. 24th retiring "and mixed up with the 25th N.I.

"2. I proceed to state the details furnished to me by the officers, and "of occurrences as the regiments continued their advance towards the "enemy's position.

"On nearing the enemy, the difficulties and obstacles to the advance "in line increased, and it was frequently impassable but in sections; and "within fifty yards of the guns was a tank or pond partially filled with

"water, and surrounded by scraggy trees and stumps, and the ground very
"much broken.

"Two companies were here obliged to file in rear. Thus it happened
"that the centre and several companies on the left were brought up nearly to
"the muzzles of the guns in masses, and in much disorder, and were received
"when within a few yards of the guns by a tremendous discharge of grape
"and musketry. But, still the regiment never for an instant wavered,
"but pressed forward, taking the guns and position at the bayonet's point
"without firing a shot.

"Large bodies of infantry in position, on a rising ground on the right
"and left, continued to pour in their fire, and bodies of cavalry also were in
"rear of the position.

"I may here remark that the grenadier company of the regiment
"having experienced less difficulty, carried the part of the position opposite
"them before the rest of the regiment.

"Lieutenant Lutman assisted Private Stanfield of the grenadiers to spike
"one gun. The grenadiers were then forced back, but again advanced on
"the charge, at the command of Captain Travers, and again carried the
"guns, and a second gun was spiked by Sergeant Lear, of the same
"company.

"Captain Travers fell, cut down by a tulwar. Colonel Brookes was seen
"at this time by Lieutenant Lutman in engagement with three men armed
"with tulwars, who rushed out from under their guns. They were all
"bayoneted by men of the grenadiers. Soon afterwards Colonel Brookes
"was seen to fall close by the guns.

"The Brigadier (Pennycuick) and the Major of Brigade, Captain C. R.
"Harris were also killed at the guns.

"Major Henry Harris was mortally wounded and carried to the rear.
"Major Howell Paynter was dangerously wounded in the advance. Captain
"Shore fell at the guns. The two officers carrying the colours, Lieutenant
"Collis and Ensign H. Phillips were both struck down by grape within a
"few yards of the muzzles of the guns. Lieutenants G. Phillips, Woodgate,
"and Payne fell at the guns. Thus, in the short space of time that
"elapsed between the advance at the double time and during the struggle
"on the part of the regiment to hold the position they had so gallantly
"won, thirteen officers were killed and ten wounded.

"The men were quite exhausted by their exertions and the rapid
"advance made for so long a distance, completely unsupported in the
"attack, is it to be wondered at that the regiment retreated? In the retir-
"ing the few officers found it impossible to conduct it with regularity and
"order.

"Whole companies, as I have shewn, were mixed up together in the
"advance, and this, added to the difficulties of the ground they had to
"retrace (already detailed), prevented the regiment being reformed until
"clear of the jungle. When I again advanced the regiment was met by the
"Adjutant-General of the Army.

"The regiment went into action with 32 officers and 1,000 bayonets, "(exclusive of the band). The loss in officers is 'thirteen' killed and "ten wounded, and as far as it can at present be ascertained two hundred "and thirty-one non-commissioned officers and men were killed, and two "hundred and sixty-six wounded.

"(Signed) A. BLACHFORD,
"Captain-Commanding 24th Regiment.

"To Major Ponsonby, A.A.G.,
"Army of the Punjaub."

"Camp, Chillianwallah,
"Punjaub,
"28th January, 1849.

"Dear Sir,

"Having had the honour to be nominated by Lord Gough, "Lieutenant-Colonel of the 24th Regiment, and the severity of Lieutenant "Colonel Paynter's wound entirely incapacitating him from writing, I feel it "my duty to acquaint you with the share taken by the regiment in the "battle of Chillianwallah, on the 13th inst., with the rebel forces of Shere "Singh.

"You will be grieved to perceive by the enclosed returns that the "regiment sustained very severe loss.

"I was with my former regiment, the 29th, in the battle, at another "point of the field, and therefore personally, saw nothing of the 24th, but "I have carefully ascertained every particular from Major Blachford (who "commanded at the close of the action) and the other surviving officers, "and I am happy to assure you, most confidently, (in which I am fully "supported by the official despatch of Brigadier-General Campbell, com- "manding the 3rd Infantry Division) that, although in the very moment "of victory, after the capture of some 20 guns, many of which the regiment "spiked, it was compelled by the onset of thousands, (while shattered and "confused by the heavy fire it had encountered and was sustaining) to retire "for a while, yet the bravery of the noble corps, led by that gallant soldier, "Lieutenant-Colonel Brookes, was most distinguished.

"I lament to state that in this desperate conflict, actually at the "muzzles of the enemy's guns, when three field officers, and ten others "were killed, including the two ensigns (Collis and Phillips) who carried "the colours, the Queen's colour was unhappily lost. Its staff had been "broken in two, and one of the men is reported to have wrapped the colour "round his body, but he was afterwards killed, and all endeavours to find "any trace of it have hitherto been vain. The Regimental colour was for a "time on the ground, but was brought off uninjured.

"On the morning of 13th of January the army advanced to this
"place in order of battle. We found a dense and most perplexing jungle
"of low thorn bushes, about two miles in depth, between us and the
"enemy's position. They were encamped with their rear to the river Jhelum
"(about a mile distant from it) and occupied an immense line, far out-
"flanking ours on either hand ; the distance between us and them probably
"three miles.

"Lord Gough's first intention (after driving in an outpost of the enemy)
"seems to have been to encamp, and to defer the attack till next morning ;
"but the enemy, doubtless well aware that we should have to fight them
"under extreme disadvantage in the jungle, boldly came out with 50 or 60
"guns, and about 30,000 men of all arms, including their best troops,
"placed themselves in array, and fired upon us. The battle then com-
"menced, about 1 o'clock, and lasted till sunset. At the close of it, the
"enemy retired, completely beaten ; we having taken and spiked some 40
"of their guns. But, apprehension lest they should (having such numbers
"at their disposal) get round to our rear and destroy the wounded and the
"baggage of the army, induced Lord Gough to withdraw us from the
"jungle, the further border of which we had reached, and with us only 12
"of the captured guns were brought away.

"During the night which was dark and stormy, the Sikhs, knowing the
"ground completely, crept out and carried off the rest. They must have
"had difficulty in unspiking them, as they know little of the proper mode
"of doing so, but I believe they have effected it.

"Since the battle the army of the Punjaub has remained encamped on
"this ground, the enemy continuing opposite to us ; and it is understood
"that we shall have to await the arrival of General Whish's army from
"Moultan, that fortress having surrendered on the 22nd inst.

"The wounded officers are doing well. Major (now Colonel) Paynter
"was shot through the lungs, and at first, was not expected to survive, but
"he is now considered out of danger, though the ball has not been found.
"He has 12 months leave to the hills. Lieutenant (now Captain) Williams
"was desperately wounded with sword cuts ; his hand severed at the wrist,
"and his skull fractured, but there is every hope of his recovery, and the
"others will be fit for duty after a few months.

"I solicit your good offices in favour of Mrs. Colonel Brookes and Mrs.
"Captain Lee, to obtain for them the highest rates of pension available for
"widows of officers killed in action.

"The destruction of accoutrements has been, I am sorry to say, very
"great. Those of the killed were all lost, and many of the wounded threw
"theirs off to facilitate getting away to the rear. The men *wore their dress
"caps in the action*, and this sort of head dress is always found ill-suited for
"hard work in battle. Many fell off and were lost in the charge and
"meleé, and it seems to be on such occasions the soldier's great desire to
"rid himself of so inconvenient an appendage. The forage cap is far

24TH REGIMENT.

"better for service, though doubtless something more protective than that "might be devised.

"Lord Gough has at my request recommended the son of the late "Major H. W. Harris, Mr. John FitzCharles Lock Harris, for an ensigncy "in the 24th. I trust you will give your support to the application.

"Our wounded men are doing well, and seem very cheerful. I wish we "could hope to be recruited with men of similar description. If some of "the Four Company Depôts were allowed to volunteer we might probably "be so—

"I have the honour to be, dear Sir,
"Yours very faithfully,
"M. SMITH.
"Lieutenant-Colonel,
"Commanding 24th Regiment.

"To Lieut.-General Ellice,
"Colonel, 24th Regt."

STATE OF HER MAJESTY'S 24TH REGIMENT.

Camp, Chillianwallah, 28th January, 1849.

From the original return at War Office.

	Lieutenant Colonels.	Majors.	Captains.	Lieutenants.	Ensigns.	Staff.	Sergeants.	Corporals.	Drummers.	Privates.	Total, exclusive of Officers.
Strength engaged on the 13th January, 1849	2	2	7	14	5	1	47	45	18	955	1065
Deduct, killed in action, 13th January, 1849	2	1	4	3	3	..	4	7	1	213	225
Remaining ..	..	1	3	11	2	1	43	38	17	742	840
Deduct, wounded in action, 13th January, 1849 ..	..	1	2	5	..	1	14	15	1	248	278
Fit for duty in the Field after the action ..	..	..	1	6	2	..	29	23	16	494	562
All other absentees, viz.:—Sick, Depôt at Agra, and recruits on march to join ..	..	..	2	5	2	6	7	2	3	92	104
Total strength in India after the action ..	..	1	5	16	4	7	50	40	20	834	944

(Signed) M. SMITH, Lieut.-Colonel,
Commanding 24th Foot.

REGIMENTAL ROLL OF KILLED, DIED OF WOUNDS, AND MISSING.

OFFICERS.

Lieutenant-Colonel:—Robert Brookes, Commanding the Regiment.
Brigadier and Lieutenant-Colonel:—John Pennycuick, C.B., K.H., Commanding 5th Brigade.
Major:—Henry William Harris.

Captains:—

Charles Lee	Charles H. Harris, Brigade-Major, 5th Brigade
Robert Wm. Travers	John T. Shore.

Lieutenants:—

G. Phillips	J. A. Woodgate, Interpreter to the Regiment
O. B. Payne	Wm. Phillips.

Ensigns:—

H. C. B. Collis | Alexander Pennycuick.

NON-COMMISSIONED OFFICERS AND MEN.

Sergeant-Major:—J. Coftee.   *Colour-Sergeant:*—W. Davies.

Sergeants:—

T. Lear | J. Webster.

Corporals:—

G. Evans	W. Runchey	H. Webb
J. Sheriff	J. Wilkes	F. Howell
W. Pattenden		

Drummer:—E. Doughty.

Privates:—

W. Allsworth	S. Andrews	J. Williams	J. McMullin	W. Gardner	J. Pittman
J. Amos	J. Bailey	R. Windle	J. Mohan	T. Hanscombe	D. Shea
J. Bowman	G. Bird	J. Armett	M. Moore	C. Lawrence	C. Simson
J. Burgess	J. Byers	W. H. Bailey	T. Morrish	W. Pearson	J. Twigg
J. Butcher	R. Campbell	W. Barnett	J. Newman	T. Priest	W. Smith
T. Bryne	D. Clifford	E. Barr	W. Oakley	W. Rampling	J. Welch
T. Carpenter	R. John Coates	C. Barnes	T. Osborne	I. Robinson	A. Whittell
S. Carter	R. Cockerton	R. Burchett	T. Parker	T. Savage	W. Tobyn
W. Cuthbert	W. Coult	W. Bone	P. Quick	J. Morton	R. Edmonds
G. Dean	T. J. O'Donoghue	J. Brewer	J. Roxberry	J. Lake	W. Ebnieby
P. Fowlk	G. Egan	H. Cork	J. Saunders	I. Rostert	J. Enright
G. George	J. Fergusson	E. Everest	W. Seirs	E. Shea	J. Flinn
G. Hardman	W. Fletcher	M. Green	J. Summergill	G. Smith	P. Flinn
J. Henshaw	G. Harrison	J. Hanlon	J. Townsend	J. Tyers	G. Gibson
J. Horsfall	W. Hobson	J. Haston	C. Whitehead	T. Atkinson	J. Hill
T. Hughes	D. Houlston	S. Smith	T. Biddle	J. Burton	T. S. Hall
J. Jutin	E. Tudle	W. Sladen	S. Bingham	J. McCullock	W. Hucker
T. Joblin	T. Mackay	J. Tebble	J. Connelly	H. Meeds	B. Johnson
W. Lakin	B. Magill	J. Slattery	J. Dudley	J. Pratt	J. Lamb
C. Lander	C. Mayo	W. Walsh	J. Kemming	J. Terry	J. Murphy
P. McColey	C. Mitchell	H. Wrightman	O. Loyd	J. Tulley	J. Averton
J. McReary	J. O'Connor	P. Dales	T. List	W. S. Duffan	J. Patience
T. Merchant	N. Pulling	J. Delmage	J. Walker	J. Edwards	R. Pratt
T. Pocock	T. Regan	T. Ellice	F. Battlestone	W. Francis	J. Riddle
R. Porter	C. Rochford	W. Giles	J. Eginton	G. Harris	J. Shaw
W. Selby	W. Ryder	J. Goodchild	J. Elliott	J. Hicks	W. Groner-Simmonds
J. Sharp	G. Saunders	T. Grandy	S. English	W. Jervis	
P. Westneat	J. Wakefield	R. Harding	H. Farmer	E. Johnson	W. Thompson
D. Wheeler	J. Warren, 2nd	W. Hopkins	C. Green	T. Kelson	
W. Willis, 1st	W. Welton	J. Kelly			

DIED OF WOUNDS.

Corporal:—W. Bugden.

Privates:—

J. Hawkins | J. Morris | J. Atwell

MISSING.

Privates:—

G Barrington	W. H. Medlam	W. Nicols	R. Lang	M. Betson	T. Cresswell
J. Barry	M. Whealan	J. Carrier	E. Meade	T. Cleenen	P. Managan
J. Bradbrook	Sandford	J. Clarke	J. Phillips	P. Devaney	T. Murphy
G. Evans	J. Wood	W. Cross	J. Sovation	J. Killeen	A. Weldon
E. Fry	T. Chapple	B. Henry	G. Worley	P. Murphy	J. Hunter
C. Lancaster	W. Nevard	F. Lang	J. Bentley	R. Smith	T. Lancaster

All those missing may be included among the dead.

BATTLE OF GOOJERAT.—The 24th remained with the army in camp at Chillianwallah, which was every day becoming more unsanitary, until the middle of February, when it was discovered that the Sikh army had decamped at night, leaving its fires burning. Lord Gough at once broke up his camp on 15th February and started in pursuit. Coming up with the enemy on 20th February, he encamped close around the fort and city of Goojerat—a holy place of the Sikhs. On the following day was won the victory of Goojerat, in which the Sikh army was routed and finally dispersed.

On the morning of 21st February, 1849, the army of the Punjaub, perhaps the finest brought together in India, was drawn up opposite the Sikh position in one long magnificent line, covered by its divisional artillery and skirmishers. The fifth brigade, commanded by Brigadier Alex. Carnegy, 27th Bengal Native Infantry, and consisting of H.M. 24th, and the 25th Bengal Native Infantry, formed the left centre brigade of the long line. The 24th, under command of Lieutenant-Colonel Matthew Smith and mustering twenty-nine officers, forty sergeants, twenty-seven corporals, seventeen drummers, and five hundred and eighty-one privates, was the right regiment of its brigade, the front of which was covered by skirmishers, composed of No. 7, and the light company 24th, under Lieutenants Sweton Grant, G. F. Berry, J. Hinde, and Lawrence Archer, 96th, attached. During the tremendous cannonade that followed the gradual British advance, the regiment was for some time under fire of the enemy's artillery, but fortunately escaped without a single casualty. The most remarkable incident connected with the regiment was the daring attempt of a party of Sikh sowars, evidently picked men, who got round the right flank of the line, swept along the rear, and made a dash at the commander-in-chief, wounding Lieutenant Stannus, the officer in command of the escort. They then broke through the line close to the grenadiers of the 24th, who, in the excitement of the moment, seeing the Sikhs in front of them and forgetful of their own companies extended beyond, opened fire and emptied every saddle. Although the Sikhs, who were early abandoned by their Afghan allies, made a gallant stand at certain points, their overthrow was complete, and the afternoon saw the remains of the host in the far distance, in flying crowds, enveloped in clouds of red dust. The main body took the direction of Peshawur, whither they were followed by General Gilbert's division, to whom they eventually laid down their arms, at Rawul Pindi. The 24th and some native regiments were sent after the fugitives, who had taken the direction of the Bimber Pass into Cashmere. From thence the 24th returned to Goojerat two days afterwards, bringing back with it two Sikh guns.

The regiment remained in camp at Goojerat until the final subjection of the Sikhs and the breaking up of the "Army of the Punjaub," when it was told off for Wuzeerabad. Accordingly it crossed to the left bank of the Chenab, where the native city is situated, and encamped at a distance of about seven miles from it, on the way to Ramnuggar. Temporary barracks subsequently replaced the tents, and there the depôt with the women and children, which had been left behind at Agra on the opening of the campaign, rejoined the regiment on 24th January, 1850.

Annexed are some additional papers of interest in connection with the campaign in the Punjaub.

REMARKS BY GENERAL SIR CHAS. JAS. NAPIER, G.C.B.,
Commander-in-Chief in India,
ON THE CHARGE AT CHILLIANWALLAH.

From a letter to Major Kennedy, published in *Life and Opinions of Sir Chas. Napier*, vol. iv., pp. 349-52.

"I felt sure that your wish must be to do justice to your comrades in "your book, and it was with this object that I enquired about poor "Pennycuick's conduct. I thought it probable some officer would write "an account of the campaign, and my position as commander-in-chief "offered me more opportunities than others had of doing so impartially, "my only interest being that of doing justice to a heroic officer's memory.

"That the 24th charged at too great a distance may be admitted, and "the question resolves itself into this.—By whose order was the charge "made? All my enquiries satisfy me that Lieutenant-Colonel Pennycuick "did not order the charge. That no man did. That it arose from a "general impulse.

"1. The ground is said to have concealed the enemy; no man knew "how far that enemy was from him.

"2. Pennycuick's brigade was isolated; the brigade on his right had "obliqued to the right in advancing.

"3. The 24th regiment was also isolated; the two Sepoy regiments on
"the right and left of the 24th were not up in time, the jungle being too
"dense to preserve the line; thus the 24th advanced with its flanks
"exposed.

"4. In this state, no view in front, a heavy fire from the enemy, the
"line broken by the jungle, sections doubling in rear of each other and
"doing their best to form up when possible, no man seeing above a few
"yards before him, no officer, I say, could be heard by a regiment, no
"officer would attempt to be heard. The commander could only address
"himself to those files immediately around him. On this subject no man
"who has ever led a regiment against an enemy in fire and through
"broken ground, as I have done and therefore now speak from experience,
"can doubt what I say. All that a commanding officer can do is to dash
"on with those about him, cheering and trusting that all those of his
"regiment out of his sight will close up to him as the jungle clears, and
"the loud cheering marks the ground he gains.

"5. In these circumstances the 24th Regiment and Colonel Pennycuick
"were placed; and the excitement of danger, the desire to close with the
"enemy, the cheers of the soldiers to encourage each other as they
"struggled through the jungle—all conduced to change an advance in
"quick time to a rush forward by a common impulse. Of course, the
"shout to charge would be echoed along the line by hundreds without
"orders.

"6. There was nothing then for a brave and able commander to do
"but what Colonel Pennycuick did—dash forward, cheering on his men,
"and by his example supporting the impulse he could not check, and
"ought not to check. There were but two things to do—to run on or run
"off: the 24th chose the nobler one. Had Colonel Pennycuick acted
"otherwise he would have been unworthy to command in battle.

"7. I have now shewn, from carefully collected evidence, that Colonel
"Pennycuick did not order the charge at such a distance as 150 (1,200?)
"yards, but necessarily joined in it. We have then to enquire, did this
"charge succeed or fail? The 24th took the enemy's guns and broke his
"centre. It was master of the position, and the glory of Pennycuick
"and his regiment was complete—but they were alone in their glory,
"isolated, unsupported, and the enemy rallied and destroyed them. The
"intrepid Pennycuick and his unflinching soldiers fell around the guns
"they had so nobly won. Such is my defence of this hero's conduct,
"gathered from many mouths, and the British army may justly be proud
"of him. It is easy to say a regiment advanced too quickly—if so, follow
"it up and support it. I beg distinctly to say I find no fault with any
"man in this battle—much less with any regiment. I merely state what
"I believe to be real facts relative to the 24th Regiment and its com-
"manders—their conduct has never been surpassed by British soldiers
"on a field of battle. Among others, I collected my information from
"Sir Colin Campbell, who, in my opinion, was the man who decided the
"battle when the crisis hung upon the wheeling-up of the two right
"companies of the 61st Regiment. But for that manœuvre, I do not see
"how the 61st could have escaped the fate of the 24th Regiment. The
"destruction of the last separated the wings of the army, and the change
"of front and advance made by the 61st and 46th (N.I.) united them
"again. Sir Colin's decided and daring conduct was described to me by
"an officer on his staff."

CHILLIANWALLAH ROLL OF OFFICERS.

Showing the Distribution and Casualties on 13th January, 1849.

(The names of Officers *not present in the action* are in Italics)

Rank.	Name.	Date of Reg. Com.	Casualties.	Remarks.
Colonel	*Robert Ellice*, L.G.	*2 Nov.*, *1842*		Comdg. Troops, Malta. Dead.
Lieut.-Col.	Robt. Brookes, K.H.	28 April, 1846	Killed	Comdg. Regiment.
,,	John Pennycuick, C.B., K.H., C.	7 April, 1848	Killed	Comdg. 5th Brigade
Major	H. W. Harris	14 April, 1846	Killed	
,,	Howell Paynter	28 April, 1846	Wounded	Retired as Lieut.-Col. 21 Dec., 1849. Died of his wounds
Captain	*John Harris, M.*	*11 May*, *1830*		In command of Hill Depôt, Landour. Ret. as Lt.-Col., 1849. Dead
,,	A. G. Blachford	7 Aug., 1841		Afterwards Major-Gen. retired. Dead
,,	W. Gust. Brown	10 May, 1844	Wounded	In command of Light company. Afterwards Gen. W. G. Brown. Died 1886
,,	Chas. Lee	12 April, 1844	Killed	
,,	*C. H. Ellice*	*8 Aug.*, *1845*		A.D.C. at Malta. Afterwards Sir C. H. Ellice, A.G. Died 1888
,,	R. W. Travers	3 April, 1846	Killed	In command of Grenadier company
,,	C. R. Harris	14 April, 1846	Killed	Brig.-Major of Pennycuick's Brigade
,,	*Ed. Wodehouse*	*28 April, 1846*		In command of Depôt at Chatham. Now Gen. Wodehouse
,,	L. Howe Bazalgette	7 April, 1848	Wounded	Died as Major, 2nd Batt. 24th
,,	J. Saunders Shore	20 Oct., 1848	Killed	
Lieutenant	*Francis Spring*	*22 April, 1842*		Depôt at Chatham. Killed at Jhelum, 1857
,,	J. H. Lutman	16 June, 1843		Retired as Major, 1862. Now living
,,	G. E. L. Williams	22 Aug., 1844	Wounded	Retired as Captain. Living in Ceylon
,,	*T. C. Skurray*	*8 April*, *1842*		Depôt at Chatham. Ret. as Major. Now living
,,	Sweton Grant	19 Jan., 1844		Orderly Officer to Brig.-Genl. Colin Campbell Comdg. Div. Died as Captain, 1849
,,	A. J. Macpherson	26 July, 1844	Wounded	Now Lieut.-Col. Ret.
,,	R. Aubin Croker	5 Oct., 1844	Wounded	Died at Peshawur, 1855 or 1856
,,	G. F. Berry	25 April, 1845	Wounded	Succeeded to command of Light company. Now Major-Genl. G. F. de Berry
,,	C. Mackechnie	3 April, 1846		Retired. Now living in Canada
,,	G. Phillips	3 April, 1846	Killed	Light company
,,	*Walter Cuming*	*3 April, 1846*		Promoted from 35th. Not joined at date of action

24TH REGIMENT.

Rank.	Name.	Date of Reg. Com.	Casualties.	Remarks.
Lieutenant	J. B. Thelwall	3 April, 1846	Wounded	Regimental Orderly Officer. Afterwards Major-General J. B. Thelwall, C.B., Indian Staff Corps. Dead
,,	W. Hartshorn, Adjt.	3 April, 1846	Wounded	Now Major. Retired
,,	C. M. Drew	3 April, 1846		Retired. Died in Australia ?
,,	*W. Selby*	*28 April, 1846*		Name appears in Army List, January, 1849, but had retired previous to the battle
,,	F. Clark	9 Oct., 1846		Exchanged as Captain to 4th Foot. Dead
,,	*Oliver T. Graham*	*10 May, 1841*		Left the regiment at Heylah Camp
,,	H. P. Thicknesse Woodington	25 Aug., 1846		Afterwards in Holy Orders. Chaplain on Indian Establishment. Dead
,,	Orlibar T. Payne	7 April, 1848	Killed	
,,	J. A. Woodgate	7 April, 1848	Killed	Regimental Interpreter
,,	*T. Maling Greensill*	*20 Oct., 1848*		Left in command of Depôt, at Agra. Killed at Delhi, 1857
,,	Wm. Phillips	20 Oct., 1848	Killed	Carrying the Queen's Colour
,,	H. M. Burns	*23 June, 1848*		Exchanged from 62nd Foot. Not yet joined
Ensign	H. C. Collis	7 April, 1846	Killed	Carrying the regimental Colour
,,	W. H. D. Baillie	14 April, 1846		Afterwards in 82nd Foot. Retired. Now Member Legislative Council, New Zealand
,,	H. J. Hinde	13 Nov., 1846		Died at Sialkote, 1854
,,	*R. G. A. de Montmorency*	*25 Aug, 1846*		Retired as Capt., 1866
,,	*J. C. W. Kippen*	*31 March, 1848*		Retired
,,	Alex. Pennycuick	18 July, 1843	Killed	Son of Brig. Pennycuick
,,	*F. W. A. Parsons*	*19 Aug., 1848*		Afterwards Adjt., R. Renfrew Mil. Dead
,,	*R. H. Holland*	*20 Oct., 1846*		Afterwards Capt., 22nd Foot
Paymaster	Geo. Ferrier	29 March, 1842		Lieut. 1 January, 1838. Died at Murree, 1854
Qr.-Master	Jas. Price	16 Aug., 1842		Died at Wuzeerabad, 1848
Surgeon	G. K. Pitcairn	*5 Oct., 1843*		Sent home sick at the commencement of the campaign. Afterwards Surgeon, 5th D. G., in Crimea
Asst.-Surg.	W. Hanbury	3 April, 1846		Afterwards Surg., 33rd Foot. Dead
,,	W. J. Furlonge, M.D.	3 April, 1846		Died at Wuzeerabad, 1850
,,	*J. Grant, M.D.*	*13 Oct., 1841*		From 28th Foot. Not joined
Attached	J. Lawrence Archer, Lt., 96th Foot	22 Dec., 1843		Attached to the Regiment at his own request. Joined at Ramnuggar, and served through the campaign. In command of a company, 24th Regiment. Ret. as Major, half-pay. Dead
,,	A. Gordon, Surgeon, 52nd Foot			In medical charge, 24th Regiment

General G. F. de Berry has kindly revised this roll, and supplied the explanatory remarks.

List of Promotions subsequent to the Action of Chillianwallah, 13th January, 1849.

By Order of the Right Honble. the Commander-in-Chief in India, subject to Her Majesty's approval. *

Major H. Paynter, to Lieutenant-Colonel vice Brookes, killed in action
    ,, *M. Smith, from 29th Foot, to Lieut.-Col.* ,, Pennycuick, killed in action
Brevet-Major J. Harris, to Major ,, Paynter, promoted
Captain A. G. Blachford, to Major ,, H. W. Harris, killed in action
Lieutenant F. Spring, to Captain ,, C. Lee ,, ,,
    ,, J. H Lutman, to Captain ,, R. W. Travers ,, ,,
    ,, G. E. L. Williams, to Captain ,, C. R. Harris ,, ,,
    ,, F. C. Skurray ,, ,, J. Harris, promoted
    ,, S. Grant ,, ,, A. G. Blachford, promoted
    ,, A. J. Macpherson ,, ,, J. S. Shore, killed in action
    ,, R. A. Croker ,, ,, *W. G. Brown, promoted Major, 29th Foot*
Ensign W. D. H. Baillie, to Lieutenant ,, G. Phillips, killed in action
    ,, H. J. Hinde ,, ,, O. B. Payne ,, ,,
    ,, R. G. A. Montmorency ,, ,, J. A. Woodgate, killed in action
    ,, R. Halahan, from 18th Foot, to Lieutenant ,, F. Spring, promoted
    ,, A. R. Mowbray, from 29th Foot ,, ,, J. H. Lutman, promoted
    ,, J. Stewart, from 98th Foot ,, ,, G. E. L. Williams, promoted
    ,, J. C. Goodfellow, from 10th Foot ,, ,, F. C. Skurray ,,
    ,, F. Stanford, from 53rd Foot ,, ,, S. Grant ,,
    ,, R. H. Travers, from 10th Foot ,, ,, A. J. Macpherson ,,
    ,, G. Wedderburn, from 53rd Foot, to Ensign ,, H. C. B. Collis, killed in action.

---

* N.B.—The promotions shewn in italics were subsequently cancelled in England; Captain and Brevet-Major John Harris becoming Lieutenant-Colonel, and Captain W. G. Brown, Major, 24th Regiment.

CHAPTER X.

1850-61.

Punjaub Honours—The Indian Mutiny—Another Second Battalion added—Home.

1850-52.

CHAKO PLATE.
1856-68.

AT Wuzeerabad the 24th received its six months "donation-batta" for the Punjaub campaign.* Of the stay of the regiment in the temporary cantonments, now long since abandoned and overgrown, there is not much to be chronicled. It lasted through 1850-51. Intense heat and frightful dust-storms marked the hot seasons, and were productive of a good deal of sickness and ophthalmia. The regiment lost several officers and a good many men. The dust-storms—one of which is recorded to have continued five days—were a not unfrequent source of accidents, and one day a sergeant of the regiment (Sergeant Wardle) fell into a well in the cantonment, and was drowned. Nor were heat and dust the only ills. When the snows melted in Cashmere the Chenab overflowed its banks, and, though a mile and a half distant, converted the camp into a vast sheet of water, so that all duties had to be performed with bare feet and trousers rolled above the knees.

The right wing of the regiment, under Major C. H. Ellice, was sent to Lahore, to escort back treasure. The grenadier companies of the 24th and 10th Foot, with colours and band, formed the guards of

---

* A grant of extra pay, according to rank, given according to old Indian custom at the end of a campaign. On such occasions the men were allowed a fixed number of days to spend it, during which they were left to their own devices, officers being advised to keep out of their way and not to interfere with them, if possible.—MS. Notes, by General G. F. de Berry.

honour to Lord Dalhousie, at the Grand Durbar, held at the neighbouring city of Wuzeerabad, on 19th and 27th December, 1851, on the occasion of the visit of the Maharajah, Ghoolab Singh.

On the retirement of Lieutenant-Colonel Howell Paynter, C.B., on 8th August, 1851, Major C. H. Ellice obtained his regimental vacancy, Captain Wodehouse succeeding to the majority, and Lieutenant and Adjutant Hartshorn to the company. In February, 1852, two companies of the regiment proceeded to Sialkote, about thirty-eight miles from Wuzeerabad and eighteen from the Cashmere stronghold of Jummas, which had been fixed upon as the site of a new cantonment. The rest of the regiment followed in December.

1853-56.

A notification was received on 6th March, 1853, dated Horse Guards, 20th December, 1852, stating that Her Majesty had been graciously pleased to approve of the 24th Regiment bearing on the regimental colours and appointments the word "PUNJAUB," in consideration of the services of the regiment in the campaign of 1848-49, and that the words "CHILLIANWALLAH," "GOOJERAT," be borne in addition thereto, in commemoration of the battles fought at those places, on 13th January and 21st February, 1849.

The regiment remained at Sialkote until 1st November, 1854, when it marched for Peshawur, arriving there on 28th November. In cantonments in that fair, but fever-haunted, valley, a few miles from the famous Khyber Pass, the regiment spent the next three years, far remote from the stirring events of the Russian war time.

On January 17th, 1855, a flying column, under Colonel W. G. Brown, 24th, was sent out to bring in the Sirdar Hyder Khan (son of Dost Mahomed), an emissary from Cabul to the Governor-General of India, who was on his way to Peshawur and had been detained by the tribes in the Khyber Pass. The advance of the column, under Captain Berry, 24th, was composed of the grenadier company 24th, and the rifle company 9th Bengal Infantry, the latter commanded by Captain Donald Stewart, now Sir Donald Stewart, G.C.B., recently commander-in-chief in India. The tribesmen had in the meantime thought better of the matter, and Hyder, with his following, clad in the uniforms and accoutrements of the British Sepoys massacred at Cabul in 1842, were met about five miles out of Peshawur. Both forces halted, and the Afghan camp was formed on the plain beside the Khyber road, about four miles outside the city.*

During its stay at Peshawur, the regiment suffered very severely from malarial fever, having on one occasion between five and six hundred men in hospital at once. The head-quarters and healthy men were moved out into the district, batches of convalescents being sent to join them as they recovered, and were kept moving by short marches till the hospitals were emptied, and the health of the men fairly restored.†

On 19th September, 1856, on a general parade at Peshawur, the new pattern clothing—tunics in place of coatees, and chakos of new shape—was taken into wear. The Enfield rifle was issued to the regiment at this period, in place of the old smooth-bore musket.

In December, the same year, the regiment proceeded from Peshawur to Rawul Pindi, "moving by easy stages, on account of its sickly state."

---

* "The tribesmen around Peshawur are very predatory in their habits, constantly coming in to steal. Horses are their particular vanity. The thieves don't trouble themselves by walking into the stable through the door, they prefer to cut a hole through the mud wall. A cordon of sentries, always loaded, surround the cantonment—in our time the old muzzle-loader was in vogue, the bullet being split into four to act as slugs—indiscriminate firing was going on all night; either from sentries, or from 'Chokedars' (private watchmen) always semi-tamed hill men. You were supposed to be safe from the depredations of the tribe your Chokedar belonged to by paying the black mail his wages represented. . . . . . . On one of these nightly raids, a captain of 'Ours,' Thelwall, discovering a party of cattle-lifters, from the Khyber, in the compound of his bungalow, who were paying unauthorised attention to his horses, saluted them with a few rounds from his unerring rifle. The wounded were picked up and carried off by their companions. The result of this little episode was that the entire clan bound themselves by an oath to murder Thelwall's wife and child; so, to prevent mischief, he sent his family away for a time. Murders were common both in and in the vicinity of cantonments. Visiting the guards in Peshawur at night was a service of danger, for it sometimes happened, and no one knew when it might occur, that a party of these 'Budmashes' sprang from some dark hiding place by the roadside and attacked officer and orderly, slashing at men and horses with their keen tulwars and long knives. Even going to mess it was customary to carry a loaded revolver. The knowledge that everyone went about armed in all probability prevented many an outrage." Lieutenant-Colonel Macpherson, *Rambling Reminiscences.*

† MS. Notes by General G. F. de Berry.

1857-58.

At Rawul Pindi the regiment lay on the memorable 13th May, 1857, when a Council was held to consider the tidings of revolt arrived from Delhi and Meerut. Brigadier Neville Chamberlain, who had been invited to the conference, urged the immediate formation of a flying column, ready to pounce down on any point where mutiny might show itself. The 24th, under Lieutenant-Colonel W. G. Brown, was at once despatched to Jhelum for that purpose, and on arrival there, on 20th May, was ordered on to Wuzeerabad; but, after crossing the Chenab, was ordered back to Rawul Pindi, where it arrived on 8th June. Two days afterwards, three companies 24th (Nos. 6, 7, and Light), under command of Major E. Wodehouse, were sent to hold the fort and ferry at Attock, relieving a like detachment of the 27th Inniskillings.

On 1st July, 1857, three companies 24th (Nos. 1, 2, and 3), under Brevet-Colonel and Lieutenant-Colonel C. H. Ellice, were ordered from Rawul Pindi to Lahore, and on 4th July, Colonel Ellice received instructions to march with these companies, numbering two hundred and eighty-five of all ranks, three horse artillery guns, and a detachment of Native Cavalry, to Jhelum, to disarm the 14th Bengal Native Infantry and detachments of the 39th Native Infantry, who were known to be ripe for revolt.

On nearing the cantonments, on the morning of 7th July, after a night march of twelve and three-quarter miles from Deenah, Colonel Ellice heard these regiments had mutinied. He pressed on with the guns and cavalry, and was met by the officers, who were making their escape, pursued by the fire of their own mutinous Sepoys. The latter retired on perceiving his force and took refuge in their lines, previously loopholed, occupying strongly the fortified keep, or guard room, which commanded the whole position. The Sepoys numbered over a thousand, all armed and well provided with ammunition; Colonel Ellice had with him under three hundred infantry and three guns available for the task of assaulting a well-posted enemy from an open plain. He attacked from a flank, and drove the mutineers from line to line of huts, till he reached a position from which to make an assault on the keep, which was carried by the men of the 24th Regiment with the greatest gallantry. The Sepoys had lost heavily, and what remained of them were now retreating hastily across the plain. The affair up to this point had been absolutely and entirely successful, and the position brilliantly carried with small loss. At this moment, unfortunately, Colonel Ellice was desperately wounded (shot through neck, leg, and right shoulder, and horse killed,) and had to be carried off the field, the command devolving on the next senior officer, Colonel Gerrard, 14th Bengal Native Infantry. The fugitive mutineers retired to a walled village, some distance from the cantonments, and made a fresh stand. The infantry and guns followed them up and recommenced the attack. Unfortunately one of the guns was unlimbered within musket shot of the village, and fell short of ammunition. The horses were killed, and in the endeavour to drag the gun further back several lives were sacrificed.

It was now 4 o'clock in the afternoon, the men had been marching since 12 the previous night, and since 4 o'clock a.m. had been fighting under the scorching sun of the Punjaub in July. They were utterly exhausted from the excessive heat and want of food, the rations having failed to come up. It was therefore determined to hold the position already gained and not resume the attack till next morning. In the night the Sepoys retreated from the village, but the pursuit being vigorously pushed, on the morning of 8th July, the result was the entire destruction of the Jhelum mutineers. This engagement was highly creditable to the weak force engaged, and more particularly to the 24th Regiment, which on this occasion, though in great numerical inferiority, drove a vastly superior force with heavy loss from a singularly advantageous position.

It was a day of great responsibility, as not only had Colonel Ellice to attack the mutineers at once, after a long, fatiguing march in the month of July—for in the days of the mutiny, no matter the odds, one was bound "to go at them"—but he had to tell off a party to watch the town and a wing of irregular cavalry (Liptrot's Irregulars in garrison at Jhelum) who were suspected of wavering, and actually in the end did mutiny, thus greatly weakening the force at his disposal for the attack on the lines.

The regimental casualties were: Captain F. Spring, killed;* Colonel Ellice and Lieutenant R. C. Streatfeild,† dangerously wounded; Lieutenant E. P. Chichester,‡ severely wounded; two sergeants, one corporal, and nineteen privates, killed; forty-eight privates, wounded.

One hundred and fifty of the mutineers were killed in their lines; the remainder (excepting one hundred and fifty who escaped to the territories of the Maharajah Ghoolab Singh), were taken prisoners and executed summarily.

The following letters relate to the affair :—

[COPY]

"Sir,
                                    "Jhelum,
                                   "8th July, 1857.

"I have the honour to report for the information of H.E. the Com-
"mander-in-Chief that yesterday morning, agreeably to the instructions
"received from Col. Ellice, commanding a detachment 24th Queen's and
"three guns of European Horse Artillery, together with some of the Mooltan
"Foot and Horse, I paraded the men of the 14th regiment N.I. for the pur-
"pose of withdrawing all the Sikhs and Punjabees, and on his arrival in the
"morning, for the disarming of the down country men. The men were
"paraded at 4½ o'clock a.m., the Sikhs were marched off, and on the
"appearance of the force under Col. Ellice on the parade ground, I
"attempted to explain to the men that they would be called upon to give
"up their arms for the present; but that if they continued to behave as
"well as they had hitherto been doing, that they would get them back, and
"that the 14th regiment would still be borne on the strength of the army.
"I had scarcely uttered the words when the whole of the Grenadier com-
"pany commenced loading their firelocks, and although every effort was
"made by myself and my officers to dissuade the men, they loaded, and as
"we retired from among them towards the approaching force, they fired on
"us, which hastened our movements. They then broke, and fled towards
"the lines and quarter guard, which latter place they held for a consider-

---

* Captain Francis Spring, father of the late Captain W. E. D. Spring. See chap. xv.

† Afterwards Colonel Robert Champion Streatfeild, Chief Paymaster, Home District. Died at Canterbury, 8th August, 1891, aged 56.

‡ Lieutenant Edmund Prideaux Chichester. Retired from the Service as Captain 7th Dragoon Guards. Died 1869.

"able time, although under a severe fire from the guns, and indeed were
"in possession of it until Col. Ellice himself headed a most daring and
"brilliant advance, when it was taken by our party, with, I regret to say, the
"loss of Col. Ellice's services, he having fallen there severely wounded in
"two places. Being the next senior officer present, I then took command,
"and seeing that the mutineers were retiring on the left, I ordered the guns
"forward towards the 39th N.I. lines, directing them to blow up the
"magazine of that regiment, which most fortunately was done by the second
"shot, on which the Sepoys in a large body commenced retreating towards
"the river. I immediately limbered up, and, with the whole of the avail-
"able cavalry, followed at full speed in the hope of cutting them off. They
"however made for a large village, which they took possession of. Major
"Brown having made arrangements for preventing their escape downwards
"by placing a large body of cavalry to cut them off, and as the lines had
"not been quite cleared of the mutineers, I returned with the guns to the
"left of the lines, into which they fired with great effect, turning out the
"mutineers in great numbers. They were followed up by our men, and as
"soon as they had cleared the huts, I advanced towards the village with
"2 Cos. H.M.'s 24th on the left, the guns in the centre, and the other
"Cos. H.M.'s 24th on the right, flanked on either side by cavalry. It was
"now nearly 2 o'clock in the day, and the men had been on their legs since
"12 o'clock the previous night, having marched from Deenah, and had been
"fighting the whole time since their arrival at Jhelum. Before attacking
"the village, I called a halt to refresh the men and horses, and immedi-
"ately sent off to the camp to get the breakfasts, which the Artillerymen
"did receive, but not a scrap could I get for the men of H.M. 24th, and it
"was not till 4 o'clock p.m. that I could get them even a drain of liquor.
"During this time I kept the men out of fire, and made my arrangements
"for the storming of the place, by directing the flanking companies to
"advance in skirmishing order (under cover of a heavy fire from the guns)
"till within 120 yards or so, when they were to close and make a rush into
"and clear the place. As soon as this had been done, I ordered up the
"Artillery to within 400 yards of the village, to keep down the fire of the
"mutineers as much as possible. Everything was progressing well, when
"the Artillery fell short of ammunition, and were obliged to retire, leaving
"one gun and a tumbril behind. On seeing this from the village I followed
"after, and on finding how matters stood, I was forced to recall our men
"and reformed in the open, protecting the lines by placing a large body of
"horse on the left, and connecting them by a chain of sentries with the
"guns which were placed in position on the left flank of the lines, our right
"flank being protected by infantry and cavalry. As night came on (with-
"out our being attacked) I placed a party some 250 yards in advance of the
"guns, under an European officer, as an outlying picquet. Several attacks
"were made on Capt. Lind's cavalry on the left ; he has, I hear, made
"several prisoners, but as I ordered that officer off early this morning to
"scour the country below this, I am unaware of their number at present. I

"beg to state that all prisoners taken, belonging to my late regiment, have
"been shot as soon as brought in, and that fifteen have already suffered
"death.

"Signed. J. G. GERRARD, Lt.-Col.,
"Commanding at Jhelum.

"CASUALTIES.

"*H.M. 24th.*—1 Field Officer wounded severely ; 1 Captain Officer (since
"died) ; 2 Subaltern Officers, severely. 2 Sergeants, 1 Corporal,
"21 Privates, killed. 1 Corporal, 48 Privates, wounded.

"1/3 *H.A.*—Men, 1 killed ; 7 wounded. Horses, 19 killed ; 8 wounded.

"Signed. J. G. GERRARD."

[COPY]

"Jhelum,
"11th July, 1857.
"Sir,

"With reference to No. 4 telegraph message, received by me
"yesterday afternoon, and calling for a report of the particulars of the
"engagement with the mutineers of the 14th N.I. at Jhelum by a detach-
"ment of H.M.'s 24th regiment under the command of Colonel Ellice, on
"the morning of the 7th July, '57, I beg to state for the information of
"General Gowan, commanding in the Punjaub, that I have been informed
"by Colonel Gerrard, who succeeded to the command of the forces when
"Col. Ellice fell severely wounded and carried off the field, that a report
"detailing all particulars and casualties, was duly forwarded by him the
"next day, under care of the Brigade-Major Rl. Pindee. Agreeably, how-
"ever, to instructions contained in the message received by me, I now en-
"close a duplicate of the report sent in by Col. Gerrard, and in forwarding
"the same, I would beg most particularly to bring to the notice of General
"Gowan the distinguished gallantry of Col. Ellice, who led the attack on
"the guard room, when the artillery were unable to silence the fire of the
"mutineers, and there received his very severe wound. I have also
"most favourably to mention Capt. Macpherson, who succeeded
"to the command of the detachment when Capt. Spring was mortally
"wounded, and brought the detachment out of action ; likewise the gallantry
"of the whole of the Subaltern officers, namely Lieuts. de Montmorency,
"S. Burns, Lieut. Chichester and Lieut. Streatfeild. The two latter
"wounded, the former officer severely in the arm, and the latter wounded
"in both legs, the right amputated. The detachment lost a third of its
"strength in killed and wounded.

"I have the honour to be, Sir,
"Your most obedient Servant,
"W. G. BROWN,
"Col. and Lt.-Col.,
"Commanding H.M.'s 24th Regt.

"To the Asst.-Adjutant-General,
"Lahore."

During this period, and for months afterwards, the regiment was in ceaseless movement. On 8th July a detachment, under Lieutenant R. H. Holland, marched from Rawul Pindi towards Jhelum, and back on 10th July. On 11th-13th July, Major Wodehouse's detachment was brought back from Attock to Rawul Pindi, which had become provisionally the provincial seat of government. The weather was exceedingly hot, and twelve men of the detachment died of sunstroke in one day on the march. On 12th July, Captain R. T. Glyn marched with a detachment towards Jhelum, to protect the sick and wounded, and returned to Rawul Pindi on 18th July.

Colonel Brown, who had been specially ordered to Jhelum to assume command of the troops there, received instructions on 10th July to march to Trimmoo Ghât, to co-operate with Brigadier John Nicholson in destroying the mutinous 46th Native Infantry. The troops started early next morning, but, on reaching Soubrial, were countermanded to Lahore. Meanwhile the regimental head-quarters, under Major Wodehouse, had marched from Rawul Pindi for Lahore, leaving a depôt at the former place. They were joined *en route* by Colonel Brown, with orders for their return to Rawul Pindi, a detachment of two hundred and fifty men, under Major Wodehouse, going on to Lahore and Umritzur, to form part of a movable column at the latter station, under Colonel Boyd. No. 2 company 24th, under Captain de Montmorency, from Jhelum, was sent to Jullundur; and Nos. 1 and 3 companies, under Captain A. J. Macpherson, were ordered to hold the fort of Phillour. At this time the regiment lost a valuable officer in Captain Thos. Maling Greensill,* who was accidentally killed with the army before Delhi, while serving as field engineer.

---

* Captain Greensill, who was a cousin of the present General Lord Roberts, G.C.B., obtained his first commission in the 24th Foot in 1846. The circumstances of his death are thus related by General Sir Henry Norman, in a private letter to Colonel Symons, dated India House, 1st August, 1883 : " In reply to your letter, all I can say is that Captain Greensill was at the Metcalfe Picquet at Delhi on the night on which he was mortally wounded. He was on duty with it as assistant field engineer, and had occasion to go beyond the sentries in the dark. I am not quite certain as to the purpose for which he went, but, as the enemy often came close to the picquet, I know officers sometimes went beyond the

In August, cholera broke out among Major Wodehouse's detachment, at Umritzur, and caused twenty-five deaths. On 1st September (the Mahommedan festival of Ede) the Hill Station and Sanatorium at Murree, in charge of Captain G. F. Berry, 24th, (now Major-General G. F. de Berry) which was crowded with wounded officers and families, was attacked by the hillmen, at the instigation of some Hindustani fanatics sworn to the Koran to destroy the station and all in it. The first warning of an intended attack was given by a native servant of Lady Lawrence, who was a visitor at the station. The assailants entered the station at one end next morning and gutted a house, but were driven out with loss. The ladies and families were removed to the European barracks, and with the scanty force within his reach—one hundred and fifty European soldiers (invalids of various corps), one hundred and eighty Sikhs (Dogras), of the 2nd Punjaub Infantry, hastily summoned from a place called the Flats about four miles distant, and some volunteers improvised from residents and visitors—Captain Berry (with whom was Lieutenant Crutchley, 24th) held the place during a three days' blockade, until the arrival of reinforcements, when small columns were sent out which dispersed the insurgents, burned their villages, and brought in over two hundred prisoners known to have been implicated in the attack. For these measures Captain Berry received the thanks of the Punjaub government and of Sir Sydney Cotton, commanding the division. *(See Appendix—Services of Officers.)*

In October 1857, Captain Berry was sent to Lahore to raise two battalions of Sikh police, one for the Delhi district, just wrested from the rebels, the other for Benares. These battalions, numbering

---

sentries to lie down and listen for any signs of movement. At other times after dark, small parties used to go out to clear away the bushes, which, until a late period of the siege, impeded the view of the sentries of the picquet. Possibly he may have been visiting a party engaged in this work. Be this as it may, the essential part of the story is that Greensill did go beyond the sentries in the dark in the performance of his duty, and that in coming back he was challenged, and either because he was not very quick in answering, or the sentry was hasty, he was fired at and mortally hit. I understood that on returning he came opposite a different sentry to the one he had passed in going out, and that the sentry who fired had no idea that any of our people were in front. It was an unlucky accident, but no blame was attributed to anyone."

twelve hundred men, were raised, clothed, armed, and equipped in two months. The first, now the 45th Bengal Native Infantry, or Rattray's Sikhs, was sent to its destination as soon as complete. The other, known as Berry Sikhs, afterwards the 2nd Bengal Police battalion, proceeded under command of Captain Berry, by forced double marches, to Cawnpore, where it arrived in February, 1858, and did good service with Brigadier Maxwell's column, before Calpee.

In November, 1857, No. 6 company 24th was sent from Umritzur to Gogaira, and the Jullundur and Phillour detachments rejoined Major Wodehouse at Umritzur. In December the head-quarters from Rawul Pindi arrived at Umritzur, where Colonel W. G. Brown assumed command of the movable column there.

In January, 1858, a draft from England, under Lieutenant-Colonel Blachford, joined at Umritzur, and Major E. Wodehouse was sent to take charge of the depôt left at Rawul Pindi. In March, the head-quarters were moved from Umritzur to Ferozepore, whither they were followed, a few days later, by a detachment left under Lieutenant-Colonel Blachford at Umritzur, and in May by the depôt and women and children from Rawul Pindi, in charge of Major Wodehouse.

On 3rd June, 1858, the 24th (2nd WARWICKSHIRE) Regiment was once more augmented by a second battalion, which was formed at Sheffield under Brevet-Colonel and Lieutenant-Colonel C. H. Ellice. (See chap. xi., *Services of the Second Battalion.*)

On 28th June, 1858, General the Honble. Edward Finch, C.B., *(Appendix B.)* was appointed colonel of the regiment, in the room of General Robert Ellice, deceased.

On 29th June, 1858, the following letter was received at head-quarters :

" Adjutant-General's Office,
" Head-quarters, Allahabad,
" 22nd June, 1858.
" Sir,
" The services performed by a detachment of the 24th regiment at " Jhelum on the 7th July last, in a severe action with the armed mutineers " of the late Bengal N.I., having been brought to the notice of the Com-

"mander-in-Chief, I have the honour by his direction to request that you will express to the officers and men who were engaged, His Excellency's approval of their conduct on that occasion.

"I have, &c.,
"(Signed.) N. PAKENHAM,
"For Adjt. Genl."

On 14th July, Lieutenant-Colonel Blachford assumed command of the first battalion at Ferozepore, on Colonel W. G. Brown proceeding to Calcutta to take up the duties of brigadier.

1859-60.

On 31st January, 1859, the 1st battalion at Ferozepore detached seven officers, twelve sergeants, four drummers, and three hundred and four rank and file, under Major Lutman, to Seria, to join a movable column under Major Chamberlain, 1st Irregular Cavalry. Major Lutman's detachment rejoined the battalion, 2nd April, 1859.

Details (invalids) of the regiment, in charge of Captain Munnings, (who had been regimental adjutant in 1857-58), were on board the passenger ship *Eastern Monarch*, Captain Morris, when, owing to an explosion in the spirit room, she caught fire and burnt to the water's edge, at Spithead, on 3rd June, 1859, on arrival from Kurrachee. Captain Munnings received the thanks of Colonel Allan, the senior military officer, and of Captain Morris, for his coolness and judgment on this most trying occasion.*

On 30th December, 1859, the 1st battalion, which was still at Ferozepore, received orders to hold itself in readiness to proceed on active service to China; but the order was countermanded on 6th January, 1860. On 9th March, 1860, Major E. Wodehouse obtained a lieutenant-colonelcy, *vice* Blachford, retired on half-pay. On 3rd September, 1860, Colonel Brown proceeded to Delhi, as first-class brigadier.

On 7th January, 1861, the 1st battalion was thrown open to volunteering, preparatory to its return home. The volunteering lasted four days, and was superintended by Major Dickson, 51st Light Infantry. Three sergeants, one corporal, five drummers, and two

---

* See account in *Times* newspaper, June, 1859.

hundred and eighty-six privates of the battalion elected to transfer their services to other corps remaining in India. The following address by Brigadier Sanderson to the 1st battalion, on leaving India, is extracted from Station Orders, Ferozepore, 21st January, 1861:

"No. 5. In saying farewell to H.M. 24th Regiment of Foot, the "brigadier feels that it does not lie with him to more than advert to the "fifteen years of its memorable service in India, now terminating its "share in the arduous campaigns of 1848-49; and especially the "part it played at the battle of Chillianwallah, where so many of its "officers and men fell, and regarding which the despatches of the day "state that the conduct of the regiment, and especially its exertions, "elicited the admiration of the general commanding.

"As to its marching and counter-marching, its toil and exposure, and "gallant deeds during the terrible crisis of 1857-58, when on the endurance "and valour of European officers and soldiers hung the destiny of the "East—the estimate of such services belong to the highest authority. "The brigadier can presume, therefore, to speak only of its conduct whilst "under his orders, which he can say truly has been such as to command "his respect and admiration."

[COPY]
"Head-quarters, Bombay,
"21st March, 1861.

"GENERAL ORDER.
"Her Majesty's 24th regiment of foot is about to leave for England, "after a prolonged stay in India.

"Sir William Mansfield (C.-in-C. Bombay army), has much pleasure in "testifying to the good conduct and discipline by which this regiment has "been distinguished throughout its Indian career, in the most difficult cir- "cumstances of war and in quarters.

"Her Majesty's 24th foot took a leading part in the Indian Campaign, "including the battles of Chillianwallah and Goojerat, and was much "employed subsequently, in 1857, in maintaining order in the Punjaub "when that great province was denuded of troops on account of the siege "of Delhi.

"To have formed part of the small body of troops which upheld the "honour of England in India in the eventful year of 1857, is a proud recol- "lection for this regiment, which will be handed down hereafter amongst "the most glowing traditions of their records. By order of His Excellency "Lieut.-General Sir R. W. Mansfield, K.C.B.

"(Signed)   C. H. SOMERSET, Colonel,
"Depy. Adjt. Genl. H.M.'s. Forces, Bombay.
"To Lt.-Col. Wodehouse,
"Commanding H.M.'s 24th Regt."

The battalion marched from Ferozepore for Mooltan on 22nd January, 1861.

The head-quarters and seven companies, under Colonel Wodehouse, left Mooltan on 16th February, and steaming down the River Indus, arrived at Kurrachee on 5th March, 1861.

A detachment of three companies, under Brevet-Major A. J. Macpherson, arrived at Kurrachee by the same route on 1st March.

The head-quarters embarked at Kurrachee for England on 22nd March, on board the transport ship *Sirocco*, and disembarked on 27th July, 1861, at Portsmouth, where the depôt, over four hundred strong, was awaiting them. Major Macpherson's detachment left Kurrachee on board the *Phœbe Dunbar* on 26th March, and arrived at Portsmouth on 14th September, 1861.

Major-General the Honble. J. Finch, the colonel of the regiment, died on 25th November, 1861, and Major-General Pringle Taylor, K.H. *(Appendix B.)* was appointed to the vacant colonelcy on the following day.

[185]

CHAPTER XI.

1858-74.

Services of the First Battalion, 1862-74—Services of the Second Battalion, 1858-74.

SERVICES OF THE FIRST BATTALION.

1862-74.

CHAKO PLATE.
1868-80.

AFTER its return from India, the first battalion was quartered at Gosport and Portsea until September, 1862, when, under command of Colonel Wodehouse, it proceeded by march route to Aldershot, and was quartered in the North Camp. The marching-in strength was twenty-eight officers, forty-four sergeants, thirty-nine corporals, twenty drummers, and seven hundred and twenty privates. It remained at Aldershot until 28th April, 1864, when it moved to Shorncliffe, detaching companies to the Western Heights, Dover. On 29th March, 1865, it embarked for Kingston, and proceeded to the Curragh Camp. In August it moved into the Beggars Bush barracks, Dublin, with detachments at Ship Street and Portobello, where it remained during the winter. Great excitement was caused at this time by the Fenian plots then rife. A large body of men, well provided with arms and trained to organised action, was known to the authorities to be at the disposal of a secret council, and on the watch for an opportunity to attempt a rescue of political prisoners in the Dublin gaols. The precautions against such attempts rendered the duties exceptionally severe. Strong picquets were posted at the different prisons, the streets were patrolled at night, and the troops held in constant readiness to turn out. In February, 1866, the battalion went back to the Curragh.

On 21st June, 1866, the battalion, which was still at the Curragh, was presented with new colours by the Countess of Kimberley, the wife of the lord lieutenant, at a grand divisional parade ordered for the purpose. The old colours having been trooped, the new colours, garlanded with roses—the colours subsequently carried in Zululand—were handed by Majors R. T. Glyn and R. H. Travers to the countess, who delivered them to the ensigns, with an appropriate address, to which Colonel Wodehouse replied on behalf of the regiment The old colours—one of them the relic of Chillianwallah—were borne off the parade under an escort of the battalion, and were subsequently deposited in the Beauchamp Chapel, an annexe of the old parish church of St. Mary, Warwick.*

---

* The following appeared in a local paper, at the time:

"St. Mary's Church, Warwick.

"A few months ago a handsome sculptured monument was placed in the north transept of the above church to the memory of Lieutenant-Colonel Louis Howe Bazalgette and Major Thomas Clark, of the 2nd battalion 24th regiment, by their brother officers of both battalions.

"The regiment, having been presented with new colours, were wishful that the old ones should be placed over the monument.

"A detachment of the regiment having arrived at 12 noon from the Depôt at Sheffield, the ceremony took place. The officers present were: Captains Johnston, Logan, and Tongue; Lieutenants G. A. Lee and Ellis Lee; and Ensigns Bennett and Pryce.

"The detachment was met at the station by the staff and band of the 1st Warwickshire Militia, who were under the command of Captain and Adjutant Vaughan.

"Headed by the band the party marched to the church, where the detachment presented arms, the band played the National Anthem, and the colours were carried into the church by the two ensigns and placed over the monument.

"The colours bear the marks of having been in numerous engagements, and are very much cut by shots. They were taken and retaken by the enemy more than once, and three officers who bore them were killed in battle. The blood of one is still visible on the colour staff."

Another account, referring to Private Richard Perry, 24th regiment, who saved the regimental colour at Chillianwallah, adds:—

. "Perry died at Warwick, in the year 1855, and was buried in St. Mary's Churchyard, and it is singular that the colours which he so nobly and gallantly saved at the imminent risk of his life, should be, twenty years afterwards, placed within a few feet of where his remains were interred."

On 8th August, 1866, a detachment of three companies, under Major R. T. Glyn, was sent to Londonderry, and a subaltern's party to Greencastle Fort. On 16th August the battalion arrived at Belfast, and on 30th September, 1866, embarked, under command of Colonel E. Wodehouse, for Malta, in the SS. *Pennsylvania* The strength embarked was thirty officers, thirty-two sergeants, sixteen drummers, and six hundred and twenty rank and file. The following were the officers embarked:

Colonel E. Wodehouse, commanding.
Majors R. T. Glyn and R. H. Travers.
Captains H. J. Hitchcock, W. J. M. Crawford, J. Foot, W. M. Dunbar, C. F. Lloyd, and W. A. H. Plasket.
Lieutenants J. M. G. Tongue, J. C. Thomas, W. M. Brander, H. A. Harrison, W. Hitchcock, H. R. Farquhar, F. Hibbert, G. A. Lee and E. Lee.
Ensigns R. Upcher, F. Carrington. H. B. Moffat, R. R. Corcor, T. Melvill, L. H. Bennett, J. G. Syms, F. P. Porteous, and C. C. Allen.
Paymaster F. F. White.   *Lieutenant and Adjutant* J. F. Caldwell.
Quarter-Master W. Charters.
Surgeon J. Coates.   *Assistant Surgeon* G. F. Duffey.

Although its stay had been short, the battalion was very popular at Belfast, and the streets and river banks were thronged with spectators to bid it good speed. A detachment, under Brevet Major A. J. Macpherson, consisting of Captain R. O'Mahoney; Lieutenants R. C. T. Athill, R. H. B. Airey, and Geo. Paton; Ensign Wm. Hughes; twelve sergeants, five drummers, and one hundred and twelve rank and file, was left at home to form a depôt with the 14th Depôt battalion at Sheffield. The Service companies arrived at Malta on 12th October, 1866, and landed on Fort Manoel Island next day. After fifteen days' quarantine, owing to the existence of Asiatic cholera in the United Kingdom, they marched into quarters at Fort Verdala, with a company in St. Clements retrenchment.

On 13th February, 1867, Major R. T. Glyn was promoted to lieutenant colonel, *vice* Colonel E. Wodehouse, who retired on half-pay. The following address subsequently appeared in regimental orders:

"In bidding farewell to the regiment in which the whole of his military "career has been passed, and which he had the honour of commanding "for more than 6 years, Colonel Wodehouse begs to return his most sincere "and cordial thanks to the officers and non-commissioned officers for the "support which they have invariably accorded him in maintaining the "discipline and general efficiency of the regiment, and to the whole body "of men for the ready and cheerful manner in which his orders have been "obeyed.

"It has ever been his aim and object, as far as was consistent with his "position, to keep up an easy intercourse with all ranks, to familiarize him-"self with their wants and wishes, and by such means to promote their "comfort and well-being.

"In the good feeling and unanimity that pervades the regiment, he has the "justifying assurance that his efforts have not been unsuccessful. He has "endeavoured to impress upon all under his command the advantage of "regarding the regiment as their home; for thirty years it has been a happy "home to him, and he now parts from it with the deepest regret.

"Such being his feelings, he need hardly add that as long as life is "spared to him he will continue to take the warmest interest in all that "concerns the honour and prosperity of the regiment; and, in every sense "of the word, he bids his gallant comrades farewell.

"By Order. (Signed) H. R. FARQUHAR,
"*Lieut. and Adjt. 1-24th Regt.*"

The battalion moved from Verdala to Floriana barracks in February, 1868. During this period it received the Snider rifle, in place of the Enfield. In September, 1869, it removed from Floriana to Fort Ricasoli, detaching two companies to Zabbar Gate, and one to Salvatore.* Under instructions dated Horse Guards, 1st April, 1870, medical officers were no longer borne on the strength of the regiment.

On 29th February, 1872, the 1st battalion 24th embarked at Malta, in the Indian troopship *Jumna*, for Gibraltar, where

---

* While at Malta the young officers of the 24th were instrumental in founding the Malta racecourse. The first race ridden on the now well-known "Mars-a-course" was a match between Lieutenant Teignmouth Melvill and an officer of another regiment.

it arrived 5th March. The following were the officers embarked:

Lieut.-Colonel Colonel R. T. Glyn, commanding.
Major H. J. Hitchcock.
Captains Dunbar, Harrison, Farquhar, and Mostyn.
Lieutenants Wardell, Airey, Carrington, Melvill, Syms, Boothby, Ealand, Browne and Curteis.
Sub-Lieutenant Haughton.   *Quarter-Master* Charters.
Lieutenant and Adjutant Corcor.   *Paymaster* White.
Surgeon-Major Coates, M.D.   *Assistant Surgeon* Hickson.

During the ensuing winter, Lieutenant and Adjutant Corcor died of pneumonia, and was succeeded in the adjutancy by Lieutenant Teignmouth Melvill.

On 28th April, 1873, the battalion moved from Europa Flats and Windmill Hill to the South front. The brigade depôt at Brecon was formed this month. (See *Services Second Battalion*.)

H.R.H. the Field Marshal Commanding-in-Chief was pleased, by Horse Guards letters, dated 5th and 10th June, 1873, to express his approval of the SPHYNX being worn on the forage caps of the officers and on the collars of the tunics and kersey frocks of the non-commissioned officers and men of the 24th Regiment, and also of the same being adopted for the officers' mess and scarlet patrol jackets.

In March, 1874, the battalion moved from the South to Buena Vista barracks, and on 28th November, the same year, the head-quarters embarked in the troopship *Himalaya* for the Cape of Good Hope. In a local general order of the same date, His Excellency the General Commanding the Garrison, recorded his approval of "the admirable manner" in which the head-quarters paraded, without a single absentee or unsteady man, and of the "manner in which the battalion embarked, which reflects high credit on all."

The following officers embarked with the head-quarters:

Lieut-Colonel Colonel R. T. Glyn, commanding.
Captains Brander and W. Degacher.
Lieutenants Carrington, Porteous, Dickinson, Halliday, Browne, Curteis, Cavaye, and Daley.
Sub-Lieutenant Hodson.   *Paymaster* White.
Lieutenant and Adjutant Melvill.   *Quarter-Master* Charters.
Surgeon Hickson.

SERVICES OF THE SECOND BATTALION.
1858-74.

The present Second Battalion—the third the regiment has raised—was organized at Sheffield on 3rd June, 1858, under the command of Colonel and Lieutenant-Colonel C. H. Ellice, C.B., being first recruited by the transfer of one hundred and fifty-four men from the 1st battalion.*

The new battalion removed from Sheffield to Bury, Lancashire, in July, and back to Sheffield in September. In November it underwent its first inspection, by Lieutenant-General Sir Harry Smith, G.C.B., commanding the Northern District.

On 3rd May, 1859, colours were presented to the battalion by Susan, Baroness Wharncliffe; and in June, the battalion, numbering thirty-two officers, thirty-nine sergeants, twenty drummers, and seven hundred and twenty rank and file, with fifty-four women and forty-eight children, moved to Aldershot, and was quartered in the West block, permanent barracks. It was among the troops reviewed on 9th July, 1859, by Her Majesty and H.R.H. the Prince Consort, during their stay in Aldershot camp in the summer of that year. A short time since, Her Majesty was graciously pleased to present to the officers' mess of the battalion a photogravure from a painting of the event.

The battalion remained at Aldershot until an unfortunate fracas with some of the Tower Hamlets Militia, on Christmas Day, led to its removal from the station, on 31st December, 1859. Two companies were sent to Winchester, and the rest to Portsmouth, where they embarked in the *Urgent*, for Cork, arriving on 29th February, 1860. The depôt companies were separated, and on 13th March, the Service companies of the battalion, numbering three field officers, seven captains, eighteen subalterns, six staff-sergeants, forty-three sergeants, twenty-one drummers, and seven hundred and fifty-five

---

* According to a Parliamentary return, there were three thousand and thirty-six Warwickshire men serving in the army this year.

rank and file (with sixty-seven women and sixty-six children) embarked in the *Donald McKay* for Mauritius. The following were the officers embarked :

Lieut.-Colonel C. H. Ellice, commanding.
Majors Honble. D. Finch and L. H. Bazalgette.
Captains T. Clark, F. C. D'Epinay Barclay, W. V. Munnings, E. W. Kent, W. P. Gaskell, E. T. Tarte, and H. J. Hitchcock.
Lieutenants E. T. Dunne, W. Franklin, H. B. Pulleine, A. C. Hallowes, R. N. Surplice, R. S. W. Leech, E. H. B. Sawbridge, W. R. B. Chamberlin, Oliver Goldsmith, and C. A. Hewett.
Ensigns G. V. Wardell, H. Dewe, R. B. Airey, T. H. Yonge, W. Hitchcock, Geo. Paton, C. J. Bromhead (Adjutant), W. M. de Rune Barclay, and regimental staff.

The battalion landed in Mauritius on 23rd May, 1860, eight companies going into the Line barracks and two into the Citadel. It did duty in Mauritius until October, 1865, during which time it was twice broken up in detachments, viz.: *July, 1860, to June, 1861*—two companies at Flacq, with a detachment at Grande Rivière Sud-Est, four companies at Port Louis, with an officers' detachment at Cannonier's Point, and a sergeants' party at Réduit, and head-quarters and staff at Mahébourg. *June, 1862, to June, 1863*—head-quarters, staff, and two companies at Mahébourg, four companies at Cannonier's Point, two companies at Flacq, with a detachment at Grande Rivière Sud-Est, one company at Petite Rivière, and one at the Citadel, with a sergeants' party at Réduit.

On 5th-6th October, 1865, the battalion embarked at Port Louis, in the ships *Devonport* and *Star of India*, for British Burmah. It landed at Rangoon, 2nd-10th December, 1865, and went into cantonments. In 1866 the battalion supplied two lieutenants and forty-four non-commissioned officers and men, as a body guard to the chief commissioner of British Burmah on his state visit to Mandalay. The party was absent on this duty from 18th October to 13th December, 1866.

On 6th May, 1867, a party of the 24th, under Lieutenant W. T. Much, was sent from the detachment stationed at Fort Blair, Andaman Islands, to ascertain the fate of the captain and crew of the ship *Assam Valley*, who were reported to have landed on the Little Andaman, and to have been murdered by the natives there. The steamer *Arracan* left Port Blair with the party on the day mentioned, anchored for the night in East Bay, and next day ran along the South coast of the island, and cast anchor about a mile and a half from a rock supposed to have been the scene of the massacre. The second cutter was manned and sent in, and a landing effected through a very heavy surf, the men wading to shore through five feet of water. The party marched towards the rock, the first cutter moving along outside to cover those on shore. They had not advanced far, when the natives began to show themselves and discharge their arrows. About fifty yards from the rock, a skull was picked up, which was afterwards pronounced to be that of an European. After the party had expended its ammunition in replying to the natives, a signal of recall was made; but, in the attempt to repass the surf the second cutter capsized and was washed away, and an officer of the 9th Bengal Infantry, a volunteer with the expedition, was drowned. Covered by the fire of the first cutter, the party on shore then marched back to East Bay, but all attempts to get boats into the bay failed. After finding the bodies of four men, partially buried, the party moved back to their first landing place, where a raft was sent into them. Lieutenant Much and another were swept off the raft by the surf, and were dragged on shore terribly exhausted. A volunteer crew was then made up on board the steamer, composed of Assistant-Surgeon Douglas, M.D., and four soldiers of the 24th, who pluckily took the steamer's gig into the surf, but, finding that the boat was filling fast, put back again. A second attempt was more successful, and five of the shore party were brought off safely and put into a boat outside the surf. A third trip brought off the rest. The expedition returned to Port Blair the next day.

The conduct of Dr. Douglas and the four soldiers with him was brought to the notice of H.R.H. the Field Marshal Commanding-in-Chief by the Commander-in-Chief in India, (Sir William Mansfield, afterwards Lord Sandhurst), with the result that the VICTORIA CROSS was bestowed on the officer and men in question: Assistant Surgeon Douglas, M.D., and Privates Thomas Murphy, James Cooper, David Bell, and William Griffiths, all of the 2nd Battalion 24th regiment. (See *Victoria Cross Roll, appendix A.*) A special note was directed to be made of the services of Lieutenant Much, (Horse Guards Letter, 27th December, 1867).

This year the battalion again supplied a body-guard to the British commissioner, on his annual visit to the court of the "Golden Foot," consisting of one captain, two lieutenants, one assistant-surgeon, and seventy-two non-commissioned officers and men, which proceeded to Mandalay on 19th September, and returned to Rangoon, 7th November, 1867. In 1868 the battalion lost over one hundred non-commissioned officers and privates (the picked men of the corps) who went home for discharge on the completion of the first term of their limited engagement.

The battalion left Rangoon, by wings, for Madras, *en route* to Secunderabad, Deccan; the left wing on 31st December, 1868; the right wing on 1st January, 1869. On arrival at Madras, they proceeded to Arconam, where they remained from 9th to 16th January, when they proceeded by rail to Tadpurie, where a twenty-nine days' march to Secunderabad began. The battalion arrived at Secunderabad on 16th February, 1869, after a most successful journey, three infants only having died on the way. It remained at Secunderabad until November, 1872.

During this period, after the reduction of the first battalion from twelve to ten companies, a draft, consisting of one captain, one lieutenant, one sergeant, three corporals, and one hundred and ninety privates joined from the depôt, on 22nd January, 1871. With the exception of twenty-two men who had been with the battalion before, all were young soldiers of seven or eight months' service. The battalion was then seventeen in excess of its established strength.

On 25th February, 1872, the battalion was supplied with the Snider rifle.

After inspection by Major-General De Saumarez, at Secunderabad, 28th August, 1872, the battalion was opened for volunteering, preparatory to returning home. Five sergeants, eight corporals, and one hundred and eighty-four privates volunteered to corps in India. On 14th November, 1872, the battalion commenced its march to Bombay, for embarkation, and, without casualty of any kind, arrived at Goolburgha, 28th November, 1872, and went under canvas there until 30th November, when it proceeded by half battalions to Poonah, by rail. On 2nd-3rd December, 1872, it embarked, under Major D'Epinay Barclay, at Bombay, in the Indian troopship *Euphrates*, and, after a singularly rapid and favourable voyage through the Suez Canal, reached Spithead on 22nd January, 1873, landed at Portsmouth four days later, and proceeded to Warley, Essex, where it was joined by its depôt-companies, and also the depôt of the 1st battalion.

On 1st April, 1873, the whole of the regular, militia, and volunteer forces of the United Kingdom were reorganized. Great Britain and Ireland were divided into military districts and sub-districts, and in each sub-district was established, under the command of a colonel, a brigade depôt, consisting of the depôt-companies of two battalions of the line, and the permanent staff of two battalions of militia. All the local corps of rifle volunteers were placed under the command of the colonel of the brigade depôt. The 24th (2nd WARWICKSHIRE) Regiment was assigned to the twenty-fifth (subsequently twenty-fourth) sub-district, embracing the counties of Cardigan, Radnor, Brecon, and Monmouth, with a brigade depôt at Brecon. Brevet Colonel E. Wodehouse, half-pay, 24th regiment, was appointed to command the brigade depôt. Colonel Wodehouse was selected for the command of a brigade at the autumn manœuvres on Dartmoor this year.

In September, 1873, Captain C. J. Bromhead, who, with other officers of the battalion, had volunteered for service on the Gold Coast, and Lieutenant Lord Gifford, accompanied Sir Garnet, now Viscount Wolseley, to Ashantee. For their services with the Ashantee expedition, the former received a brevet-majority, and the latter, a half-pay company and the VICTORIA CROSS. (See *Victoria Cross Roll, Appendix A*.)

In November, 1873, the battalion received the Martini-Henry rifle, in place of the Snider. In December, the battalion moved from Warley to Aldershot, and was quartered in the North camp, with the depôts of the 31st and 70th attached.

On 14th November, 1874, Colonel and Lieutenant-Colonel Thos. Ross retired on half-pay, Major D'Epinay Barclay obtaining the lieutenant-colonelcy, and Captain Dunbar the majority.

[195]

CHAPTER XII.

1875-78.

Services of the First Battalion : Griqualand—Kaffir War of 1877-78 – Proceeds to Natal.

Services of the Second Battalion—Kaffir War of 1878—Proceeds to Natal.

Services of the Mounted Infantry of the Regiment.

SERVICES OF THE FIRST BATTALION.

1875-77.

GLENGARRY CAP BADGE,
1871-1882.

THE voyage from Gibraltar was accomplished without a casualty, and on 2nd January, 1875, the battalion landed at Cape Town and procceded by rail to Wynberg Camp, where it was joined by a draft under Major H. J. Degacher that had arrived prior to the disembarkation, and a few days later by the detachment left at Gibraltar, under Major H. B. Pulleine, on the embarkation of the headquarters. On 4th February, 1875, the battalion moved from Wynberg Camp into the Main barracks, Cape Town.

On 6th May, 1875, Captain E. B. Sawbridge, Lieutenants F. W. Curteis and J. P. Daly, five sergeants, three corporals, two drummers, and ninety-four privates, proceeded by rail from Cape Town to Wellington, *en route* to Griqualand West, on account of disorders at the Diamond Fields.* The detachment was followed,

---

* A number of malcontents at the Diamond Fields had formed a " Digger's Association," with the avowed purpose of setting up a republic. Over seven hundred armed men were openly drilled by Germam and Irish Fenian officers.

on 15th May, by a second, under the personal command of Colonel R. T. Glyn, with Major H. J. Degacher,* Captains H. A. Harrison and W. Degacher, Lieutenants F. Carrington, J. D. Dickinson, and E. S. Browne, ten sergeants, six corporals, five drummers, and one hundred and seventy-nine privates. Included in this detachment were two sergeants, one corporal, one bugler, and thirty-six privates armed with the short snider rifle and provided with corduroy pantaloons and leggings, who were to be employed as mounted infantry. The men had been selected as able to ride, and, as it was proposed to purchase horses for them at Hope Town, saddles and bridles were sent with them. An officer and twenty-five men, Royal Artillery, with two Armstrong guns, accompanied the party.

The two 24th detachments united at Hope Town on 12th June, 1875, and on 19th June entered Griqualand West and marched to Kimberley (Diamond Fields), where they were reviewed by His Excellency Lieutenant-General Sir Arthur Cunynghame, commanding the troops in South Africa, in the presence of Governor Southey. The ringleaders of the disaffected party were arrested immediately on the arrival of the troops, who, immediately after the review resumed their march to Barkly, where they arrived on 2nd July, and remained in camp until 11th October, 1875. They then commenced their return march to the old colony, moving, at the rate of from twelve to twenty-three miles a day, by Hope Town, Colesberg, and Cradock to Port Elizabeth, where they arrived on 2nd November, 1875, and proceeded in the mail steamer *European* to Cape Town. By the general's order, Colonel Glyn and Lieutenant Carrington preceded the battalion by mail-cart.

The Mounted Troop was completed with horses on 20th June, 1875, and, under command of Lieutenant F. Carrington, instructor of musketry, and Lieutenant Dickinson, in the course of a week became fairly efficient, and rode and drilled well. They were employed on patrols, and as an advance guard during the march from Hope Town to the Diamond Fields. Their number was reduced to

---

* Major H. J. Degacher and Captain W. Degacher, brothers, had recently changed their name from Hitchcock to Degacher.

twenty men in July, and in October the troop was broken up and the horses sold.

On 25th December, 1875, a detachment, consisting of Major H. J. Degacher, commanding, Captains W. M. Brander, and T. Rainforth, Lieutenant E. O. Anstey, six sergeants, six corporals, three drummers, and one hundred and thirty-five privates was sent from Cape Town to East London, and in January, 1876, was reinforced by a detachment under Lieutenant Cavaye. On 7th August, 1876, a detachment, composed of Captain G. V. Wardell, Lieutenant Cavaye, five sergeants, two drummers, and seventy-seven rank and file was sent to the island of St. Helena On 18th April, 1877, the detachments at East London returned to head-quarters, Cape Town, under command of Major Pulleine.

On 2nd June, 1877, a detachment, consisting of Captain Much, Lieutenant the Honble. U. de R. B. Roche, three sergeants, two drummers, and sixty-three rank and file was sent from Cape Town to Natal.

On 3rd August, 1877, the battalion embarked at Cape Town in H.M.S. *Orontes* for passage to East London, *en route* to King William's Town. It was joined by Captain Wardell's detachment, from St. Helena, and a draft from England under Captain Russell Upcher and Lieutenant C. J. Atkinson. The battalion disembarked at East London on 6th-7th August, 1877, and proceeded by rail to King William's Town, where it was subsequently joined by Brevet Major Much's detachment from Natal, and by a company ("G") which had been left at East London at the time of disembarkation.

1877-78.

THE KAFFIR WAR.—In the month of August, 1877, Colonel Glyn, then commanding the 1st battalion 24th and the Eastern Frontier military district, received information of Kaffir and Fingo disturbances in Galekaland and the Idutywa Reserve, which caused him to despatch Lieutenant and Adjutant Melvill to report on the state of affairs there. Soon after that officer returned with valuable information. Colonel Glyn accompanied His Excellency the Governor and High Commissioner (Sir Bartle Frere) to Butterworth, to interview the chiefs and headmen of the various tribes. Kreli, the chief of the Galekas and paramount chief of the Amakosa tribes, refused to meet the Governor, and soon after the return of the latter from the Transkei, the tribe took up arms against the Government.

Various military movements followed. Among other arrangements a Mounted Troop was again formed in the battalion, at the end of September, 1877. Komgha was occupied by a detachment under Captain Russell Upcher, consisting of three subalterns, eight sergeants three drummers, and one hundred and eighty-nine rank and file, with detached subalterns' parties, under Lieutenant Anstey, at Pullen's Farm, and under Lieutenant Heaton at Impetu. "A" company, under Lieutenant Cavaye and the Honble. U. de R. B. Roche, proceeded to Fort Cunynghame at the same time.

Lieutenant and Adjutant Melvill, with an escort of four mounted men of the battalion, crossed the Kei by the general's order, and was present at the affair on the Butterworth river on 3rd October, 1877, when the enemy's country was entered by the colonial forces, and the Galekas were driven back with loss and their huts burned for a distance of three miles. After an interview with Commandant Griffiths, commanding the colonial forces, Lieutenant Melvill returned to King William's Town.

On 6th October, 1877, Captain Wardell assumed command of the Komgha post, which was reinforced by "A" company, under Lieutenant Cavaye, and "B" company, under Lieutenant Spring.

On 19th November, Lieutenant Cavaye, with sixty men, was sent to Draaibosch, to endeavour to intercept Mackinnon, a half-caste T'Slambi chief, who had made his way into the colony with a small following. In this they were unsuccessful, Mackinnon having effected a junction with his brother N'dimbi. Lieutenant Cavaye's party returned to Komgha. On 20th November, "G" company, under Captain Rainforth and Lieutenant Atkinson, was sent to Caboosie post, and thence to Gray's farm, where it was stationed, with one sergeant and fifteen men of the Mounted Troop under Lieutenant Coghill, 1st battalion 24th, and a party of Royal Artillery, the whole under the command of Lieutenant-Colonel Walker, Scots Guards, assistant military secretary.

On 25th November, 1877, Colonel R. T. Glyn, 1st battalion 24th, took command of the force, and on 8th December following—on which date the Imperial troops were ordered to cross the Kei—was appointed to command in the Transkei, with the rank of colonel on the staff.

Colonel Glyn, with his staff, and the mounted men 1st battalion 24th under Lieutenant Clements, left King William's Town on 9th December, and reached Ibeka, in the Transkei, on 11th December. He was followed by the detachments from Pullen's farm, Komgha, and Kei road, which reached Ibeka on 22nd December, and by His Excellency Sir Arthur Cunynghame, who arrived on Christmas Day. Captain R. Upcher, who had been detached to "The Springs," had a brush meanwhile with the enemy in the Mnyameni bush, in which four Kaffirs were killed and forty horses captured

On 27th December, 1877, a field force was organised in the following columns :

> HEAD-QUARTER COLUMN.—Colonel R. T. Glyn commanding; Lieutenant A. A. Morshead, District Adjutant; Lieutenant G. F. G. Hodgson, Orderly Officer; "G" company 1st battalion 24th, made up to one hundred and eighty men, under Captain Rainforth; twenty-three mounted men 1st battalion 24th, under Lieutenant Clements; Naval Brigade (H.M.S. *Active*,) under Commander Wright, R.N., with rocket-tube; Frontier Armed Mounted Police Cavalry and Artillery, with three seven-pounder guns; and Native Levies (Fingoes,) eleven hundred men.
>
> LEFT COLUMN.—Captain Russell Upcher, 1st battalion 24th, commanding; "F" company 1st battalion 24th, one hundred and thirty men; Royal Artillery, two seven-pounder guns; Royal Marines with rocket-tube; Frontier Armed Mounted Police; and Native Levies (Fingoes,) five hundred men.
>
> RIGHT COLUMN.—Major Hopton, 88th regiment, commanding; "A" company 1st battalion 24th, under Lieutenant Cavage, sixty men; "E" company, 88th Regiment; Royal Artillery with rocket-tube; Frontier Armed Mounted Police; and Native Levies (Fingoes,) five hundred men.
>
> FOURTH COLUMN.—Major Elliott, civil commissioner and resident magistrate, Tembuland, commanding; Frontier Armed Mounted Police, one hundred and fifty men; and Native Levies (Fingoes,) two thousand men.

The force proceeded through Galekaland towards the sea, and the head-quarters and left column from Ibeka; the fourth column from the Idutywa reserve; the right column from "The Springs." The right column cleared the country from the Butterworth and Kei rivers to the Qora river, at the mouth of which it joined the head-quarter column, which had cleared the difficult kloofs of the Qora. The left column, moving down the Shixeni ridge, cleared the country between the Qora and Shixeni. The fourth column cleared that between the Shixeni and the Bashee. Whilst these operations were in progress, "B" company 1st battalion 24th, under Major Logan and Lieutenant Palmes, was guarding Ibeka. The head-quarter column camped at the head of the Nxaxa, and on 29th December took up a position on the high ground above the Qora river, sending out the Fingoes as patrols, who, coming up with the enemy in dense bush, attacked and routed them, capturing nine hundred and ten head of cattle and some horses, and over one hundred women and children, who were sent under escort to Ibeka. On 30th December the head-quarter column passed through the Manuba Forest, and two days later crossed the Qora on a barrel raft and took up a position near the sea overlooking the Injuga river, where it was joined by Captain Russell Upcher's column, which had worked down the Shixeni range without much difficulty, scouring the country and capturing five hundred head of cattle.

During this month (December, 1877,) and the succeeding months, Major and Brevet Lieutenant-Colonel H. B. Pulleine, 1st battalion 24th, was employed at King William's Town in raising a body of infantry, called Pulleine's Rangers, of which he was commanding officer; and which, after active service on both sides of the Kei, was disbanded in August, 1878.

On 1st January, 1878, the Galekas having also broke into rebellion, the right column, which had cleared the country on the right of the head-quarter column, was left on the right bank of the Qora to keep the country clear between that river and the Kei, and to render aid in the colony if needed. The infantry of the head-quarter and left columns, with the waggons, spare ammunition, supplies, etc., were sent to Malan's station, the Injuga river being impassable.

On 3rd January, Colonel Glyn, with one hundred mounted men 1st battalion 24th and Frontier Armed Mounted Police, two Armstrong guns, and one thousand three hundred Fingoes, crossed the Injuga and passed through the rough and broken country towards the Quabora. The Udwessa Forest was then scoured, the enemy hastily retreating, leaving behind five hundred head of cattle. During these operations H.M.S. *Active* was kept off the coast under steam, between the mouths of the Injuga and Bashee, to render aid if needed. On 9th January, Fort Warwick, Impetu, which had been erected by "D" company, under Captain Wardell, was surrounded by Kaffirs, and defended by the company until relieved by a column from Komgha under Colonel Lambert, 88th regiment.

On 13th January, 1878, Colonel Glyn, with a force composed of nine officers and two hundred and ninety-three men (of which two officers and one hundred and thirty-seven men were 1st battalion 24th and the rest Royal Artillery, Royal Marines, and Frontier Armed Mounted Police), marched from Ibeka to Quintana, halting there about 1 p.m., when news was brought that the Kaffirs were collecting in large numbers between the right of the right column under Major Owen, 88th regiment, and the Kei. Colonel Glyn pushed on, reaching Major Owen's camp about 4.30 p.m., when the combined columns at once attacked the enemy, who were lodged in a strong position at Neumarka, and in great force. The action lasted an hour and a half, the enemy making a resolute stand for three-quarters of an hour before they began to retreat. They were followed until darkness compelled the troops to return to camp. Owing to the nature of the ground, it was impossible to ascertain the exact loss of the enemy, but fifty lay dead on the ground where the action had taken place, and several were found in the kloofs, having died of their wounds. Various minor detached movements followed, in which several thousand head of cattle and sheep were captured.

On 24th January, 1878, the whole of the Imperial and Colonial forces at head-quarters, Ibeka, were reviewed by His Excellency Sir Arthur Cunynghame, K.C.B., commanding the forces.

On 27th January, news having been brought from Komgha that a large body of Kaffirs, with some cattle, had been driven across the

Kei into the Mnyameni bush, a column, under Captain Russell Upcher, 1st battalion 24th,—composed of "G" company 1st battalion 24th, under Captain Rainforth, and parties of the Naval Brigade, Frontier Armed Mounted Police, Cavalry, and Artillery—was sent out from Ibeka to a place near Quintana. The enemy was found to be in force near the Tala Bush, and on 29th January were attacked by the column (which had been reinforced by the mounted infantry—1st battalion 24th, twenty-five Frontier Armed Mounted Police, and three hundred Fingoes) and driven from their position with the loss of forty killed and four hundred head of cattle and ten horses taken. The casualties on our side amounted to one man of the Naval Brigade and five Fingoes wounded.

On 6th February, 1878, Lieutenant Carrington, 1st battalion 24th, joined head-quarters, Ibeka, at the head of a body of Colonial cavalry which he had raised under the name of the Frontier Light Horse. Colonel Glyn having received information that a very strong force of Kaffirs, under Kreli, Sandilli, and other great chiefs, were meditating an attack, either on Ibeka or Quintana, despatched a small column, under Captain Robinson, Royal Artillery, to Tutura, mid-way between the two stations, so as to be in readiness to support either.

On 7th February, 1878, about 5 a.m., Captain Upcher learned that the Kaffirs—four thousand to five thousand Galekas and Gaikas, under Kreli and Sandilli—were advancing on his camp at Quintana. The action that ensued was described by His Excellency Sir A. Cunynghame as "the most disastrous to the enemy of any yet 'fought.'"

Upcher's force consisted altogether of fourteen officers and four hundred and twenty men, or, counting Fingoes, five hundred and sixty men, and included two companies 24th. On hearing the news he at once struck his tents and posted men in the shelter-trenches that had been dug on the lines traced out for a fort. "G" company 1st battalion 24th, under Captain Rainforth and Lieutenant Carrington with his Frontier Light Horse, were sent out to patrol the country to the northward, with instructions to fire and retire before the Kaffirs, so as to draw them on well within the range of the shelter-trenches—orders which were carried out admirably. They came upon two divisions of Kaffirs, estimated at one thousand five hundred men each, who, in spite of the heavy fire from the nine-pounder and seven-pounder guns and the rockets of the Naval Brigade, advanced very steadily to within nine hundred yards, when they came within range of the rifles, and on the left flank to within four hundred yards, being constantly reinforced by fresh Kaffirs coming over the hill in their rear. After about twenty minutes the Kaffirs broke both in front and flank, and the Frontier Light Horse charging out drove them into the Mnyameni bush. A strong division of Kaffirs was then seen approaching the right flank, and a party—including fifty men 1st battalion 24th under Lieutenant Atkinson—was sent out to intercept them. They were attacked, and after a stubborn resistance were driven off. Captain Rainforth, with "G" company, and Lieutenant Carrington, with the Frontier Light Horse, were engaged with this party. Captain Upcher and Lieutenant Anstey, with "F" company, and the Naval Brigade attacked another body of Kaffirs to the right front, and drove them off with heavy loss. By 10 a.m. the enemy was out of range, and the pursuit ceased. The casualties in Captain Upcher's force were two men wounded, one horse killed and two wounded in the Frontier Light Horse, and two Fingoes killed and seven wounded. The Galekas acknowledged a heavier loss than on any previous occasion. The total number of Kaffirs killed was estimated at over two hundred and sixty.

His Excellency Sir Arthur Cunynghame reported in terms of unqualified praise of "the high state of drill and discipline and the "admirable instruction of the 1st battalion 24th," which bade him fully "endorse the statement of Captain Upcher regarding the "excellence of their skirmishing and the heavy loss thus inflicted on "the enemy." Captain Upcher, who received the thanks of the general "for the excellent way in which he handled his force and the perfect "success he obtained," received a brevet-majority for his services.

The column under Captain Robinson, Royal Artillery,* arrived

---

* Captain Robinson, Royal Artillery, made special mention of the good marching of fifty men of the 1st battalion 24th who were with his detachment. They were each carrying one hundred rounds of ball ammunition, and accomplished seven miles in an hour and a half, the ground being very slippery.

from Tutura about 8.30 a.m., after the Kaffirs had been broken, and helped to follow them up to the Mnyameni bush. The Mnyameni and Tala Bushes were cleared during the succeeding days by patrols from Captain Upcher's column.

On 20th February, 1878, No. 6 company 1st battalion 24th (made up to one hundred men,) under Captain Mostyn, was sent to Fort Beaufort to help in clearing the Water Kloof and Schelm Kloof, two fastnesses that had given much trouble in the old wars. They burned Tini Macomo's kraal and cleared the Schelm Kloof, capturing a good many cattle. The company was relieved by a company of the 90th Light Infantry, and returned *via* King William's Town to Ibeka, Transkei, which was reached on 13th April, 1878.

On 16th March, 1878, the band of the 1st battalion, which had been left behind in King William's Town and drilled in artillery, left that station with two seven-pounder muzzle loading guns for Izeli and Mount Kempt, where they did good service with the newly-arrived Second Battalion of the regiment, and returned on 7th April. They were sent out again on 29th April, and were present in the actions at Intaba-ka-N'doda, and at Isidengi and Mount Kempt, returning to King William's Town on 12th May.

Meanwhile, on 3rd May, 1878, a combined movement of all the forces in the Transkei was commenced, for the purpose of driving the enemy towards the Bashee river, in which Major Boyes, resident magistrate in Tembuland, co-operated with a force of Tembus.

On 4th May, Colonel Glyn, with the mounted men of the battalion and two troops of Frontier Armed Mounted Police, crossed the Bashee and marched to Saville's shop, in Bonvanaland, (whither Captain Harrison, 1st battalion 24th, had been sent with a convoy to form a camp,) to meet the sons of Moni, the Bonvana chief. On 8th May the camp was moved into the Cwebe Forest, Bonvana land, which on the following day was surrounded by Colonel Glyn's forces, but the enemy had escaped. Colonel Glyn, with the mounted infantry and paid Fingoes, made a four days' patrol through Bonvanaland, capturing some cattle and interviewing the Chief Pali, after which the forces returned to their several stations in Galekaland.

From 13th to 28th May the 1st battalion band, with their guns, were with the 2nd battalion in Fort Black.

On 3rd June, 1878, the head-quarters, four companies, and the remaining companies at the outposts of the 1st battalion were inspected at Ibeka by the new commander of the forces, Lieutenant-General the Honble. T. A. Thesiger, C.B., now Lord Chelmsford, and the battalion was ordered to be concentrated at that station. Accordingly, "G" company marched in from Quintana, "B" company from Malan's station, and "H" company from Beechenwood.*

On 20th June, 1878, Colonel Glyn returned from Ibeka to King William's Town, Major and Brevet Lieutenant-Colonel Pulleine taking over the command at Ibeka. The war was now virtually at an end, and on 28th June, 1878, the Colonial Government proclaimed an amnesty.

The following letter was communicated to the regiment at this period:

"Horse Guards,
"War Office, S.W.,
"5th June, 1878.

"Sir.—I have the honor to acquaint you that the F.M. Commander-in-"Chief has perused with great satisfaction the precis of the operations on "the Eastern Frontier of the district under your command from the 24th "April to the 1st ult., transmitted with the letter addressed by you to the "Quarter-Master-General on the latter date.

"H.R.H. has especially noted that two guns were manned by the band "of the 1st battalion 24th regiment during the action on the 30th April, "and he considers that the cheerful spirit thus evinced for the general "interest and benefit of the public service is most creditable.

"I have the honor to be, etc.,
"(Signed) R. C. H. Taylour, D.A.G.

"The Genl. Officer Commanding,
"C. G. Hope."

---

* During the occupation of the Transkei the battalion threw up four earthworks: Fort Glyn, at Ibeka; Fort Owen, at Quintana; Fort Nixon, at Malan's station; Fort Upcher, at Beechenwood.

Kreli, the prime mover of all the mischief on the frontier for many years past, was still at large, and on 12th July, 1878, a party of thirty-five men, 1st battalion 24th, ten of them mounted, under Lieutenant and Adjutant Melvill, were sent from Ibeka to the Udwessa Forest to drive out all Galekas found therein and to endeavour to capture the fugitive chief.

The party took waggons with them, and had to find their own road and make drifts through one or two streams. A body of Fingoes were disposed round the forest, and on 18th July Kreli and his followers were discovered, and followed till sundown. Three prisoners were taken, but Kreli escaped, and no traces were found of him until 23rd August, although frequent patrols were sent by day and night into Bonvanaland as well as Galekaland.

The troops now began to move back from the Transkei to King William's Town, and on 8th August, 1878, Colonel Glyn handed over the command of the Transkei to the Colonial Government, the detachment in the Udwessa Forest still remaining, under Lieutenant and Adjutant Melvill. On 23rd August, 1878, Lieutenant Melvill learned from a prisoner that Kreli was hiding at his mother's kraal, in Bonvanaland, and made a night march thither; but, as on many another occasion, the wily chief once more escaped. The colonial officer, whose place he was holding, having arrived, Lieutenant Melvill handed over the spoor to him, and on 25th August retired with his mounted men to King William's Town.

On 17th August, 1878, Captain Harrison and Lieutenants Spring and Roche, with "B" company 1st battalion 24th, consisting of four sergeants, five corporals, two drummers, and seventy-four privates, marched from King William's Town to the mouth of St. John's, or Umzinvarboo, river, in Pondoland, where a settlement had been purchased from the Pondo chief, N'quaci. The British flag was hoisted there for the first time by Lieutenant-General the Honble. T. A. Thesiger, C.B., on the 24th August, 1878, and an earthwork, to which the name of Fort Harrison was given, was thrown up by the detachment. "B" (since "H") company remained at St. John's river mouth throughout the period of the subsequent Zulu War.

The troops had not long returned, ere the menacing aspect of affairs in Natal summoned the battalion to that colony, whither the 2nd battalion had already gone.

On 25th September, 1878, "C" and "D" companies 1st battalion, under command of Major and Brevet Lieutenant-Colonel Pulleine, left King William's Town for East London, *en route* to Durban, Natal. On arrival, "D" company remained at Durban, "C" company proceeding to Pietermaritzburg.

These were followed by "A," "E," "F," "G," and "H" companies, under command of Colonel Glyn, C.B., which embarked on 25th November, landed at Durban, and reached Pietermaritzburg on 28th November, 1878.

Before leaving the Cape the following letter was received by Colonel Glyn from His Excellency Sir Bartle Frere, G.C.B. :

" Government House, Cape Town,
"2nd September, 1878.

"MY DEAR GLYN.—I send a small silver box for cigars etc., which I "trust you and the Officers of H.M. 1st battalion 24th will permit me to "place on their mess table as a souvenir of the time when I was their "guest, and of the grateful sense I shall always entertain of your hospitality "during the trying months I lived in your barracks at King William's Town "and your men defending the frontier during the Kaffir war of 1877-78. "With kindest regards to all my old friends round the mess table, believe "me ever,

" My dear Glyn,
"Very sincerely yours,
"(Signed) H. B. FRERE.

"Colonel Glyn,
"1st battalion 24th Regt."

SERVICES OF THE SECOND BATTALION,

1875-78.

Kaffir War of 1878—Proceeds to Natal.

On 21st July, 1875, Lieutenant-Colonel Barclay exchanged to the 66th Regiment with Colonel G. V. Watson, who commanded the 2nd battalion 24th until his retirement on half-pay, 8th June, 1877.

The battalion removed from Aldershot to Dover in August, 1875, and on 11th October furnished the guard of honour on the embarkation for India of H.R.H. the Prince of Wales. On 21st June, 1877, the battalion left Dover Citadel for Chatham.

The serious aspect of affairs on the Eastern Frontier of the Cape Colony at the close of the same year, led to a call for reinforcements, and on 28th January, 1878, a telegraphic despatch from the Horse Guards directed the 2nd battalion 24th to be held in readiness to embark for the Cape. The 2nd battalion 24th, 90th Light Infantry, and a battery Royal Artillery were at once put under orders. Major-General the Honble. F. Thesiger, C.B. (afterwards Lord Chelmsford) was appointed to the Cape command, with local rank of lieutenant-general, in the room of Lieutenant-General Sir A. Cunynghame, K.C.B., whose period of staff service had expired.

Being the furlough season, many of the men were on leave, but with the exception of a very few whose letters of recall did not reach them early enough, all joined at the time appointed, and on 1st February, 1878, the battalion left Chatham by two special trains for Portsmouth, where it embarked in H.M. troopship *Himalaya*, and started next day. The strength embarked was twenty-four officers, eight staff-sergeants, thirty-nine sergeants, forty corporals, sixteen drummers, and seven hundred and forty-six privates.

The officers who embarked with the battalion were :

24TH REGIMENT.

Lieut-Colonel H. J. Degacher, commanding.
Majors W. M. Dunbar and Wilsone Black.
Captains W. R. B. Chamberlin, R. N. Surplice, J. M. G. Tongue, J. F. Caldwell, Farquhar Glennie, and A. G. Godwin-Austen.
Lieutenants W. Penn Symons, H. M. Williams, W. Sugden, C. D'A. Pope, Gonville Bromhead, G. S. Banister, H. G. Mainwaring, Q. M'k. Logan, H. J. Dyer, and F. Godwin-Austen.
Sub-Lieutenants C. V. Trower and T. L. Griffiths.
Staff: *Paymaster* J. Mahoney, hon-major; *Adjutant* J. J. Harvey, lieutenant; *Quarter-Master* Bloomfield.

After a fine passage, the *Himalaya* reached Simon's Bay on 28th February, remained a few days to coal and make good some repairs, getting under weigh again on 6th March, and sighting East London on 9th March. The day being favourable for crossing the bar, "B" and "C" companies, under Major Dunbar, were landed at once in surf-boats. The bar and heavy surf render landing at East London a slow and ofttimes dangerous operation, and not until 11th March was the last company got ashore. As fast as trains could be procured for them, the companies were hurried off to King William's Town, and thence marched to the front. By 14th March all had moved out to the posts assigned to them, with the exception of "D" company, which was left to garrison Fort Glamorgan, East London.

The cause of this hurry was that Sandilli, the famous Gaika chief, had eluded the Colonial forces, under Commandant-General Griffiths, which had been sent towards the junction of the Thomas and Kei rivers to make a combined movement against him, and, availing himself of the bush along his line of march, had escaped from his location, situated to the north of the Amatola and Caboosie mountains, and, turning the easternmost point of the latter, had got into the Döhne bush, and thence into his old fighting ground in former wars, the central and highest part of the range of mountains— Guilli-Guilli, Buffalo, and Izeli—extending from Middle Drift to Komgha, at the foot of which lies the great Perie bush, where the Buffalo river takes its rise.

The tops of these mountains are large plateaux, well supplied with grass and water, but intersected by deep ravines and rocky bush. So precipitous is the ground, and so thickly is it wooded, that only on the

P

very verge of a ravine, or *kloof*, is discovered the unsurmountable obstacle it presents to an advance in some direction, which a short distance off appeared perfectly easy. The slopes of these table-lands were defended by similar obstacles; dense bush, full of rocks, ravines, and trees of enormous growth; the ascent becoming steeper as one advances, until in most cases it terminates in a precipitous face of rock, or *krantz*, of great height. Few points in these krantzes are accessible to the natives, fewer still to Europeans. Indeed, the difficulties and intricacies of the country must be seen to be properly understood. However well known the country may have been in former wars, no actual knowledge of it for military purposes was at hand; even the white settlers and their labourers living on the skirts of the forest were ignorant of the main paths through it and over the mountains. In fact, the rebels were in vast natural fortresses, where they had ample supplies of wood, water, and grass, besides their store of mealies (Indian corn), which latter they sought to replenish by nightly raids on the neighbouring Fingo locations at the foot of the hill. Nor had they any lack of ammunition, as later on they were seen from Mount Kempt actively engaged in drill and target practice. As Sandilli had made a long stand in this country during the old war, the general was anxious to prevent any permanent occupation of the tract by the rebels, whilst, at the same time, it was of the greatest importance to prevent their passing further west into the Colony, spreading rebellion among those whose loyalty was very doubtful. His objects therefore were—

1. To close all outlets by which any large bodies with cattle and horsemen might escape.
2. To prevent any isolated parties who had escaped from re-forming and reaching locations where they could do mischief.
3. That every post should have a garrison sufficient to protect stores and to form a rallying-point for the well-affected.
4. To avoid any isolated attacks on the rebels, but, if possible, to take concerted action against them.

With these objects the 2nd battalion 24th, which, with a detachment Royal Artillery, was the only regular force in this part of the country, was split up into detachments of one, two, or three companies, each detachment forming the nucleus of a column, consisting of European volunteers and Fingo levies.

From the time it landed, the battalion was engaged in marching, patrolling, or waylaying paths leading to the rebel position, up to Sunday, 17th March, 1878, when the general arranged a combined attack for the following day.

The idea was that the three columns, moving respectively from Baillie's Grave, the Keiskamma Hoek, and Fort Merriman, should sweep the kloof and table-land to the west and north of the Guilli-Guilli into the Buffalo Valley bush. At the foot of this range, and at the mouth of the valley, were two companies 2nd battalion 24th, commanded by Major Wilsone Black, and attached to the column under Lieutenant-Colonel Law, Royal Artillery. The second part of the operations was to be the driving, in a north-easterly direction, of the Buffalo Valley bush and Murray's krantz, the outlets of which were guarded by a column commanded by Lieutenant-Colonel Degacher. Another column, composed of Colonial forces, was stationed at the head of the Gwengwe Valley, at Izidengi.

The companies were posted as follows :—

Beginning from the right, at Izeli post, were "G" and "H" companies (Captains Glennie and Caldwell), attached to Colonel Degacher's column; next came the two companies under Major Black before mentioned; "F" (Captain R. N. Surplice) at Haynes' Mill, the entrance to the enormous kloof known as the Buffalo Poort; and "E" (Brevet Major Chamberlin) at the Perie mission station, where the Christian Kaffirs were strongly suspected of rebel sympathies. This last company had left King William's Town on 12th March, with "A" company (Captain Tongue), for Fort White, a post that had witnessed many a fight in the old war; but at Green river, Major Dunbar, who was in command of the convoy, received orders to detach one of the companies to the Perie mission station. "E" company was sent, and thus became part of Major Black's command, whilst Major Dunbar went on with "A" company to Fort White, which was put in a thorough state of defence, and where he received orders to take up a position on the Intaba-ka-N'doda for the 18th March. Prolonging the line, at Hudson's store, was "B" company (Captain Godwin-Austen), with instructions to support the Colonial column, under Commandant Brabant. Finally, on the extreme left, was "C" company (Lieutenant H. M. Williams), attached to the column commanded by Colonel Evelyn Wood, V.C., C.B., 90th regiment, also destined to attack the heights.

On 18th March, the general (the Honble. F. Thesiger) took up his position at Haynes' Mill, but the column of Colonial forces, under Commandant Brabant, allowed itself to be lured away by the sight of some cattle, and commenced the attack before Colonel Wood arrived, so that it became impossible to carry out the original plan of advance. On the 19th the operations were resumed; the enemy was driven as intended, and the upper valley shelled from Haynes' mill. On the 20th the general moved round to Mount Kempt by the Gwengwe valley, passing as he did so Lieutenant-Colonel Degacher's column, which on the first day of the attack had taken up, at daybreak, a strong position in this valley from Izeli post. The general ordered the column to make a night march, *via* Frankfort, for the same destination, the long detour being necessary, as the path through the valley of Izidengi and Mount Kempt was found impracticable for guns and ammunition wagons. On arriving at Mount Kempt in person on the 21st, the general found the volunteer forces retiring from the plateau, the alleged reason being the difficulty in obtaining rations. Many of the volunteers were desirous of leaving for their homes, their terms of engagement being about to expire. The projected attack did not, therefore, take place, and the general returned to King William's Town to concert fresh arrangements for the clearing of the bush. All this time the officers and men were without covering of any kind; tents only having arrived on 21st March.

The movements of the two companies under Major Wilsone Black may be taken as an example of the work throughout the campaign. On 17th March, "F" company, as before stated, marched from Haynes' mill to join "E" at Perie mission station. On the 18th, together they waylaid the bush paths, returning to camp towards sunset for a hasty meal, after which they fell in and were all night on picquet duty. On the 19th they were ordered to Hayne's mill, to ascend the first open ground in the poort above the mill, where a demonstration was made in support of two guns, Royal Artillery, and a rocket detachment, Royal Navy, which shelled the kloofs in the Poort. At dusk, with detachments of the Naval brigade added, they proceeded to watch the ground as far as the second drift, where they communicated with "A" company, through a fearfully tempestuous night. On the 20th and 21st they were again employed in guarding the guns by day and watching the approaches by night. All this time, the Kaffirs made nightly attempts to pillage the mealie gardens, but on every occasion were driven back by the fire of the "sections of fours," which during this war were employed instead of the regulation double sentries and picquets. One night a Kaffir crept so near to Major Black, who was asleep, as nearly to grasp the rein of his pony grazing by his side. The cheerful spirit in which the men, mostly young soldiers, bore the hardships they had to endure was most creditable, and elicited the warm commendation of the general.

The movements of "B" and "C" companies may also be related. "B" company mounted the Rebula heights, and on arrival found Commandant Brabant's force, which, being mounted, had preceded the infantry, coming out of action with the loss of both men and horses. The company bivouacked on the heights, and next day descended to a lower plateau, skirmishing through the bush towards the edge of the krantz above Haynes' mill, driving the rebels before it, and at nightfall returning to occupy its previous bivouac. Next morning it remained inactive, owing to the dense mist shrouding the mountain, and on the 21st beat the bush back to Baillie's Grave.

"C" company marched with Colonel Wood's column from the Keiskamma Hoek to the Guilli-Guilli heights, and, supported by Carrington's Horse, drove a large body of rebels from a lower plateau thereon, and bivouacked on the ground. On the 19th, half the company being left to guard the bivouac, the rest co-operated with the Colonial forces in beating the Gozo bush, and on the 21st took part in the operations between Gozo and Baillie's Grave, retiring to the Keiskamma Hoek next day.

On 27th March the general took up his quarters on Mount Kempt, a high bleak mountain on the north of the Buffalo Poort, overlooking a wide range of country towards King William's Town. Colonel

Degacher's detachment had arrived on the 23rd, together with two seven-pounder guns manned by the band of the 1st battalion 24th, from King William's Town (see p. 204.) These guns were pushed up the mountain by a path cut through the bush. The 24th detachment, with the volunteer corps and Fingoes, lined the bush from Izidingi to Mount Kempt, where should have been the Colonial force, which took upon itself to return on the 21st, on the plea of obtaining rations. On the 28th the attack was made, commencing as on the previous occasion from the Keiskamma Hoek. The general, from Mount Kempt, witnessed the operations of "B" and "C" companies, in clearing three separate clumps of bush immediately beneath him, and afterwards personally complimented them on the "admirable manner" in which the service had been performed. The Kaffirs were driven from the plateau and confined to the bush of the Buffalo Poort, but the latter is of such vast extent that there were not men enough to drive it. A thousand Fingoes were telegraphed for from the Transkei, and the troops in the meantime were employed in watching, and cutting roads through the bush.

On 3rd April, "G" and "H" companies had a hard day's work. Lieutenant-Colonel Degacher having been ordered to push a reconnaissance on to Murray's krantz, a plateau separating the Buffalo Poort from the Gwengwe valley. The companies paraded at 9 a.m., and, preceded by a mounted volunteer corps, gained the krantz by a road three miles long, which they had previously cut through the bush. No Kaffirs were seen until about the close of the day, when they opened fire at about fifty paces from the edge of the krantz overlooking Haynes' mill. The companies formed and charged into the bush in open files, but the Kaffirs were down the side of the krantz before the men could get at them. A half company of "H," under Lieutenant G. H. Banister, caused some anxiety. Carried away by the ardour of the pursuit, they neither heard the order not to follow beyond the edge of the krantz, nor the bugles sounding the "halt," and soon found themselves at the bottom of the ravine. The valley was full of Kaffirs, and the impetuous act might have turned out very seriously; but the half company somehow disentangled itself without further damage than one man fainting from over-exertion. The commanding officer was pleased with the desire evinced by the men to close with the enemy on their own ground—ground so favourable to the latter, and so much the reverse to Europeans. The companies returned to camp long after dark.

The Transkei Fingoes having arrived, the Buffalo Poort was driven on 5th April by one thousand seven hundred and seventy-seven Fingoes, led by European officers. Very few Kaffirs were found; the delay having, no doubt, enabled them to get away in small numbers at a time.

The general now issued orders for breaking up the forces around the Buffalo range, but before this could be completed intelligence was received of the presence of large bodies of Kaffirs at Intaba-ka-N'doda, a curiously shaped hill on the west of Baillie's Grave, and at the end of a large valley, the Zanyorkwe. The Fingo levies were ordered off at once, and a small force under Lieutenant-Colonel Law, Royal Artillery, with which was Captain Tongue's company 2nd bat'alion 24th, marched to Baillie's Grave. "B" and "C" companies were also ordered to make a forced march to the same place with Colonel Wood's force.

On 6th April the rebels were attacked, and defended themselves well, but were driven from the bush on the appearance of Wood's column. Captain Tongue's company ("A" company) was noted in official despatches as having done twenty-four hours harassing work and made excellent practice at the rebels. From a rocky eminence it covered the advance of the first division of Fingoes, and subsequently beat the bush. During the night the rebels broke away in various directions, but about 7 a.m. on the 7th, a body of one hundred and fifty to two hundred being seen passing near Baillie's Grave into the Pine bush, "A," "B," and "C" companies were sent out to intercept them. The Tutu bush was driven and forty Kaffirs killed, among whom were two chiefs. "A" company lost Private J. Collins, killed while skirmishing in the bush.

As the bands of rebels appeared to be quite demoralized and dispersed, the general returned to King William's Town to make arrangements for replacing the volunteers, whose periods of service had expired. "A," "B," "G," and "H" companies were then collected at King William's Town, the remaining companies being stationed as follows: "C" at Baillie's Grave; "D," Fort Glamorgan; "E," Perie mission station; "F," Haynes' mill.

On 29th April, 1878, active operations recommenced, the objective being the Intala Ka Udoda, where the rebels had again collected in large numbers. The companies 2nd battalion 24th at King William's Town were moved to Baillie's Grave, where they were joined by "C" company there stationed, and from the first day of the attack by "E" company, from Perie station. These six companies were reinforced by five companies 90th Light Infantry and two guns Royal Artillery from the Fort Beaufort district, which continued to serve with the 2nd battalion 24th to the end of the war.

On 30th April, before daybreak, a combined movement was made by two small columns under Colonel Evelyn Wood, one beating the bush on the right side of the Zanyorkwe valley, in the direction of Intaba-ka-N'doda; the other, with the two seven-pounder guns moving towards the open ground to the westward, and a force of five companies 2nd battalion 24th, with four seven-pounder guns, under Lieutenant-Colonel Degacher, to occupy the ground where the guns were to be placed in position. Colonial troops were placed between the regulars. By 6.15 a.m. Colonel Degacher's force had occupied the heights around the Intaba-ka-N'doda. One of Colonel Wood's columns suffered some loss, having two officers and seven men killed and wounded. About 8 a.m. the flag signallers requested that "C" company, 2nd battalion 24th, which had been told off to follow the Frontier Light Horse to a ridge between the Zanyorkwe and Congo valleys, should be allowed to descend into the valley. This was granted, and "B" company was sent from Colonel Degacher's force to support it. Major Wilsone Black went with the latter. Together the companies worked their way up the opposite side, inflicting heavy loss on the enemy. On this occasion the Kaffir women facilitated the escape of the men by forming up in front of them, and thus preventing our men from firing. In his report on the day's operations, the general observed that " the Kaffirs fought with determination at " certain points, but the ground they endeavoured to hold was far too " extended for their force, and they were quite overweighted by the "presence of so many Europeans, as the ten companies present in the "field worked through the bush in the most creditable manner."

Some unimportant movements followed on the succeeding days; but it was soon discovered that the rebels had abandoned the Zanyorkwe valley for the Buffalo range. It was, therefore, decided to follow them up, and attack them on the plateau to the west of Buffalo Poort, where they had remained unmolested since 5th April. The battalion was now distributed as follows: "E" company, in charge of the guns at Baillie's Grave; "C," "G," and "H" companies, at a drift about three miles distant from Haynes' mill and two miles from a path, known as "Wood's path," which had been cut by "B," "C," "E," and "F" companies from the foot of the bush to the top of the plateau; "F" company, at Haynes' mill; "A" and "B" companies, at Isidengi, whence they were moved the day before the attack to Mount Kempt.

On 8th May, 1878, a column, under Colonel Wood, was to ascend from the Rabula river; a Colonial column was to move by the path near the mission station; whilst a third column, under Colonel Degacher, composed of two of the 24th companies from the drift and a Fingo corps, was to move up Wood's path. "A" and "B" companies, under Major Dunbar, were to operate from Mount Kempt with a column commanded by Major Buller, C.B. "G" company was to move on Haynes' Mill, replacing "F" company—which was to support Haynes' Fingoes in blocking "Buller's path," the only known outlet for the rebels. Owing to a mistake of the Fingo leader this was missed, whereby many rebels were subsequently enabled to escape.

The companies under Colonel Degacher paraded at 2 a.m. and marched to the foot of Wood's path. Here a long delay occurred, as the Fingoes did not arrive, and Major Black had to be sent after them. The excuse given by their commander was that the heavy rains of the preceding night had so chilled the men that they could not be got to move. (It is well known that the natives cannot stand cold or wet.) This caused the column to arrive on the plateau rather late, the delay being increased by the darkness and the dense overhanging bush, through which the column thrice lost its way. The plateau was driven as directed, and the columns met at a point to the eastward of it without finding any rebels. Here the Frontier Light Horse, from Mount Kempt, under their commander, Major Buller, C.B., crossed the front and entered Buller's path, supposed to be guarded by "F" company and Haynes' Fingoes. Soon afterwards heavy firing was heard, and a staff officer brought tidings that the Frontier Light Horse had been suddenly fired upon and had lost two officers and several men killed and wounded. The hospital stretchers of the 24th were asked for and sent up, with "H" company as a reinforcement. The entrance to the path was situated at the apex of an angle formed by precipitous cliffs, disguised by trees growing amidst the rocks on their sides, so that their tops presented the appearance of ordinary bush. On coming under fire, the company extended, so that its left touched the right of the Frontier Light Horse, and, led by its officers, charged past with a cheer into what was believed to be bush, but was brought up by an unseen krantz; the true entrance to the path, directly in front of the Frontier Light Horse, not having been pointed out. All engaged then laid down, and it was decided to wait till some Fingoes should turn the position; but before this could be done, some of the latter, mistaking the direction, got into the open and under fire, seeing which all jumped up simultaneously—Frontier Light Horse, 24th, and the rest—and the place was "rushed," the Frontier Light Horse losing one man in the meleé, as also did the Fingoes.

Whilst this was in progress "A" and "B" companies, under Major Dunbar, were actively engaged in carrying some of the Kaffir positions about the foot of Mount Kempt. On each occasion the enemy fled into an accessible bush. On 9th May, these companies again descended from Mount Kempt and drove the bush in the western part of the Buffalo Poort, on which occasion Captain Godwin-Austen, commanding "B" company, was slightly wounded.

This was the last combined movement made. The rebels were completely broken up, and it only remained to continue harassing them to prevent them reassembling in any number. With this object the battalion was posted as follows: "A" and "B" companies under Major Dunbar, at Mount Kempt; "F" company at Isidengi;

"C" company, Haynes' mill; "D," "E," and "H" companies, under Major Black, at Intaba-ka-N'doda, where they threw up an earthwork, called Fort Black. "G" company was ordered to Fort Glamorgan, East London, to relieve "D" company, under Captain Symons, which joined Major Black.

On 2nd June, 1878, Major Black, with "D" and "E" companies, was sent to the Gozo heights to relieve the 90th Light Infantry ordered to Natal. They remained there until the 9th July, experiencing much rough and bitterly cold weather, as also did the companies on Mount Kempt.

Early in June the veteran chief, Sandilli, was shot by a party of Fingoes whilst endeavouring to escape from the Buffalo Poort. His two sons being captured soon after, the Gaiekas were left without chiefs, and powerless for any serious mischief. Thus the Kaffir War of 1877-78 —the sixth—came to an end, and on 28th June, 1878, the Colonial Government proclaimed a general amnesty.

As a fitting conclusion to the foregoing events, the thanks of the Colonial House of Assembly were voted to the lieutenant-general commanding, and to the officers and men of the imperial Land and Naval forces engaged.

The positions held by the 2nd battalion 24th were one by one made over to the Colonial forces, and on 12th July, 1878, seven companies of the battalion were collected in camp on an open site in the Buffalo Poort bush, to refit after the hard work gone through. A week later a telegram arrived ordering the battalion to Natal, where war with Cetewayo, the Zulu king, was imminent.

Leaving the women and children and heavy baggage behind at King William's Town, the battalion—numbering twenty-one officers, five staff-sergeants, thirty-four sergeants, twenty-nine corporals, fifteen drummers, and six hundred and sixty-three privates—embarked by half battalions at East London on 24th and 26th July, and, landing at Durban, marched to Pietermaritzburg, arriving there on 6th August, 1878.

A small mounted troop, which had been formed under Lieutenant W. Sugden soon after the arrival of the battalion at the Cape, preceded it overland to Natal.

SERVICES OF THE MOUNTED INFANTRY OF THE REGIMENT.

The first mounted troop possessed by the regiment consisted of thirty-six men of the 1st battalion, under command of Lieutenant F. Carrington (the battalion instructor of musketry), and Lieutenant Dickinson. They received their horses, as before stated, at Hope Town in June, 1875. After much useful service at the Diamond Fields, the troop was broken up on the return of the 1st battalion from Griqualand in October, the same year.

Early in 1877 it was decided to form a corps of mounted infantry for service in South Africa, of which Lieutenant F. Carrington, 1st battalion 24th, was appointed commander. On 21st April that year Lieutenants F. Carrington and E. S. Browne, with a party of two sergeants, one drummer, and thirteen privates of 1st battalion, left Cape Town and—being joined by the men who had been mounted in Griqualand, and had been left on the Eastern Frontier on the return of the battalion to Cape Town—proceeded to Newcastle, Natal, where, with a like party of the Buffs, they were formed into a squadron of mounted infantry and sent into the Transvaal, then just annexed to the Cape. Whilst stationed at Victoria, Transvaal, in August, 1877, the mounted infantry was ordered to escort Sir Theophilus Shepstone in an official tour through the Transvaal and along the Zulu border, which lasted till November, when Lieutenant Carrington returned to the Cape to raise a volunteer force of cavalry there, which, under the names of Carrington's Horse and the Frontier Light Horse, served in the Transkei during the war of 1878. On Lieutenant Carrington's departure, Lieutenant E. S. Browne, 1st battalion 24th, assumed command of the mounted infantry in the Transvaal, which was augmented by forty men of the 80th regiment, and accompanied Sir Theophilus Shepstone to Pretoria.

In June, 1878, part of the squadron, including fifteen men of the 24th regiment, proceeded to the south-west border of the Transvaal with the Secretary for Native Affairs, and then joined the force under Colonel, afterwards Sir Edward, Lanyon, engaged in quelling a native rising in Griqualand West. In August, 1878, Lieutenant Browne returned to Pretoria, and proceeded in command of the remainder of the squadron into Sekukuni's country. The squadron remaining in Griqualand formed part of Colonel Lanyon's force in the operations in September-October, 1878, in the extreme north-east of Griqualand, during which it was frequently engaged with the natives, and took part in the decisive action at Galetza heights, where Private Power, 1st battalion 24th, distinguished himself.

The head-quarters of the squadron, under Lieutenant Browne, on the march to Sekukuni's country, were placed under the command of Major J. C. Russell, 12th Lancers, and were engaged in the reconnaissance in force, under Colonel Rowland, V.C., and in the action at Tolyani's Stadt. In December, 1878, the squadron moved to the Zulu border, and, having been reinforced by the detachment from Griqualand—under Lieutenant Davis, the Buffs—was attached to No. 3 column of Lord Chelmsford's army, under command of Colonel R. T. Glyn, C.B. It was present at the affair at Sirayo's kraal, and part of it was destroyed at Isandhlwana on 22nd January, 1879.

On the outbreak of the Kaffir war, in the autumn of 1877, a mounted troop was again formed in the 1st battalion, then at King William's Town, under command of Lieutenant Coghill, and afterwards of Lieutenant Clements. The troop was actively employed throughout the operations in the Transkei in 1877-78. On the arrival of the 2nd battalion in the country, a mounted detachment was likewise formed, which was employed, under Lieutenant W. Sugden, in the operations in the Perie bush in 1878 When the Kaffir war was over, seventeen of the mounted men of the 1st battalion and Lieutenant W Sugden's detachment of the 2nd battalion marched overland to Natal, with the column under Colonel Evelyn Wood. On the way, they were detained some time at Kokstadt, owing to the state of affairs in Pondoland. On the outbreak of the Zulu war they were attached to No. 1 column of Lord Chelmsford's army, under Colonel Pearson, the Buffs, with which they served in the action at Gingindhlovu, and in all the subsequent operations of that column.

The surviving portion of the squadron with Colonel Glyn's column, reinforced by a party of the 4th King's Own, in March, 1879, joined Brigadier-General Sir Evelyn Wood's force in the north of Zululand, and was present at the action of Inhlobani, 28th March, 1879, where Private Power again distinguished himself (he was granted the medal for distinguished conduct in the field), and at that of Kambula Hill on the following day. On the latter occasion the squadron fought on foot during the Zulu attack, and afterwards, mounting, took part in the pursuit. During this action Lieutenant E. S. Browne won his Victoria Cross. (See *Appendix A, Victoria Cross Roll.*) Reinforced by twenty men from the 1st battalion 24th, the squadron continued with Sir Evelyn Wood's column, and was present at the reconnaissance in force at Ulundi, 3rd July, 1879, the battle of Ulundi, and in all the subsequent movements of the force. The men rejoined their battalions at the end of the war.

CHAPTER XIII.

1878-79.

Services of the First and Second Battalions in the Zulu War—ISANDHLWANA—RORKE'S DRIFT—Re-formation of the First Battalion, and Services of both Battalions to the end of the War.

1878-79.

AFTER its arrival in Natal, in August, 1878, the 2nd battalion remained encamped for about three months at Pietermaritzburg, busily employed in drilling and refitting. Several field days took place under Lord Chelmsford (Lieutenant-General Honble. F. Thesiger), who at this time ordered the distance between files in attack formation to be doubled.*

War with the Zulu king Cetewayo being a foregone conclusion, and in point of fact a mere question of time, orders were issued for the troops to move gradually towards the frontier, more to allay the alarm among the border farmers than for any purpose of attack, as the preparations for any movement on our side were still incomplete in the extreme.

The first to start were "F," "G," and "H" companies of the 2nd battalion, under Major Black, which marched on 30th October, 1878, to Pott's Spruit, a farm in rear of the abandoned frontier-post of Fort Buckingham, on the Tugela.† The remainder of the battalion

---

* The fact that charging home in mass with the short stabbing *umkonto* (assegai), used for slaughtering cattle, was a special feature in Zulu tactics, and had been used with overpowering effect in the wars of extermination waged by the Zulus against neighbouring tribes during the preceding generation, appears to have been entirely ignored, although Native Irregulars were to form a considerable portion of the force to be sent into the field.

† Fort Buckingham was erected in 1861, where Cetewayo, then the leader of all the restless spirits in the Zulu nation, of which he was known as "the feet," (his father, the sagacious old Panda, being "the head") caused great alarm by appearing on the border with a large *impi* (army), afterwards alleged to have been a gigantic hunting-party. The post was intended to watch certain drifts on the Tugela, of which Middle Drift was the most important.

followed soon after, under Major Dunbar—Lieutenant-Colonel Degacher, C.B. having been appointed to command the Greytown district and frontier—and encamped at Greytown, where it was joined by N. 5. Royal Artillery, under Major Harness, the battery that had served with it in the Old Colony War.

In December, 1878, four companies of the 1st battalion, lately arrived from Kaffraria, marched through Greytown, for Helpmakaar, a high plateau of great extent overlooking the junction of the Blood and Buffalo rivers, Rorke's Drift in the latter, and a wide expanse of Zulu territory. Opposite to it was the Ingutu mountain, on which was the kraal of the Chief Sirayo, one of Cetewayo's principal men, whose sons had given much umbrage to the Natal Government by a raid into the colony after some runaway women. To this position the 2nd battalion, under Lieutenant-Colonel Degacher, C.B. soon followed, together with Harness' battery, Royal Artillery. A column was formed at Helpmakaar, under Colonel R. T. Glyn, C.B., 1st battalion 24th regiment, to which Lord Chelmsford attached himself with his staff.

The plan of invasion comprised four columns of attack, the common objective of which was Cetewayo's chief kraal Ulundi, which, as the bracketed distances below indicate, was about equidistant from the several points of rendezvous.

1st Column.—Colonel Pearson, 3rd Buffs, commanding: 2nd battalion Buffs, six companies 99th Foot, a Naval Brigade with a Gatling gun, four seven-pounder guns Royal Artillery, a company Royal Engineers, a squadron Mounted Infantry, some Natal Volunteers, and a Native contingent, to penetrate to Ulundi (fifty-five miles) by the most direct line from Fort Williamson, near the mouth of the Tugela, where a bridge of boats was thrown across.

2nd Column.—Colonel Anthony Durnford, Royal Engineers, commanding: Colonial Zulus, with a rocket detachment Royal Artillery, to enter Zululand by Middle Drift (forty-five miles).

3rd Column.—Colonel R. T. Glyn, C.B., 1st battalion 24th, commanding: Seven companies 1st battalion 24th, the whole eight companies of the 2nd battalion 24th, Harness' battery Royal Artillery, a squadron of Mounted Infantry, the Natal Mounted Police and Volunteers, and two battalions of Colonial Zulus under European officers and non-commissioned officers; in all about four thousand three hundred men. Of the 1st battalion 24th four only out of the seven companies were at first with the column, one company remaining at Helpmakaar, and two others being still at Durban at the close of the year.*

4th Column.—Colonel Evelyn Wood, V.C., C.B., 90th Light Infantry, commanding: 1st battalion 13th Light Infantry, 90th Light Infantry, six seven-pounder guns Royal Artillery, and Colonial Levies: to move from Conference Hill (fifty-five miles) into the town of Utrecht, in the Transvaal, as its base.

As before stated, Colonel Durnford's column consisted exclusively of natives. The other three were about equal in Europeans, but the 1st and 3rd were strongest in point of numbers, having more natives attached to them.

The actual strength of the 3rd Column, under Colonel Glyn, C.B., was: Staff and Departments, twenty; Royal Artillery, with six seven-pounder guns and two rocket-batteries, one hundred and thirty-two; Infantry, one thousand two hundred and seventy-five; Cavalry, three hundred and twenty; Native Contingent, two thousand five hundred and sixty-six; conductors, drivers, voorloopers, etc., three hundred and forty-six. Total, four thousand six hundred and fifty-nine officers and men. Besides the troop and battery horses, there were with the column forty nine horses, sixty-seven mules, one thousand five hundred and seven draught-oxen, two hundred and twenty Cape waggons, and eighty-two carts.

Cetewayo had received an ultimatum, in which he was desired to comply with certain demands on the part of our Government—one being the disbanding of his army—under threats of an invasion of his territories by a certain date; but, as it was well known there was not the slightest prospect of the ultimatum being accepted, the 3rd column

---

* These two companies, Brevet Major Upcher's and Captain Mostyn's, marched from Durban for Pietermaritzburg early in January, 1879. Mostyn's company marched into Isandhlwana camp on 21st January, as related on a subsequent page. Upcher's followed, and went to Helpmakaar.

moved down to Rorke's Drift, where Rorke's Farm, the only building in the immediate neighbourhood standing under the Oscarberg or 'Tsiyane Hill, was appropriated as a commissariat depôt and base hospital, and "B" company 2nd battalion 24th, under Lieutenant Gonville Bromhead, told off to guard it.

Two ponts, or ferries, were established in the river a little above the drift, of size sufficient to carry over one of the large Cape waggons or a company of infantry at a time. The spans (ox-teams) and mounted men were to cross by the drift. These ponts were not quite ready—nor indeed was anything else—but, as the 11th January, 1879, was the date fixed by the ultimatum for the commencement of hostilities, it was decided to cross the Buffalo River on that day.*

The operation was carried on as follows:—On the Natal side, where the pontoons were constructed, a ledge of rocks rises to a height of fifty feet, commanding the opposite side for a considerable distance. Along this ledge the troops were drawn up before break of day, and the guns placed in position; a thick fog obscuring the view long after the sun had risen. A party of mounted infantry crossed first, then the four companies 1st battalion 24th; the Native battalions and the remainder of the troops followed; the 2nd battalion 24th, with the artillery, being kept on the ledge to cover the passage of the force. The 2nd battalion 24th soon followed, and each company on crossing took up the formation of the 1st battalion 24th, and opened, fan like, till a large semicircle was formed, with the flanks resting on the river. By night time the camp had been formed in Zululand; a native battalion on the right, then the mounted men and artillery in the centre, other two battalions 24th and a Native battalion on the left.

---

* Before leaving Helpmakaar, an incident took place which was afterwards remembered with melancholy interest by the officers of the 2nd battalion:—The officers of the 1st battalion having a few bottles of wine left, invited those of the 2nd battalion to dine with them, and, it being close to the 13th January, the thirtieth anniversary of the battle of Chillianwallah, where the 1st battalion suffered so severely, two of the officers, Captain Wm. Degacher and Lieutenant Porteous, proposed a toast: "That we may not get into such a mess, and have better luck this time." The toast was drunk. Only a few days later, not one of the 1st battalion 24th who drank the toast was left alive, and five officers of the 2nd battalion had also been killed.

After the waggons for the infantry had got over it was too late for the guns, which crossed next day. The work was most fatiguing. The officers and men were kept toiling at the pontoons under a broiling sun until late in the afternoon before they got any food, and even then the waggons had not all been brought over, and the work had to be continued late into the night and on the following day. The column remained in this camp some days, patrolling, reconnoitring, and waiting for the completion of the preparations for the advance—preparations which were still further delayed by the heavy rains, of which the hot burning sun and fog of the day of crossing were a sure prelude. It was the beginning of the rainy season, and many delays from this cause and the utter want of roads were to be expected.

On 12th January, 1879, the first fight of the war took place. It was a small affair directed against the Ingutu Mountain, or, as it was familiarly known to the troops, Sirayo's kraal. The clearing of this mountain was necessary, as it completely blocked the road to Ulundi, and, like most hills in South Africa, having sharp precipitous sides, or krantzes, and a table-land summit, it formed quite a natural fortress. The Bashee flows along its western base—an insignificant stream, fordable everywhere when not in flood—and joins the Buffalo a few miles below Rorke's Drift. The attack was to be made by the 1st battalion 24th, under Captain Wm. Degacher, and a Native battalion under Major Black, 2nd battalion 24th, attached to it for the day, who were to ascend the eastern shoulder of the hill, whilst the 2nd battalion 24th, under Lieutenant-Colonel Degacher, with another Native battalion, swept round the westernmost base of the mountain and came in front of Sirayo's kraal. The kraal is not on the mountain proper, but upon a rocky knoll at its foot, nearly shut in by steep krantzes all round. Lord Chelmsford, who had come round from Major Black's party, ordered the troops to form line and scramble up the steep sides of the knoll. This had to be done, but on reaching the top the kraal was found to be abandoned. It was looted and burnt, and the troops returned to camp. About thirty of the enemy had been killed, including one of the chief's sons. On our side the loss was one man of the Native contingent, besides a few wounded. It was afterwards discovered that the 1st battalion 24th had worked up to the edge of the krantz overlooking the kraal, and, knowing it to have been abandoned, were indulging in good-natured chaff at the energy displayed by their comrades of the 2nd battalion.

As there was found to be very heavy marshy ground in the valley of Bashee, through which the advance would have to be conducted, Major Dunbar was sent on ahead, on the 16th January, with the four left-wing companies of the 2nd battalion 24th and some Native pioneers to construct a road and make a depôt of firewood, the country ahead being destitute of fuel. The detachment was ordered to encamp on the far side of the river, close under a krantz of Sirayo's Mountain, a dangerous position as was thought at the time, and particularly on the 19th January, when Captain Symons, 2nd battalion 24th, rode out to warn Lieutenant-Colonel Degacher, who was in command of the picquets, that the General had received reliable information that three Zulu *impis* (armies) had left Ulundi to attack the column, and that he must be very careful of his right flank.

This information did not delay the intended advance on the following day. On 20th January, 1879, about 8 a.m., No. 3 column marched from Rorke's Drift for Isandhlwana Hill, a distance of about nine miles. The camp was formed at the foot of Isandhlwana Hill, between 2 and 3 p.m., and at 5 o'clock the same evening the four companies 2nd battalion 24th, under Major Black, came into the camp from the Bashee Valley. The drifts and gradients between the Buffalo and Isandhlwana were alike bad, and there were repeated breakdowns owing to overloading of the waggons, in spite of the repeated orders issued on the subject. As it would have been impossible for the rear of the column to have reached the camping ground the same night without leaving many waggons behind, permission was obtained for this portion to halt on the last rise before descending to a small mountain stream which runs past the foot of Isandhlwana Hill towards the Buffalo River. An awkward drift in this little stream was stopping the waggons. A camp was therefore formed beside a small kraal on the left of the road, which, like all Zulu kraals, was surrounded by a stone fence, and would not have made a bad defensive post. Here a company of the 1st battalion 24th, under Captain Mostyn and Lieutenants Daly and Anstey, came up on their way to join their battalion. They were in high spirits; had had a long march that day and dreadful roads up country; feared they would not be in time; but, "Thank goodness, here we are at last," Captain Mostyn said. As the drift was blocked, they pitched their camp with the rear guard for the night, and marched into Isandhlwana camp with it next morning, 21st January. The number of companies of the 1st battalion with No. 3 column was thus raised to five. Brevet Lieutenant-Colonel Pulleine, who had joined the column from Pietermaritzburg a few days previously, took over the command of the 1st battalion from Captain Degacher.

ISANDHLWANA.

The camp at Isandhlwana—Isandula it was called in the public prints of the time—which was destined to acquire so tragic a place in the regimental annals, must now be briefly described.

On leaving the little stream before mentioned, the track ascends steeply till it crosses a rocky neck of land connecting the Isandhlwana Hill with a small *kopjie* or rocky knoll—afterwards known as Black's Kopjie. Isandhlwana Hill itself is of remarkable shape, small in size by comparison with the hills round about, but standing out well from its surroundings; it has been likened in form to a couchant lion. From the officers of the 1st battalion 24th it received the *sobriquet* of the "Little Sphynx," owing to its striking resemblance to the regimental badge. The camp was pitched along the eastern declivity and extended across the road, the tents of the 1st battalion 24th being on the eastern slope of Black's Kopjie; next on their left, but on the other side of the road, those of the mounted infantry, mounted police, and volunteers; then the Royal Artillery with six guns; next to them the tents of the 2nd battalion 24th, and on the extreme left the two battalions of the 3rd Natal Native Contingent. The tents of each corps were pitched in front of its waggons. The hospital and head-quarters' tents were a little in rear of the waggons of the mounted troops and artillery. The camp thus faced the Izipezi Hill, having a fine slope in front intersected by water courses, wet and dry, and with broken ground on the flanks. Its line of picquets extended from a spur of the Ingutu range on its left to the right rear of Black's Kopjie on its right.

Good as this position might have been against European troops, compelled by the nature of the ground to operate from the open in front, it afforded no protection whatever against Zulus, accustomed from childhood to bound from crag to crag and to charge up hill with an agility surprising to Europeans, and to whom, therefore, the rocky broken ground on the flanks was no more serious obstacle than a ploughed field to our soldiers at home. This opinion was shared at the time by officers of the regiment and others. A field-officer of the 2nd battalion 24th, being on duty with the picquets on 21st January, expressed his strong misgivings to the staff-officer whose duty it was to point out the ground to be occupied, and remarked that the broken ground was no protection, and that there was not even a picquet in rear. " Well, sir," was the answer, " if you are " nervous, we will put a picquet of the pioneers there."* This picquet was posted on the road leading over the neck, but is believed to have withdrawn before morning and not replaced, as when the 2nd battalion 24th marched out of camp on the 22nd all the native pioneers were taken to make the track passable for the guns. It should be said that the staff-officer referred to was himself not satisfied with the position ; he spoke in its favour only from a sense of his official position, and afterwards said that never in all his life had he experienced so strong a presentiment of coming evil as on that day and the following morning (22nd January) when he left the camp for the front.

On the night of 21st January the picquets were posted as follows : covering the right flank and resting on the slope of Black's Kopjie was a company of the 1st battalion 24th, under Lieutenant Hodson.

---

* The same day the late Lieutenant and Adjutant Melvill, 1st battalion 24th, remarked to the field-officer above mentioned, who was looking out to the front : " I know what you are thinking of by your face, sir ; you are abusing this camp, and you are quite right ! These Zulus will charge home, and with our small numbers we ought to be in laager, or, at any rate, be prepared to stand shoulder to shoulder."

"G" company 2nd battalion 24th, under Lieutenant Pope,* then took up the line, and its sentries extended nearly to the front of the Royal Artillery camp; from this point round to the left the front was covered by Native Contingent picquets, the ground there not being so good for defence as on the right, where a ledge of rocks was pointed out to Lieutenant Pope as affording a capital position against an enemy approaching from the front or right front.

Both the 24th companies were strongly posted, provided always they were not attacked from the rear or left rear over the neck, which, from the nature of the enemy, was just as likely as not; indeed, in the end the camp was so attacked. It appears that the 24th picquets were replaced by mounted videttes at 4 a.m., on the 22nd instant.† The native picquets‡ were pushed forward in the daytime as far as the

---

* This was the only company of the 2nd battalion 24th on duty on the night of 21st January. It was to have been relieved next morning by "H" company of the same battalion, but owing to the orders received in the middle of the night "H" company marched out with the rest of the battalion before dawn on the 22nd, and the ill-fated "G" company was never relieved, although withdrawn into camp at 4 a.m.

† MS. Diary of Lieutenant Pope, 2nd battalion 24th, afterwards found on the field of battle.

‡ These native battalions were not much to be trusted, for not only was the colonial Zulu, bred in the midst of Natal civilisation, a much tamer animal than Cetewayo's warriors, but he was mistrustful of his stranger officers with whom he had been but a very short time associated. A few of these officers had served in the regular army, but the greater part were new to their work. The non-commissioned-officers were, as a rule, bad, and it would have been better to do without them altogether. In the first place, being on foot, they could not be expected to keep up over long distances that their mounted officers and the nimble native soldiers could traverse, and in their speed over rough ground lay the chief value of these levies. Again, as a body of men they were objectionable. It having been determined to give the natives some kind of European drill, old soldiers were sought for, and the first comer that could show that he had served in the regular army was accepted; character was not much looked to, with the consequence that the natives, who have a very high appreciation of the way a white man conducts himself, had often very bad examples set before them. A mistake was also made in attempting European drill instead of the tribal organisation that had acted well in previous frontier alarms. Their officers never expected them to stand a shock; if used as scouts or, in pursuit, as a kind of light cavalry, they would have done good service, especially if led by their own magistrates or Europeans whom they knew, and under their own headmen. The native races of South Africa readily follow white men whom they know and respect.

Ingutu Hill, where the enemy first appeared on the following morning; by night they were drawn nearer, forming a semicircle round the native camp and resting on the slopes of Isandhlwana Hill. The distance of the picquets from camp was about half-a-mile, but on the left it was much more.

On the same day (21st January) Major Dartnell had been sent out with his natives and the Natal Mounted Volunteers, and Commandant Lonsdale with two native battalions, to examine some ground to the south-east of the camp, near a stronghold known as Matyana's kraal. These officers took different directions, but met in the evening and proposed to bivouac together, a day's provisions having been sent out to them from camp. From their bivouac, at the eastern extremity of the N'dhlazgazi range, so large a number of Zulus were seen towards sunset on a range of hills, to the eastward, which culminates in the Izipezi Mountain, and may be called the Izipezi range, that Dartnell sent a note to camp saying they considered the forces at their disposal too small to attack, unless reinforced by two or three companies of the 24th in the morning. This decided the course of events on the morrow.

At 1.30 a.m. on 22nd January, 1879, a staff-officer came to Lieutenant-Colonel Degacher with an order for the 2nd battalion 24th to be under arms by daybreak. The men were to be roused without noise or lights, and were to turn out in light-marching order with one day's preserved rations. Four guns Royal Artillery, the Mounted Infantry, and Native Pioneers were warned for the same time.

Accordingly, at 4 a.m., "A," "C," "D," "E," "F," and "H" companies 2nd battalion 24th, with the 1st battalion 3rd Natal Native Contingent, the mounted troops, and four guns, the whole under Colonel Glyn, C.B., 1st battalion 24th, marched out of Isandhlwana camp on a very dark morning and took the direction of the Izipezi Hill. Left behind were "G" company 2nd battalion 24th, which was on picquet, with its officers, Lieutenants Pope and Godwin-Austen; also Quarter-Master Bloomfield, Quarter-Master-Sergeant Davis, and the non-commissioned officers and men on guard, on duty, or in hospital, making a total of three officers, two staff-sergeants, six sergeants, and one hundred and fifty-eight men of the 2nd battalion. Besides the above, Bandmaster Bullard and four boys were left behind. All the bandsmen had been detailed to remain, but at the last moment were ordered out with every available stretcher, the commanding-officer being informed that Lord Chelmsford had directed that no ambulances should accompany the force. The ambulances, two in number, nevertheless went out. It was to this chance that the bandsmen of the battalion owed their lives. The colours of the Second Battalion were unfortunately left in the camp; for not only was the battalion short of officers, but experience gained in the Kaffir war had proved how impossible it was to take the colours when out bush-fighting or scaling krantzes, and on some such expedition the column was supposed to be bound.

The base of the hill, on which the Zulus had been seen, was reached about 6 a.m., and here—the ground being much intersected by dongas (water courses) and rocks—the four guns had to be left, Major Black, with two companies 24th, remaining with them as escort. The natives were sent straight up the hill; the Mounted Police and Volunteers went round to the southern side; whilst the four remaining companies 2nd battalion 24th, following Lord Chelmsford, wound round the northern base, halting and resting on a neck connecting the hill attacked with a smaller one to the north. The Zulus retired as the natives advanced, and were soon retreating up a valley in a north-easterly direction towards the Ingutu Mountain; in point of fact, they were wheeling round to join in attacking the camp. The mounted men were sent after them; and two companies, under Major Dunbar, were ordered to support the police and natives, who were engaged but could make no headway.

About 9 a.m. a mounted police orderly rode up to where the general stood and delivered a despatch; having done which and answered a few questions, he rode off to where the two companies 2nd battalion 24th were resting, and began talking to the men. Colonel Degacher noticing that the news he communicated to them caused great excitement, asked the cause, and was told: "He says, "sir, that the camp is being surrounded and attacked!" This was startling intelligence; but as there was no stir among the staff or sign of anything unusual, the men were told not to let the police orderly chaff them, as, if true, " We should all be marching back as fast as we " could." The men, however, were much impressed, believing that the orderly on his way had seen more than was reported in the despatch.

The despatch was from Lieutenant-Colonel Pulleine: " Report " just come in that the Zulus are advancing in force from the left " front of the camp." Lord Chelmsford evidently did not attach much importance to the information, as he was content with sending two officers with a telescope to the top of a neighbouring hill, to reconnoitre towards the camp. These officers reported that all seemed quiet; and Lord Chelmsford soon after gave the order that the troops should not return to camp, but bivouac for the night. A few officers were ordered back to make the necessary arrangements, among whom was Sub-Lieutenant Griffith, 2nd battalion 24th, doing duty as a commissariat officer.

It must be remembered that the men had been called up at 1.30 a.m. on an intensely dark night, and as no lights were allowed to be struck, all their small belongings, of such comfort to a soldier campaigning, were of necessity scattered about the tents. They had brought with them only their ball-bags, haversacks, and water-bottles; and to collect and pack all the articles left behind in the camp—the epuipment of a battalion—there were only the company left on picquet and a few stray men. Whilst discussing how the order was to be carried out with as little confusion and loss to the men as possible, Lieutenant and Adjutant Dyer, 2nd battalion 24th, remarked that he had perhaps better ride back with Lieutenant Griffith and help the quarter-master. So the two young officers rode away, and rode to their death.

Griffith, a young officer, thoughtful beyond his years, took a gloomy view of matters. From his serving in, and indeed being quite a leading spirit with, the Commissariat, none knew better than he the incompleteness of the arrangements, owing to the badness of the roads, and the precariousness of the supplies at this, the rainy, season. Besides, all had heard the "reliable information" about the three Zulu *impis*. Now an *impi* represents ten thousand men. It was the fashion at the time to deride the Zulu formation of attack; but it is difficult to understand why this was so, except for the English propensity to underrate our enemies, especially those with black skins. Their formation seemed well-adapted to our modern idea of tactics. It consisted of what the Zulus termed the *horns*, the *chest*, and the *body* of the army, corresponding with our wings, support, and reserve. It was the duty of the horns—which really took the shape of horns, converging inwards—to circle round the flanks of the enemy, only a few men forming the points of the horns, which gradually increased to ten, twelve, or more at the base. The enemy once encompassed by the horns, the chest advanced in open, but deep, order; then followed the body in a dense mass, with crushing effect. When one reflects, besides, how reckless of life the Zulus were reputed to be, it is difficult to conceive why the formation was held so cheap; but so it was.

About 10 a.m., one of the Native battalions, under Commandant Browne, arrived near the place where the head-quarter staff had halted. It was ordered to return to Isandhlwana camp; at the same time an order was sent to Lieutenant-Colonel Harness, Royal Artillery, to march with his guns and escort towards the proposed bivouacing ground. A little later, the general proceeded over the high ground to the other side of the hill, where Major Dartnell had been skirmishing with some of Matyani's tribe, with the intention of forming a fresh camp near the Amangene stream. The two companies left with Colonel Degacher joined the two under Major Dunbar about noon, to find that fighting with Matyani's people was over. The police had killed about thirty of the enemy, and more had been despatched by the Native contingent, who had worked through the different caves and hiding-places in the hill-sides. The four companies then rested a good half-hour, for the way had been long since morning, the hill steep, and the day intensely hot. They then followed the general, who with his staff was seen in the distance.

Lord Chelmsford reached the site he had selected for the new camp about 1 p.m. (about which hour the camp at Isandhlwana was carried by the Zulus.) Soon after his arrival he received a report from a native that the Zulus were near Isandhlwana Hill, and that heavy firing was taking place. On this, Lord Chelmsford and his staff galloped to the top of an adjoining hill, whence the camp was visible; but, seeing the tents standing and all apparently quiet, concluded that the report, like a previous one received from a native source, was unfounded.

About 2 p.m. Lord Chelmsford, with the mounted volunteers, started on his return to Isandlhwana, leaving Colonel Glyn to command the new camp. The four companies 2nd battalion 24th, under Lientenant-Colonel Degacher, had arrived at the new camping ground about three-quarters of an hour, when Major Harness, Royal Artillery, came in with his guns and the escort of 2nd battalion 24th, under Major Black, who went straight to the commanding officer, saying, "Colonel, have you heard the news? They say the camp is attacked and surrounded! We were well on our way to help them; but they have brought us back here."* There was no time for explanation, for Major Gosset, aide-de-camp to Lord Chelmsford, was seen galloping in, and by 4.15 p.m. all were marching back to Isandhlwana as hard as their legs would carry them. It would be impossible, wrote one who was of the party, to describe the anxiety felt by all ranks; how eyes were strained towards the camp, how long those thirteen miles seemed, although the men marched splendidly, racing over the ground.

It appears that soon after Lord Chelmsford left the Amangene bivouac, he met Colonel Russell returning with the mounted infantry from an unsuccessful pursuit of the retreating Zulus earlier in the day. The combined party moved leisurely on, when another

---

* It appears that Colonel Harness had orders to take his guns to the new camping ground by an easier route than was followed by the troops. On the way, he received a message from Commandant Browne: "Come in every man, for God's sake! The camp is surrounded, and will be taken unless helped at once." On receipt of this message, Harness, who had previously noticed shells bursting in the air in the direction of Isandhlwana, about 12 noon, indicating that the two guns left in camp there were "in action," felt bound to start back without delay. He had got about one-and-a-half miles on his way, when a peremptory order from Lord Chelmsford compelled him to retrace his steps to the bank of the Amangene.

It was afterwards learned that when the shells were seen, the two guns in camp were throwing shrapnell into a large mass of the enemy, which appeared almost stationary, about three thousand four hundred yards away on the left front of the camp.

message was received from Commandant Browne, saying that "there "was a large body of the enemy between him and the camp." This did not occasion more uneasiness than former reports and warnings, as from the summits of different neighbouring hills, at various times during the day and almost within the last half-hour, the camp had been seen with tents standing, and all apparently quiet. Commandant Browne's battalion was picked up on the road, and the force again proceeded on its way, the mounted men leading.

About 3.30 p.m., when some five miles from Isandhlwana Hill, a solitary horseman was seen in the distance. This proved to be Commandant Lonsdale. Having to return on duty to the camp, he had ridden up unsuspectingly within ten yards of the tents shortly before, when he had suddenly been fired upon, and escaped as by a miracle. The men he had seen in the camp in red coats proved to be Zulus arrayed in the clothing of the defenders. The camp was in the hands of the enemy.

Lord Chelmsford at once despatched Major Gosset to bring up Colonel Glyn's force from the Amangene, and forming the Native battalion with the men with rifles in the front rank, and the mounted Europeans as a third rank in rear, he moved on a couple of miles further, and there halted to await the arrival of Colonel Glyn's men, who came up about 6.30 p.m.

The 2nd battalion 24th had now marched some twenty-three miles, the last nine of which had been covered by it in two hours; for it was 4.5 p.m. when the order to return was given to Colonel Glyn, and allowing fifteen minutes for the men to get on their accoutrements and fall in, to collect water parties, etc., it must have been 4.20 p.m. at the least, or perhaps nearer the half hour, when the order to march off was given. Lord Chelmsford was found on low ground, by a small stream, where the men hurriedly filled their water-bottles. He addressed a few words to them. "Whilst we were "skirmishing in front," he said, "the Zulus have taken our camp. "There are ten thousand Zulus in our rear, and twenty thousand in "our front; we must win back our camp to-night, and cut our way "back to Rorke's Drift to-morrow." And the men answered, with a cheer, "All right, sir; we'll do it."

When the general ceased speaking, preparations were made for the advance. The mounted men were sent to the front; the guns were kept in the centre, on the track, with a half-batttalion of the 2nd battalion 24th on either side of them; the two Native battalions were placed on the outer flanks. In this formation, at about 6.30 p.m., the troops resumed the advance, the infantry moving by fours from the left of companies, at company intervals, so as to be ready at once to form line. At 7 p.m. they were still two miles from the camp, and darkness was coming on rapidly; unfortunately there was no moon, and with the declining light the difficulties of the march increased; men and horses kept falling into dongas and over rocks, and the Native battalions made matters worse, despite the efforts of their officers, by crushing in on the troops as if for protection. These men were now a positive source of danger, as on the first sign of an enemy they would certainly have broken up any formation taken by the battalion, and friend and foe would have been undistinguishable. By this time it was so dark that the mounted men were called in and formed in two bodies in rear of the infantry.

By 7.45 p.m., but half-a-mile separated the column from the camp. Nought could be seen but the outlines of the hills—the Sphynx-like form of Isandhlwana—the neck of Black's Kopjie—standing out in bold relief against the sky; and at their base, impenetrable darkness. A halt was made; the infantry formed line and fixed bayonets. The death-like silence around was soon broken by Harness' guns firing shrapnel against the neck and Black's Kopjie. But no war-cry came—no answering shot; nought but the rolling echoes of our own guns. The advance was then resumed to within three hundred yards of the camp, when another halt was ordered, and the battalion fired a few random volleys into the darkness without eliciting a reply. The left half-battalion, under Major Black, was sent straight to its front to occupy Black's Kopjie, and to give a cheer as a signal this had been done. Soon came the cheer, and the line again advanced towards its night's resting place on the ridge of the neck, crossing an angle of the camp in so doing, stumbling and treading over the debris and worse; but the before unwelcome darkness now hid all details.

To some who had heard them, came back the words uttered before the war by an old frontier Boer who had fought against the Zulus in his youth:—"God save you, sir," said he, "from ever seeing a "camp or homestead sacked by Zulus."*

What happened in Isandhlwana camp while the 2nd battalion was away with Lord Chelmsford on the fatal 22nd January, 1879, must now be told. As but six men of the 1st battalion 24th escaped the massacre, the details in possession of the regiment are necessarily meagre in the extreme.

The troops left in the camp that morning consisted of "A," "C," "E," "F," and "H" companies 1st battalion 24th; "G" company and a few details 2nd battalion 24th, two guns and seventy men Royal Artillery, thirty men of the Mounted Infantry, eight Mounted Volunteers and Police, two companies 1st battalion 3rd Natal Native Contingent, two companies 2nd battalion 3rd Natal Native Contingent, and ten Native pioneers.

On 11th January, 1879, Colonel Anthony Durnford, Royal Engineers, commanding No. 2 column, which was to enter Zululand by Middle Drift, received orders from Lord Chelmsford to move with his Mounted Basutos, Rocket Battery, and a battalion of Native Contingent to Rorke's Drift, to be prepared to follow No. 3 column. He encamped at Rorke's Drift, on the left bank of the Buffalo, on 21st January, and there, at 6 a.m. on the 22nd, received further orders to advance at once with all his mounted men and the rocket battery to Isandhlwana Camp, and, as senior officer, take over the command. The camp was meanwhile in charge of Major and Brevet Lieutenant-Colonel Pulleine, 1st battalion 24th.

After the departure of the 2nd battalion 24th, at 4.30 that morning, nothing occurred until 8 a.m., when a report reached

---

* It is only just to the Zulus to say that they used no torture. They gave no quarter—slaying outright every living thing they came across; but no single case of torture was proved against them. The wild stories current at the time, and repeated in the English papers, were untrue.

Colonel Pulleine, from a mounted party about two thousand yards to the north-east of the camp, that three columns of Zulus were approaching the camp from the north-east. The men fell in in front of the 2nd battalion 24th camp, and Colonel Pulleine then sent off the despatch by the police orderly before mentioned, which reached Lord Chelmsford at 9.30 a.m. The Zulus retired almost immediately, one of the columns passing out of sight towards the north-west.

About 10 a.m., Colonel Durnford and his party arrived in camp. Hearing that Zulus had been seen in the neighbourhood, Colonel Durnford at once proposed to attack them. Colonel Pulleine strongly protested against such a course as contrary to the written instructions he had received, which were to remain in camp and to defend it if attacked.* According to the testimony of a special-service officer who was present, and afterwards escaped from the camp, Colonel Pulleine went into his tent and brought out his written orders, to which Colonel Durnford demurred, so far as to say, " Well, my idea is, that wherever Zulus appear, we ought to attack. I " will go alone, but, remember, if I get into difficulties, I shall rely on " you to support me." Colonel Durnford then despatched one of his own troop of natives to protect his waggons, which had not yet come in; two companies of Native Levies and some mounted Basutos under Lieutenant Raw and Captain Barton (with which went Captain Shepstone, political agent with Colonel Durnford), were sent to reconnoitre the heights to the north of the camp, whilst Durnford himself, with his two remaining troops of Natives, the Rocket Battery, and a company of Native Infantry as escort for the latter, descended into the plain in front of the camp, with the intention, it is thought, of creating a diversion in favour of Lord Chelmsford, who was supposed to be engaged somewhere in front.

Before starting Colonel Durnford directed a company 1st battalion 24th to occupy the heights fifteen hundred yards to the north of the camp. This was the first fatal error, leading, as it ultimately did, to

---

* On the best hearsay authority, these "written instructions" were to the following effect: "You will be in command of the camp during the absence of Colonel Glyn; draw in your line of defence while the force is out, and draw in your infantry outposts accordingly, but keep your cavalry videttes well advanced."

the further scattering of the scanty force of defenders. About noon, as the men were preparing for dinner, firing was heard on the height where this outlying company, which was under command of Lieutenant Cavaye, had been posted. It appeared that, after marching three or four miles and ascending some high ground, Lieutenant Raw and his Basutos had sighted a Zulu *impi*, about a mile off, in line and extending its left. The Basutos fell back gradually. Whilst the main body of the impi made direct for Isandhlwana, its right horn pushed on towards the head of a valley to the northward of the hills on the left of the camp, and, crossing a neck which connects these hills with the Ingutu ranges, began to descend into a valley to the west of this neck, where it came within range of Cavaye's company, which was overlooking the valley, and opened fire on them at eight hundred yards. The Zulus, however, did not turn aside to attack the company, but streamed on, to carry out their usual encircling tactics. Captain Shepstone, leaving Raw and his men, returned to camp to report to Colonel Pulleine, who objected to detaching more men from the camp; but, on Captain Shepstone saying, " I assure you affairs are very serious," he agreed to send out Captain Mostyn's company, which climbed the heights, and extended along the crest between the main body of Cavaye's company and a detached section under Lieutenant Dyson, posted five hundred yards to its left. The line was prolonged to the right by a company of natives. They were scarcely in position when the two companies were ordered to fall back, as the Zulus were menacing the front of the camp. Mostyn's and Cavaye's companies descended the hill and halted on nearing Captain Younghusband's company, which had been sent to their support, and which was now in echelon with them on their left; all three companies in extended order, facing northward, towards the hill from which Mostyn and Cavaye had retreated, at about four hundred yards from it. This was somewhere about 12.30 p.m. Colonel Pulleine had thus one-half his infantry a thousand yards away from the camp, through the necessity of supporting a company that ought not to have been sent out. Masses of Zulus, who had swarmed quickly up the hill, were now half-way down the slope, and still working round to the westward. The companies

s

were firing volleys, and Cavaye's ammunition was running short. Wardell's and Porteous' companies 1st battalion 24th, and Lieutenant Pope's, 2nd battalion 24th, were extended in front of the camp, facing east, the two guns being on their left front and the mounted men on their right front.

Whilst this was going on, Colonel Durnford, with his mounted men, had outstripped his rocket battery, and ascending a ridge away to the left front of the camp, had advanced a mile beyond it, when intelligence was brought to him by two Natal carabineers that a large force of Zulus was endeavouring to surround him. Soon the enemy came in sight. Durnford's men commenced a retreat in good order, firing by alternate troops, which continued for about two miles, when they came on the remains of the rocket battery which had been surprised by a body of Zulus, who, springing suddenly from a donga (watercourse) a hundred yards away, fired a volley which disposed of the native escort and frightened the mules. A hand-to-hand fight followed, in which Major Russell, Royal Artillery, five out of the eight Europeans, and all the mule drivers were killed. The struggle was still going on when Durnford arrived on the scene. Continuing his retreat, and opening fire on all favourable ground, Durnford finally made a decided stand at the watercourse, in front of the camp, where he was reinforced by the mounted men from the camp.

It was now close upon 1 p.m., and, so far as can be ascertained, the troops in camp occupied the following positions:—On the left, facing the north, Younghusband's, Mostyn's, and Cavaye's companies extended in the order already stated. Two companies of natives were extended on Cavaye's right front, and near them were the guns, firing towards the east. To the right of the guns was one company 1st battalion 24th, in extended order, facing east; the remaining company 1st battalion 24th filled up the space between this and the company 2nd battalion 24th under Lieutenant Pope, which was extended in front of their camp, also facing east and across the waggon track. Further on, and rather in advance, was Durnford's party.

The pressure on the right flank was not so great as on the left, being kept back by the fire of the mounted men; but on the left the defenders were forced back, and had to take up a fresh position about three hundred yards from the camp. This movement, although it concentrated the regulars, left the natives rather more exposed at the angle of the position taken up by the 24th. The camp was in the same state as the troops had left it when the 2nd battalion 24th marched out that morning, wholly without defence. Soon after the firing had begun, Captain Alan Gardner, 14th Hussars, brought an order from Lord Chelmsford for Colonel Pulleine to forward tents and supplies to the troops camping away. To this Colonel Pulleine returned an answer, addressed to "Staff Officer" (which is supposed to have reached its destination about 3 p.m.,) "Heavy firing to the left of our camp. Cannot move at present."

The Zulu advance, once begun, was so rapid that all thought of laagering was out of the question; neither must it be forgotten that had the attempt been made, the site would necessarily have been confined to the ground occupied by the camp, about the commissariat stores, that is, to ground commanded on all sides.

Moving steadily onward from the north-east, some thousands strong, in loose but deep horse-shoe formation, the Zulus directed their left horn round the right flank of the camp, while their right turned our left, and descended into the valley at the back of Isandhlwana Hill. The central mass came straight at the camp.

About 1 p.m. our men saw themselves outnumbered, six to one, by an enemy pressing onward from all sides, regardless of the heaviest losses. When the Zulu centre had come within two hundred yards of the angle in the defensive line, the Native Contingent broke and fled, leaving a gap, through which masses of Zulus at once swarmed.

This was the beginning of the end. The now isolated lines were taken in front and rear; the guns were mobbed and rendered powerless. "Before the men could turn round, before even they could fix "bayonets," said an eye-witness, "the Zulus rolled up Mostyn's* and

---

* Many months afterwards a diamond ring was picked up on the field of Isandhlwana. By means of an advertisement, the finder was enabled to identify the ring as having belonged to Captain Mostyn, and restored it to that officer's family.

Cavaye's companies, and in a few minutes they were slaughtered to a man. Younghusband's company being further off and nearer the rock, was enabled to reach a ledge on the southern side of Isandhlwana." There their bodies were found lying together in a clump, and that of their gallant captain was identified. Two other companies of the 24th, one of them being "G" company, 2nd battalion, under Lieutenant Pope, also had time to close, and made a determined stand until their ammunition was exhausted, when they were overpowered, and died where they stood. Paymaster White's body was found to the left of the 2nd battalion 24th camp. He had apparently been fighting with the companies on the left. In the 1st battalion 24th camp the bodies of the slain lay the thickest of all. A determined stand appeared to have been made behind the officers' tents, where lay seventy dead. The body of Colour-Sergeant Wolf, 1st battalion 24th, was recognized, surrounded by twenty of his men. Further down the slope of the hill, about sixty men lay together. Among them were the bodies of Captain Wardell, 1st battalion 24th, and Lieutenant and Adjutant Dyer, 2nd battalion 24th. Quarter-Master Pullen, 1st battalion 24th, was last seen in the 1st battalion 24th camp, where he was encouraging the men to stem the advance of the Zulu's left horn. But little is really known of the conflict in and around the camp. So swift was the disaster that it is easy to understand that the few survivors should be unable to give any very reliable or consecutive account of the details. The evidence of the dead, as afterwards found and buried where they lay, told the one unvarying tale of groups of men fighting back to back until the last cartridge was spent. Zulu witnesses, after the war, all told the same story: "At first we could make no way against the soldiers, but "suddenly they ceased to fire; then we came round them and threw "our spears until we had killed them all."* By 1.30 p.m. no white

---

* The Regimental Records of this date, in speaking of the disaster, say: "Turn where we will, the same story of the disaster is traced in broad characters; extended formations against savages whose hand-to-hand fighting was alone to be feared, and failure of ammunition. When this failed, there was no hope. It is known that Quarter-Master Bloomfield, 2nd battalion 24th, met his death while trying with others to untie the ammunition boxes on the mules, and that mules with

man was alive in Isandhlwana camp. According to one account, the last survivor was a drummer of the 24th, who was seen to fling his short sword at a Zulu.

A few white men followed the natives down a dry watercourse towards a drift in the Buffalo, four miles away. But so rapid was the pursuit, that dismounted Europeans had no chance of escape. Lieutenants Melvill and Coghill reached and crossed the Buffalo, losing therein the colour of their battalion which they had striven so hard to save, and parting with their lives on the Natal bank of the stream. Six privates of the First Battalion escaped the massacre, viz. :—

Private J. Williams, Officer's groom.†
„ J. Bickley } Bandsmen.
„ E. Wilson }

Private H. Grant } With the
„ W. Johnson } Rocket
„ J. Trainer } Battery.

RORKE'S DRIFT.

On the night of the disaster, the 2nd battalion 24th lay upon their arms on the crest of the neck connecting Isandhlwana Hill with Black's Kopjie. Some biscuit was found in one of the pillaged waggons in the corner of the camp crossed on the way to the neck; but there was no water, and all were too thirsty to eat. It was a night of incessant alarms and scares, caused by the Native troops attempting a stampede or opening a wild objectless fire into the darkness. A line of ill-omened beacons—the flames of burning

---

ammunition boxes on them were to be seen plunging and kicking over the field, maddened with fear. No arrangements had been made for the distribution of ammunition, and it may be mentioned that appliances for the purpose were asked for when the Second Battalion was still at Greytown. An answer came in due time, stating 'the articles applied for are not in store.' The letter further observed: 'However useful and necessary such appliances may be in European warfare, it is not expected that they will be required in a war such as the troops are about to enter upon.'"

† Private Williams was groom to Colonel Glyn, and was ordered by Lieutenant and Adjutant Melvill to take the colonel's spare horse and make his way from Isandhlwana camp as best he could.

homesteads—marked the Natal border, and when a great burst of flame arose where Rorke's post was supposed to be, many thought it had shared the fate of Isandhlwana camp, and that Helpmakaar would soon follow.

It was absolutely necessary these depôts should be recovered at all costs, so, on 23rd January, 1879, ere yet it was light, the march was resumed, and Rorke's Drift reached at 9 a.m. The mounted men led the way, a wing of the 24th and a Native battalion followed; next came the guns, then Major Black's two companies, which had passed the night on the Kopjie, and the remaining natives as a rearguard. To the astonishment of all, no opposition was encountered, although as the troops, after clearing the broken ground in rear of Isandhlwana, were moving along the high land between it and Sirayo's Mountain, a strong force of Zulus was seen on the left flank, moving in the opposite direction towards Isandhlwana. They appeared to be not more desirous of attacking the column than the latter, with only sixty rounds of ammunition per man left, were of attacking them, and both columns kept their lines of march. Again did the miles seem long and weary; again, after crossing the Bashee stream, where all hastily filled their bottles with the longed-for water, eyes were painfully strained to the front. "Again too late," was the thought when heavy smoke was seen rising from Rorke's Drift, and Zulus retiring therefrom; but, in the words of Lord Chelmsford's despatch: "To our intense relief, however, the waving of hats was "seen from the inside of a hastily-erected entrenchment, and infor-"mation soon reached me that the gallant garrison of this post, some "sixty men of the 2nd batttalion 24th Regiment under Lieutenant "Bromhead, and a few volunteers and departmental officers, the "whole under Lieutenant Chard, Royal Engineers, had for twelve "hours made the most gallant resistance I have ever heard of, "against the determined attack of some three thousand Zulus, "three hundred and seventy of whose dead bodies surrounded the "post."

The Defence of Rorke's Drift, by Lieutenant Gonville Bromhead and "B" company 2nd battalion 24th is best explained by Lieutenant Chard's official despatch :

"Rorke's Drift,
"25th January, 1879.

"Sir,—I have the honour to report that on the 22nd instant I was
"left in command at Rorke's Drift by Major Spalding, who went to
"Helpmakaar to hurry on the company of the 24th Regiment ordered
"to protect the ponts.

"About 3-15 p.m. on that day I was at the ponts, when two men
"came riding from Zululand at a gallop, and shouted to be taken across
"the river. I was informed by one of them, Lieutenant Adendorff of
"Londsdale's regiment (who remained to assist in the defence), of
"the disaster at Isandhlwana camp, and that the Zulus were advancing
"on Rorke's Drift. The other carabineer rode off to take the
"news to Helpmakaar.

"Almost immediately I received the message from Lieutenant
"Bromhead, commanding the company of 24th Regiment at the camp
"near the commissariat stores, asking me to come up at once.

"I gave the order to inspan, strike tents, put all stores, etc. into
"the waggon, and at once rode up to the commissariat store, and
"found that a note had been received from the third column to state
"that the enemy were advancing in force against our post, which we
"were to strengthen and hold at all cost.

"Lieutenant Bromhead was most actively engaged in loopholing and
"barricading the store buildings and hospital, and connecting the
"defence of the two buildings by walls of mealie-bags and two waggons
"that were on the ground.

"I held a hurried consultation with him and Mr. Dalton, of the
"commissariat, who was actively superintending the work of defence
"(and whom I cannot sufficiently thank for his most valuable ser-
"vices), entirely approving of the arrangements made. I went
"round the position, and then rode down to the pont and brought
"up the guard of one sergeant and six men, waggon, etc.

"I desire here to mention the offer of the pont man, Daniells, and
"Sergeant Milne, 3rd Buffs, to moor the ponts in the middle of the
"stream and defend them from their decks with a few men. We
"arrived at the post at 3.30 p m. Shortly after, an officer of Durnford's

"Horse arrived and asked for orders. I requested him to send
"a detachment to observe the drifts and ponts, to throw out outposts
"in the direction of the enemy, and check his advance as much as
"possible, falling back upon the post when forced to retire and
"assisting in its defence.

"I requested Lieutenant Bromhead to post his men, and having
"seen his and every man at his post, the work once more went on.

"About 4.15 the sound of firing was heard behind the hill to our
"south. The officer of Durnford's returned, reporting the enemy
"close upon us, and that his men would not obey his orders, but were
"going off to Helpmakaar, and I saw them, apparently about one
"hundred in number, going off in that direction.

"About the same time, Captain Stephenson's detachment of Natal
"Native Contingent left us, as did that officer himself.

"I saw that our line of defence was too extended for the small
"number of men now left us, and at once commenced a retrenchment
"of biscuit boxes.

"We had not completed a wall two boxes high, when, about
"4.30 p.m., five or six hundred of the enemy came in sight around
"the hill to our south, and advanced at a run against our south wall.
"They were met with a well-sustained fire, but notwithstanding their
"heavy loss, continued the advance to within fifty yards of the wall,
"when they met with such a heavy fire from the wall and cross-fire
"from the store that they were checked, but taking advantage of the
"cover afforded by the cook-house, ovens, etc., kept up a heavy fire.
"The greater number, however, without stopping, moved to the left
"around the hospital, and made a rush at our north-west wall of mealie
"bags, but after a short, but desperate, struggle, were driven back
"with heavy loss into the bush around the work.

"The main body of the enemy were close behind, and had lined
"the ledge of rocks and caves overlooking us about four hundred
"yards to our south, from whence they kept up a constant fire,
"and advancing somewhat more to their left than the first attack,
"occupied the garden, hollow road, and bush, in great force.

"Taking advantage of the bush which we had not cut down, the
"enemy were able to advance under cover close to our wall, and in

"this part soon held one side of the wall, while we held the other. "A series of desperate assaults were made, extending from the hospital "along the wall as far as the bush reached, but each was most "splendidly met and repulsed by our men with the bayonet, Corporal "Schiess, Natal Native Contingent, greatly distinguishing himself by "his conspicuous gallantry.

"The fire from the rocks behind us, though badly directed, took "us completely in reverse, and was so heavy that we suffered "very severely, and about 6 p.m. were forced to retire behind the "entrenchment of biscuit boxes.

"All this time the enemy had been attempting to force the hospital, "and shortly after set fire to its roof.

"The garrison of the hospital defended it room by room, bringing "out all the sick that could be moved before they retired; Privates "Williams, Hooke, R. Jones, and W. Jones, 24th regiment, being "the last men to leave, holding the doorway with the bayonet, their "ammunition being expended.

"From the want of interior communication, and the burning of the "house, it was impossible to save all. With most heartfelt sorrow, I "regret we could not save these poor fellows from their terrible fate.

"Seeing the hospital burning, and the desperate attempts of the "enemy to fire the roof of the stores, we converted two mealie bag "heaps into a sort of redoubt, which gave a second line of fire all "round, Assistant-Commissary Dunne working hard at this, though "much exposed, and rendering valuable assistance. As darkness "came on we were completely surrounded; and, after several attempts "had been gallantly repulsed, were eventually forced to retire to the "middle, and then the inner wall of the kraal was on our east. The "position we then had we retained throughout. A desultory fire was "kept up all night, and several assaults were attempted and repulsed, "the vigour of the attack continuing until after midnight; our men, "firing with the greatest coolness, did not waste a single shot, the "light afforded by the burning hospital being of great help to us.

"About 4 a.m. on the 23rd the firing ceased, and at daybreak the "enemy were out of sight over the hills to the south-west. We "patrolled the grounds, collecting the arms of the dead Zulus, and "strengthened our defences as much as possible. We were removing "the thatch from the roof of the stores, when, about 7 a.m., a large "body of the enemy appeared on the hills to the south-west.

"I sent a friendly Kaffir who had come in shortly before with a "note to the officer commanding at Helpmakaar asking for help. "About 8 a.m. the third column appeared in sight, the enemy, who "had been gradually advancing, falling back as they approached. I "consider the enemy who attacked us to have numbered about three "thousand. We killed about three hundred and fifty.

"Of the steadiness and gallant behaviour of the whole garrison I "cannot speak too highly, I wish especially to bring to your notice "the conduct of Lieutenant Bromhead, 2nd battalion 24th regiment, "and the splendid behaviour of his company ("B"); Surgeon Rey-"nolds, Army Medical Department, in his constant attention to "the wounded under fire where they fell; acting Commissariat-officer "Dalton, to whose energy much of our defences were due, and "who was severely wounded while gallantly assisting in the defence; "Assistant-Commissary Dunne; acting Storekeeper Bryne (killed); "Color-Sergeant Bourne, 2nd battalion 24th regiment; Sergeant "Williams 2nd battalion 24th regiment (wounded dangerously); "Sergeant Windridge, 2nd battalion, 24th regiment; Corporal "Schiess 2nd battalion 3rd Natal Native Contingent (wounded); "Privates Williams and Jones 2nd battalion, 24th regiment; "M'Mahon Army Hospital Corps, R. Jones and H. Hook 2nd "battalion, 24th regiment, and Roy, 1st battalion 24th regiment.

"The following return shows the number present at Rorke's Drift, "22nd January, 1879:

"Twelve wounded (list already forwarded by medical officer), of "whom two have since died, viz., Sergeant Williams, 2nd battalion "24th regiment, and Private Beckett, 1st battalion 24th regiment, "making a total killed of seventeen.

"I have, &c.,

"(Signed) J. M. CHARD, Lieutenant, R.E.
"To Colonel Glyn, C.B., Commanding 3rd Column.
"Forwarded.

"(Signed) R. T. GLYN, Colonel, Commanding 3rd Column."

Major Gonville Bromhead, V.C.

The following are extracts from an account published by the Rev. G. Smith, Acting Chaplain to the Forces at Rorke's Drift :*

"Rorke's Drift,
"3rd February, 1879.

"About 3 o'clock p.m., or shortly after, several mounted men arrived "from the camp at Isandhlwana, and reported the terrible disaster which "had occurred. Lieutenant Bromhead, commanding the company ("B") "of the 2nd battalion 24th regiment, at once struck his camp, and sent down "to Lieutenant Chard, R.E., who was engaged with some half-a-dozen men "at the ponts on the river, to come up and direct the preparations for "defence, as, in the absence of Major Spalding, the command of the post "devolved upon him. The windows and doors of the hospital were blocked up with mattresses, &c., loopholes made through the walls both of the 'hospital and storehouse. A wall of mealie and other grain bags was 'made, enclosing the front of the hospital and running along the ledge of "the rocky terrace to the stone wall of the kraal, which has been described "as coming from the far end of the storehouse at right angles to the front "of that building, down to the edge of these rocks. A praiseworthy effort "was made to remove the worst cases in hospital to a place of safety ; two "waggons were brought up after some delay, and the patients were being "brought out, when it was found that the Zulus were so close upon us that "any attempt to take them away in ox waggons would only result in their "falling into the enemy's hands. So the two waggons were at once utilised "and made to form part of the defensive wall connecting the right hand "front corner of the storehouse with the left hand back corner of the "hospital, about forty paces long ; sacks of mealies forming the remainder "and being also used as barricades underneath and upon the waggons. A "barricade, filling up the small space between the left front corner of the "storehouse and the stone wall of the kraal before referred to, and the "blocking up of the gates of the kraal itself, made the outer defensive "works complete. The men worked with a will, and were much encouraged "by the unremitting exertions of both the military officers, the medical "officer, and Assistant-Commissary Dalton, all of whom not merely "directed but engaged most energetically in the construction of the "barricades. The water-cart in the meantime had been hastily filled and "brought within the enclosure. The pontman Daniells, and Sergeant "Milne, 3rd Buffs, offered to moor the ponts in the middle of the stream "and defend them from their decks with a few men. But our defensive force "was too small for any to be spared, and these men subsequently did good "service within the fort. About 4.30 p.m. the Zulus came in sight, coming

---

* The Rev. Geo. Smith was subsequently appointed chaplain to the forces, in recognition of his services at Rorke's Drift.

"round the right-hand end of the large hill in our rear; only about twenty
"at first appeared, advancing in open order. Their numbers were speedily
"augmented and their line extended quite across the neck of land from
"hill to hill. A great number of dongas on their line of approach, a stream
"with steep banks, the garden with all its trees and surroundings, gave
"them great facilities for getting near us unseen. The garden must have
"soon been occupied, for one unfortunate Contingent corporal, whose
"heart must have failed him when he saw the enemy and heard the firing,
"got over the parapet and tried to make his escape on foot, but a bullet
"from the garden struck him, and he fell dead within a hundred and fifty
"yards of our front wall. An officer of the same corps who had charge of
"the three hundred and fifty natives before referred to, was more fortunate,
"for being mounted he made good his escape and 'lives to fight another
"day.'

"But the enemy are upon us now, and are pouring over the right shoulder
"of the hill in a dense mass, and on they come, making straight for the
"connecting wall between the storehouse and the hospital; but when they
"get within fifty yards the firing is altogether too hot for them. Some of
"them swerve round to their left past the back and right end of the hospital,
"and then make a desperate attempt to scale the barricade in front of that
"building; but here too they are repulsed, and they disperse and find cover
"amongst the bushes and behind the stone wall below the terrace. The
"others have found shelter amongst numerous banks, ditches, and bushes,
"and behind a square Kaffir house and large brick ovens, all at the rear of
"our enclosure. One of the mounted chiefs was shot by Private Dunbar,
"2nd battalion 24th regiment, who also killed eight of the enemy, in as many
"consecutive shots, as they came round the ledge of the hill; and as fresh
"bodies of Zulus arrive they take possession of the elevated ledge of rocks
"overlooking our buildings and barricades at the back, and all the caves
"and crevices are quickly filled, and from these the enemy pour down a
"continuous fire upon us. A whisper passes round amongst the men: 'Poor
"Old King Cole is killed.' He was at the front wall, a bullet passed through
"his head, and then struck the next man upon the bridge of the nose, but
"the latter was not seriously hurt. Mr. Dalton, who is a tall man, was
"continually going along the barricades, fearlessly exposing himself and
"cheering the men, and using his own rifle most effectively. A Zulu ran
"up near the barricade; Mr. Dalton called out—'pot that fellow,'
"and himself aimed over the parapet at another, when his rifle dropped, he
"turned round quite pale, and said that he had been shot. The doctor was
"by his side at once, and found that a bullet had passed quite through,
"above the right shoulder. Unable any longer to use his rifle (although
"he did not cease to direct the fire of the men who were near him), he
"handed it to Mr. Byrne, who used it well. Presently, Corporal C. Scammel,
"Natal native contingent, who was near Mr. Byrne, was shot through the
"shoulder and back; he crawled a short distance and handed the remainder
"of his cartridges to Lieutenant Chard, and then expressed his desire for a

"drink of water; Byrne at once fetched it for him, and whilst giving it to
"him to drink, poor Byrne was shot through the head and fell dead instantly.
"The garden and the road—having the stone wall and thick belt of bush as
"a screen from the fire of our front defences—were now occupied by a large
"force of the enemy; they rushed up to the front barricade and soon
"occupied one side whilst we held the other; they seized hold of the bayonets
"of our men, and in two instances succeeded in wresting them off the rifles,
"but the bold perpetrators were instantly shot. One fellow fled at Corporal
"Schiess, of the Natal native contingent, (a Swiss by birth, who was a
"hospital patient), the charge blowing his hat off; he instantly jumped upon
"the parapet and bayonetted the man, regained his place and shot another,
"and then, repeating his former exploit, climbed up the sacks and bayonetted
"a third; a bullet struck him in the instep early in the fight, but he would
"not allow that his wound was a sufficient reason for leaving his post, yet
"he has suffered most acutely from it since. Our men at the front wall
"had the enemy hand-to-hand, and, besides, were being fired upon very
"heavily from the rocks and caves above us in our rear. Five of our men
"were here shot dead in a very short space of time; so by 6 p.m. the order
"was given for them to retire to our retrenchment of biscuit boxes, from
"which such a heavy fire was sent along the front of the hospital, that
"although scores of Zulus jumped over the mealie bags to get into the
"building, nearly every man perished in that fatal leap; but they rushed to
"their death like demons, yelling out their war-cry of 'Usutu, Usutu.'
"Shortly after, they succeeded in setting the roof of the hospital on fire at
"its further end. As long as we held the front wall, the Zulus failed in
"their repeated attempts to get into the far end room of the hospital,
"Lieutenant Bromhead having several times driven them back with a
"bayonet charge. When we had retired to the retrenchment, and the
"hospital had been set on fire, a terrible struggle awaited the brave fellows
"who were defending it from within. Private Joseph Williams fired from
"a small window at the far end of the hospital. Next morning fourteen
"warriors were found dead beneath it, besides others along his line of fire.
"When their ammunition was expended, he and his companions kept the
"door with their bayonets, but an entrance was subsequently forced, and
"he, poor fellow, was seized by the hands, dragged out, and killed before
"their eyes. His surviving companions were Private John Williams
"(No. 1395), and two patients. Whilst the Zulus were dragging forth their
"late brave comrade, they succeeded in making a hole in the partition with
"an axe, and got into another room, where they were joined by Private
"Henry Hooke, and he and Williams turn about, one keeping off the
"enemy and the other working, succeeded in cutting holes into the next
"adjoining rooms. One poor fellow (Jenkins) venturing through one of
"these, was also seized and dragged away, but the others escaped through
"the window looking into the enclosure towards the storehouse, and, running
"the gauntlet of the enemy's fire, most of them got safely within the retrench-
"ment. Trooper Hunter, Natal mounted police, a very tall young man, who

"was a patient in hospital, was not so fortunate, but fell before he could
"reach the goal. In another ward Privates 593, W. Jones, and 716, R. Jones,
"defended their post until six out of the seven patients in it had been re-
"moved. The seventh was Sergeant Maxfield, who was ill with fever and
"delirious. Private R. Jones went back to try and carry him out, but the
"room was full of Zulus and the poor fellow was dead. The native of
"Umkungba's tribe who had been shot through the thigh at Sirayo's kraal,
"was lying unable to move; he said that he 'was not afraid of the Zulus,
"but wanted a gun.' When the end room in which he lay was forced,
"Private Hooke heard the Zulus talking with him; next day his charred
"remains were found amongst the ruins. Corporal Mayer, Natal native
"contingent, who had been wounded under the knee with an assegai at
"Sirayo's kraal, Bombadier Lewis, Royal Artillery, whose leg and thigh
"were much swollen from a waggon accident, and Trooper R. S. Green,
"Natal mounted police, also a patient, all got out of the little end window
"into the enclosure. The window being high up, and the Zulus already
"within the room behind them, each man had a fall in escaping, and had
"then to crawl (for none of them could walk) through the enemy's fire,
"inside the retrenchment. Whilst doing this, Green was struck in the
"thigh with a spent bullet. Some few escaped from the front of the
"hospital, and ran round to the right of the retrenchment, but two or
"three were assegaied as they attempted it. Whilst the hospital was thus
"gallantly defended, Lieutenant Chard and Assistant-Commissary Dunne,
"with two or three men, succeeded in converting the two large pyramids
"of sacks of mealies into an oblong and lofty redoubt, under heavy fire,
"blocking up the intervening space between the two with sacks from the
"top of each, leaving a hollow in the centre for the security of the wounded,
"and giving another admirable and elevated line of fire all round. About
"this time the men were obliged to fall back from the outer to the middle,
"and then to the inner wall of the kraal, forming our left defence. The
"Zulus do not appear to have thrown their assegais at all, using them
"solely for stabbing purposes. Corporal Allen and Private Hitch both
"behaved splendidly. They were badly wounded early in the evening, and,
"incapacitated from firing themselves, never ceased going round and serving
"out ammunition from the reserve to the fighting men. The light from
"the burning hospital was of the greatest service to our men, lighting up
"the scene for hundreds of yards around; but before 10 p.m. it had burned
"itself out. The rushes and heavy fire of the enemy did not slacken till
"past midnight, and from that time until daylight a desultory fire was kept
"up by them from the caves above us in our rear and from the bush and
"garden in front. At last daylight dawned, and the enemy retired round
"the shoulder of the hill by which they had approached. Whilst some
"remained at their posts, others of our men were sent out to patrol, and
"returned with about one hundred rifles and guns and some four hundred
"assegais, left by the enemy upon the field; and round our walls, and
"especially in front of the hospital, the dead Zulus lay piled up in heaps.

"About three hundred and fifty were subsequently buried by us. They
"must have carried off nearly all their wounded with them. Whilst all
"behaved so gallantly, it was hardly possible to notice other exceptional
"instances, although all their comrades bore testimony to such in the
"conduct of Colour-Sergeant Bourne,* 2nd battalion 24th regiment, Ser-
"geant Williams, 2nd battalion 24th regiment, (dangerously wounded—
"since dead), Sergeant Windridge, 2nd battalion 24th regiment, and
"Privates M'Mahon, Army Hospital Corps, and Roy, 1st battalion
"24th regiment. It was certainly of the utmost strategegical importance
"that this place should not be taken. Perhaps the safety of the remainder
"of the column, and of this part of the colony, depended on it."

According to Zulu estimates, the aggregate strength of their *impis* was fourteen thousand men, and their loss at Isandhlwana not less than one thousand men. At Rorke's Drift, four hundred bodies were found.†

Three years afterwards, on 13th April, 1882, a memorial window, placed by the regiment in the ancient church of St. John's Priory, Brecon, was unveiled and dedicated by the Lord Bishop of St. David's. The memorial brass, mounted on black marble, bears the following inscription :—

---

* Colour-Sergeant Bourne received the distinguished service medal for his services at Rorke's Drift. He was subsequently promoted to a commission as quarter-master of his battalion.

† With the instincts of a warrior race, the Zulus were not slow to recognize the worth of their opponents. Many stories of the gallantry displayed were related by them after the war. One of the sons of the chief Sirayo spoke of a very tall dark officer, killed at the waggons at Isandhlwana : "A very brave man was killed near one of them. I don't know whether he was an *inkos'* (officer), for when I saw him after he had been killed, his coat had been taken off, but he had red stripes on his trousers, and wore brown gaiters. He was a very tall dark man, and when we were rushing over the camp he jumped on a waggon and kept firing, first on one side and then on the other, so that no one could get near him. We all saw and watched him, and we all said what a brave man that was. I think he was an *inkos*. All who tried to stab him were at once bayonetted or knocked over. He kept his ground a long time. At last, one shot him."

Another *induna*, or chief, related his encounter with an officer when some Zulus were surrounding a party of "red soldiers" on the neck at Isandhlwana. Two officers "with pieces of glass in their eyes" (afterwards ascertained to have been Lieutenants Pope and Godwin-Austen) came forward, shooting at them with their revolvers. One fell by a gunshot, and the other, after firing his revolver several times and hitting the *induna* in the neck, left side, and left leg, shared the fate of his brother officer.

To the Glory of God,

AND IN MEMORY OF 22 OFFICERS AND
655 NON-COMMISSIONED OFFICERS AND MEN
OF THE 24TH REGIMENT,
WHO FELL IN ACTION, OR DIED OF WOUNDS AND DISEASE,
IN THE SOUTH AFRICAN CAMPAIGNS OF 1877-8-9,
THE EAST WINDOW IN THIS CHURCH
IS ERECTED BY THEIR COMRADES PAST AND PRESENT.

1ST BATTALION.

[The names in succession of the officers, and 429 N.C.O.'s and men.]

2ND BATTALION.

[The names in succession of the officers, and 226 N.C.O.'s and men.]

Of the above, 21 officers and 590 non-commissioned officers and men were killed in action on the field of Isandhlwana, Zululand, on the 22nd January, 1879, and in the defence of Rorke's Drift on the 22nd and 23rd January, 1879.

THEY GAVE THEIR LIVES FOR QUEEN AND COUNTRY.

JESU MERCY.

NOMINAL ROLL OF THE OFFICERS AND MEN OF THE 1st BATTALION 24TH REGIMENT KILLED AT ISANDHLWANA AND RORKE'S DRIFT.

KILLED IN ACTION AT ISANDHLWANA.

Major and Lieutenant-Colonel H. B. Pulleine, commanding.
Captain W. Degacher, acting-major.

" A " Co., *Lieut.* C. W. Cavaye.   " F " Co., *Capt.* W. E. Mostyn,
" C " Co., *Capt.* R. Younghusband,   *Lieut.* E. O. Anstey,
       Lieut. G. F. G. Hodson.   *Lieut.* J. P. Daly.
' E ' Co., *Lieut.* F. P. Porteous,   " H " Co., *Capt.* G. V. Wardell,
       2nd Lieut. E. H. Dyson.   *Lieut.* Atkinson.

Adjutant Lieutenant Teignmouth Melvill.
Paymaster Hon. Major F. F. White.   *Quarter-Master* James Pullen.
Staff-Officer to *Brigadier-General* R. T. Glyn, C.B.   *Lieutenant* N. J. A. Coghill.
Sergeant-Major Frederick Gapp.   *Quarter-Master-Sergeant* Thomas Leitch.
Sergeant-Instructor of Musketry George Chambers.
Paymaster-Sergeant George Mead.   *Armourer-Sergeant* Henry Hayward.
Drum-Major Robert Taylor.   *Orderly-Room-Clerk* Gerald Fitzgerald.
Sergeant-Cook Alfred Field.

Colour-Sergeants:

James Ballard	William Edwards	Fred H. Wolfe.
Thomas Brown	William Whitfield	

Sergeants:

Peter Ainsworth	Thomas Fay	Michael Hornibrook
George Bennett	James Fowden	William Parsons
Daniel Bradley	David Gamble	Alfred Piall
John Clarkson	Edward Giles	John Smedley
William Coholan	John Greatorex	Joseph Smith
Thomas Cooper	Christopher Heppenstall	George Upton.
John Edwards		

Lance-Sergeants:

John Milner | John Reardon

Corporals:

Nicholas Ball	Richard Davis	Matthew Miller
Peter Bell	Edward Everett	Harry Richardson
James Lawler	John Franks	John Rowden
John Bellhouse	John Knight	John Tarbuck
Alfred Board	Patrick Markham	Robert Williams.

Lance-Corporals:

Richard Abbott	George Hadden	John Murphy
Thomas Bushby	John Hewitt	Henry Weatherhead
William Chadwick	David Horgan	Thomas Young.

Drummers:

William H. Adams	Charles Osmond	Daniel Trottman
Charles Andrews	Thomas Perkins	Alfred Wolfendale
George Dibden	Timothy Reardon	James Wolfenden.
John F. Orlopp	John Thompson	

Privates:

Thomas Allingham
Edward Amos
Alfred Atkins
Joseph Bailey
Elijah Baker
John Barry
John Barry
Elias Barsley
John Bartles
Claude Bastard
Robert Beadon
John Benham
Alfred Bennett
Richard Bennett
Robert Benson
Noah Betterton
Joseph Birch
John Bishop
Robert Blackhurst
James Blower
Frederick Bodman
Samuel Bolton
John Boylan
James Bray
John Breese
John W. Brew
Jeremiah Broderick
Joseph Brown
William Brown
Frederick W. Bugby
James Bull
Timothy Burke
William Burns
William Burke
William Butler
Joseph Cahill
Jeremiah Callanan
James Camp
Michael Campbell
James Cantillon
Henry Carpenter
Peter Carrol
James Casey
Edward Ceiley
William Chalmers
James Chatterton
William Chepman
John Christian
Alfred Clarke
Michael Clarke
Henry Clements
William Clutterbuck
Albert Cole
James Coleman
Daniel Collins
Thomas Collins
Thomas Colston

George Conboye
Cornelius Connelly
John Connelly
Samuel Connors
James Cook
Henry Cooper
Richard Coughlan
James Cox
Thomas Cox
Martin Cullen
Aaron Davies
William Davies
Edward Davis
Mark Diggle
Thomas Diggle
John Dobbin
William Dobbs
Christopher Donohoe
Michael Doran
John Dorman
Patrick Dowde
William Dredge
Thomas Duck
George Duckworth
John Duffy
Edward Dugmore
Francis Dunn
John Dyer
John Edwards
William Edwards
Thomas Egan
William Egan
George Elderton
William Eldrington
Owen Ellis
Henry Ellison
James Ellsmore
David Evans
John W. Evans
Thomas Evry
John Faircloth
William Farmer
George H. Fay
Michael Ferris
Thomas Fitzgerald
Edward Flint
William Flood
James Fortune
William Freeman
Thomas Gilder
John Gillan
Charles Gingell
George Glass
Ashley Goatham
Charles Goddard
George Goodchild
Thomas Goss

William Green
William Gregg
William Gregson
George Griffiths
Isaac Hale
John Hall
Jacob Hannaford
Thomas Harkin
John Harman
Daniel Harney
Denis Harrington
Thomas Harris
William Harris
William Haydon
John Haynes
James Hedges
Charles Hemmings
James Hibbard
William H. Hicken
Thomas Hicks
Thomas Higgins
James Hind
John Hitchen
William Holden
John Holland
John Horn
Charles Hornbuckle
William Hough
Edwin Hughes
John Hughes
John Hughes
Owen Hughes
Thomas Hughes
Alfred Iggulden
Frederick Ilsley
Ernest Ivatts
James Jenkins
Matthew Jenkins
William Jenkins
George Johnson
Henry Johnson
John Johnson
Joseph Johnston
William Johnston
Alexander Johnstone
George Johnston
James Johnston
Evan Jones
John Jones
John Jones
Thomas Jones
William Jones
William Jones
John Keane
James Keegan
Andrew Kelly
Finton Kelly

24TH REGIMENT.

James Kelly
John F. Kelly
Nelson Kempsell
John Kempster
James Knight
John Lamb
Thomas Lambert
Robert Leech
John Lawrence
Thomas Leaver
John Lee
Henry Lewis
Richard Lewis
James Ling
John Linnane
Stephen Lippett,
George Lisbeck
George Lloyd
William Lockett
Charles Lovell
Charles Lowe
Richard Lowe
James Lycett
John Lyons
Miles McDonald
Matthew McFarlane
John McHale
Hugh A. Mack
John J. Mackensie
George R. Mace
Charles Mahoney
Martin Maloney
Cornelius Maney
William Mann
Luke Marley
Henry Marsh
David Martin
John H. Meredith
Charles Millen
Patrick Miller
Richard Moore
John Morgan
William Morgan
George Morris
Richard Morse
John Murphy
Patrick Murphy
John Murray
Patrick Nash
Alfred Newberry
Thomas Newberry
Edward Nicholas
Walter Nicholas
E. Nicholls
William E. Nye

Privates—continued:
William Oakley
George Odey
James Ogden
James Padmore
Thomas Painter
Robert Parry
Henry H. Patterson
John Peters
James N. Phillips
John Phillips
Jabez R. Pickard
Samuel Plant
James Plunkett
Augustus Pollen
William Pope
Uriah Pottow
Henry Powell
John Proctor
George Prosser
John Prosser
Walter Pugh
William Pugh
James Quirk
Edward Remington
William Retford
George Richards
Mitchell Richardson
John Rigney
John Rittman
William Roberts
Henry Rogers
Patrick Roubrey
Henry Rowman
Walter Rule
Frederick Russell,
Thomas Rutter
James Ryan
George Salter
Frederick Sarney
Henry Sears
William Sellwood
Frederick Sharp
Robert Shaw
Daniel Shea
Henry Sheather
John Shrimpton
Robert Silcock
Walter Skelton
Edwin Smith
Charles Smith
Charles Smith
George Smith
James Smith
Thomas Speed
Samuel Stansfield

Henry Stevens
William Stevens
Edward Strange
John Sullivan
Patrick Sullivan
Patrick Sutton
Richard Swoffer
Reuben Tate
Edward Taylor
James Ferry
John Thomas
John B. Thomas
Thomas Thornett
Charles Throssell
Henry Tillison
Thomas Tinneny
George Todd
Joseph Townsend
James Tulett
Edward Turner
Edward Trowell
William Theobald
George Vines
Edward Walker
Edward Waller
Thomas Walsh
Thomas Walsh
William Walton
Joseph Warner
William Watkins
John Watley
Henry Watts
Thomas Webb
William Welsh
John Whelan
Thomas Whelan
Arthur Wilkinson
Frederick Wilks
Ellis Williams
Evan Williams
James Williams
John Williams
Matthew Williams
Thomas Williams
Thomas Williams
William E. Williams
John Wilson
Samuel Wilson
William Wisher
James Wood
John Woolley
Enoch Worthington
Robert Wright
Elijah Whybrow.

Boys:
Thomas J. Harrington | — Richards.

Killed in Action at Rorke's Drift.

Privates:

William Beckett | William Horrigan | Joseph Williams

These Men Died of Disease in the Kaffir War, 1877-78.

Privates:

T. Johns	A. Coxall	J. Norman
T. Carmody	T. Scaplehorne	R. Sheehan
I. Scannell	T. Cairns	G. Mitchell
P. Barrett	W. Dodimead	J. Cross
A. Bailey	G. Holt	J. Edwards
W. Young	J. McCarthy	J. Healey

NOMINAL ROLL OF THE OFFICERS AND MEN OF THE 2ND BATTALION 24TH REGIMENT KILLED AT ISANDHLWANA AND RORKE'S DRIFT.

Killed in Action at Isandhlwana.

Lieutenants:

C. D'A. Pope | F. Godwin-Austen | H. J. Dyer.

Sub-Lieutenant T. L. G. Griffith. *Quarter-Master* E. Bloomfield.

Bandmaster H. Bullard.

Quarter-Master-Sergeant H. G. Davis.

Sergeants:

I. Lines	W. Shaw	H. Carse
C. Chew	J. Ross	W. J. G. Reeves.
G. Wilkins		

Lance-Sergeants:

J. Mc'Caffry | H. Haigh.

Corporals:

J. Henshaw	J. M. Low	H. Mortlock
G. Sims	T. Thompson	W. Greenhill.

Drummers:

J. Anderson | J. Holmes.

Lance-Corporals:

J. Bryan | J. Elvy | W. Jenkins | H. Morris.

Privates:

J. Quinn	J. Flyn	D. Phillips
J. Mc'Guire	G. Horrocks	R. Howells
T. White	W. Hawkins	R. Evans
W. Mockler	J. Jones	P. Smith
S. Sherwood	M. Broderick	C. Long
E. Malley	J. Kelly	T. Jones
J. Smith	T. Kennedy	R. Emerson

24TH REGIMENT.

Privates—continued.:

T. Lynch	J. E. Hill	J. Lewis
E. Edwards	J. King	E. Martingale
R. Smith	R. Nobes	T. Marsh
D. Pritchard	J. Machin	F. Moore
G. P. Brierly	J. Davis	J. Morrisey
T. Jones	T. Neagle	J. Morgan
W. Jones	T. Quelford	J. Murphy
B. Latham	A. Farr	G. Mc'Doon
J. Mack	J. Allen	S. Poole
R. Stephens	S. Bevan	S. Popple
T. Vedler	S. Bennett	H. Price
J. Watkins	J. Bryne	J. Price
J. White	R. Buckley	T. O'Keefe
G. Wood	A. Bray	W. Rees
J. Bryant	F. Bridgewater	W. Rice
J. Carrell	M. Cleary	J. Roche
T. Cornish	W. Charles	M. Roche
J. J. Davis	F. Cherry	W. Shean
S. Hacker	G. Davis	C. M. Smith
C. Hall	D. Davis	H. Smith
J. Hudson	J. Dowle	D. Smith
R. H. Hopkins	M. Donegan	F. Smith
J. Mc'Cormack	J. Edwards	W. Terrett
H. Slade	J. Earish	D. Thomas
G. Thompson	T. Finn	A. Treverton
T. Bull	G. Fitton	S. Walker
J. Hall	D. Flyn	E. Williams
J. Davis	J. Fry	E. Williams
M. Furtune	T. Fox	E. Williams
E. Lewis	W. Gee	E. Williams
G. Williams	G. Ghost	J. Williamson
T. Montgomery	W. V. C. Griffiths	J. Wright
F. Perkins	W. Hall	J. Young
P. Mc'Caffry	F. Hughes	J. Scott
W. Waterhouse	J. Hunt	E. Waters
H. Bishop	J. Healy	J. Mulroy
A. Byard	W. Johnson	B. Hall
E. Turner	J. Jones	W. Shuttleworth
S. Mc'Cracken	E. Jones	J. Barton
M. Fitzpatrick	A. Jones	A. Whitman
G. Watson	J. Llewellyn	T. Saunders.

Boys.

J. S. Mc'Ewan	D. Gordan	J. Gurney.

KILLED IN ACTION AT RORKE'S DRIFT.

Sergeant R. Maxfield.

Privates:

J. Scanlon	J. Williams	G. Hayden
T. Cole	J. Chick	R. Adams.
J. Fagan		

DIED OF WOUNDS AT RORKE'S DRIFT.

Lance-Sergeant T. Williams.

KILLED IN ACTION OR DIED PREVIOUS TO ISANDHLWANA.

KILLED.
Private T. Collins.

DIED.
Sergeant A. Stratton.   *Corporal* L. Davies.

Privates:

S. Stanton	E. Stephens	W. Boulter
W. Shaw	B. Meek	A. Jones
W. Ritchie	T. Tandy	J. L. Bradley
T. Davies	E. Richards	H. Hughes
J. Ford	J. Gorman	G. Partridge
W. R. Davies	H. Robinson	J. Brailsford.
A. Careless		

DIED AFTER ISANDHLWANA AND RORKE'S DRIFT.
2nd Lieutenant R. W. Franklin.

DIED AT GREYTOWN.
Private Cronin.

DIED.
Privates:

R. Wittaker | J. Williams | G. James | J. Farr | C. Foster.

Lance-Sergeant D. Jones.

Lance-Corporals:

C. Fowan | T. Haslan.

Colour-Sergeant H. Cuthbert.

Privates:

T. Jones	W. Davenport	J. Boyle
G. Brooks	T. Sullivan	J. Bryan
T. Clayton	W. Lyons	A. Lemmond.
G. Ricks	A. Dorrell	

DIED AFTER THE BATTALION CAME DOWN COUNTRY.

F. Taylor | G. Delaney | F. Cope | E. Bennett.

TOTAL LOSSES.

1st Battalion	445, including	16 officers.
2nd Battalion	232, ,,	6 officers.
Total	677, ,,	22 officers.

Re-formation of the First Battalion—Subsequent Services of both battalions to the end of the War.

As soon as tidings of the disaster at Isandhlwana reached England, volunteers were called for to re-form the First Battalion, and a draft of five hundred and twenty non-commissioned officers and men, furnished by the following regiments : 1st battalion 8th, 1st battalion 11th, 1st battalion 18th, 2nd battalion 18th, 1st battalion 23rd, 2nd battalion 25th, 32nd, 37th, 38th, 45th, 50th, 55th, 60th, 86th, 87th, 103rd, 108th, and 109th was collected at Aldershot, under the command of Lieutenant-Colonel H. F. Davies, Grenadier Guards. The draft embarked at Woolwich, in the *Clyde*, on 1st March, 1879 ; Captains Brander and Farquhar Glennie and Lieutenant T. J. Halliday, 24th regiment, and a number of special service officers proceeded with the draft.

The *Clyde* had an uneventful voyage until 4th April, 1879, when she ran upon a reef seventy miles east of Simon's Bay, between Dyer's Island and the mainland. The sea was perfectly smooth at the time, and the troops were all got safely on shore by 11.30 a.m., except two companies, which were left on board two hours longer to look after the baggage. These companies had not long landed, when, with the rising of the tide, the ship slid off the reef and suddenly went down, all clothing, books, etc., being lost in her. The chief officer of the *Clyde* had previously been despatched to Simon's Bay, where he arrived at 10 p.m. the same night, and early on the morrow the *Tamar* arrived, took the draft on board, returned to Simon's Bay, and on 7th April started for Durban, arriving there on the 11th. The troops were at once landed and marched up country, reaching Pietermaritzburg on 18th April ; Ladysmith, 29th April ; and Dundee, 4th May.

At Dundee the 1st battalion was re-formed with "D" and "G" companies 1st battalion 24th, which had remained at Helpmakaar, under command of Brevet-Major Russell Upcher, since the first arrival of the battalion there ("D" becoming "A" company.) "B" company, which was still at St. John's River ("B" became "H" company), and "B," "C," "D," "E," and "F" new companies formed from the draft The acting officers of the re-formed battalion were :—

    Major W. M. Dunbar, commanding.
    Major J. M. G. Tongue. *Acting-Major* Wm. Brander.
    Captains Brevet-Major Russell Upcher ("A" company), Rainforth, ("G" company), A. A. Morshead ("B" company), L. H. Bennett ("D" company), Honble. G. A. V. Bertie, Coldstream Guards ("E" company).
    Lieutenants W. Heaton, ("F" company), C. R. W. Colville, Grenadier Guards ("C" company), R. A. P. Clements, (Acting Quartermaster), — Weallens, W. W. Lloyd.
    Sub-Lieutenants W. A. Birch, J. D. W. Williams, W. C. Godfrey, M. E. Carthew Yorstoun, Robt. Scott-Kerr, R. Campbell, Honble. R. C. E. Carrington.
    Captain C. P. H. Tynte, Glamorgan Militia, *Lieutenant* St. Le Malet, Dorset Militia, *Lieutenant* E. P. H. Tynte, Glamorgan Militia, E. R. Rushbrook, Royal East Middlesex Militia, *Second Lieutenant* Lumsden, 2nd Royal Lanarkshire Militia.

On 13th April, 1879, previous to the re-formation of the battalion, a reorganisation of the forces under Lord Chelmsford was promulgated :—

The 1st division, in two brigades, under Major-General Hope Crealock, C.B., was to operate from the Tugela. Wood's force was to remain independent, under the name of Brigadier-General Wood's Flying Column.

The remainder of the troops in the Utrecht district, in which were both battalions 24th, were to constitute the second division under Major-General Newdigate, and operate from Landman's Drift. The cavalry brigade was ordered to join the northern column.

On 13th May, 1879, the new 1st battalion 24th left at Dundee, under command of Colonel R. T. Glyn, C.B., marched to join Major-General Newdigate's division, and on 7th June was formed into a brigade with the 58th and 94th regiments, under Colonel Glyn, C.B. The brigade marched towards Ulundi, and on 27th June arrived within ten miles of that place. Leaving two companies in laager at Entonganini, the remainder of the battalion advanced with its division, carrying ten days' rations and no tents, towards Umsenbarri, joined

General Wood's column, and formed laager and built a stone fort on the banks of the Umvelosi. The whole of the mounted men, including the mounted infantry under Lieutenant and Local Captain E. S. Browne, 24th regiment, crossed the river and reconnoitred as far as Ulundi.* In the battle which followed there, Colonel Glyn's brigade was present, with the exception of the 1st battalion 24th, which with detachments of other corps was left in the entrenched camp on the Umvelosi, under Colonel Bellairs, C.B. On 4th July, the Zulu power being regarded as broken, the brigade retraced its steps to Entonganini, where it lay during the great storm of wind and cold of 6th-8th July, 1879. It subsequently returned to Landman's Drift.

On 26th July the battalion received orders to march to Durban, to embark for England. Moving by Dundee, Greytown, and Pietermaritzburg to Pine Town, it encamped, and there at a brigade parade, on 22nd August, 1879, the *Victoria Cross* was presented to Lieutenant E. S. Browne. " H " (late " B ") company, having rejoined from St. John's River, the battalion, under command of Colonel R. T. Glyn, C.B., numbering twenty-four officers, forty-six sergeants, thirty-six corporals, eleven drummers and seven hundred and sixty-seven privates, embarked in the transport *Egypt* on 27th August, 1879, landed at Portsmouth on 2nd October, and marched into quarters in the New Barracks, Gosport.

The 2nd battalion remained at Rorke's Drift from its arrival there on 23rd January, 1879, until the middle of April. The privations to which the officers and men were subject were at first very great. The battalion had nothing but what it stood in. There were no tents, no covering of any sort; all they had to shelter them from the cold sleet and rain that fell nightly, converting the enclosed space into a slough of mud, was their thin kersey frocks. The sick list increased alarmingly, and, to make matters worse, the medicines

---

* Captain Lord William Beresford, 9th Lancers, and Sergeant O'Toole, Frontier Light Horse, received Victoria Crosses for gallantly rescuing Sergeant Fitzmaurice, 1st battalion 24th Mounted Infantry, who was disabled by his horse falling and rolling on him, in front of an advancing body of Zulus during the reconnaissance.

having been burnt with the hospital, all that remained at the disposal of the medical officers, then and for some time afterwards, was contained in the small field companions they carried with them. It speaks volumes for the healthiness of the Natal climate, that during these three months the battalion only lost one officer, Lieutenant Reginald Franklin, and twelve men by death, and two officers and thirteen men invalided.

At the beginning of April, half of the battalion, under Lieutenant-Colonel Degacher, moved to Dundee; four companies, under Brevet Major Black, remaining at Rorke's Drift. On the advance of the northern column from Landman's Drift, two companies ("G" and "H") 2nd battalion 24th, under Brevet Major C. J. Bromhead, were brought down from Dundee to that post; but it having been decided to construct a strong fort at Kopjie Alleine, Captain Harvey moved up with "H" company, and Major C. J. Bromhead joining with "F" company, under Lieutenant H. Mainwaring, the two companies speedily converted the small earthwork they had found on arrival into a substantial closed redoubt. On 3rd June, 1879, this detachment had the melancholy duty of furnishing a guard of honour and escort to the mortal remains of the Prince Imperial of France, whose body was escorted by the battalion from Kopjie Alleine to Landman's Drift and Dundee on its way to Pietermaritzburg. Captain Harvey, with "H" company and a party of Native pioneers, was also employed in constructing another fort on the Itelezi ridge, which Major-General Marshall, commanding the lines of communication in Zululand—who was much pleased with the work—named Fort Warwick, in honour of the regiment. To replace "H" company, "B" company, under Brevet-Major Bromhead, which had been sent up from Rorke's Drift to a post near Conference Hill, wood-cutting, was moved to Kopjie Alleine. The battalion remained in these positions until after the battle of Ulundi, 4th July, 1879, when a redistribution of companies took place.

After the second division was broken up on 28th July, 1879, Sir Garnet, now Lord, Wolseley, who had arrived to supersede Lord Chelmsford, took "F" and "H" companies, 2nd battalion 24th, under Major C. J. Bromhead, as his special escort. They accompanied him to Ulundi and in all his movements until the conclusion of peace. These companies then fell back on Isandhlwana, completing the burial of the dead there, and afterwards marching to Pietermaritzburg, where they arrived on 6th October, to await the battalion head-quarters. Sir Garnet Wolseley had selected the 2nd battalion 24th for an expedition against Sekukuni, but on his arrival at Utrecht, on 9th September, 1879, he brought the news that the battalion was ordered to Gibraltar. Sir Garnet took the opportunity of presenting their *Victoria Crosses* to Brevet Major Gonville Bromhead and Private Robert Jones. He had already given one to Private Henry Hook at Rorke's Drift. Two other Rorke's Drift men, Corporal Allen and Private Hitch, received their crosses from the hands of Her Majesty at Netley. (See *Victoria Cross Roll, Appendix A*.)

The march of two hundred and fifty miles down country began on 29th September, and on 14th October the remaining companies entered Pietermaritzburg, where great demonstrations awaited " the battalion that saved Natal." The march was resumed on 21st October, and after some delay in camp at Pinetown, awaiting transport, the battalion embarked in the SS. *Ontario*, reached Gibraltar on 12th February, 1880, and went into quarters in the Casemate barracks.

CHAPTER XIV.

1879-81.

The Story of the Colours—Lieutenants Melvill and Coghill—Services of both battalions to 1881.

THE STORY OF THE COLOURS.

HELMET PLATE, 1879-81.

TO avoid digressions in the preceding chapter, it has been thought best to give the Story of the Colours in Zululand as a separate narrative. The details are briefly these :—

When the companies of the 1st battalion were with No. 3 column of Lord Chelmsford's army, of which Colonel R. T. Glyn, C.B., was in command, they had with them the Queen's Colour of the battalion, the regimental colour having been left with the detachment remaining at Helpmakaar.

On the fatal 22nd January, 1879, when it was evident that all was lost in Isandhlwana camp, Lieutenant and Adjutant Melvill, 1st battalion 24th, received special orders from Lieutenant-Colonel Pulleine, to endeavour to save the colour. "You, as senior subaltern," that officer is reported to have said, "will take the colour, and make your way from here." Accompanied by Lieutenant A. J. A. Coghill, 1st battalion 24th, who was orderly officer to Colonel Glyn, but had remained in camp on account of a severe injury to his knee, Melvill rode off with the colour, taking the same direction as the other fugitives. Both officers reached the Buffalo, although, owing to the badness of the track, the Zulus kept up with them and continued throwing their spears at them. The river was in flood, and at any other time would have been considered impassable. They plunged their horses in, but whilst Coghill got across and reached the opposite bank, Melvill, encumbered by the colour, got separated from his horse and was washed against a large rock in mid-stream, to which Lieutenant Higginson, of the Native contingent, who afterwards escaped, was clinging.* Melvill called to him to lay hold of the colour, which Higginson did, but so strong was the current that both men were washed away. Coghill, still on his horse and in comparative safety, at once rode back into the stream to their aid. The Zulus by this time had gathered thick on the bank of the river and opened fire, making a special target of Melvill, who wore his red patrol jacket. Coghill's horse was killed and his rider cast adrift in the stream. Notwithstanding the exertions made to save it, the colour had to be abandoned, and the two officers themselves only succeeded in reaching the opposite bank with great difficulty, and in a most exhausted state. Those only who know the precipitous character of the Natal side at the spot, can fully realize how great must have been the sufferings of both in climbing it, especially of Coghill with his wounded knee. They appear to have kept together, and to have got to within twenty yards of the summit when they were overtaken by their foes and fell.

On 4th February, 1879, Lieutenant-Colonel Black, who in a previous reconnaissance had found the bodies of Melvill and Coghill close to a large boulder, against which they appear to have stood to fight, for around them lay several dead Zulus, set out with a search-party, to endeavour to find the Queen's Colour. After erecting a cairn of stones over the bodies of the two officers where they lay, the party descended into a glen through which the Buffalo runs in deep curves, about four hundred yards below where Melvill crossed. First the case was found, then the crest, lastly, at a spot fifty yards higher up, the colour itself was lifted from the water where it had become wedged between the stones. The party returned to Rorke's Drift and handed over the colour to Colonel Glyn, the men of the 2nd battalion turning out and giving a hearty cheer as the trophy was brought in. Next day it was taken under escort to Helpmakaar and

---

* Melvill's watch was found to have stopped at ten minutes past two, probably the time when he was washed off his horse.

given over to the two companies then representing the 1st battalion.

On 14th April, 1879, the bodies of Lieutenants Melvill and Coghill were buried beside where they fell. A marble cross was subsequently placed over the spot by His Excellency Sir Bartle Frere and his staff, bearing the inscription :—

> In Memory of Lieutenant and Adjutant Teignmouth Melvill and Lieutenant A. J. A. Coghill, 1st battalion 24th regiment, who died on this spot, on 22nd January, 1879, to save the Queen's Colour of their regiment.

And on the reverse side :—

> For Queen and Country.   Jesu Mercy.

While the 1st battalion was at Gosport during the summer after its return home, Her Majesty expressed a wish to see the rescued colour. Accordingly, on 28th July, 1880, Lieutenant-Colonel J. M. G. Tongue, with Lieutenants Weallens and Phipps, and an escort of four colour-sergeants, carried the colours to Osborne, where Her Majesty attached a wreath of immortelles to the pole of the Queen's Colour.* The case bears the following inscription :—

---

* The original wreath with which Her Majesty was graciously pleased to decorate the Queen's colour is now preserved in possession of the officers' mess of the 1st battalion of the regiment. The illustration is taken from a photograph.

THIS WREATH
WAS PLACED ON THE
QUEEN'S COLOUR OF THE 1ST BATTALION 24TH REGIMENT
BY
HER MAJESTY QUEEN VICTORIA,
TO COMMEMORATE THE DEVOTED GALLANTRY OF
LIEUT. AND ADJUTANT T. MELVILL AND LIEUT. N. J. A. GOGHILL,
WHO GAVE THEIR LIVES TO SAVE THE COLOUR FROM THE HANDS
OF THE ENEMY ON 22 JANUARY, 1879, AND IN RECOGNITION
OF THE NOBLE DEFENCE OF RORKE'S DRIFT.
AS A LASTING MEMORIAL OF HER GRACIOUS ACT,
A FACSIMILE OF THE WREATH IN SILVER WAS COMMANDED
TO BE BORNE ON THE
QUEEN'S COLOUR OF BOTH BATTALIONS OF THE REGIMENT.
AUTHORITY DATED 15TH DECR., 1880.
QUEEN AND COUNTRY.

The following letters were subsequently received, and ordered to be entered in the Regimental Records:—

"Horse Guards,
"War Office, S.W.,
"31st July, 1880.

"Sir,

"I have the honour, by the desire of the Field Marshal "Commanding-in-Chief, to subjoin for your information the following "extract from a letter dated Osborne, 28th July, 1880, from Lieut.-General "The Right Hon. Sir Henry Ponsonby, K.C.B.: 'The Queen received "'the Colour party of the 1st battalion 24th Foot, to-day, and decorated "'the Queen's Colour with a wreath in memory of Melvill and Coghill.

"'Her Majesty wishes that this wreath should always be borne on this "'Colour.' And I am to request that you will be pleased to cause the same "to be entered in the Regimental Records.

"I have the honour to be, Sir,
"Your obedient Servant,
"(Signed) C. H. ELLICE, A.G.

"The Officer Commanding 1st Battn. 24th Foot, Gosport."

"Horse Guards,
"War Office, S.W.,
"15th December, 1880.

"Sir,

"I have the honour, by desire of the Field Marshal Command-"ing-in-Chief, to acquaint you, that:—'As a lasting token of her act in "'placing a wreath on the Queen's Colour, 1st battalion 24th Regiment, "'to commemorate the devotion displayed by Lieuts. Melvill and Coghill "'in their heroic endeavour to save the Colour on the 22nd of January, 1879, and of the noble defence of Rorke's Drift, Her Majesty has been graciously pleased to command that a silver wreath shall in future be borne round the staff of the Queen's Colour of the 24th Regiment.' And I am to request that you will convey Her Majesty's gracious command to the 1st battalion of that corps, now serving under your command.

"I have the honour to be, Sir,
"Your obedient Servant,
"C. H. ELLICE, A.G.*

"Major-General Radcliffe,
  "Commanding at Colchester."

A notification had before appeared in the *London Gazette*, of 2nd May, 1879, that Lieutenants Melvill and Coghill, had they survived, would have received the Victoria Cross. (See *Victoria Cross Roll*, *Appendix A.*)

Both the Queen's and Regimental colours of the 2nd battalion were also in the camp at Isandhlwana, having been left there when the battalion marched out twith Colonel Glyn, on the morning of the 22nd January, 1879. The pole, crown, and case of one of the colours were afterwards recovered and carried by the battalion to Gibraltar, where new colours were afterwards presented to the battalion by Lord Napier of Magdala, on behalf of Her Majesty, and thence to India. On arrival in India, the pole was offered to Her Majesty through Lord Napier. The Queen's gracious acceptance of the trophy, and the curious circumstances of the recovery, are recorded in the following letters from Sir John Cowell and Major C. J. Bromhead, by whom the pole was brought home. It should be added that a broken portion of the other colour pole was also found afterwards, and is now in possession of the officers' mess of the battalion.

"Windsor Castle,
"15th March, 1881.
"Sir,
    "I am commanded by the Queen to inform you that Her Majesty has had much pleasure in receiving the colour-staff and crown of the Colour of the 2nd battalion 24th Regiment, which were recovered after the battle of Isandhlwana, and which were offered to the Queen by you and the officers of the battalion.

---

* The same communication was addressed to the officer commanding the 2nd battalion at Secunderabad.

"The staff and crown were delivered to Her Majesty by Major C. J.
"Bromhead by her desire, and they now occupy a place of honour in the
"armoury of the castle, where they will be preserved, with a record of
"their recovery.
"Believe me, &c.,
"(Signed) J. COWELL.

"To Lt.-Col. Degacher, C.B.,
"Commanding 2nd Batt. 24th Regt."

"Heatherlands, Parkstone,
"Dorset, 19th April, 1881.

"Sir,
"In compliance with your instructions I have the honour to
"submit the following particulars relating to the recovery of the Staff and
"Crown and Colour Case of the Colours of the 2nd battalion 24th
"Regiment, which were lost at the capture of the Camp at Isandhlwana,
"on the 22nd of January, 1879, and are now deposited at Windsor Castle.
"The Staff was found by Lieutenant N. Sadlier, King's Dragoon Guards,
"in a Kraal, some two miles from the battle-field, on the 21st May, 1879,
"(when covering the Cavalry reconnaissance, in force, under Major
"General F. Marshall, C.M.G.,) and returned by him to the regiment at
"Rorke's Drift the same day. The Kraal was unfortunately burnt before
"being fully searched.
"The Crown was found by a wood-cutting party of the 2nd battalion
"24th regiment, in the month of March, 1879, in the garden of a Farm
"situated on the Natal bank of the Buffalo, some four miles from Rorke's
"Drift, and about five miles from the battle-field.
"The Crown may have been dropped there by a Zulu after the repulse
"at Rorke's Drift, as the Farm lay in the route taken by the Enemy, and
"was burnt by them that day.
"The Colour Case was found by a detachment 2nd battalion 24th
"Regiment on the 23rd September, 1879, in the bed of the River
"Amanganyanna (Black Water), three-quarters of a mile from the battle-
"field, and at the point crossed by the fugitives.
"This river was carefully searched until it joins the Buffalo three miles
"lower down, but without further success.
"It would appear that the Crown and Colours had been removed from
"the Staff by some one accustomed to do so, as the articles were found
"separate, and no savage would understand how to unscrew the Crown
"from the Staff, and that found shews no sign of violent handling.

"I have the honour to be, Sir,
"Your obedient Servant,
"(Signed) C. J. BROMHEAD,
"Brevet Major, half-pay, 24th Regiment.

"Major-General
"Sir John Cowell, K.C.B.,
"Master of the Household."

CONTINUATION OF SERVICES, 1880-81.

At Gosport a new band, formed of volunteers from other regiments, joined the 1st battalion. All men of the battalion who desired, were retransferred to their original corps, being replaced by drafts from the brigade depôt. In May, 1880, Colonel Glyn, C.B., retired on half-pay from the battalion which he had commanded for thirteen years.

On 6th August, 1880, Brevet Colonel W. M. Dunbar was promoted to regimental lieutenant-colonel, *vice* Colonel Glyn.

On 28th September, 1880, Lieutenant-Colonel Wilsone Black, C.B., succeeded Colonel W. M. Dunbar in command of the battalion.

On 16th November, 1880, the South African war medals were distributed to the battalion.

On 26th November, 1880, the 1st battalion, under command of Lieutenant-Colonel Wilsone Black, C.B., numbering two field officers, seven captains, nine subalterns, two staff, thirty-eight sergeants and four hundred and ten rank and file, proceeded by rail from Portsmouth to Colchester, there to be stationed. Since its arrival in England, the battalion had taken on three hundred and fifty-eight, and struck off seven hundred and nine, men.

As before stated, the 2nd battalion, under Lieutenant-Colonel Degacher, C.B., reached Gibraltar on 12th February, 1880. On 31st July, in the same year, on receipt of news of the Maiwand disaster in Afghanistan, the battalion was ordered to be held in readiness for embarkation for India. New colours had been received from England, and as Her Majesty had intimated her wish that the battalion should receive them at her hands, and had delegated their presentation to the Governor, Lord Napier of Magdala, the ceremony had to be performed before the departure of the battalion. The 6th August, 1880, was fixed for the ceremony.

The men made a goodly show as they paraded on the Alameda on the afternoon of that day. After trooping the old relic, the colour pole and crown before mentioned—the escort for which was furnished by "B" company, of Rorke's Drift memory—a hollow square was formed. His Excellency having dismounted, the new colours were handed to him by Captains J. J. Harvey and H. M. Williams, and were by him delivered to Lieutenant Smyly and Sub-Lieutenant Neave, who received them kneeling. In the course of his speech, Lord Napier said:

" At Isandhlwana, your comrades overwhelmed by countless numbers, " with ammunition exhausted, fell in the ranks in which they had fought, " dauntless to the last, and surrounded by the enemy's slain. Their " Queen's colour was saved by the devotion of Lieutenants Melvill and " Coghill, but at the sacrifice of their own lives. Five officers and one " hundred and seventy-three non-commissioned officers and men of your " battalion fell in defence of the camp. Who can ever forget the heroic " history of Rorke's Drift! The prompt resolution of the gallant Bromhead, " fully appreciating the importance of the post and determined to defend it " to the last! The skill and courage of the engineer, Lieutenant Chard, "and the noble conduct of the garrison? What words can convey " sufficient praise for Private Joseph Williams, who defended the entrance " to the hospital while his comrades were removing the sick, and gave his " life to save theirs! Never were Victoria Crosses won better than those " with which Her Majesty decorated Major Bromhead, Corporal William " Allen, and Privates John Williams, William Hook, Frederick Hitch, " Robert Jones, and William Jones. Thirteen times has the Victoria " Cross been won by the 24th regiment since 1867. The history of your " regiment is one of which you may well be proud; it is a noble " heritage."

On 12th August, 1880, the 2nd battalion 24th embarked in the *Orontes*, reached Bombay on 1st, and Poonah on 2nd September. On 15th September the battalion was very unexpectedly sent off from Poonah, again by rail, to Secunderabad, Deccan.

A general order (No. 57), received in February, 1881, signified Her Majesty's pleasure that the 24th (2nd Warwickshire) Regiment should bear upon its colours and appointments, in addition to previous distinctions, the words, "SOUTH AFRICA," in commemoration of its services there in the campaigns of 1877-78-79.

CHAPTER XV.

1881-92.

The Regiment named the "South Wales Borderers"—Services of the First Battalion—Services of the Second Battalion.

SERVICES OF THE FIRST BATTALION.

ON 1st July, 1881, in consequence of the new territorial organisation of the army, the time-honoured title of the 24th (or 2nd Warwickshire) Regiment was ordered to be discontinued, and the 1st and 2nd battalions, then stationed respectively at Colchester and at Secunderabad, to be styled the First and Second Battalions of the South Wales Borderers. The facings were changed from *grass-green* to *white*, with gold, *rose-pattern* lace. At the same time, the Royal South Wales Borderers Militia Rifles (late the Royal Radnor and Royal Brecknock Militias) and the Royal Montgomery Militia Rifles were ordered to be styled, respectively, the 3rd and 4th battalions South Wales Borderers, and their uniforms (*green*, facings *scarlet*, lace *black*) to be altered to that to be adopted by the line battalions of the regiment.

On 25th February, 1882, Colonel Wilsone Black retired from the command of the 1st battalion, on appointment to the staff, as adjutant and quarter-master general at Halifax, Nova Scotia.

On 29th of April the regiment was ordered to adopt as a quickstep, "Men of Harlech," in place of "Warwickshire Lads." (See *Appendix C.)*

The following communication, bearing the like date, was also received:—

"Horse Guards,
"War Office,
"29th April, 1882.

"Sir,

"By desire of H.R.H. the Field-Marshal Commanding-"in-Chief, I have the honour to acquaint you that Her Majesty has "been graciously pleased to command that the victories of "'BLENHEIM,' 'RAMILLIES,' 'OUDENARDE,' and 'MALPLAQUET' "shall be inscribed on the colours of the South Wales Borderers, "and the same shall be recorded in the next issue of the *Queen's* "*Regulations and Orders for the Army,* in addition to their present "achievements.

"I have the honour, etc.,

"(Signed) G. J. WOLSELEY, Adjutant-General.

"The Officer commanding, Colchester."

On 14th August, 1882, on the occasion of a partial mobilisation of the reserves in consequence of the war in Egypt, one hundred and two non-commissioned officers and men rejoined the colours at Colchester. The battalion was specially commended by the civil authorities for its activity at a fire in Queen Street, Colchester, on the night of 18th-19th August. On 29th August, the battalion (seven companies), under Lieutenant-Colonel Tongue, proceeded by rail from Colchester to Manchester, and was quartered for a year in Salford barracks, giving detachments at Birmingham and Chester.

A general order of 1st September, 1882, signified Her Majesty's commands that the dates "1806" be added to "Cape of Good Hope," and "1877-78-79" to "South Africa," on the regimental colours and appointments.

On 26th September, 1883, the battalion proceeded by rail from Salford to Liverpool, crossed to Dublin, and from thence to Kilkenny, furnishing detachments at Waterford, Killarney, and Duncannon Fort.

On 6th April, 1844, General Sir Charles Ellice, G.C.B., was appointed colonel, *vice* General Pringle Taylor, K.H., deceased.

On 31st January, 1885, Colonel George Paton, C.M.G., succeeded to the command, *vice* Colonel Tongue, appointed commandant of the School of Musketry at Hythe. On 28th September, the same year, the battalion proceeded to the Curragh. Whilst at the Curragh, the regiment lost the services of Captain W. E. D. Spring, 1st battalion, who died at Harrogate, 13th January, 1886, to the great regret of his brother officers.

In August, 1886, three companies proceeded to Belfast, in aid of the civil power, and were subsequently reinforced by two others.* One of them went to Galway, and three others rejoined at the Curragh when the disturbances were over. On 18th October, 1886, the battalion removed from the Curragh to Birr. The following extract from District Orders, dated Adjutant-General's Office, Dublin, 12th October, 1886, was published for general information :—

"H.S.H. the Commander of the Forces has much pleasure in notify-"ing to the Troops in the Command that the Lords of the Treasury have "approved of the payment of a pecuniary reward to Corporal Roach, 1st "battalion South Wales Borderers, in recognition of his gallant conduct "during the riots in Belfast, under the following circumstances : Corporal "Roach pursued a rioter armed with a revolver, and notwithstanding that "the latter turned and threatened to fire, the corporal ran in upon him, "arrested him, and handed him over to the civil power."

The battalion was still at Birr at the time of the celebration of Her Majesty's Jubilee, in June, 1887. On 29th September that year it removed to Dublin, and was quartered in the Richmond Barracks.

General Sir Chas. Ellice, the colonel of the regiment, having forwarded to the Right Honble. Sir Henry Ponsonby a photograph of the officers killed at Isandhlwana, 22nd January, 1879, for Her Majesty's acceptance, the following reply was received :—

"Osborne, 24th December, 1887.
"MY DEAR ELLICE,
"The Queen was much pleased by your sending her the photo-"graph of the officers of the 24th who were killed at Isandhlwana, "and though touched by the sad recollections it arouses, Her Majesty "is glad to receive these portraits of those who died whilst gallantly "doing their duty.
"Yours very truly,
"(Signed)   H. PONSONBY."

On 24th February, 1888, Colonel Paton, C.M.G., retired; and on 9th June following, Lieutenant-Colonel Farquhar Glennie succeeded to the command of a battalion, and exchanged with Lieutenant-Colonel C. J. Bromhead, who proceeded to join the 2nd battalion in Burmah.

---

* An attack by a mob on an Orange procession on 31st July resulted in serious rioting, during which some sixty persons were injured, eleven of them fatally.

On 13th November, 1888, General E. Wodehouse was appointed colonel, *vice* Sir Chas. Ellice, G.C.B., deceased. The battalion was under canvas in the Phœnix Park during the summer of 1889, the Richmond Barracks being in the hands of the engineers. During its stay in Dublin, typhoid fever was rife in the battalion, especially among the officers.

On 14th December, 1889, the battalion, under command of Major Moffat, embarked at Kingston for Portsmouth, where it arrived on 17th December, and proceeded to Aldershot.

In July, 1891, the battalion marched from Aldershot to London to keep the streets on the occasion of the State visit of the German Emperor to the Guildhall, returning by march route to camp on the completion of the duty.

In May, 1892, the battalion sent a team from Aldershot to the Military Tournament, in London, which carried off the first prizes in bayonet exercise and bayonet combat.

On 9th June, 1892, Colonel Farquhar Glennie, having completed the regulation period of four years' command of the battalion, retired on half-pay, and was succeeded by Major G. S. Banister.

SERVICES OF THE SECOND BATTALION.

Services in Burmah, 1881-92.

The battalion remained at Secunderabad from the date of its arrival, in 1880, until 31st December, 1883, when it proceeded to join the Camp of Exercise, at Bangalore. It remained in camp there until 1st February, 1884, when it proceeded by rail to Fort St. George, Madras, detaching a company to Malliapuram.

On 1st December, 1884, a detachment—consisting of Captain Heaton, Lieutenant Sugden, five sergeants, five corporals, and one hundred and fifty privates—was sent to Fort Blair, Andaman Islands.

On 3rd May, 1885, the detachment at Malliapuram under Captain Logan was employed in suppressing an outbreak of Moplahs,* near Tirur, in which Corporal Mooney and Privates Lynch and Fryer were wounded severely, and Private Coughlin slightly. A notification was afterwards received, dated 12th May, 1885, stating that the commander-in-chief considered the duty to have been promptly and well carried out by Captain Logan and his men.

On 20th April, 1886, the detachment at the Andaman Islands was relieved by a like party under Major Harvey and Lieutenants Moore and Cooke.

On 4th May, 1886, the battalion—consisting of twelve officers, two warrant officers, seven staff sergeants, twenty-two sergeants, twenty-four corporals, thirteen drummers, and six hundred and forty-seven privates, with thirty-seven women and fifty-one children—embarked for Rangoon, where it landed by wings on 9th and 10th May. The King of Burmah had been deposed, and his possessions, now Upper Burmah, had been annexed to the Indian Empire, and placed under the Chief Commissioner of British Burmah

---

* A turbulent sect of Mahomedan fanatics.

(Lower Burmah) and his assistants, from 26th February previous.

On 6th August, 1886, a detachment, consisting of Major Clements, with Lieutenants Kelly, Parker, and King, with two hundred and twenty non-commissioned officers and men was sent by rail and river to Thayet-Myo, whither it was followed on 19th September by another party, consisting of Major Heaton, Lieutenant Reed, and one hundred men. The right wing of the battalion, under Colonel Upcher, and the left wing under Colonel Bromhead, proceeded to Thayet-Myo and Tonghoo respectively on the 2nd December following.

During the years 1886-87-88 the battalion was constanty engaged in the pacification of Upper Burmah, and between September, 1886, and November, 1888, had three privates killed and fifty-six non commissioned officers and men, who died of wounds, or of disease induced by the ardous work gone through in the fever-haunted jungles. The following illustrative incidents have been recorded :—

On 14th August, 1886, " A " company, made up by " E " company to one hundred and five rifles, marched out of Thayet-Myo. On 18th October it returned with only five men fit for duty. Two had been killed in action, twenty-one had died of fever ; the remaining seventy-seven were attending hospital.

On 13th September, 1886, Major Clements, in command of fifty rifles of the battalion, was proceeding from the village of Myo Thit to the military post of Taindah. Sergeant Neave and six men formed the advanced guard. After six miles, the flank groups had to close on the track, as the jungle was impenetrable on either side. Shortly after they had closed, a volley was fired into them at fifteen yards. Privates Head and Lewis fell dead; Sergeant Neave and Privates Bickley and Loxton were severely wounded. Private Loxton propped himself up and opened fire on the Dacoits, who now appeared on all sides. His conduct was afterwards especially brought to notice. Major Clements quickly brought up some men and dispersed the enemy, but not before he was himself wounded.

On 4th and 5th October, 1887, Major Harvey, 2nd battalion 24th then in command of the frontier posts to the north and west of Thayet-Myo—with Lieutenant Way and forty rifles of the mounted infantry of the battalion, and Captain Alban with thirty-one mounted infantry of the 7th Bombay Native Infantry whom he picked up on his way, after a very trying march in single file of sixty-seven miles, the last fifty-two of which was done in fourteen hours in rain and over the roughest of jungle tracks, surprised and killed the noted Dacoit leader, Bo Shwè.

The Dacoits were encamped in huts on the hills, and numbered about one hundred and fifty. They were completely taken by surprise at mid-day, and fled without making any resistance, leaving their leader and ten of their number dead, many wounded, forty guns, their camp as it stood, and much ammunition. The gang was pursued for two miles through dense jungles, over ground quite impossible for the ponies of the mounted infantry to travel.

This exploit was considered one of the smartest performed in Upper Burmah. Major Harvey was promoted to a brevet lieutenant-colonelcy, and afterwards received the D.S.O. for his services in command of the Lower Burmah Karens. Major R. A. P. Clements also received a brevet lieutenant-colonelcy and the D.S.O. for his services in Upper Burmah, where he was twice wounded. Captain Upcher also received the D.S.O. for his services with the battalion in Burmah.

The battalion arrived by wings at Rangoon from Thayet-Myo and Tonghoo on 5th and 9th November, 1888. Major Harvey having been selected for service on the staff in Burmah, Major Heaton assumed command of the battalion, which embarked at Rangoon on 10th November in the I.M.S. *Clive*, and arrived at Calcutta on 14th November. Thence it proceeded to Bareilly, where Colonel Bromhead took command.

In March, 1889, the battalion proceeded from Bareilly to Ranikhet, returning to Bareilly in November the same year.

On 27th July, 1890, the regiment lost a distinguished officer in Brevet Lieutenant-Colonel Harvey, D.S.O., who died of cholera, to the sincere regret of all ranks.

24TH REGIMENT. 283

The following remarks by Sir Frederick Roberts, G.C.B., the commander-in-chief, were published in Battalion Orders of 17th October, 1890 :—

"I inspected the 2nd battalion South Wales Borderers at Ranikhet "in April last, and was much pleased with the appearance and turn-out of the "men. The Report shews the battalion to be thoroughly efficient, and "reflects great credit on Colonel Bromhead. The conduct of the men has "been good, and has considerably improved since last year. Great care "and attention are paid to the Regimental Institutions, and the comfort "and welfare of all ranks are well looked after."

On 17th October, 1890, two companies left Ranikhet for Allahabad, the rest of the battalion following in November.

On 22nd January, 1891, a letter was received from the Right Honble. Sir Henry Ponsonby, enclosing, by command of the Queen, a photogravure of the Royal Review at Aldershot, in 1859, in which the battalion took part, for the officers' mess.

On 7th February, 1891, to the great sorrow of all ranks of the regiment, and of his many friends in and out of the service, Major Gonville Bromhead, V.C. (of Rorke's Drift), succumbed to an attack of typhoid fever.

The following telegraphic message was received from the Commander-in-Chief on the sad occasion :—

"Please let all ranks of the South Wales Borderers know how much "the Chief sympathizes with them in the loss of Major Bromhead, V.C., "who behaved with such conspicuous gallantry at Rorke's Drift, and so "well supported the reputation of his distinguished regiment."

The battalion, under command of Colonel W. P. Symons, C.B., is still (June, 1892) at Allahabad.

CHAPTER XVI.

NOTES ON THE COSTUME AND EQUIPMENTS.
1742-1873.

PRIVATE, 1742.

ALTHOUGH the regiment was raised in 1689, there appears to be no evidence in existence regarding the particular costume worn until 1742. No doubt the clothing was red, and probably the facings (the lining of the coat coming prominently into view when the lapels and cuffs were turned back) would be green. The first really authentic information is obtained from the work entitled "*The Cloathing of His Majesty's Troops, etc., etc., 1742*" (copy in the British Museum), which gives a coloured engraving of a soldier of every regiment then existing. The illustration represents that of the 24th regiment. The large and broad skirted coat is of red cloth; the lapels and cuffs green; the skirts, however, lined white; the latter a departure from the general order of things, as the facings and skirt linings were at that period almost invariably of the same shade.

There seems to have been some particular regimental distinction in this, for, if an *Army List* for 1758 is consulted, it will be found that the 24th is credited with having willow green facings, *lined with white*. This is repeated until 1787, and then discontinued.* The coat is trimmed with narrow white lace, having

---

* Millan's *Complete System of Camp Discipline*, 1747, gives a list of infantry regiments with their facings, and quotes the 24th as having "willow green facings, lined white."

a green stripe; the button-holes are also bound with it. This lace may have been intended to strengthen the coat; it was, however, ornamental and characteristic. Most regiments had different patterns, which, together with the various hues of the facings, was all that distinguished one corps from another; numbers, though used, as far as precedency of regiments was concerned, did not show on the buttons.

The waistcoat of 1742 was cut very long in the body, of red cloth, and bound with white lace; the breeches the same colour; the leggings, white.

The next information is found in the picture of a grenadier of the regiment at Windsor Castle, by David Morier, an able artist, who executed a number of military pictures for the king, about 1750-52.

The coloured illustration, p. 62, represents the picture in question. All grenadiers wore the tall mitre-shaped cap, having on the lower part a red flap, thereon the "White Horse" of Hanover, with the motto "*Nec aspera terrent.*" The upper part, of cloth, was of the colour of the facings, willow green; embroidered in crewel work, with the royal cipher in white and the crown above. The coat and skirts still continue large and easy, the lining of the latter being depicted in Morier's picture as of willow green. Whether this is a mistake on his part, or whether the skirts were now actually green, will possibly never be cleared up; the fact that white linings are specially mentioned in the *Army Lists* up to 1787 is not evidence of a conclusive character; such things were often repeated year after year, long after they had fallen into disuse. The lace on the coat, it will be noticed, has two green stripes. Though called grenadiers, their occupation as such was gone; no hand grenades had been thrown for twenty years or more, and of their peculiar equipment nothing was left but the high caps originally intended to increase the appearance, and the brass-mounted match case, an empty relic, destined to remain attached to the cross-belt for sixty or seventy years, a special mark of the grenadier company.

There is no evidence of the officers' costume at this period, unless it exists in family portraits, but doubtless, as in the case of officers of other regiments, whose dress is known, it would consist of a voluminous wide-skirted red coat, faced with willow green, laced with narrow silver lace and a silver aiquillette on the right shoulder, the sword suspended from a waistbelt under the waistcoat, and a crimson silk sash over the left shoulder. Battalion officers, like the men, had three-cornered cocked hats, but laced with silver, displaying on the left side the black cockade of the reigning house of Hanover. Grenadier officers wore a cap in shape like that of the men, but handsomely embroidered in gold and silver.

Regiments of infantry had received a number early in the century, in conformity with their order of precedence, which, however, was used as little as possible; there seemed a dislike to it in the official mind, and regiments were invariably designated by their colonel's name, but it being found desirable to have an additional form of distinction beyond the facings and the varied patterns of regimental lace, a warrant was issued 21st September, 1767, requiring that the number of the regiment should appear on the buttons, hitherto quite plain.

GRENADIER, 1768

By warrant, in 1768, the cloth grenadier cap was abolished, and a new one of bearskin introduced, having in front the badge of the king's crest (lion and crown) in white metal on a black ground. This, it may be observed, was common to all grenadiers.

The illustration represents a grenadier of the regiment in the uniform conformable to the new regulations of 1768, taken from a MSS. work in the Prince Consort's library, Aldershot.

It will be noticed that the coat has become a very much closer fitting garment, a turned-down collar, or cape as it was then called, has appeared, the lapels across the chest very much smaller than before, serving little more than to shew off the lace-looped button-holes on them.

The Royal Warrant of 19th December, 1768, is full of detail on every point connected with the uniform of the infantry, both men and officers. The private soldier's lace had become a matter of strict regulation. In the case of the 24th, the lace was white, with two stripes, one red and one green, the loops being square-headed, and set on at equal distances.

This pattern of lace was worn by the private soldiers until the alteration of 1824. The loops themselves were set on by twos somewhere towards the end of the century, and so remained until 1855; in fact, when the tunic was first authorised.

The officer's costume was as follows :—scarlet coats lapelled to the waist with green cloth lapels, three inches wide, fastened back by silver buttons (having the regimental number), and placed at equal distances; the cape, or collar, also of green cloth turned down, and fastened by one button-hole to the top button of the lapels. Small round green cuffs, three inches and a half deep, having four buttons and button-holes, cross pockets in line with the waist, having four buttons; skirts lined and turned back white; this latter the regulation for all, and therefore now of no particular significance to the regiment. The button-holes throughout edged with narrow silver lace.

Officers of the grenadier company wore an epaulet of silver lace and fringe on each shoulder; battalion officers one on the right shoulder only, white waistcoat and breeches, black linen gaiters with black buttons; crimson silk sash, tied round the waist (until recently worn over the shoulder); a silver gorget with the king's arms engraved thereon, fastened to the neck with green silk rosettes and ribbons; hats laced with silver, and the usual black cockade.

Grenadier officers wore the back bearskin cap like the men, but the king's crest in gilt upon the black metal; they carried fusils (a short musket), and had white shoulder belts and pouches.

Battalion officers carried the espontoon, a light steel-headed pike, with a small cross-bar below the blade, seven feet in length, used with graceful effect in the salute.

Sergeants had buttons of white metal, and narrow loops of plain white tape; hats laced with silver, silk shoulder knots, and crimson and green worsted sashes; they carried swords from a shoulder belt and halberds, the latter a light ornamental kind of battle-axe with a long shaft.

Annual regimental inspections by general officers had been instituted quite as early as 1709, but the earliest inspection return of the 24th which has been preserved is dated Carlisle, May 15th, 1750. General Onslow, after detailing the state of the equipments, etc., states that "the two colours are in good order, there are twenty "drummers, and that the men have very good white gaiters, as well as "marching gaiters."

Another, dated Exeter, May, 1751, gives few details.

The next one to be found, dated Dublin, 16th May, 1771, adds "the regiment has a band of music."

Others, soon after, in 1773 and 1774, dated respectively Galway and Dublin, state "the officers' uniform is red, faced green, white lining, "square pockets, buttons numbered."

The uniform of 1768 remained almost unaltered till about 1790; cross-belts were however introduced for the men, that is the bayonet belt removed from the waist to the shoulder, and a brass breastplate, (probably oval in form with the regimental number engraved thereon) affixed to the latter.

The officers' swords were also ordered to be suspended in a white shoulder belt, over the right shoulder, ornamented with a silver oval breastplate, but of what design, in the absence of any authority, cannot be arrived at. The espontoons also discontinued.

The coloured illustration, p. 76, represents an officer, 1792. The outline of the figure and details of the cut of the uniform are taken from E. Dayes' beautiful series of coloured engravings of the infantry, in the British Museum. It will be noticed that the gaiters are shorter than formerly, only reaching to the knee; the collar is also worn turned up, the button and silver loop, originally used to fasten it down, still retained on it only as ornament, destined however, as will afterwards be seen, to develope into two buttons and two loops of silver lace, and so to remain on the officers' coat collars till 1855, more than half a century after its original purposes or uses had lapsed. The coat had become still more scanty, and the waistcoat also shrinking quite up to the waist.

The private soldier's uniform of this date was extremely like that of the officer's in cut, but with loops of the regimental lace (white, with a green and a red stripe) to all the button-holes.

Towards the end of the century, following the general fashion of the day, it was decided to fasten the coat in front down to the waist, completely hiding the white waistcoat.

The warrant of 1796 directed that for officers the lapels were to be continued down to the waist, and to be made either to button over occasionally (making what now would be called a double-breasted coat) or to fasten close with hooks and eyes all the way to the bottom, in which case the green lapel, with its silver-laced loops round the button-holes, would shew, being buttoned back, the stand-up collar very high and roomy, to admit the large neck-cloth coming into fashion.

It may be that at this time also the white piping or edging round the collar, cuffs, pockets, and coat generally was introduced, and also the custom of wearing the buttons and silver loops by *twos*, instead of singly, as hitherto.

The jacket for the rank and file was single-breasted, having ten buttons and loops of regimental lace down the front, probably arranged in twos, the lace serving no other purpose than that of ornament. The button now, and for probably the last ten years, in use, was of hard white metal, about five-eighths of an inch in diameter, perfectly flat, the number 24 raised in the centre, surrounded by a very narrow ring or circle formed in a small and neat pattern of laurels. The old white woollen waistcoat with sleeves became practically the shell jacket worn for undress or fatigue duties, though still and for many years afterwards called the "waistcoat."

Horse Guards warrant, dated 22nd April, 1799, directed officers and men of infantry (except the flank companies) to wear their hair queued, to be tied a little below the upper part of the collar of the coat, and to be ten inches in length, including one inch of hair to appear below the binding.

w

The cocked hat worn by the men was discontinued by general order, dated February, 1800. The three-cornered old-fashioned shape had been out of use some time, the hat having only two corners, and being worn across, even with the shoulders. A cylindrical shako took its place. This head-dress was made of lacquered felt, ornamented with a large oblong brass plate in front, some six inches high, thereon engraved the regimental number, with the king's crest, surrounded by a trophy of drums, standards, etc. A red and white worsted tuft was fixed in front, rising from a black cockade.

The officers, however, still retained the cocked hat, wearing it fore and aft, ornamented with a large red and white feather. This head-dress was used all through the earlier stages of the Peninsular war, and, in most cases, at least a year after the order was issued for its discontinuance.

The illustration represents an officer of the regiment about the year 1808, the same costume being, as a rule, worn up to 1811, the tops of the lapel often worn turned back, shewing the green facing and a little of the silver lacing.* Bright blue pantaloons were much worn, and it may be noticed that the old-fashioned knee-boot, or possibly gaiter, had given way to the universally adopted Hessian boot, with tassels. With the beginning of the century, the officers brought into use a very handsome oval silver breastplate, worn in the centre of the shoulder-belt supporting the sword. It was a matted silver

OFFICER, 1808.

---

* The officers' silver lace was plain vellum pattern at this time, very narrow, probably not more than a quarter of an inch in width,

plate with a beaded edge. In the centre, an eight-pointed bright silver star, very much raised; in the middle of the latter "XXIV.," with a girdle thereon, "2nd Warwickshire Regiment." The officers' silver buttons worn now were rather plain, without device or ornament of any kind other than the number 24 engraved in the centre, the shape very convex, almost amounting to a half globe.

Chevrons for the non-commissioned officers were introduced by an order dated July, 1802; sergeant-majors to be distinguished by four, sergeants by three, and corporals by two chevrons on the right arm; the first of silver lace, the second of the plain white tape lace, and the third of the red and green white-striped regimental lace. For a considerable period the staff-sergeants had worn silver lace on their coats, and continued to do so until 1855, notwithstanding the fact that the officers' lace (as will be shewn) was changed to gold in 1831.

By the year 1808 it became clear to the authorities that too much time was taken up in making and dressing the queue, time better spent at drill now that soldiers were so much wanted at the front. To the joy of the sufferers, this troublesome appendage was abolished by an order dated 20th July, 1808. "The hair to be cut short in "the neck, and a small sponge added to the rest of the soldier's "necessaries, for the purpose of frequently washing his head."

December, 1811. A War Office order authorized infantry officers to wear a cap of a pattern similar to that of the men, also permitting them to wear a regimental jacket to button over the breast and body (double-breasted, in fact), and a grey overcoat, also grey pantaloons or overalls, as the private men. This was the service dress used by officers during the later Peninsular and the Waterloo campaigns.

1814. The general costume of the regiment was as follows:—officers, long-tailed scarlet coat for parade, levees, etc., green lapels buttoned back by ten silver buttons (as last described), and silver lace loops (vellum pattern) set on by twos. The coat collar of green cloth, with two buttons and silver loops on each side, cuffs with four buttons and loops by pairs, cross pockets (in line with the waist) with the same; skirts turned back white, the skirt ornament (where the points of the turnbacks met, replacing, in fact, the buttons absolutely necessary with the old voluminous skirts) being—so old lacemen's books tell us—silver embroidered "admiral's" stars, 24 in centre, on green cloth. The white turnbacks had an edging of the regimental silver lace down the outsides, meeting under the star; there was also a triangle of lace in the small of the back between the coat buttons. The coat generally, the collar, cuffs, and pockets piped or edged white. White breeches with black leggings worn for home, and grey trousers for active service. The coloured illustration, p. 134 represents an officer in the service dress of 1814.

The long straight sword, black leather scabbard, gilt mounting, with crimson and gold sword knot, was worn according to regulation, suspended in a frog from a light buffalo leathern shoulder-belt, the latter ornamented with the regimental silver breastplate already described. Officers of the light company carried the light infantry sabre, suspended by slings from the shoulder-belt (on service, however, this weapon was often used by other officers), a crimson sash being worn round the waist.

It was quite customary at this period, judging from the evidence of miniatures, corroborated by the evidence of the inspection returns,* for officers of the 1st battalion serving in the East Indies to wear single-breasted scarlet coats with the silver lace loops (by twos) in front on the scarlet cloth.

Officer's rank distinguished by the silver epaulet, according to the instructions laid down in the general order, dated February, 1810. Field Officers wore two, a colonel having a crown and a star in gold on the strap; a lieutenant-colonel, a crown; major, a star; captains and subalterns, including the quarter-master, wore one silver epaulet on the right shoulder. Officers of the flank companies, two silver shoulder wings, with grenades or bugles thereon respectively. The adjutant wore, in addition to his epaulet, an epaulet strap, without fringe, on his left shoulder.

The epaulettes of field officers and captains, together with the wings

---

* Inspection Return, 1816. 24th Regiment, 1st Battalion, Dinapore. "The officers' jackets are without lapels, single-breasted, like the men; and the wear of officers is white linen pantaloons and white half-gaiters. Field officers, half-boots."

of captains of flank companies, were edged with silver bullion; those of the subalterns, with silver fringe. Paymaster and surgeon wore the regimental coat, single-breasted, without epaulet or sash, the sword being suspended by a plain waistbelt under the coat.

Private soldiers had single-breasted red cloth jackets, laced across the chest with square-headed loops of the regimental lace (before described) four inches long, set on in pairs. Lace round the high green collar (shewing a white frill in front), also round the green shoulder straps, terminating in small white shoulder tufts; in the flank companies with a wing of red cloth trimmed with stripes of regimental lace and edged with an overhanging fringe of white worsted; gaiters and breeches as officers.

Sergeants dressed like privates, but in finer cloth, having the chevrons of their rank on the arm, which, together with their coat lace, was of fine white tape; sash, crimson worsted with a green stripe. They carried a straight sword in a shoulder-belt with a brass breastplate, as worn by the men, their other weapon being the halberd, which had a plain steel spear-head with crossbar, not unlike the "espontoon" formerly carried by the officers, the old battle-axe-headed halberd having fallen into disuse about 1792.

The head dress for officers was a light felt cylindrical chako of felt with black leather peak, a black cockade and small red and white tuft on the left side (green or white for light infantry or grenadiers respectively) a gilt oval plate in front, surmounted by a crown, thereon the cipher G.R., with the regimental number; across the front, a festoon of red and gold cord, with tassels on the right side. That for the men of similar make, but the cords and tassels of white worsted. On service, cap covers worn, of black japanned material.

In 1816, the neat and serviceable felt cap was laid aside, and the broad-topped heavy chako introduced, its shape being more in accordance with foreign fashion, then, as before, our chief guide in such matters. It was eleven inches in diameter at the top, and seven and a half deep, brass chin scales, which, when not required, could be fastened up to the cockade in front, ornamented with an upright white feather, twelve inches high, and a brass plate in front with the regimental number. The light company had a green feather,

Grenadier companies on home service and in cold climates were directed to wear high bearskin caps, a head dress which during the busy war time had fallen into disuse. The officers' chakos had silver lace two inches wide round the top, and a three-quarter inch silver lace round the bottom. On the lace immediately below the high feather appeared the black cockade, in the shape of an oval boss of black cord, a regimental button in the centre; the ornament in front taking the form of a small circular silver burnished plate, having 24 in gold between two gold laurel leaves, this plate being surrounded in turn by four narrow circles—the inner one black, next silver lace, the next red, and the outer one silver lace again; the whole connected with the black cockade by a short silver scale loop. Silver chin scales worn, generally fastened up to the cockade with black ribbon.

Short-tailed coats or jackets for all ranks were abolished in 1820, and two years afterwards the breeches and leggings. The same year a circular was issued, calling attention to the fact that "the gorget formed "part of the officer's equipment." This ancient ornament seemed falling into disuse; whether this circular restored it to its former position is doubtful. It is difficult to find any evidence from portraits or miniatures that it was used, or had indeed been used for some time. Finally, in 1830, it was obligingly abolished.

According to the regimental records, a new set of accoutrements was ordered for the regiment by its colonel, General Sir David Baird, Baronet, G.C.B., "and the patterns of the breastplates, buttons, and lace were altered." This would principally refer to the equipments of the rank and file.

The old brass breastplate (design unknown) would undoubtedly be replaced by a square one of the pattern which lasted until 1855. It had a raised star, nearly filling the plate; in the centre of it a girdle, surmounted by a crown, on it "Warwickshire," and within the girdle 24 in floriated characters; below the girdle, but partially on the star, a sphinx, with the motto, "Egypt;" below that again, quite at the foot of the plate, a label bearing the word "Peninsula." The old flat buttons would be replaced by a smaller pattern, still of white metal, and the white lace with the red and green stripes was changed to one with a single red stripe.

There are indications that about this period, or perhaps a little before, the old oval officer's breastplate had given way to a new one of square oblong shape, also of silver. It will be found slightly referred to in the year 1828.*

In 1826 the private soldier's coat altered in shape, the lace loops across the chest of the new pattern, white with one red stripe, made broader at the top, tapering down narrower towards the bottom, and the lace taken off the skirts.

1826. OFFICERS' COSTUME. Chakos, as before described, but half an inch higher, the silver lace round the top now a handsome pattern, called "flower and ring," regimental lace at bottom.

Long-tailed coats, the skirt ornaments as before, the general cut of the coat much as in 1814, excepting that the green lapels were cut rather broad, forming what was known as the cuirass breast; the collar also was of the so-called Prussian shape, cut square and fastened up the front, precluding the possibility of wearing the shirt collar and large black neckcloth so conspicuous only a few years before.

The white piping or edging on the coat pretty much as described for 1814. Epaulettes were also under the same regulations, but had become much larger, the strap of silver lace (two and a quarter inches fine check pattern), the crescent filled in rough bullion with a silver rose at each end, the fringe some three and a quarter inches deep. The wings worn by the officers of the flank companies very handsome; the strap and crescent as for battalion officers, thereon gold grenades or bugles, the wing part (over the shoulder at right angles to the strap embroidered with silver, shell pattern, as for Highland officers) on scarlet cloth, edged over the shoulders with short bullion fringe. The skirt ornaments worn by these officers were silver embroidered grenades or bugles respectively.

The dress trousers worn very full, Cossack shape, of light blueish

---

* The writer of these notes has never come across a specimen, or even seen a copy of the design of this particular plate; indeed its wear would be for so short a time, at most seven years, that very few would be made, and those soon melted up when out of use.

grey cloth, and trimmed down the outer seam with silver lace, two and a half inches wide, oak pattern, a green silk stripe woven into it on each side.

Light company officers wore whistles and chains; a blue "great coat," otherwise frock coat, was authorised for undress, the crimson sash worn with it, and the sword suspended in a frog from a black leathern waistbelt.

For balls, levees, etc. the coat was worn with white kerseymere breeches, silk stockings, and shoebuckles, the sword being carried in a belt under the coat. See illustration.

OFFICER,
1826,
LEVEE DRESS.

So much lace had been introduced on to the coats of many regiments since the commencement of the century, notably so in the case of the 24th, that the authorities issued special orders to inspecting officers to report upon any deviations from the established dress regulations.

Accordingly, on the 23rd October, 1828, the following was handed in:* "The "major-general has to report that, previous "to March last, light blue trousers, with "silver lace, costing four pounds, and a "silver waistbelt, costing one pound fifteen "shillings, were introduced for dress by "Lieutenant-Colonel Fleming, but the "only deviation from regulation which now "exists are having badges placed on the breastplate, costing eighteen "shillings, and a trifling alteration in the wings of the flank "companies."

In December, 1828, the officer's chako was considerably altered, being reduced to six inches in height, all the silver lace removed; and, to the surprise of many, the time-honoured Hanoverian black cockade

---

* By the officer who inspected the 24th.

also disappeared—never since this date worn on the chakos of infantry officers; it lingered till recently on those of rifle regiments, and still occupies a place, in a somewhat modified manner, on the cocked hats of the staff. The only ornament in front of the new chako was a new universal pattern gilt star plate with crown over, about six inches by five inches in size; in the centre of it regiments were allowed to place what regimental devices they pleased; probably the 24th placed a silver star thereon, with a gilt girdle, and the regimental number in the centre.

Gold cap lines were introduced, having a heavily braided festoon in front, terminating in two tassels, looped up to one of the coat buttons. The men had similar chakos with a small brass star plate, with white— and the light company green—cap lines. A month afterwards the feather was ordered to be white for the whole, light infantry excepted, still remaining, however, twelve inches high.

The very large amount of lace on the coats of officers of the regiment was shared by the officers of many other regiments in the army who wore lace, whilst some regiments, by no means undistinguished, wore none at all on the coat beyond the single epaulet and the skirt ornaments. It was determined by the authorities to make all alike in this respect, hence the warrant of February, 1829, authorising the well-known double-breasted coatee, which remained, with scarcely any alteration, the dress of officers until the Crimean war.

The coatee worn by the 24th had two rows of silver buttons down the front in pairs; a green collar, Prussian shape; on each side two loops of regimental silver lace, the old vellum pattern, nine-sixteenths of an inch wide; green cuffs, with a scarlet slash, thereon four silver loops and buttons in pairs; white turnbacks to the skirts, the extremities still ornamented with the embroidered silver stars as before; scarlet slashed pockets on the skirts placed obliquely, with silver lace loops by pairs; the collar, coat, cuffs, pockets, etc. all edged with a very narrow white piping. The difference in the amount of lace may be estimated from the fact that the old coatee required twenty yards, whereas the new one only took four and a half yards. Large silver epaulettes worn on both shoulders by all ranks of officers, (for the first time in the case of captains and subalterns of infantry,) excepting the grenadiers and light infantry—who wore large curbchain wings strictly according to the new regulation. The epaulet strap was of silver, vellum pattern, striped with green silk; the fringe varied a little according to rank, the field-officers being distinguished by gold crowns and stars on the strap.

The new Oxford mixture was now authorised instead of the old blue grey trousers, and a blue forage cap with a broad stiff top was, for the first time, authorised.

1830. A red fatigue jacket was substituted for the white one hitherto worn by the rank and file; fusils also substituted for the halberds, so long carried by the sergeants.

The recently introduced cap lines were suddenly abolished by the comprehensive warrant of 1830, marking the accession of William IV. The tall feathers were reduced to eight inches, a green ball tuft ordered to be worn by the light infantry, musicians to be universally dressed in white, and, lastly, (what was of great importance to the 24th) the officers of the regular army ordered to wear gold lace.

The coatee remained precisely the same, but in every part "gold" was substituted for "silver" lace and appointments; consequently at mess (the full dress coatee always being worn at this period) no less than three different costumes might be seen—the heavily silver-laced coatee of 1828, the silver-epauletted coatee of 1829, and the gold-laced garment of 1830!

The officer's gilt button* (see illustration, p. 275) would be introduced at this time, and also a new breastplate to be worn, as before, on the sword shoulder-belt. It was a square, or rather oblong, plate, bright gilt, in the centre 24 in raised silver, surmounted by a silver sphinx; this again surmounted by a gilt crown, and encircled by two gilt laurel branches. This handsome ornament remained in use until 1855.

1832. FIELD OFFICERS ORDERED TO USE BRASS SCABBARDS. A red seam down the trousers authorised January, 1833. Next year

---

* The wave or curved border gives this button a very good appearance, and was adopted by many other regiments at the same time.

a new forage cap adopted by the officers, of dark blue cloth, with black oakleaf band, and 24 in gold in the centre.

Officers' undress consisted of a single breasted blue frock coat, with gilt buttons, shoulder straps edged with gold lace and terminating in gilt metal crescents, the sword carried in the frog of a black waistbelt over the crimson sash.

By royal warrant, dated October 10th, 1836, the red striped lace worn by the rank and file was abolished, and a plain white tape lace took its place, but each regiment was allowed to retain the peculiar method of wearing it. The 24th, therefore, continued to wear its tape loops by pairs; sergeants were directed to wear double-breasted coatees without any lace across the chest, white epaulettes, or wings.

Coloured lace was still worn by the drummers, the pattern being white with short diagonal red stripes across, besides the ordinary parts of the coat being laced after the manner of the coatees worn by the rank and file; the back and side seams, and the arm seams, were also covered with this lace; five or six chevrons of it also worn on each arm, and large white wings ornamented the shoulders.

The coloured illustration, p. 144, represents a private soldier, 1840.

The band at this period were dressed in white double-breasted coatees; collar, cuffs, and skirt turnbacks of green, with large epaulettes of green worsted; broad white stripes on the trousers, and the chako ornamented with a red ball or tuft.

In 1844 a new chako for the infantry was authorised, sometimes called the "Albert hat," six and three-quarter inches high, one-quarter less in diameter at top than at bottom; thus completely altering the appearance of the head dress.

The grenadier fur caps also discontinued, for those regiments still using them.

Officers lost the fine handsome chako plate they had been wearing since 1829, a smaller one sufficing; it also consisted of a universal gilt star, crown over, four and a half inches in diameter; in the centre 24, surrounded by a girdle, thereon "2nd Warwickshire;" resting on the girdle a sphinx, with motto, "Egypt;" a small wreath of laurels surrounded the girdle, and immediately below it two small labels, bearing "Cape of Good Hope" and "Peninsula;" on seven of the larger star rays, the words "Talavera," "Fuentes d'Onor," "Salamanca," "Vittoria," "Pyrenees," "Nivelle," "Orthes."

The men still continued to wear their old cap ornament—a small circular brass plate with the regimental number, crown over it.

1845. The sergeants lost their red and green sashes, and others of crimson introduced.

1848. The undress uniform of infantry officers was altered very considerably by the discontinuance of the blue frock, and the introduction of a scarlet shell jacket with regimental facings.

Possibly this change may not have affected the officers of the 24th to any great extent, the regiment being in India, and it is believed that shell jackets had been for some time worn in that country. A black patent leather sling sword-belt was ordered to be worn with the shell jacket, and a great coat of grey cloth adopted.

Coloured engravings of the advance of the 24th at Chillianwallah depict the regiment wearing shell jackets and forage caps with white covers. This, however, appears to be a mistake. Thackwell, in his "Sikh War," mentions the "Albert Hats," worn by the regiment on that occasion, and the following extract from a letter, written by Lieutenant-Colonel M. Smith, dated Chillianwallah, 28th January, 1849, clearly indicates what was worn:

"The men wore their dress caps in the action, and this sort of "head-dress is always found unsuited for hard work in battle. Many "fell off and were lost in the meleé, and it seems to be, on such "occasions, the soldier's great desire to rid himself of so inconvenient "an appendage. The forage cap is far better for service, though "doubtless something more protective than that might be devised."

1850. A plain shoulder belt, without the brass breastplate, to carry the men's pouches, authorized the bayonet being hung in a frog from a waistbelt. This change, however, was not probably carried out immediately.

The coloured illustration, p. 170, represents an officer in full uniform at this period; though not well adapted for field movements, on the parade ground it was one of the handsomest costumes ever worn.

1855. The coat tails of the whole army disappeared, and frock coats or tunics took the place of the old coatee. The first issue was double-breasted, the buttons of brass at equal distances; no white lace used, excepting round the buttons on the cuffs and skirts; the coat edged and piped with white cloth all over; dark blue trousers, with a red welt, introduced; the chako made smaller and lighter, officers' and sergeants' sashes worn over the left and right shoulders respectively.

At the next issue the tunic was made single-breasted; officers' rank now distinguished by the amount of gold lace worn, and by crowns and stars on the collar. A double-breasted blue frock-coat adopted for undress, with gilt regimental buttons and a plain stand-up collar, the crimson silk sash worn over it, and the sword carried in a white leather sling belt.*

1866. The peculiar drummers' lace (previously described) used by the regiment for half-a-century was done away with, and the universal pattern (white, with red crowns) adopted.

1867. The officers' black sword scabbard replaced by a steel one, and a patrol jacket substituted for the blue frock-coat.

1868. The slashed cuff on the tunic discontinued, and pointed cuffs introduced. Officers allowed to wear for levees, etc., a gold and crimson sash, gold-laced trousers and sword-belt, the chako ornamented with gold lace, the old star replaced by a garter and crown, the number inside, surrounded by a wreath of laurel in high relief. See illustration, p. 185.

About 1873, white clothing for the band was discontinued, and soon after the shell jackets worn by the men were abolished, loose scarlet frocks being adopted for undress.

S. M. MILNE.

---

* The chako very much smaller, and ornamented with a small star plate crown over, the regimental number in the centre in black. See illustration, p. 171.

APPENDIX.

A.

VICTORIA CROSS ROLL OF THE REGIMENT.

FIRST BATTALION.

LIEUTENANT AND ADJUTANT TEIGNMOUTH MELVILL,
LIEUTENANT N. J. A. COGHILL (killed 22nd January, 1879):

Lieutenant Melvill, 1st battalion 24th Foot, on account of the gallant efforts made by him to save the Queen's Colour of his regiment after the disaster at Isandhlwana; and—

Lieutenant Coghill, 1st battalion 24th Foot, on account of his heroic conduct in endeavouring to save his brother officer's life, would have been recommended to Her Majesty for the Victoria Cross had they survived.—*London Gazette*, 2nd May, 1879.

LIEUTENANT EDWARD S. BROWNE (now Major 2nd battalion South Wales Borderers):

For his gallant conduct on 29th March, 1879, when the Mounted Infantry were being driven in by the enemy at Inhlobani, in galloping back and twice assisting on his horse—under a heavy fire and within a few yards of the enemy—one of the mounted men, who must otherwise have fallen into the enemy's hands. —*London Gazette*, 17th June, 1879.

Cross presented at Pine Town Camp, Natal, 22nd August, 1879.

SECOND BATTALION.

ASSISTANT-SURGEON C. M. DOUGLAS, M.D. (now Brigade Surgeon, retired.)

PRIVATES D. BELL (now a pensioner), J. COOPER (dead), W. GRIFFITHS (killed at Isandhlwana, 22nd January, 1879), and T. MURPHY (now a pensioner.)

For the very gallant and daring manner in which, on 7th May, 1867, they risked their lives in manning a boat and proceeding through a dangerous surf to the rescue of some of their comrades who formed part of an expedition that had been sent to the Island of Little Andaman by order of the Chief Commissioner of British Burmah, with the view of ascertaining the fate of the captain and seven of the crew of the ship *Assam Valley* who had landed there, and were supposed to have been murdered by the natives.

The officer who commanded the troops on the occasion reports: "About an hour later in the day Dr. Douglas and the "four privates referred to, gallantly manning the second gig, made "their way through the surf almost to the shore; but, finding their "boat half filled with water, they returned. A second attempt by "Dr. Douglas and party proved successful, five of us being passed "through the surf to the boats outside. A third and last trip got "the whole of the party on shore safe to the boats."

It is stated that Dr. Douglas accomplished these trips through the surf to the shore by no ordinary exertion. He stood in the bow of the boat and worked her in an intrepid, seamanlike manner, cool to a degree, as if what he was doing was an act of everyday life. The four privates behaved in an equally cool and collected manner, rowing through the roughest surf, where the slightest hesitation or want of pluck on the part of any of them would have been attended with the gravest risks. It is reported that seventeen officers and men were thus saved from what otherwise must have been a fearful risk, if not certainty of death.—*London Gazette*, 17th December, 1867.

LIEUTENANT LORD GIFFORD (Brevet Major, late Middlesex Regt.):

For his gallant conduct during the operations in Ashantee, and especially at the taking of Becquah. The officer commanding the expeditionary force reports that Lord Gifford was in command of the scouts after the army crossed the Prah, and that it is no exaggeration to say that, since the Adansi Hills were passed, he daily carried his life in his hands in the performance of his dangerous duties. He hung upon the rear of the enemy, discovering their positions and ferreting out their intentions, with no white man with him. He captured numerous prisoners. Sir Garnet Wolseley brings him forward for this mark of royal favour, and more especially for his conduct at the taking of Becquah, into which place he penetrated, with his scouts, before the troops entered, when his gallantry and courage were most conspicuous.—*London Gazette*, 28th March, 1874.

LIEUTENANT GONVILLE BROMHEAD (afterwards Major 2nd Battalion South Wales Borderers, dead):

For gallant conduct at the defence of Rorke's Drift, on the occasion of the attack by the Zulus, 22nd and 23rd January, 1879. The lieutenant-general commanding reports that had it not been for the firm example and excellent behaviour of Lieutenants Chard, Royal Engineers, and Bromhead, 24th Regiment, the defence of Rorke's Drift would not have been conducted with the intelligence and tenacity which so eminently characterized it. The lieutenant-general adds, that the success must in a great measure be attributable to the two young officers who exercised the chief command on the occasion in question.—*London Gazette*, 2nd May, 1879.

Cross presented by Sir Garnet Wolseley, at Utrecht, in September, 1879.

PRIVATE JOHN WILLIAMS (now Army Reserve):

Was posted with Private Joseph Williams (1st battalion 24th Foot) and Private Wm. Horrigan (1st battalion 24th Foot) in a distant room of the hospital at Rorke's Drift, 22nd and 23rd

January, 1879, which they held for more than an hour, so long as they had a round of ammunition left. As communication was for a while cut off, the Zulus were enabled to advance and burst open the door; they dragged out Private Joseph Williams and two patients and assegaied them. While the Zulus were occupied with the slaughter of these men, a lull took place, during which Private John Williams, with two other patients, who were the only men left alive in this ward, succeeded in knocking a hole through the partition and taking the two patients into the next ward, where he found Private Hook.—*London Gazette*, 2nd May, 1879.

PRIVATE HENRY HOOK (now a pensioner):

Private John Williams and Private H. Hook, together—one man working, whilst the other fought and kept the enemy at bay with his bayonet—broke three other partitions, and were thus enabled to bring eight patients through a small window, into the inner line of defence.—*London Gazette*, 2nd May, 1879.

Crosses presented by Sir Garnet Wolseley at Rorke's Drift.

PRIVATE WILLIAM JONES (now a pensioner):
PRIVATE ROBERT JONES (now a pensioner):

In another ward facing the hill, at Rorke's Drift, on 22nd and 23rd January, 1879, Privates William Jones and Robert Jones defended the post until six out of the seven patients it contained had been removed. The seventh, Lance-Sergeant Maxfield, 2nd battalion 24th Foot, was delirious with fever. Although they had previously dressed him, they were unable to induce him to move. When Private Robert Jones volunteered to endeavour to carry him away, he found that he had been stabbed by the Zulus, as he lay on his bed.—*London Gazette*, 2nd May, 1879.

Cross presented to Private Robert Jones, by Sir Garnet Wolseley, at Utrecht, September, 1879.

CORPORAL WILLIAM ALLEN (dead),
PRIVATE FRED. HITCH (pensioner):

It was chiefly due to the courageous conduct of these men at Rorke's Drift that communication was kept up with the hospital at all. Holding together, at all costs, a most dangerous post, raked in reverse by the enemy's fire from the hill, they were both severely wounded; but their determined conduct enabled the patients to be withdrawn from the hospital, and when incapacitated by their wounds from fighting they continued, as soon as their wounds had been dressed, to serve out ammunition to their comrades through the night.—*London Gazette*, 2nd May, 1879.

Crosses presented by Her Majesty, in person, at Netley.

NOTE ON MEDALS FOR DISTINGUISHED SERVICE.

COLOUR-SERGEANT FRANK BOURNE, "B," company, 2nd battalion 24th Regiment, now Lieutenant and Quarter-master Bourne, 2nd battalion South Wales Borderers, and—

PRIVATE JOHN ROY, one of eight men of the 1st battalion 24th Regiment (five of them patients in hospital) who were with the detachment at Rorke's Drift, received medals for Distinguished Service in the Field for their conduct at the defence, 22nd and 23rd January, 1879.

PRIVATE POWER, 1st battalion 24th Regiment, received the medal for Distinguished Conduct in the Field for gallant conduct with the Mounted Infantry on various occasions, particularly at Galetza Heights and Inhlobane. He was killed by a fall from a horse while his battalion was at Kilkenny, in Ireland.

A tombstone has been erected to his memory in the parish churchyard, by his officers and comrades.

B.

SERVICES OF OFFICERS.

Airey, R. H. B.   Ensign, 24th Regiment, 30th April, 1858; lieutenant, 7th January, 1862; captain, 3rd August, 1872; exchanged to 9th Regiment; retired as major. Royal Humane Society's medal.

Ancram, W., Earl of.   Colonel, 24th Regiment, 1747-52. A.D.C. at Fontenoy (dangerously wounded). Present at Culloden. Afterwards General the (4th) Marquis of Lothian, K.T.; colonel, 11th Dragoons. Died, 1775.

Anstey, E. O.   Lieutenant, 1st battalion 24th Regiment, 9th March, 1873. Abroad in Kaffir war, 1877-78. Killed at Isandhlwana, 22nd January, 1879.

Armitage, P. T.   2nd lieutenant, 76th Regiment, 19th October, 1878; lieutenant, 24th Regiment, 7th July, 1880; captain, 28th November, 1885. Zulu war, 1879 (medal and clasp). Burmah, 1887-89 (medal and clasp). Adjutant, 1st Volunteer battalion South Wales Borderers.

Atkinson, C. T.   Lieutenant, 24th Regiment, 28th February, 1875. Served in the Kaffir war, 1877-78. Killed at Isandhlwana, 22nd January, 1879.

Austen.   See Godwin-Austen.

Baird, Sir David, Bart., G.C.B., K.C., Colonel, 24th Regiment, 1807-29. Entered the army, 1772. Taken prisoner by Hyder Ali in 1780, and treated with great cruelty for nearly four years. Captured Pondicherry, 1792. Stormed Seringapatam, 1799. Commanded Indian army sent to Egypt, 1801. Recaptured the Cape of Good Hope, 1806. Commanded a division at Copenhagan, 1807; and at Corunna, 1809 (loss of arm). General commanding the forces in Scotland. Died, 1829.

APPENDIX.

BALCARRES, ALEX., (6th) EARL OF. Lieutenant-colonel commanding 24th Regiment in America, 1777-82. Afterwards general and colonel, 63rd Foot. Died, 1825.

BANISTER, G. S. Ensign, 24th Regiment, 8th July, 1868; lieutenant, 28th October, 1871; captain, 5th February, 1879; major, 15th August, 1885; lieutenant-colonel, 9th June, 1892. Kaffir war, 1877-78, including the operations against the Galekas. Zulu war, 1879 (medal and clasp). Now commanding 1st battalion of the regiment.

BARCLAY, F. C. D'EPINAY. Ensign, 12th Regiment, 27th April, 1849; lieutenant, 15th July, 1853; captain, 24th Regiment, 5th March, 1858; major, 29th October, 1866; lieutenant-colonel, 14th November, 1874. Exchanged to 66th Regiment, 1875. Major-general, retired. Served with 12th Regiment in Kaffir war, 1851-53 (medal). Dead.

BAZALGETTE, L. H. Ensign, 24th Regiment, 26th January, 1838; lieutenant, 24th September, 1841; captain, 7th April, 1848; major, 30th March, 1858. Punjaub war, 1848-49; severely wounded at Chillianwallah (medal and clasp). Died, 1866.

BEAUCHAMP, C. G. Lieutenant, South Wales Borderers, 25th August, 1886. Burmah, 1887-89 (medal and clasp).

BENNETT, L. H. Ensign, 24th Regiment, 12th January, 1866; lieutenant, 12th May, 1869; captain, 23rd January, 1879. Exchanged to 90th Regiment. Transferred to Pay Department 15th September, 1881; honorary major, 15th September, 1891. Served in Zulu campaign, 1879; battle of Ulundi (medal and clasp).

BERESFORD, J. 2nd lieutenant, South Wales Borderers (from non-commissioned officer, 1st battalion 24th Regiment), 8th June, 1881; lieutenant, 1st July, 1881. Burmah, 1887-89 (medal and clasp). Half-pay.

BERRY. See DE BERRY.

BIRCH, A. W. 2nd lieutenant, 24th Regiment, 26th March, 1879; lieutenant, 17th May, 1879; captain, 15th May, 1885. Zulu war, 1879 (medal and clasp).

BLACHFORD, A. G. Ensign, 24th Regiment, 12th November, 1825; lieutenant, 12th December, 1826; captain, 17th August, 1841; major, 14th January, 1849; brevet lieutenant-colonel, 7th June, 1849; brevet colonel, 7th June, 1855; lieutenant-colonel, 30th March, 1858. Punjaub war, 1848-49; succeeded to the command of the regiment at Chillianwallah. Present at Goojerat (medal and two clasps). Retired as major-general, 9th March, 1860. Dead.

BLACK, WILSONE, C.B. Ensign, 42nd Highlanders, 11th August, 1854; lieutenant, 9th February, 1855; captain, 9th January, 1857; exchanged to 6th Regiment, brevet major, 5th July, 1872; major, 1st April, 1873; exchanged to 24th Regiment, 1st December, 1875; brevet lieutenant-colonel, 31st December, 1878; went on half-pay, 25th February, 1882; brevet colonel, 31st December, 1882. Passed Staff College. Served in the Crimea from 14th June, 1855 (medal, clasp for Sevastopol, and Turkish medal). Kaffir war, 1878, including attack on Intaba-ka-N'doda. Zulu war, 1879 (medal and clasp, mentioned in despatches, and C.B.). Brigade major, Nova Scotia. Assistant adjutant-general in Canada, and in Scotland and at Gibraltar. Appointed to command the troops in Jamaica, with local rank of major-general, 18th March, 1891.

BLAKE, JOHN. Ensign, 24th Regiment, 1767; captain in Saratoga campaign (twice wounded). Commanded a brigade in Egypt, 1801. Brevet colonel and lieutenant-governor of Landguard Fort. Died, 1806.

BLOOMFIELD, E. Quarter-master, 2nd battalion 24th Regiment (from sergeant-instructor of musketry), 24th September, 1873. Served in Kaffir war, 1878. Killed at Isandhlwana, 22nd January, 1879.

BOURNE, F. Honorary lieutenant and quarter-master, 2nd battalion 24th Regiment (from non-commissioned officer, 2nd battalion

24th Regiment), 21st May, 1890. Served in Kaffir war, 1878; also in Zulu war, 1879, including the defence of Rorke's Drift, 22nd-23rd January, 1879 (mentioned in despatches, medal and clasp, and medal for distinguished service in the field). Served in Burmah, 1887-89 (medal and clasp).

BRADFORD, S. S. 2nd lieutenant, South Wales Borderers, 5th February, 1887; lieutenant, 26th March, 1890. Burmah, 1887-89 (medal and clasp).

BRANDER, W. B. Ensign, 24th Regiment, 24th August, 1860; lieutenant, 16th May, 1862; captain, 13th February, 1867; major, 29th February, 1879; retired on pension, with honorary rank of lieutenant-colonel, 1880. Served in the Kaffir and Zulu wars, and was mentioned in despatches for "skill and judgment in selecting a landing place and camping ground at the wreck of the steamship *Clyde*, in 1879" (medal and clasp).

BROMHEAD, C. J. Ensign, 24th Regiment, 30th August, 1859; lieutenant, 20th February, 1863; was adjutant; captain, 17th October, 1872; brevet major, 1st April, 1874; major, 1st July, 1881; lieutenant-colonel, 31st January, 1885; colonel, 31st January, 1891; half-pay, 1891. Appointed to command 24th Regimental District, 1892. On special service in Ashantee, 1873-74 (mentioned in despatches, brevet of major, medal and clasp). Zulu war, 1879 (medal and clasp). Burmah, 1887-89 (medal and clasp).

BROMHEAD, GONVILLE, V.C. Ensign, 24th Regiment, 20th April, 1867; lieutenant, 28th October, 1871; captain, 23rd January, 1879; brevet major, 23rd January, 1879; major, 4th April, 1883. Served in Kaffir war, 1878; Zulu war, 1879, and commanded "B" company, 2nd battalion 24th Regiment, at the defence of Rorke's Drift, 22nd-23rd January, 1879 (mentioned in despatches, brevet of major, medal and clasp), and received the Victoria Cross for his conduct on that occasion. *(See Victoria Cross Roll, Appendix A).* Served in Burmah, 1887-89 (medal and clasp). Died at Allahabad, 7th February, 1891.

⁎ The two last named officers were brothers.

BROMHEAD, J., C.B. Ensign, 24th Regiment, 1795; left the regiment, as captain, in 1807. Lieutenant-colonel commanding 77th Regiment at the storming of Badajos, in 1812. Commanded 77th Regiment and 5th Fusiliers in the retreat at El Bodon, formed them into square and marched through the French cavalry to rejoin Wellington (gold medal and C.B.). Died, 1837.

˳ Lieutenant-Colonel John Bromhead, C.B., was son of Captain John Bromhead, who, like his brother, Captain Benjamin Bromhead, was an officer in the 2nd battalion 24th Regiment, afterwards 69th Regiment, when first formed. Both these last named served at Belle Isle, Martinique, and Grenada.

BROOKS, R., K.H. Ensign, South Gloucester Militia; ensign, 9th Regiment, 16th May, 1811 (on bringing a draft of militia volunteers); lieutenant, 23rd August, 1813; captain, unattached, 27th August, 1825; captain, 24th Regiment, same year; captain, 69th Regiment, same year; major, 69th Regiment, 3rd May, 1831; lieutenant-colonel, unattached, 27th April, 1846; exchanged next day to 24th Regiment. Served with the 9th Regiment in the Peninsula, 1811-14 (three times wounded, medal and five clasps); also in America, and with the army of occupation in France. Served with the 69th Regiment in North America and the West Indies. Killed, in command of the 24th Regiment, at Chillianwallah, 13th January, 1849.

BROWN, W. G. Ensign, 24th Regiment, 7th July, 1825; lieutenant, 11th May, 1830; captain, 10th May, 1844; major, 29th Regiment, 15th January, 1849; lieutenant-colonel, 24th Regiment, 21st December, 1849; brevet-colonel, 28th November, 1854; major-general, 1864; lieutenant general, 1877; general, 1883; Colonel, 83rd Regiment, 29th May, 1873. Served at Chillianwallah with the 24th Regiment (wounded), and at Goojerat with the 29th Regiment (medal and clasp). Commanded a brigade in India at the period of the Mutiny. Dead.

BROWNE, E. S., V.C. Ensign, 24th Regiment, 23rd September, 1871; lieutenant, 28th October, 1871; captain, 12th May, 1880; major, 2nd November, 1885. Kaffir war, 1878; Zulu war, 1879, with the mounted infantry, including engagements

APPENDIX.   313

at Inhlobani Mountain *(See Victoria Cross Roll, Appendix A)*, and Ulundi (mentioned in despatches), and in the operations against Sekukuni (medal and clasp). Deputy assistant adjutant general for musketry, Bengal.

BURNETT, J. J. 2nd lieutenant, 24th Regiment, 11th August, 1880; lieutenant, 1st January, 1881; captain, 20th September, 1886. Transferred to Pay Department, July, 1886. Served in South Africa, 1879—Zulu campaign, action of Inyezane, battle of Ginginhlow, and relief of Etshowe (medal and clasp).

BURNS, H. M. Ensign, 62nd Regiment 20th May, 1842; lieutenant, 23rd June, 1848; exchanged to 24th Regiment *(see page 169)*; captain, 24th Regiment, 25th July, 1856. Dead.

BURNS, S. J. J. Ensign, 24th Regiment, 11th May, 1848; lieutenant, 1862; captain, 21st February, 1862. Died in Dublin, 1865.

BUTLER, T. P. Ensign, 56th Regiment, 25th August, 1854; lieutenant, 13th July, 1855; retired, April, 1856. Rejoined the army, as ensign, 24th Regiment, 23rd April, 1858; lieutenant, 7th December, 1858; retired, November, 1862. Served in the Crimea (medal and clasp and Turkish medal).
  ⁎ Now Sir THOMAS PIERCE BUTLER, (10th) Baronet, of Ballin Temple and Garryhundon, County Carlow.

CALDWELL, J. F. Ensign, 24th Regiment, 28th May, 1858; lieutenant, 15th November, 1861; adjutant, 1st battalion; captain, 30th October, 1866; major, 5th February, 1879; lieutenant-colonel, 1st July, 1881; colonel, 1st July, 1885. To command 27th Regimental District, 12th July, 1887. Kaffir war, 1877-78 (medal and clasp).

CAMPBELL, REG. Sub-lieutenant, 24th Regiment, 26th March, 1879; lieutenant, 7th July, 1880; captain, 9th January, 1886. Zulu war, 1879 (medal and clasp). Burmah, 1886-89 (medal and clasp). Station staff officer, Sialkote.

CANNING, A. 2nd lieutenant, South Wales Borderers, 11th April, 1888; lieutenant, 6th March, 1891. Egypt, 1882 (medal and clasp, and Khedive's star). Soudan, 1884 (two clasps). Soudan, 1885 (clasp).

CARRINGTON, SIR FRED, K.C.M.G. Ensign, 24th Regiment, 4th May, 1864; lieutenant, 13th February, 1867; captain, 16th February, 1878; brevet major, 11th November, 1878; brevet lieutenant-colonel, 29th November, 1879; colonel, 26th January, 1884. Commanded Frontier Light Horse in Kaffir war, 1877-78 (medal and clasp). Commanded Transvaal Volunteers against Sekukuni in 1878-79, and left wing Cape Mounted Rifles, 1879-83. Commanded the Colonial Forces in the Basuto war (severely wounded); the 2nd Mounted Rifles, Bechuanaland Field Force, in 1884; the Police Battalion in Bechuanaland, in 1885; the Colonial Forces in Zululand, in 1888. Commanding Border Police in Bechuanaland. Half-pay, 24th Regiment.

CAVAYE, C. W. Lieutenant, 24th Regiment, 30th December, 1871. Kaffir war, 1887-88. Killed at Isandhlwana, 22nd January, 1879.

CHAMBERLIN, T. Ensign, 24th Regiment, 1793; lieutenant, 1795; captain, 1797: major, 1804; brevet lieutenant-colonel, 1811; lieutenant-colonel, 24th Regiment, 1813; half-pay, 1814; retired, full pay, 8th Royal Veteran Battalion, 1819. Died, 1828. Served in Canada; Egypt, 1801; Cape, 1806; and Peninsula (gold medal for Talavera).

CHAMBERLIN, W. R. B. Ensign, 24th Regiment, 1st May, 1858; lieutenant, 21st October, 1859; captain, 16th May, 1865; brevet major, 1st October, 1877; brevet lieutenant-colonel, 18th October, 1879. Retired.

CHURCH, H. B. Ensign, 5th January, 1858; lieutenant, 24th September, 1858; exchanged to 24th Regiment, captain, 3rd November, 1867; major, and retired as honorary lieutenant-colonel, 1880. Served in Zulu campaign, 1879 (medal).

CLARK, THOMAS. Ensign, 1st West India Regiment, 26th April, 1844; lieutenant, 23rd July, 1846; regimental adjutant; captain, 27th March, 1855; to 24th Regiment, on formation of 2nd battalion; major, 24th Regiment, 29th July, 1862. Died, 1866.

CLEMENTS, R. A. P., D.S.O. Lieutenant, 24th Regiment, 2nd December, 1874; captain, 4th December, 1880; major, 24th February, 1886; brevet lieutenant-colonel, 1st July, 1887. Kaffir war, 1877-78; Zulu war, 1879, and present at Ulundi (medal and clasp). Burmah, 1885-86, as brigade-major; and was present at Obu (severely wounded) and Taindah (slightly wounded); mentioned in despatches, brevet of lieutenant-colonel, and D.S.O.

COGHILL, N. A. J. Lieutenant, 26th February, 1873. Killed at Buffalo River, 22nd January, 1879. *(See Victoria Cross Roll, Appendix A).*

CORNWALLIS, HONBLE. EDWARD. Lieutenant-general. Governor of Nova Scotia and Gibraltar. Colonel, 24th Regiment, from 1756 until his death in 1772.

CURLL, E. C. 2nd lieutenant, 24th Regiment, 14th September, 1878; lieutenant, 23rd January, 1879; captain, 5th January, 1884; Zulu war, 1879 (medal and clasp).

CUSACK, J. Quarter-master, 24th Regiment (from sergeant-major, 97th Regiment) on the formation of the 2nd battalion; afterwards captain, 8th Regiment; retired as major. Served with the 97th Regiment in the Crimea, including the siege and fall of Sevastopol, taking of the Quarries, and assaults on the Redan of 18th June and 8th September, 1855 (wounded; mentioned in despatches, medal for distinguished service in the field, Crimean medal and clasp, and Turkish medal).

DALY, J. P. Lieutenant, 24th Regiment, 28th February, 1874. Kaffir war, 1878. Killed at Isandhlwana, 22nd January, 1879.

DE BERRY, G. F. Ensign, 75th Regiment, 7th June, 1842; lieutenant, 25th April, 1845, exchanged to 24th Regiment; captain, 24th Regiment, 20th October, 1849; brevet major, 20th September, 1861; major, 1st Royal Regiment, 18th December, 1866; brevet lieutenant-colonel, 1st April, 1870; lieutenant-colonel, 56th Regiment, 29th March, 1873; colonel, 29th March, 1876. Retired from command of a brigade depôt, 1879, honorary major-general, 1883. Served with 75th Regiment at the Cape, with 24th Regiment in the Punjaub war, 1848-49, including passage of the Chenab and battle of Sadoolapore, Chillianwallah (slightly wounded), and Goojerat (medal and two clasps). Commanded at Murree, when that station was attacked by the hillmen, 1st September, 1857. Raised a corps of Sikhs, which, in January, 1858, was attached to Maxwell's column, and present in the engagements at Ooryah and Shurhurgar, and capture of Calpee (medal and clasp). Distinguished Service Reward, 26th March, 1883.

DEGACHER, H. J., C.B. Ensign, 24th Regiment, 22nd February, 1855, (under name of Hitchcock); lieutenant, 21st September, 1855; adjutant, 2nd battalion, when formed; captain, 21st October, 1859; major, 8th July, 1861, (took the name of Degacher); lieutenant-colonel, 9th June, 1877; colonel, 1st July, 1881; major-general, 8th July, 1891. Commanded 2nd battalion 24th Regiment in the Kaffir war, 1878, including the operations against the Galekas, and the attack on Intaba-ka-N'doda, and in Zulu war, 1879 (C.B., medal and clasp).

DEGACHER, W. Ensign, 24th Regiment, 31st May, 1859, (under the name of Hitchcock); lieutenant, 19th August, 1862; captain, 2nd December, 1868, (took the name of Degacher). Served in the Kaffir war, 1877-78. Killed at Isandhlwana, 22nd January, 1879. Brother of Major-General H. J. Degacher, C.B.

DEMPSTER, T. C. Ensign, 24th Regiment, 29th March, 1861; lieutenant, 16th April, 1864; adjutant, 2nd battalion; captain, 28th Regiment, 1814; paymaster, A.P.D., 1880; honorary major, 13th July, 1885. Royal Humane Society's bronze medal, for saving life at Port Louis, Mauritius, 17th March, 1863.

DERING, SIR EDWARD, (3rd) Bart., M.P. Raised the regiment, and died in command, in Ireland, 1689.

DERING, DANIEL. Colonel of the regiment, 1689 to 1691. Died in Ireland, 1691. Brother of Sir Edward Dering.

DERING, DANIEL, the younger. Son of Colonel D. Dering. Ensign in the regiment, 1704. Lieutenant-colonel and keeper of the privy purse to Frederick, Prince of Wales, father of George III. Died at Leyden, 1737.

DEWHIRST, T. Sub-lieutenant, 24th Regiment, 6th August, 1879; lieutenant, 25th July, 1883; captain, 6th March, 1891, retired. Burmah, 1887-89, (medal and clasp).

DOUGLAS, C. M., M.D., V.C. Assistant surgeon, 24th Regiment, 1st October, 1862. Retired as surgeon-major, A.M.D., with step of honorary rank, 1881. *(See Victoria Cross Roll, Appendix A).*

DOYLE, G. H. Served as captain and major, 24th Regiment, 1820-46. Afterwards General Sir C. Hastings Doyle, K.C.M.G. Colonel 87th Royal Irish Fusiliers. Dead.

DRUMMOND, GEO. DUNCAN. Lieutenant-colonel, 24th Regiment, 1808-11. Ensign, 33rd Foot, 1783. Joined 1st Foot Guards (Grenadier Guards), 1786. Exchanged as captain and lieutenant-colonel to lieutenant-colonel, 24th Foot, 1808. Wounded at Talavera (gold medal). Died in command of a brigade of the light division, 1811.

DUNBAR, W. M. Ensign, 34th Regiment, 5th January, 1855; lieutenant, 23rd March, 1855; captain, 2nd September, 1862, exchanged to 24th Regiment; major, 14th November, 1874; brevet lieutenant-colonel, 29th November, 1879; honorary colonel, 4th September, 1883, retired. Appointed gentleman-at-arms, 16th June, 1882. Served with 34th Regiment in the Crimea, from 12th July, 1855, including the siege and fall of Sevastopol and attack on the Redan, of 8th September, 1855, (Medal and clasp, and Turkish medal); also in the Indian

Mutiny, including the actions at Cawnpore, in November, 1857, seige and capture of Lucknow, relief of Azinghur, and other actions, (medal and clasp). Served with the 2nd battalion 24th Regiment in the Kaffir war, 1878, and the first part of the Zulu war of 1879. Commanded 1st battalion 24th Regiment during the latter part of the campaign, and was present at Ulundi, (brevet of lieutenant-colonel, and medal and clasp).

DYER, H. J. Lieutenant, 24th Regiment, 11th October, 1876; adjutant, 2nd battalion. Served in the Kaffir war, 1878. Killed at Isandhlwana, 22nd January, 1879. *(See page 234.)*

DYSON, E. H. 2nd lieutenant, 24th Regiment, 1st May, 1878. Killed at Isandhlwana, 22nd January, 1879.

ELLICE, R. Colonel, 24th Regiment, 1842-56. Served with the 9th Dragoons, in S. America, in 1807; deputy adjutant-general in Canada, 1809-11; major, Inniskilling Dragoons, with the army of occupation, in France, 1816-18; commanding the troops in Malta, 1848-53. Died, a general, and colonel of the 24th Regiment, 1856. Father of General Sir C. H. Ellice, G.C.B.

ELLICE, SIR C. H., G.C.B. Ensign and lieutenant, Coldstream Guards, (from Royal Military College), 10th May, 1839; lieutenant and captain, August, 1845, exchanged to 24th Regiment; major, 24th Regiment, 21st December, 1849; lieutenant-colonel, 8th August, 1851. Raised the present 2nd battalion of the regiment, in 1858. Half-pay, July, 1862; major-general, 1865; lieutenant-general, 1873; general, 1877; colonel, the South Wales Borderers, April, 1888. Served with the Coldstream Guards, in Canada, 1840-42. A.D.C. to his father, when commanding the troops at Malta. Served in India at the period of the Mutiny, and commanded the 24th Regiment at the defeat of the Jhelum mutineers, July, 1857, (dangerously wounded, horse killed under him, medal). Held various staff appointments at home, and was adjutant-general, Horse Guards, from November, 1876, to March, 1882. Died, 12th November, 1888.

ENGLAND, R. Served in the 47th Regiment from 1767 to 1782, and was present with it at Saratoga. Lieutenant-colonel commanding 24th Regiment, at home and in Canada, 1782-98, afterwards general, colonel 5th Foot, lieutenant-governor of Plymouth. Died, 1812.

FARQUHAR, H. R. Ensign, 24th Regiment, 30th December, 1859; lieutenant, 7th November, 1862; captain, 22nd December, 1869; became major, and retired as lieutenant-colonel. Was adjutant 1st battalion 24th Regiment from October, 1866, to December, 1869.

FINCH, HONBLE. D., C.B., General. Colonel, 24th Regiment, 1856 to 1861. Served with the 15th Hussars in the Peninsula, (medal and three clasps). Military secretary to Lord Combermere, in the West Indies, in Ireland, and in India, including the siege and capture of Bhurtpore, in 1825, (mentioned in despatches, brevet lieutenant-colonel, and C.B.). Died, 1861.

⁎ General Finch's nephew, the late HONBLE. D. GREVILLE FINCH, who served with the 68th Regiment in the Crimea (medal and clasp), was major, 2nd battalion 24th Regiment in 1859-61.

FLEMING, J., C.B. Ensign, 31st Regiment, 1803. Lieutenant-colonel, commanding the 24th Regiment, 1823-33. Served with the 31st Regiment in Calabria and the Peninsula, (dangerously wounded at the Coa, mentioned in despatches, medal and three clasps). Served with the 2nd West India Regiment, in the West Indies and on the coast of America, and with the 53rd Regiment in India. Afterwards Lieutenant-General J. Fleming, C.B., colonel, 27th Inniskilling Regiment. Died, 1864.

FOSTER, T. W. Ensign, 24th Regiment, 1793; lieutenant, 2nd February, 1795; captain, 16th July, 1802; major, 22nd February, 1810. In command of Peninsular 2nd battalion when disbanded. Brevet lieutenant-colonel, 1819. Died, March, 1842.

FRANKLIN, R. W. 2nd lieutenant, 24th Regiment, 11th May, 1878. Served in the Zulu campaign. Died at Helpmakaar, 1879.

FRASER, SIMON, (of Balnain). Major and lieutenant-colonel, 24th Regiment, 1762-77. Was a lieutenant in Lord Drumlanrig's Regiment of the Scots brigade, in the Dutch service, and was wounded in the defence of Bergen-op-Zoom, in 1747, when the Scots-Dutch won great distinction. He entered the British service as lieutenant in the 62nd Regiment, afterwards the 60th Royal Americans. He served under Wolfe, at the taking of Quebec, as captain in the old 78th Fraser Highlanders. He was on the staff in Germany, and at Gibraltar. He was principal aide-de-camp to the Marquis of Townshend, when lord lieutenant of Ireland, who described him as " a very intelligent and "prudent man," and employed him on various confidential missions. He commanded the 24th Regiment in America, in 1776, and was mortally wounded at the battle of Stillwater, near Saratoga, 7th October, 1777, as brigadier-general commanding the " advanced corps " of General Burgoyne's army.

GIFFORD, E. F., LORD, V.C. Ensign, 83rd Regiment, 17th April, 1869; lieutenant, 30th November, 1870, exchanged to 24th Regiment; promoted captain, half-pay, 57th Regiment, 1st April, 1874; brevet major, retired. Served in the Ashantee Expedition, 1873-74, (medal and clasp), and received V.C. for gallantry, especially at Becquah, *(See Victoria Cross Roll, Appendix A).* On the staff of Sir Garnet Wolseley, in Natal and Cyprus. In Zulu war, 1879, and took a prominent part in the capture of Cetewayo, (medal and clasp, and brevet majority). Colonial secretary—Western Australia, 1881; Gibraltar, 1882-87.

GLENNIE, FARQUHAR. Ensign, 9th Regiment, 31st July, 1860; lieutenant, 26th February, 1864; captain, 26th March, 1873, exchanged to 24th Regiment, with Captain Airey; major, 24th Regiment, 1st July, 1881; lieutenant-colonel, 9th June, 1886; colonel, 9th June, 1890. Commanded 1st battalion 24th Regiment, 9th June, 1888, to 9th June, 1892. Served with the 2nd battalion 24th Regiment in the Kaffir war, 1878, and was dangerously wounded. Served in the Zulu war, 1879, (medal and clasp).

APPENDIX. 321

GLYN, R. T., C.B., C.M.G. Ensign, 82nd Regiment, 16th August, 1850; lieutenant, 24th June, 1853; captain, 7th September, 1855, exchanged to 24th Regiment; major, 24th Regiment, 23rd July, 1861; lieutenant-colonel, 13th February, 1867; colonel, 13th February, 1872; major-general, 30th September, 1882; retired, honorary lieutenant-general, 30th September 1887. Served with the 82nd Regiment, in the Crimea, from 2nd September, 1885, (medal and clasp, and Turkish medal); with the 24th Regiment, in India, during the Mutiny, (medal); in the Kaffir war of 1877-78, first in command of the Eastern frontier, and afterwards commanding in the Transkei, (several times mentioned in despatches, and C.B.); also in the Zulu war, 1879, first in command of No. 3 column, and afterwards in command of the infantry brigade, 2nd division, and present at Ulundi, (mentioned in despatches, C.M.G., and medal and clasp). Commanded brigade depôt, at Brecon.

GODWIN-AUSTEN, H. H. Ensign, 24th Regiment, 26th December, 1851; lieutenant, 12th October, 1854; captain, 29th October, 1858, transferred to the Staff Corps; major, 18th November, 1868; lieutenant-colonel, 2nd March, 1878, retired. Served in the Burmese war of 1853, as aide-de-camp to his uncle, General Godwin, (medal and Pegu clasp). On special service with the Bhotan expedition, (clasp). Late deputy-superintendent, Trigonometrical Survey of India.

GODWIN-AUSTEN, A. G. Ensign, 89th Regiment, 11th April, 1862; lieutenant, 6th November, 1867; captain, 15th February, 1874, exchanged to 24th Regiment; major, 1st July, 1881; retired, with rank of lieutenant-colonel, 30th May, 1885. Kaffir war, 1878, wounded, (medal and clasp).

GODWIN-AUSTEN, F. Lieutenant, 24th Regiment, 28th February, 1875. Kaffir war, 1878. Killed at Isandhlwana, 22nd January, 1879.

*** The three last named officers were brothers.

GRAHAM, H. M. 2nd lieutenant, 24th Regiment, 11th August, 1880; lieutenant, 8th June, 1881; captain, 25th October, 1890. Burmah, 1885-87, (medal and clasp).

Y

GRANT, G. H. Lieutenant, South Wales Borderers, (24th Regiment,) 7th February, 1885 ; captain, 3rd November, 1891. Served in Burmese expedition, 1885-87, (medal and clasp).

GRIFFITH, T. L. Sub-lieutenant, 24th Regiment, 11th September, 1876. Kaffir war, 1878. Attached to commissariat department in Zululand. Killed at Isandhlwana, 22nd January, 1879.

HARRIS, C. R. Ensign, 24th Regiment, 17th February, 1837 ; lieutenant, 8th January, 1841 ; captain, 14th April, 1846. Killed at Chillianwallah, 13th January, 1849. *(See below, under Harris, John.)*

HARRIS, H. W.- Ensign, 54th Regiment, (from Royal Military College,) 23rd May, 1822 ; lieutenant, 27th April, 1824 ; transferred to 24th Regiment, 14th, July 1825 ; captain, 20th December, 1831 ; commanded the Grenadiers for many years ; major, 14th April, 1846. Served with the 54th Regiment in first Burmese war ; with the 24th Regiment in Canada. Killed at Chillianwallah, 13th January, 1849.

⁎ Major Harris had a brother, J. BEVERIDGE HARRIS, who served many years in the 24th Regiment, retiring as captain in 1837.

HARRIS, JOHN. Lieutenant, Warwick Militia, 1805 ; ensign, 24th Regiment, August, 1807 ; lieutenant, 21st July, 1809 ; captain, 11th May, 1830 ; brevet major, November, 1846 ; major, 14th January, 1849 ; lieutenant-colonel, 21st December, 1849 ; retired, 1849. Served at the Cape ; in the Mozambique (on board the *Astell)*, in the Nepaul and Mahratta wars ; and in the Canadian rebellion.

⁎ Lieutenant-Colonel Harris was father of CAPTAIN C. R. HARRIS, 24th Regiment, *(see above)* and of ENSIGN ALFRED HARRIS, 24th Regiment, who died in Canada.

HARRISON, H. A. Ensign, 24th Regiment, 1st April, 1859 ; lieutenant, 29th July, 1862 ; captain, 8th March, 1867 ; major, 7th July, 1880 ; retired with rank of lieutenant-colonel. Served in the Kaffir war, 1877-78, and in Pondoland, (medal and clasp).

APPENDIX.   323

HARVEY, J. J., D.S.O. Ensign, 24th Regiment, 21st March, 1865; lieutenant, 30th September, 1868; captain, 24th July, 1878; major, 9th June, 1882; brevet lieutenant-colonel, 1887. Served in Burmah in 1885-87, and particularly distinguished himself by his surprise of the noted Dacoit chief—Bo Shwè, (brevet of lieutenant-colonel, medal and clasp). Subsequently employed in command of the Lower Burmah Karen Field Force, 1888-89, (D.S.O.). Died at Ranikhet, 1890.

HARTSHORN, W. Ensign, Cape Mounted Riflemen, from sergeant-major, 24th Regiment, 29th December, 1843; brought back into 24th Regiment as ensign, February, 1844; lieutenant, 3rd April, 1846; captain, 96th Regiment, 8th August, 1851; half-pay, 1855. Served as adjutant, 24th Regiment, at Chillianwallah (wounded) and at Goojerat, (medal and two clasps). Afterwards many years adjutant, 6th Royal Lancashire Militia. Retired with rank of major.

HEATON, WILFRED. Lieutenant, 24th Regiment, 28th February, 1874; captain, 4th September, 1880; major, 28th November, 1885. Served in the Kaffir war, 1877-78; also in the Zulu war, 1879, and present at Ulundi, (medal and clasp, mentioned in despatches); also in Burmah, 1885-87, (medal and clasp).

HITCHCOCK. See DEGACHER.

HODGETTS, T. Joined the 24th Regiment in Bengal, from Europe, as private, in December, 1815. Served with the regiment in the Mahratta war, and returned home with it as sergeant. Promoted from sergeant-major to ensign and adjutant, September, 1830. Subsequently retired. Joined the pension staff at Drogheda in 1844, and from 1851 to 1867 was staff officer of pensioners at London, Canada West. Retired with honorary rank of lieutenant-colonel. Died in Canada, 1892. Lieutenant-colonel Hodgetts is believed to have been the last survivor of the Grand Army of the Deccan, serving under the Marquis of Hastings against the great Mahratta confederacy in 1816-18.

HODSON, G. F. J. Lieutenant, 24th Regiment, 28th February, 1874. A.D.C. to Sir Bartle Frere. Killed at Isandhlwana, 22nd January, 1879.

HOUGHTON, D. Served many years in the junior commissioned ranks. Raised the 45th Regiment (numbered at first as the 59th) in 1741. Colonel, 24th Regiment, 1745-47. Commanded a brigade at the battle of Val or Laffeldt, in 1747. Died a major-general in Flanders soon after.

HOWARD, T. Served in Spain and Portugal in 1705-7. Taken prisoner at the battle of Almanza, and detained two years in France. Bought the colonelcy, 24th Regiment, from the executors of Major-General Gilbert Primrose, in 1717, and held it for twenty years. The regiment from him derived its *sobriquet* of "Green Howards." Died a lieutenant-general, and colonel of the 3rd Buffs, in 1752.

HUGHES, CHAS. Ensign, 24th Regiment, 25th May, 1796; lieutenant, 1st May, 1797; captain, 28th August, 1804; major, 4th June, 1814; lieutenant-colonel, 10th October, 1835. Served in Canada; in Egypt in 1801, (medal); at the Cape; in the action with the French frigates in the Mozambique in 1810; in the Peninsula in 1813, (medal and clasp for actions on the Nive); in the Nepaul war, 1814-15, (wounded at Harriarpore); in the Mahratta war, 1816-18; and commanded the regiment in the Canadian rebellion in 1837-39. Retired on full pay, 1842. Dead.

KELLY, W., C.B. Ensign, 24th Regiment, 31st August, 1787; lieutenant, 27th June, 1792; captain, 5th September, 1795; major, 5th April, 1799; lieutenant-colonel, 22nd February, 1810; brevet colonel, 1813. Commanded the 2nd battalion in the Peninsula, 1810-14, (gold medals for Fuentes d'Onor, Salamanca, Vittoria, and Pyrenees; C.B.). Commanded the regiment in Nepaul and Mahratta campaigns. Died, 21st August, 1818.

APPENDIX. 325

LEE, C. Ensign, 77th Regiment, 8th April, 1825; lieutenant, 30th December, 1828; captain, 12th April, 1844; exchanged to 24th Regiment, through 59th Regiment, in 1845. Served with 77th Regiment at Jamaica, Malta, etc. Killed at Chillianwallah, 13th January, 1849.

LEE, G. A. Ensign, 24th Regiment, 16th May, 1862; lieutenant, 26th January, 1866; captain, 25th March, 1871; exchanged to 68th Regiment, major, 1st July, 1881; lieutenant-colonel, 27th August, 1884; colonel, 27th August, 1888; half-pay, 27th August, 1890; to command of 16th Regimental District, 1892. Served with the Soudan Frontier Field Force, in command of a reserve battalion, in 1885-86, and was present at the battle of Ginniss, (medal and clasp and Khedive's star).

LEE, ELLIS. Ensign, 24th Regiment, 8th July, 1862; lieutenant, 9th March, 1866; captain, 31st October, 1871; exchanged to 65th Regiment, major, 1st July, 1881; lieutenant-colonel, (commanding battalion,) 27th August, 1890.

LETHBRIDGE, E. Ensign, 90th Regiment, 27th February, 1867; lieutenant, 27th October, 1871; captain, 31st August, 1877; exchanged to 24th Regiment; retired, 10th April, 1885. Served in Kaffir and Zulu wars, 1877-78-79 (medal and clasp).

LLOYD, J. D. A. T. Sub-lieutenant, 24th Regiment, 4th December, 1878; lieutenant, 23rd January, 1879; captain, 15th April, 1885. Zulu war, 1879, (medal and clasp).

LLOYD, W. W. 2nd lieutenant, 24th Regiment, 12th June, 1878. Served in Zulu campaign, (medal). Retired.

LOGAN, W. B. Ensign, 24th Regiment, 5th May, 1854; lieutenant, 20th July, 1856; captain, 15th April, 1864; major, 9th June, 1877. Retired as lieutenant-colonel. Served in the Kaffir war, 1877-78 (medal and clasp).

LOGAN, Q. M'K. Sub-lieutenant, 24th Regiment, 23rd September, 1871; lieutenant, 28th April, 1876; captain, 2nd February, 1881; major, 9th June, 1886. Served with 2nd battalion in Kaffir war, 1878, and Zulu war, 1879, (medal and clasp).

LUTMAN, J. H. Ensign, 24th Regiment, and became lieutenant, 16th June, 1843; captain, 14th January, 1849; major, 17th April, 1858; retired, 1862. Served in Punjaub war, 1848-49, including the battles of Sadoolapore, Chillianwallah, and Goojerat, (medal and two clasps).

LYON, SIR J. F., K.C.B., G.C.H. Colonel, 24th Regiment, 1829-42. Commanded a company 25th Regiment, acting as marines, in Admiral Howe's great victory of 1st June, 1794. Served with the 25th Regiment in the West Indies, and with the Queen's German Regiment in Egypt. Commanded the latter as the (old) 97th Regiment in the Peninsula in 1809-10. Commanded a brigade of Hanoverian levies (distinct from the King's German Legion) in the war of liberation in Germany in 1813-14, and at Waterloo. Commanded the Hanoverian troops in France after Waterloo; afterwards commanding the troops in the West Indies. Died, 1842.

MACDONALD, HONBLE. G. Lieutenant-colonel, 24th Regiment, 1803-8; and commanded the regiment at the recapture of the Cape of Good Hope, 1806; afterwards MAJOR-GENERAL LORD MACDONALD. Died, 1832.

MACPHERSON, A. J. Ensign, 24th Regiment, 19th April, 1842; lieutenant, 26th July, 1844; captain, 14th January, 1849; brevet major, 19th January, 1858; major, 29th August, 1866; brevet lieutenant-colonel, 27th December, 1868; retired. Served in the Punjaub war, 1848-49, and was severely wounded at Chillianwallah, (medal and clasp). Served with 24th Regiment in India in 1857-58; was present at the defeat of the Jhelum mutineers, and succeeded to the command of the 24th detachment there. Afterwards in command of the 21st Punjaub Infantry. (Medal.)

₊ Lieutenant-colonel Macpherson is author of *Rambling Recollections of the Punjaub Campaign.* (London, 1889.)

APPENDIX.   327

MAINWARING, H. G.   Ensign, 24th Regiment, 23rd September, 1871 ; lieutenant, 21st September, 1873 ; captain, 7th July, 1880 ; major, 2nd November, 1885. Served in the Kaffir war, 1877-78, including the operations against the Galekas ; and in the Zulu war, 1879 (medal and clasp).

MARLBOROUGH, JOHN, DUKE OF, K.G.   Colonel of the 24th Regiment, 1702-4.

MARRIOTT, RANDOLPH.   Raised the Peninsular 2nd battalion of the regiment. Commanded 1st battalion 24th Regiment and was taken prisoner in the Mozambique, in 1810 ; major-general, 1814. Died, 1820.

MARSACK, H. C.   Lieutenant, Leicester Militia ; ensign, 46th Regiment, 1st May, 1855 ; lieutenant, 24th Regiment, 13th June, 1858 ; captain, 7th January, 1862 ; retired, December, 1863. Served with 46th Regiment in the Crimea, (medal and clasp for Sevastopol). Died, 1892. Previous to entering the British service, Captain Marsack served in the French Army, in the Foreign Legion, in Algiers.

MELVILL, TEIGNMOUTH.   Ensign, 24th Regiment, 20th October, 1865 ; lieutenant, 2nd December, 1868 ; adjutant, 1st battalion, in the Kaffir war, 1877-78, including the operations against the Galekas. Killed at Buffalo River, 22nd January, 1879. *(See Victoria Cross Roll, Appendix A).*

MOFFAT, H. B.   Ensign, 24th Regiment, 6th July, 1864 ; lieutenant, 26th February, 1867 ; captain, 4th May, 1878 ; major, 25th February, 1882 ; lieutenant-colonel, half-pay, 4th March, 1892. Passed Staff College. Was H.M. Vice-Consul at Sevastopol, from February, 1877, to November, 1878. Employed in Natal during Zulu war, 1879 (medal).

MOORE, G. K.   Transferred from 8th Regiment to 24th Regiment, as lieutenant, 12th April, 1879 ; adjutant (1st battalion), December, 1880, to August, 1882 ; captain, 15th August, 1885 ; transferred to Pay Department. Served in Zulu war, 1879 (medal and clasp).

MOORE, H. A. Lieutenant, South Wales Borderers (24th Regiment), 6th May, 1885. Served in the Burmese expedition, 1885-87 (medal and clasp).

MORSHEAD, A. A. Ensign, 24th Regiment, 13th February, 1866; lieutenant, 30th October, 1869; captain, 23rd January, 1879; major, 25th April, 1882; lieutenant-colonel, half-pay, 25th February, 1889. Passed Staff College. Served in the Kaffir war, 1877-78, as district adjutant of the Transkei and Ciskei districts, and was present in the operations against the Galekas and the engagements at Newmarke and Quintana (mentioned in despatches); also served in the Zulu war, 1879 (medal and clasp).

MOSTYN, W. E. Ensign, 24th Regiment, 29th July, 1862; lieutenant, 23rd March, 1866; captain, 31st October, 1871. Killed at Isandhlwana, 22nd January, 1879.

MUCH, W. T. Ensign, 24th Regiment, 11th February, 1862; lieutenant, 14th March, 1865; captain, 14th November, 1874; major, 31st May, 1876; lieutenant-colonel, 28th November, 1885. Commanded detachments 24th Regiment, Indian Naval Brigade, and Madras Sappers and Miners on an expedition to the Little Andaman Island, 6th-8th May, 1867, including an engagement with the savages on 7th May. Was thanked by the Commander-in-Chief in India. Commended by the Government of India, and his services specially noted by order of H.R.H. the Commander-in-Chief (brevet of major). Served in the Kaffir war, 1877-78, in the Ciskei (medal and clasp). Retired.

NORRIS, W. H. 2nd lieutenant, South Wales Borderers (24th Regiment), 6th November, 1887; lieutenant, 31st July, 1889. Retired.

PALMES, G. C. Lieutenant, 24th Regiment, 10th September, 1877; captain, 9th July, 1882; major, 9th June, 1892. Served in the Kaffir war, 1877-78, and was present in the engagement at Quintana; served in the Zulu war (medal and clasp). Now adjutant, 4th Volunteer battalion South Wales Borderers.

APPENDIX.

PATON, G., C.M.G. Ensign, 24th Regiment, 23rd August, 1859; lieutenant, 5th September, 1862; captain, 30th October, 1869; major, 19th May, 1880; lieutenant-colonel, 25th February, 1882; colonel, 25th February, 1886. A.D.C. in the operations in the Malay Peninsula, in 1875-76 (medal and clasp). Served in the Kaffir war of 1877-78, including the operations against the Galekas (medal and clasp, and C.M.G.). Commanded the 1st battalion, 1885-88; commanded 24th Regimental District from 8th June, 1889, to 13th February, 1892. Now commanding the troops in Barbadoes, with local rank of major-general.

PAYNTER, HOWELL, C.B. Ensign, 9th Regiment, 26th April, 1828; removed to 56th Regiment, 21st November, 1828, with which he served in Jamaica; lieutenant, 6th January, 1833, and transferred to 24th Regiment, in Canada; captain, 6th May, 1842; major, 28th April, 1848: lieutenant-colonel, 14th January, 1849. Served in the Punjaub war, 1848-49, including the passage of the Chenab and the actions at Sadoolapore and Chillianwallah (dangerously wounded, medal and clasp). Retired from the service, 8th August, 1851. Died of the effects of a wound received at Chillianwallah.

PENNYCUICK, JOHN, C.B., K.H. Ensign, 78th Highlanders, 31st August, 1807; lieutenant, 10th August, 1812 (anti-dated to 15th January); captain, 14th June, 1821, and placed on half-pay; exchanged to 47th Regiment, in 1825; major, unattached, 25th April, 1834; appointed to 17th Regiment, 8th May, 1835; brevet lieutenant-colonel, 23rd July, 1839; lieutenant-colonel, 12th June, 1840; exchanged to 24th Regiment, 1846. Served in Java, 1811 (medal); Bantam and Macassar, 1814; in the Burmese war, 1825-26 (medal); in Afghanistan, 1839, including the capture of Ghuznee and Khelat (medal); and afterwards in Arabia in 1841. Killed in command of the 5th brigade of the army at Chillianwallah, 13th January, 1849.

PHIPPS, A. B. 2nd lieutenant, 24th Regiment, 14th September, 1878; lieutenant, 23rd January, 1879; captain, 20th July, 1883. Served in the Zulu campaign, in 1879, including the battle of Ulundi (severely wounded, mentioned in despatches, medal and clasp). Retired.

POPE, C. D. A.   Ensign, 24th Regiment, 8th January, 1868; lieutenant, 4th February, 1871.   Served in the Kaffir war, 1878.   Killed at Isandhlwana, 22nd January, 1879.

PORTEOUS, F. P.   Ensign, 24th Regiment, 9th March. 1868; lieutenant, 22nd December, 1869.   Served in the Kaffir war, 1878.   Killed at Isandhlwana, 22nd January, 1879.

PRIMROSE, GILBERT.   Served in the Grenadier Guards from 1680 to 1708, in the Cadiz expedition, at Schellenberg (wounded), and at Blenheim, where he succeeded to the command of his battalion.   Exchanged to the colonelcy, 24th Regiment, with Brigadier Tatton, in 1708.   Died, a major-general and colonel of the regiment, 1717.

PRIMROSE, GILBERT (the younger).   Served in the 24th Regiment from 1709 to 1730, the latter years as lieutenant-colonel commanding.   Died, a brigadier-general, in Ireland, in 1739.   Is believed to have been a natural son of Major-General Primrose.

PUIZAR, MARQUIS OF.   Georges Louis le Vasseur Cougnée, bearing the French courtesy title of Marquis de Puissar, or Puizar, a young French noble, who became a refugee at the Revocation of the Edict of Nantes, and soon after married one of the ladies of the suite of the Princess Mary, afterwards the consort of King William III.   He served in the Irish war, and was colonel of the regiment from 1695 until his death, in 1701.

PULLEINE, H. B.   Ensign, 24th Regiment, 16th November, 1855 lieutenant, 4th June, 1858; captain, 15th November, 1861; major, 4th February, 1871; brevet lieutenant-colonel, 1st October, 1877.   Served in the Kaffir war, 1877-78, during which he raised and commanded a Native battalion, known as Pulleine's Rangers.   Killed in command of 1st battalion 24th Regiment, at Isandhlwana, 22nd January, 1879.

˳ Colonel Pulleine's son, Lieutenant H. P. Pulleine, is now serving with the 1st battalion 24th Regiment.

APPENDIX. 331

PULLEN, J. Quarter-master, 2nd battalion 24th Regiment (from sergeant-major), 21st July, 1877. Served in the Kaffir war, 1878. Killed at Isandhlwana, 22nd January, 1879.

RAINFORTH, T. Ensign, 24th Regiment, 6th May, 1862; lieutenant, 16th May, 1865; captain, 1st April, 1875; major, 1st July, 1881; retired, with rank of lieutenant-colonel, 1882. Served in the Kaffir war, 1877-78. Also in the Zulu war, 1879, and was present at Ulundi (medal and clasp).

ROBISON, W., C.B. Ensign, 24th Regiment, 1795; lieutenant, 24th May, 1796; captain, 25th June, 1803; major, 3rd October, 1811; lieutenant-colonel, 12th December, 1816. Passed Senior Department, Royal Military College. Served in Egypt, 1801; Cape of Good Hope, 1807-10 (deputy quarter-master-general); Java expedition, (deputy quarter-master-general) 1811-12 (repeatedly mentioned in despatches). Afterwards served in India, 1818 (C.B.). Died, 1823.

ROCHE. HON. U. DE R. B. Lieutenant, 24th Regiment, 6th September, 1876; captain, 18th June, 1881; major, 10th February, 1891. Served with the 1st battalion 24th Regiment in the Kaffir war, 1877-78 (medal and clasp); also in Burmah, 1885-87 (medal and clasp). Now deputy assistant adjutant-general in Bengal.

ROSS, T. Ensign, 90th Regiment, 23rd March, 1838; lieutenant, 18th May, 1841; captain, June, 1847; major, 22nd October, 1852; exchanged to 73rd Regiment; brevet lieutenant-colonel, 26th October, 1858; lieutenant-colonel, 24th Regiment, 5th April, 1864; colonel, 1863; major-general, 1868; honorary lieutenant-general, 1881. Commanded a large force on the Nepaul Frontier in 1859; drove the rebels from the plains of Tilawara, attacked them next day in the jungles, when the rebel army, under Bala Rao, retired to Bhotwal, where it was destroyed by Sir R. Kelly (thanks of Commander-in-chief and of Sir R. Kelly for general services on the Nepaul Frontier; medal).

RUFANE, W. Name appears as lieutenant, 24th Regiment, 1727; commanded the regiment on the coast of France, 1757. Afterwards Lieutenant-General Wm. Rufane; colonel, 6th Foot. Died, 1773.

SCOTT, T. (of Malleny, Midlothian.) Ensign, 24th Regiment, 20th May, 1761; lieutenant, 7th June, 1765; captain, 53rd Regiment, 8th October, 1777; lieutenant-colonel, Scotch Brigade (94th Foot), 1794; general, 1830. Carried the King's Colour, 24th Regiment, in the engagements at Wilhelmstahl and the Fulda, in Germany, in 1761. Served with the regiment in America, and was repeatedly engaged in scouting with parties of Indians in 1776-77. Made a very perilous journey, in the guise of a pedlar, through the American lines, to open up communication between Burgoyne's army and New York. The preceding messengers had been taken by the Americans and hanged. His diary of the journey is among British Museum Additional MSS. He served with the 53rd Regiment, under the Duke of York, in Flanders; commanded the Scotch brigade at the Cape and in India; and was in command of a Native brigade at the storming of Seringapatam in 1799. Commanded the Forces in Scotland, 1808-13. At his death, in 1841, at the age of ninety-six, he was the oldest officer in the British army.

SEYMOUR, W. Colonel, 24th Regiment, 1701-2. Was the second son of Sir Edward Seymour, leader of the Tory party in the time of William III. and Mary. Originally an officer of the Coldstream Guards. Commanded a regiment of foot at the Namur. Died, general of marines and colonel, 4th Foot, 1717.

SMITH, LIONEL. Ensign, 24th Regiment, 1794; lieutenant, 28th October, 1795. Served on the staff in North America, and on special service on the West Coast of Africa, for which he was promoted to a company 85th Regiment. Afterwards Lieutenant-General Sir Lionel Smith, G.C.B., G.C.H. Colonel, 40th Regiment. Governor of Mauritius. Died in Mauritius, 1841.

APPENDIX.   333

SMITH, M., C.B. Lieutenant-colonel, 24th Regiment (from major, 29th Regiment), 14th January. 1849. Commanded the regiment at Goojerat (medal and clasps, and C.B.). Reverted to 29th Regiment, December, 1849. Died a major-general.

SMYLY, F. P. 2nd lieutenant, 66th Regiment, 31st January, 1877 ; lieutenant, 24th Regiment, 12th April, 1879 ; captain, 15th August, 1885. Zulu war, 1879 (medal and clasp). Now adjutant, 2nd Volunteer battalion South Wales Borderers.

SPRING, F. Lieutenant, 24th Regiment, 22nd April, 1842 ; captain, 14th January, 1849. Killed in action at Jhelum, 7th July, 1857.

SPRING, W. E. D. Lieutenant, 24th Regiment, 30th April, 1875 ; captain, 1st January, 1881. Served in Kaffir war, 1878 (medal and clasp). Died, 13th January, 1886.

₊ Captain W. E. D. Spring was the son of Captain F. Spring, 24th Regiment, who was killed at Jhelum.

STACK, G. F., K.H. Ensign, 24th Regiment (from 8th Garrison Battalion), 2nd February, 1808; lieutenant, 4th December, 1806; captain, 54th Regiment, 1815 ; rejoined 24th Regiment, 1825 ; major, 24th Regiment, 26th October, 1835 ; retired on full pay, 1840 Served with the 2nd battalion 24th Regiment throughout the Peninsula, and lost an arm at Orthes (medal and five clasps). Afterwards served with the regiment in Canada.

₊ Major Stack is believed to have been the compiler of the Peninsular narrative, included in Chapter vii. of the present history.

STEWART, J. Ensign, 98th Regiment, 27th February, 1845 ; lieutenant, 15th January, 1849 ; captain, 16th April, 1858 ; staff officer of pensioners, 1863 ; major, 5th July, 1872 ; lieutenant-colonel, 1st April, 1875 ; retired. Joined the 24th Regiment after Chillianwallah, and was present with it at Goojerat (medal and clasp).

STREATFIELD, R. C. Ensign, 24th Regiment, 1853; became lieutenant paymaster, 8th June, 1858 ; honorary major, 12th August, 1868 ; honorary lieutenant-colonel, 1st April, 1878 ; honorary colonel, 1st April, 1886. Served in suppression of the Mutiny ; Jhelum, severely wounded (medal and clasp). Died, 1891.

STOYTE, J. Captain, 24th Regiment, 19th May, 1825; major, 8th January, 1841; lieutenant-colonel, 1846. Served with the 1st Royals in the Peninsula (medal and two clasps), in North Holland, and at Waterloo. Served with the 24th Regiment in Canada and India. Exchanged to the command of the 17th Regiment with Colonel Pennycuick, 1847. Died a major-general.

SUGDEN, W. Ensign, 24th Regiment, 17th November, 1866; lieutenant, 1st October, 1870; captain, 23rd January, 1879; paymaster, A.P.D., 5th April, 1882; honorary major, 5th April, 1892. Served in the Kaffir war of 1878, with 2nd battalion 24th Regiment, in command of the mounted infantry of the battalion; also in the Zulu war of 1879, and present at Gingindhlova (mentioned in despatches, medal and clasp); in the Soudan, in 1885 (medal and clasp, and Khedive's star); and with the Soudan Frontier Field Force in 1885-86 (medal).

SURPLICE, R. Ensign, 56th Regiment, 23rd July, 1855; lieutenant, 24th Regiment, 10th September, 1858; captain, 23rd March, 1866. Served in the Kaffir war of 1878 (medal and clasp). Retired as captain. Appointed H.M. Vice-Consul at Boulogne, 16th May, 1883.

SYMONS, W. P., C.B. Ensign, 24th Regiment, 6th March, 1863; lieutenant, 30th October, 1866; captain, 16th February, 1878; major, 1st July, 1881; brevet lieutenant-colonel, 17th May, 1886; brevet colonel, 1st July, 1887; regimental lieutenant-colonel, 31st January, 1891. Served with the 2nd battalion 24th Regiment in the Kaffir war, 1878; and in the Zulu war, 1879 (medal and clasp). Served in Burmah in 1885-88, as deputy assistant adjutant and quarter-master general. Organised and commanded the Mounted Infantry in Burmah (mentioned in despatches, brevets of lieutenant-colonel and colonel, and medal and clasp). Commanded the Chin-Lushai Expeditionary Force in 1889 (thanks of the Government of India, C.B., and clasp). Now commanding the 2nd battalion.

** Colonel Symons is the compiler of MS. notes, from which the present Regimental History has been largely drawn.

TATTON, W. Ensign in Cornwall's Regiment (9th Foot), 1st June, 1687; became lieutenant-colonel, 24th Regiment, 1692. Was selected as assistant quarter-master-general at the outset of the Blenheim campaign on account of his intimate personal knowledge of Germany. Present at Blenheim. Became colonel, 24th Regiment, 25th August 1704. Present at Ramillies. Exchanged to Grenadier Guards with Colonel Primrose, 1707. Died a lieutenant-general. Governor of Tilbury Fort and colonel of the 3rd Buffs, 1737.

TAYLOR, PRINGLE, K.H., General. Colonel, 24th Regiment, 1861 to 1884. Served with the late 22nd Light Dragoons in India from 1811 to 1820, including the Mahratta campaigns of 1816-18. At the capture of the hill-fortress of Copal Droog, blew open one of the gates with a galloper gun of the 22nd Dragoons, and led in the forlorn hope, when every man of the party was killed or wounded. Taylor received a ball through the lungs and body, which killed a grenadier behind him. Commanded the Cape Corps cavalry against the Kaffirs in 1823-24. Sent to restore discipline in a mutinous regiment at Malta. Commanded a brigade in British Kaffraria during the Kaffir alarm of 1856-57. Lieutenant-governor and commanding the troops in Jamacia, 1860-61. Died, 1884.

TAYLOR, W. Many years in 32nd Regiment, in which he became major in 1754. Lieutenant-colonel, 9th Foot, 1763. Colonel, 24th Regiment, 1776-93. Died a lieutenant-general, 1793.

THELWALL, J. B., C B. Ensign, 24th Regiment, 4th August, 1843; lieutenant, 3rd April, 1846; captain, 21st December, 1849; brevet major, 21st April, 1859; transferred to 94th Regiment; transferred to Bengal Staff Corps, major, 4th June, 1866; brevet lieutenant-colonel, 28th January, 1868; lieutenant-colonel, 4th August, 1869; colonel, 15th September, 1874; retired with honorary rank of major-general, 1880. Served with the 24th Regiment in the Punjaub war of 1848-49, including the battles of Chillianwallah (severely wounded) and Goojerat (medal and clasp). Served under Sir Sydney Cotton on the Eusoofzie border, 1858; Oude campaign, 1859 (mentioned in despatches, thanked by the Governor-General, C.B., and medal and clasp). Served in the Joyntah Hills during the rebellion of 1862-63. Commanded 21st Bengal Native Infantry in the Abyssinian expedition (mentioned in despatches, and medal). Dead.

TIDY, F. S., C.B. Entered the army as a volunteer, 1792. Served in the West Indies, at Corunna, Walcheren, Genoa, Waterloo (commanding 3rd battalion 14th Regiment; C.B., and medal), the Ionian Islands, and India. Lieutenant-colonel commanding 24th Regiment, 1833-35. Died at Montreal, 1835.

TIGAR, J. Promoted to quarter-master, with rank of lieutenant, from non-commissioned officer, 24th Regiment, 30th April, 1879; honorary captain, 30th April, 1889. Served in South Africa, 1877-78-79, Kaffir campaign, operations against the Galekas, Zulu campaign (medal and clasp).

TOMPKINS, J. J. Promoted to quarter-master, with rank of lieutenant, from non-commissioned officer, 24th Regiment, 26th November, 1879; honorary captain, 26th November, 1889. Served in South Africa, 1877-78-79, Kaffir campaign, operations against the Galekas, Zulu campaign, and battle of Ulundi, (medal and clasp).

TONGUE, J. M. G. Ensign, 24th February, 1857; lieutenant, 16th April, 1858; captain, 29th August, 1866; major, 23rd January, 1879; lieutenant-colonel, 29th November, 1879; colonel, 29th November, 1883. Served in India, in pursuit of rebels, 1859. Served in the Kaffir war of 1878, including the attack on Intaba-ka-N'dodu; and in the Zulu war, 1879, and present at Ulundi (medal and clasp). Commandant of the School of Musketry, Hythe, 1885-90. To command troops in Barbadoes, with local rank of major-general, 1891. Died, 1892.

TOWNSHEND, H. D. Major, 24th Regiment, 1835; lieutenant-colonel commanding, 1842-46. Served with the 41st Regiment, in America, 1813-14 (severely wounded at Fort Erie). Served with the 24th Regiment in Canada, in 1837-40. Afterwards GENERAL HENRY DIVE TOWNSHEND, colonel King's Own Scottish Borderers (25th Foot). Died, 1882.

TRAVERS, R. H. Ensign, 10th Regiment, 9th December, 1845; lieutenant, 24th Regiment, 5th January, 1849; captain, 7th August, 1857; major, 7th January, 1862; lieutenant-colonel, 48th Regiment, 12th November, 1870; commanded 48th Regiment, 1870-78; died, commandant of the school of musketry, Hythe, 1879. Served with the 10th Regiment in the operations against Mooltan. Joined the 24th after the battle of Chillianwallah, and was present with it at Goojerat (medal and two clasps).

₊ His son, CAPTAIN J. H. DU B. TRAVERS, is now serving in the 24th Regiment.

TRAVERS, R. W. Ensign, 77th Regiment, 23rd January, 1835; transferred to 24th Regiment, February, 1836; lieutenant, July, 1841; captain, 3rd April, 1846. Served with 24th Regiment in Canada. Killed at Chillianwallah, 13th January, 1849.

TROWER, C. V. Sub-lieutenant, 24th Regiment, 17th May, 1876; lieutenant, 17th May, 1877; captain, 8th October, 1881; major, 4th March, 1892; was adjutant, 25th May, 1879, to 25th October, 1882. Served in South Africa, 1877-78-79, Kaffir war, operations against Galekas and Gaikas, and Zulu war, (medal and clasp).

UPCHER, R., D.S.O. Ensign, 24th Regiment, 21st November, 1862; lieutenant, 29th October, 1866; captain, 31st October, 1871; brevet major, 11th November, 1878; major, 4th September, 1880; lieutenant-colonel, 9th June, 1882. Commanded 2nd South Wales Borderers from 9th June, 1886; brevet colonel 9th June, 1886. Commanded 1st Durham Light Infantry from 31st October, 1888. Served in the Kaffir war of 1877-78, in command of the left column, and was present in command of the troops at Quintana, (mentioned in despatches, and brevet of major); and at Kei River; also in the Zulu war, 1879, and commanded 1st battalion 24th Regiment after Isandhlwana, (medal and clasp). Served in the Burmese expedition, 1887-89, (mentioned in despatches, D.S.O., and medal and clasp).

VENNER, SAMUEL. An officer of one of the English regiments in the pay of Holland. Came to England with William of Orange. Colonel, 1691-95.

WARDELL, G. V. Ensign, 24th Regiment, 14th May, 1858; lieutenant, 23rd July, 1861; captain, 10th February, 1872. Served in the Kaffir war of 1877-78. Killed at Isandhlwana, 22nd January, 1879.

WATSON, G. V. Ensign, 66th Regiment, 9th April, 1847; lieutenant, 14th November, 1848; captain, 28th April, 1854; major, 6th February, 1863; lieutenant-colonel, 21st August, 1869; brevet colonel, 21st August, 1874; exchanged to 2nd battalion 24th Regiment, 1875; half-pay, 1877; major-general, 1885; lieutenant-general, 1888.

WAY, A. C. Lieutenant, South Wales Borderers (24th Regiment), 10th January, 1883; captain, 9th June, 1892. Served with Burmese expedition, 1885-87, (mentioned in despatches, medal and clasp). Employed with Gold Coast Constabulary, 18th July, 1889.

WEALLENS, W. 2nd lieutenant, 24th Regiment, 11th May, 1878; lieutenant, 23rd January, 1879; captain, 30th September, 1882; adjutant, 25th March, 1890. Served in Zulu war, 1879, and was present at Ulundi, (medal and clasp).

WENTWORTH, THOS. Appointed colonel 24th Regiment, from 39th Foot, in 1737. Transferred to 2nd Irish Horse (now 5th Dragoon Guards), 1745. British ambassador at Turin; became major-general. Died, November, 1747.

WHITE, F. F. Ensign, 15th February, 1850; lieutenant, 5th May, 1854; paymaster, 1st battalion 24th Regiment, 11th July, 1856; honorary major, 11th July, 1866. Killed at Isandhlwana, 22nd January, 1879.

WHYTE, RICH. Many years an officer in the 3rd Dragoons (now Hussars), in which he got his troop, 1769. Raised and commanded the old 96th Regiment (British Musketeers), of 1780-83. Colonel of the 24th Regiment, 1793-1807; became lieutenant-general. Died, 1807.

WILLIAMS, G. E. L. Ensign, 24th Regiment, 23rd April, 1841; lieutenant, 22nd August, 1844; captain, 14th January, 1849. Served in the Punjaub campaign, 1849; present at Chillianwallah (wounded in twenty-three places, medal and clasp). Retired, 1850.

WILLIAMS, H. M. Ensign, 24th Regiment, 5th July, 1864; lieutenant, 28th October, 1868; captain, 23rd January, 1879; major, 30th September, 1882; exchanged to 77th Regiment; retired. Served in South Africa, 1877-78-79—Kaffir war; operations against the Galekas and Gaikas; affair in Perie Bush; Zulu campaign (mentioned in despatches, medal and clasp).

WODEHOUSE, EDM. Ensign, 24th Regiment, 24th March, 1837; lieutenant, 15th January, 1841; captain, 28th April, 1846; major, 8th August, 1851; brevet lieutenant-colonel, 12th December, 1857; lieutenant-colonel, 9th March, 1860; brevet colonel, 1st June, 1862; major-general, 1868; lieutenant-general, 1880; general, 1881. Colonel, South Wales Borderers, 13th November, 1888. Served with the 24th Regiment in Canada and India. Commanded the 1st battalion 24th Regiment, and was selected as the first lieutenant-colonel of the Brecon brigade depôt, (now 24th Regimental District).

WORLLEDGE, A. C. Lieutenant, 24th Regiment, 7th June, 1879; captain, 2nd November, 1885; transferred to Pay Department. South African war, 1879. Served in Natal (medal).

YOUNGHUSBAND, REG. Ensign, 24th Regiment, 20th August, 1862; lieutenant, 29th August, 1866; captain, 14th March, 1876. Served in the Kaffir war, 1878. Killed at Isandhlwana, 22nd January, 1879.

SERVICES OF WARRANT OFFICERS.

BURCK, C. G. Bandmaster, 1st battalion 24th Regiment, 1871-89; warrant officer from 5th September, 1882, to 4th September, 1889.

CABORNE, J. O. Warrant officer, 5th September, 1889; now serving as bandmaster, 1st battalion South Wales Borderers.

COOKE, J. Sergeant-major, 1st battalion 24th Regiment, 22nd November, 1879; warrant officer, 1st July, 1881; sergeant-major, 4th battalion South Wales Borderers, from 20th August, 1883, to 12th January, 1891. At present sergeant-major, 24th Regimental District. Served in the Kaffir war, 1877-78 (South African medal and clasp, 1877-78).

FIELD, A. S. Promoted to warrant officer from 1st battalion South Wales Borderers as sergeant-major of the Provisional battalion, 1st May, 1891.

FIELD, J. T. Sergeant-major, 1st battalion 24th Regiment, 21st August, 1883; warrant officer, 21st August, 1883. Served in the Mounted Infantry, in the Kaffir war, 1877-78; also in the Zulu war, 1878-79 (South African medal and clasp, 1877-78-79). At present sergeant-major, 1st battalion South Wales Borderers.

GALLAGHER, H. Promoted to warrant officer as sergeant-major, 2nd battalion South Wales Borderers, 9th January, 1889. Served in the Kaffir and Zulu wars, 1877-78-79, and was present at Rorke's Drift (South African medal and clasp, 1877-78-79).

O'DONNELL, P. Promoted to Warrant officer, as bandmaster, 2nd battalion South Wales Borderers, 20th September, 1884. Served in Afghanistan, 1878-80 (Afghan medal, and clasps for Charasiab and Cabul).

SUCCESSION OF COLONELS SINCE THE FORMATION OF THE REGIMENT IN 1689.

Name. 1689-1892.	Date of Appointment.
Sir Edward Dering, Bart.	28th March, 1689
Daniel Dering	27th Sept., 1689
Samuel Venner	1st June, 1691
Louis Marquis de Puizar	13th March, 1695
William Seymour	1st March, 1701
John, Earl, afterwards Duke, of Marlborough, K.G.	12th Feb., 1702
William Tatton	25th August, 1704
Gilbert Primrose	9th March, 1708
Thomas Howard	10th Sept., 1717
Thomas Wentworth	27th June, 1737
Daniel Houghton	22nd Jan., 1745
William, Earl of Ancram	1st Dec., 1747
Honble. Edward Cornwallis	8th Feb., 1752
William Taylor	15th Jan., 1776
Richard Whyte	13th Nov., 1793
Sir David Baird, Bart., G.C.B., K.C.	19th July, 1807
Sir James Lyon, K.C.B., G.C.H.	7th Sept., 1829
Robert Ellice	2nd Nov., 1842
Honble. J. Finch, C.B.	19th June, 1856
Pringle Taylor, K.H.	26th Nov., 1861
Sir Charles H. Ellice, G.C.B.	6th April, 1884
Edmund Wodehouse	13th Nov., 1888

HONORARY COLONELS OF THE THIRD AND FOURTH BATTALIONS SINCE THE FORMATION OF THE REGIMENT IN FOUR BATTALIONS IN 1881.

1881-92.

3rd Battalion (late Royal South Wales Borderers Militia):

A. Lord Ormathwaite	30th Dec., 1876

4th Battalion (late Royal Montgomery Militia):

J. Hayward Hayward	25th June, 1879

SUCCESSION OF LIEUTENANT-COLONELS COMMANDING BATTALIONS SINCE THE LAST FORMATION OF THE REGIMENT IN TWO BATTALIONS IN 1858.

1858-92.

Name.	First Battalion.	Became Senior in the Battalion.
William Gustavus Brown		8th August, 1851
(The battalion was commanded by Lieutenant-Colonel A. G. Blachford from 14th July, 1858, during Colonel Browne's absence as brigadier.)		
Edmund Wodehouse		1st Sept., 1861
Richard T. Glyn		13th Feb., 1867
William M. Dunbar		19th May, 1880
Wilsone Black, C.B.		4th Sept., 1880
J. M. G. Tongue		27th Feb., 1882
George Paton, C.M.G.		31st Jan., 1885
Farquhar Glennie		9th June, 1888
G. S. Banister		9th June, 1892

	Second Battalion.	
Charles H. Ellice, C.B.		3rd June, 1858
Thomas Ross		5th April, 1864
F. C. D'Epinay Barclay		14th Nov., 1874
G. V. Watson		31st July, 1875
H. J. Degacher		9th June, 1877
J. F. Caldwell		9th June, 1882
Russell Upcher		9th June, 1886
C. J. Bromhead		25th Feb., 1888
W. P. Symons		31st Jan., 1891

SUCCESSION OF LIEUTENANT-COLONELS COMMANDING THIRD AND FOURTH BATTALIONS SINCE THE FORMATION OF THE REGIMENT IN FOUR BATTALIONS IN 1881.

1881-92.

3rd Battalion (late Royal South Wales Borderers Militia):

W. J. Thomas		4th October, 1876

4th Battalion (late Royal Montgomery Militia):

John Pryce Harrison		19th April, 1879
Offley John Crewe-Read		2nd May, 1882
R. J. Harrison		16th April, 1887

ROLLS OF OFFICERS

From the Monthly Army List,

1823, 1829, 1842, 1852, 1862, 1872, 1879, 1880, 1881, 1892.

OFFICERS OF 24TH REGIMENT, JULY, 1823.

Colonel	Sir David Baird, Bart., G.C.B. and K.C.	19th July,	1807
Lieut.-Col.	S. T. Popham	10th Sept.,	1818
Major	Thomas Craig	12th Dec.,	1816
,,	John Hogg	29th Oct.,	1822
Captain	L. Stewart	27th August,	1804
,,	Chas. Hughes	28th August,	1804
,,	J. C. Meacham	28th March,	1805
,,	Wm Gill	6th August,	1806
,,	Jas. Adair	20th June,	1811
,,	Pons. Kelly	10th Sept.,	1818
,,	Robert Brown	21st Oct.,	1813
,,	Edwd. Lane	22nd Oct.,	1813
,,	T. D. Franklin	10th Nov.,	1814
Lieutenant	John Ewing	28th May,	1807
,,	A. N. Findlater	15th Feb.,	1808
,,	Chas. A. Stuart	18th Feb.,	1808
,,	G. L'Estrange	19th July,	1809
,,	John Harris	21st July,	1809
,,	F. Grant	22nd July,	1809
,,	Jas. Nokes	22nd Feb.,	1810
,,	F. B. Bainbrigge	3rd May,	1810
,,	C. F. Barton	30th May,	1811
,,	Jas. Wright	21st April,	1814
,,	Alex Child	3rd August,	1815
,,	Robt. Marsh	13th Feb.,	1817
,,	Ron. Campbell	29th May,	1817
,,	A. Watson	16th August,	1818
,,	Thos. F. Smith (Adjutant)	25th June,	1818
,,	Peter Dore	21st August,	1819
,,	A. McKenzie	3rd Nov.,	1819
,,	Geo. Murray	1st Sept.,	1820
,,	H. Y. W. Hartley	1st Oct.	1820
,,	J. Q. Wall	19th July,	1815
,,	J. W. Harvey	15th March,	1814
Ensign	Alex Dirow	15th Sept.,	1818
,,	Dunc. Campbell	16th Sept.,	1818
,,	G. Frankland	1st Sept.,	1819
,,	J. A. Campbell	3rd Nov.,	1819
,,	J. B. Harris	4th June,	1816
,,	W. Campbell	25th March,	1813
,,	R. Bennett	15th March,	1821
,,	W. H. Buckley	4th Oct.,	1821
,,	W. Campbell (Paymaster)	28th May,	1818
,,	,, (Lieutenant)	6th June,	1809
Adjutant	T. F. Smith (Lieutenant)	23rd July,	1818
Qr.-Mr.	J. Murray	4th Dec.,	1817
Surgeon	J. Featherstone	9th July,	1803
Asst. Surg.	D. Kearney	11th March,	1813

OFFICERS OF 24TH REGIMENT, JULY, 1829.

Rank	Name	Date	Year
Colonel	Sir David Baird, Bart., G.C.B. and K.C.	19th July,	1807
Lieut.-Col.	E. Fleming	6th Nov.,	1823
Major	Chas. Hughes	25th June,	1824
,,	Pons. Kelly	14th April,	1829
Captain	H. D. Townshend	1st Nov.,	1821
,,	Hon. C. T. Monckton	27th March,	1823
,,	John Ewing	25th June,	1824
,,	G. Fitz. G. Stack	25th May,	1815
,,	John Stoyte	27th Jan.,	1825
,,	Wm. Andros	16th June,	1825
,,	C. Hastings Doyle	16th June,	1825
,,	C. F. Barton	12th Dec.,	1826
,,	Jas. B. Harris	15th May,	1828
,,	Rob. Marsh	14th April,	1829
Lieutenant	John Harris	21st July,	1809
,,	F. Grant	22nd July,	1809
,,	H. W. Harris	27th Sept.,	1824
,,	Daniel Riley	15th Dec.,	1825
,,	F. T. Maitland	13th Feb.,	1826
,,	F. F. Cunynghame	8th April,	1826
,,	Nich. Leslie	31st July,	1826
,,	Hy. Young	1st August,	1826
,,	A. G. Blachford	12th Dec.,	1826
,,	L. Heyland	15th May,	1827
,,	Hon. C. Preston	15th May,	1828
,,	A. G. Sterling	14th April,	1829
Ensign	W. G. Brown	7th July,	1825
,,	J. Massy Stack	26th Sept.,	1826
,,	Wm. Spring	30th Dec.,	1826
,,	F. Chetwode	5th June,	1827
,,	J. J. Greig	15th May,	1828
,,	R. C Hunter	10th July,	1828
,,	Jas. George (Adjutant)	17th July,	1828
,,	Peter Grehan	8th June,	1826
,,	P. A. Barnard	14th April,	1829
Paymaster	Alex Tovey	4th Feb.,	1819
,,	,, (Lieutenant)	11th June,	1818
Adjutant	Jas. George (Ensign)	17th July,	1828
Qr.-Mr.	Jas. Murray	4th Dec.,	1817
Surgeon	W. Byrtt	9th Sept.,	1813
Asst. Surg.	John O'Toole	11th Nov.,	1813

OFFICERS OF 24TH REGIMENT, JULY, 1842.

Colonel	Sir J. Lyon, K.C.B., G.C.H., (Lieut.-General)	7th Sept., 1829
Lieut.-Col.	H. G. Townshend	17th August, 1841
Major	John Stoyte	8th Jan., 1841
,,	C. H. Doyle	17th August, 1841
Captain	R. Marsh	14th April, 1829
,,	J. Harris	11th May, 1830
,,	H. W. Harris	30th Dec., 1831
,,	F. T. Maitland	12th April, 1833
,,	J. A. Lutman	13th Feb., 1835
,,	Daniel Riley	25th Oct., 1835
,,	Henry Young	3rd Nov., 1837
,,	Nich. Leslie	8th Jan., 1841
,,	A. G. Blachford	17th August, 1841
,,	Howell Paynter	6th May, 1842
Lieutenant	W. G. Brown	11th May, 1830
,,	Wm. Spring	1st June, 1832
,,	E. G. James	16th July, 1829
,,	J. J. Greig	21st March, 1834
,,	J. Monck Mason	25th Oct., 1835
,,	R. Wm. Travers	27th March, 1840
,,	Chas. R. Harris	8th Jan., 1841
,,	E. Wodehouse	15th Jan., 1841
,,	E. J. J. Fleming	17th August, 1841
,,	Louis Bazalgette	24th Sept., 1841
,,	T. Hodgetts (Adjutant)	13th March, 1845
,,	F. Spring	22nd April, 1842
,,	J. S. Shore	6th May, 1842
Ensign	J. G. Fitz Gibbon	25th Oct., 1839
,,	J. H. Lutman	8th Jan., 1841
,,	J. H. F. Stewart	15th Jan., 1841
,,	G. E. L. Williams	23rd April, 1841
,,	R. S. W. Hackett	17th August, 1841
,,	J. S. Payne	24th Sept., 1841
,,	P. W. C. Lipyeatt	22nd April, 1842
,,	Alf. Woodgate	6th May, 1842
Paymaster	G. A. Ferrier	29th March, 1842
Adjutant	Thos. Hodgetts (Lieutenant)	1st June, 1835
,,	,,	1st April, 1842
Qr.-Mr.	J. Murray	4th Dec., 1817
Surgeon	W. Lorimer	3rd Nov., 1837
Asst. Surg.	J. Donald	23rd August, 1839

APPENDIX. 347

OFFICERS OF 24TH REGIMENT, JULY, 1852.

Rank	Name	Date	Year
Colonel	Robert Ellice, C.G.S.	2nd Nov.,	1842
Lieut.-Col.	Wm. Gust Brown	21st Dec.,	1849
,,	Chas. Henry Ellice	8th August,	1851
Major	Aug. G. Blachford	14th Jan.,	1849
,,	Edmd. Wodehouse	8th August,	1851
Captain	Louis Howe Bazalgette	7th April,	1848
,,	Francis Spring	14th Jan.,	1849
,,	John Henry Lutman	14th Jan.,	1849
,,	Francis Chas. Skurray	14th Jan.,	1849
,,	Andrew J. Macpherson	14th Jan.,	1849
,,	R. Aubrie Croker	15th Jan.,	1849
,,	Geo. Fred. Berry	20th Oct ,	1849
,,	John B. Thelwall	21st Dec.,	1849
,,	Wm. Hartshorn	8th August,	1851
,,	Francis Clark	26th Dec.,	1851
Lieutenant	Chas. Mackechnie	3rd April,	1846
,,	Walter Cuming	3rd April,	1846
,,	C. Monteb. Drew	3rd April,	1846
,,	T. Maling Greensill	20th Oct.,	1848
,,	Hy. M. Burns	23rd June,	1848
,,	W. D. H. Baillie	14th Jan.,	1849
,,	Hy. John Hinde	14th Jan.,	1849
,,	R. G. A. de Montmorency	14th Jan.,	1849
,,	Robt. Halahan	1st Jan.,	1849
,,	James Stewart	15th Jan.,	1849
,,	Jos. Chas. Goodfellow	15th Jan.,	1849
,,	Richd. H. J. Travers	15th Jan.,	1849
,,	F. W. A. Parsons	20th Oct.,	1849
,,	Richd. H. Holland	11th Dec.,	1849
,,	W. V. Munnings	1st Feb.,	1850
,,	H. Nangle	10th April,	1849
,,	Jas. Tenant Tovey	8th August,	1851
,,	W. Price Hill	2nd May,	1851
,,	Chas. A. Mouat	16th Sept.,	1841
,,	Robert Lind	26th Dec.,	1841
,,	Saml. Head	20th Nov.,	1848
,,	Chas. P. Geneste	28th May,	1852
Ensign	Robt. L. Crutchley	23rd Nov.,	1849
,,	Fra. Freeman White	15th Feb.,	1850
,,	Sam. John Jas. Burns	11th May,	1849
,,	Chas. H. Perry	18th April,	1851
,,	Alfd. N. Cripps	16th May,	1851
,,	A. D. Hays (2nd Lieutenant)	26th Oct.,	1849
,,	T. Madden (Adjutant)	12th Dec.,	1851
,,	H. H. Austen	26th Dec.,	1851
,,	Wm. Werge	28th May,	1852
Paymaster	G. A. Ferrier	29th March,	1842
,,	,, (Lieutenant)	1st June,	1838
Adjutant	T. Madden (Ensign)	12th Dec.,	1851
Qr.-Mr.	Thos. Airey	28th May,	1852
,,	,, (Lieutenant)	15th Jan.,	1849
Surgeon	Joseph Burke	22nd Dec.,	1848
Asst. Surg.	W. Hanbury	3rd April,	1846
,,	J. L. Holloway	17th March,	1848
,,	J. A. W. Thompson	19th Nov.,	1844

APPENDIX.

OFFICERS OF 24TH REGIMENT, JULY, 1858.

Rank	No.	Name	Date	Year
Colonel		Hon. J. Finch, C.B., (Lieutenant-General)	19th June,	1856
Lieut.-Col.	1	Wm. Gust Brown (Colonel)	21st Dec.,	1849
,,	2	Chas. Hen. Ellice, C.B. (Colonel)	8th August,	1851
,,	1	Aug. G. Blachford (Colonel)	30th March,	1858
Major	1	Edmund Wodehouse (Lieutenant-Colonel)	8th August,	1851
,,	2	Louis H. Bazalgette	30th March,	1858
,,	2	Josh. H. Laye (Lieutenant-Colonel)	31st March,	1858
,,	1	John H. O. Lutman	28th May,	1858
Captain	1	Fran. Chas. Skurry	14th Jan,	1849
,,	1	Andrew J. Macpherson	14th Jan.,	1849
,,	1	Geo. Fred Berry	20th Oct.,	1849
,,	1	John B. Thelwall	21st Dec.,	1849
,,	1	Hy. M. Burns	20th July,	1856
,,	1	Richd. T. Glyn	7th Sept.,	1855
,,	1	Wm. Winniett	21st Dec.,	1855
,,	1	R. G. H. de Montmorency	8th July,	1857
,,	1	Robert Halahan	21st July,	1857
,,	1	Rich. H. G. Travers (Musketry Instructor)	7th August,	1857
,,	1	Jas. Stewart	16th April,	1858
,,	2	Richd. Henry Holland	16th April,	1858
,,	2	Richd. B. T. Thelwall	25th Nov.,	1853
,,	2	Thomas Clark	27th March,	1855
,,	2	F. C. de E. Barclay	5th March,	1858
,,	2	Richard Barter	17th April,	1858
,,	2	W. B. C. Goodison	17th April,	1858
,,	2	Montague Browne	17th April,	1858
,,	2	Thos. G. Peacocke	17th April,	1858
,,	1	W. V. Munnings	28th May,	1858
Lieutenant	1	Jas. Tenant Tovey	8th August,	1851
,,	1	Saml. Head	20th Nov.,	1848
,,	1	R. J. L. Crutchley	26th June,	1852
,,	1	S. J. J. Burns	26th Nov.,	1852
,,	2	T. Madden	11th Oct.,	1854
,,	1	H. H. G. Austen	12th Oct.,	1854
,,	1	A. W. Adcock	4th May,	1855
,,	1	Walter B. Logan	20th July,	1856
,,	1	John C. Warne	26th Feb.,	1856
,,	1	A. J. C. Birch	3rd Nov.,	1856
,,	1	Geo. Scott	8th July,	1857
,,	1	John Johnstone	21st July,	1857
,,	2	R. B. Fox	27th Nov.,	1857

APPENDIX. 349

List of Officers for 1858—(continued).

Lieutenant	2	H. Y. J. Hitchcock	21st Sept.,	1855
,,	2	T. Jones	26th Feb.,	1856
,,	2	E. T. Dunn	31st Oct.,	1856
,,	2	Wm. Franklin	16th April,	1858
,,	2	Jas. H. H. Landon	16th April,	1858
,,	2	Lucas Waring	16th April,	1858
,,	1	J. M. C. Tongue	16th April,	1858
,,	1	J. C. Thomas	16th April,	1858
,,	2	Jas. B. Scott	28th May,	1858
,,	2	H. B. Pulleine	4th June,	1858
Ensign	1	Art. Wm. Fitz Maurice	7th August,	1857
,,	1	Geo. C. Ross	9th Oct.,	1857
,,	1	Hugh B. Church	15th Jan.,	1858
,,	1	Redmond O'Mahoney	3rd March,	1858
,,	1	Thos. P. Butler	23rd April,	1858
,,	2	R. A. Farquharson	24th April,	1858
,,	2	Francis M. Pearson	25th April,	1858
,,	1	Charles H. Fellowes	26th April,	1858
,,	2	E. H. B. Sawbridge	30th April,	1858
,,	2	Wm. R. B. Chamberlin	1st May,	1858
,,	2	C. A. Hewitt	7th May,	1858
,,	2	Wm. Magill	30th April,	1858
,,	2	Geo. V. Wardell	14th May,	1858
,,	1	E. F. A. MacCarthy	21st May,	1858
,,	2	H. Y. Dewé	2nd May,	1858
,,		John F. Caldwell	28th May,	1858
,,		Rob. B. Airey	30th April,	1858
,,		A. C. Henessey	4th June,	1858
,,		F. A. H. Yonge	5th June,	1858
,,		Wm. F. Goodrich	15th June,	1858
Paymaster	1	Fra. F. White (Lieutenant, 5th May, 1854)	11th July,	1856
,,	2	Rob. C. Streatfield (Lieut., 26th Oct., 1855)	8th June,	1858
Adjutant		H. J. Hitchcock (Lieutenant)	16th July,	1858
,,		R. P. Fox (Lieutenant)	16th July,	1858
Qr.-Mr.	1	Thos. Airey (Lieutenant, 15th Jan., 1849)	28th May,	1852
,,	2	John Cusack	14th April,	1858
Surgeon	1	R. Gamble, M.D.	12th March,	1852
Asst.-Surg.	1	Richd. Wolseley	28th July,	1854
,,	1	Chas. C. Dempster	5th May,	1854
,,		Rob. Sutherland	19th Oct.,	1857

OFFICERS OF 24TH REGIMENT, JULY, 1862.

Rank		Name	Date	
Colonel		Pringle Taylor, K.H. (Major-General)	26th Nov.,	1861
Lieut.-Col.	2	Chas. H. Y. Ellice, C.B. (Colonel)	8th August,	1851
,,	1	Edmd. Wodehouse (Colonel)	9th March,	1860
Major	2	Louis H. Bazalgette	30th March,	1858
,,	2	Hon. D. G. Finch	1st July,	1859
,,	1	Richd. T. Glyn	23rd July,	1861
,,	1	Richd. H. Y. Travers	7th Jan.,	1862
Captain	1	Andrew J. Macpherson	14th Jan.,	1849
,,	1	Geo. F. Berry	20th Oct.,	1849
,,	1	Hy. M. Burns	20th July,	1856
,,	1	R. G. A. de Montmorency	8th July,	1857
,,	1	Jas. Stewart	16th April,	1858
,,	2	Thomas Clark	27th March,	1855
,,	2	F. C. D'E. Barclay	5th March,	1858
,,	2	Wm. V. Munnings	17th April,	1858
,,	2	Montague Browne (Instructor of Musketry)	17th April,	1858
,,	1	H. H. Godwin-Austen	29th Oct.,	1858
,,	2	Edm. W. Kent	31st Dec.,	1858
,,	2	Edm. F. Tarte	7th May,	1858
,,	2	Wm. P. Gaskell	1st April,	1859
,,	2	John Johnstone	5th August,	1859
,,	2	Hy. J. Hitchcock	21st Oct.,	1859
,,	2	David Gibson	26th Feb.,	1858
,,	1	W. J. M. Crawfurd	23rd Oct.,	1860
,,	2	Hy. B. Pulleine	15th Nov.,	1861
,,	1	Chas. Watkins	25th June,	1861
,,	1	Hy. Chas. Marsack	7th Jan.,	1862
,,	1	T. E. Anderson	26th July,	1858
,,	1	Sam. J. J. Burns	24th Feb.,	1862
,,	2	John Foot	16th May,	1862
,,		Alex. W. Cobham	10th April,	1847
Lieutenant	1	Alfd. Wm. Adcock	4th May,	1855
,,	2	Walter B. Logan	20th July,	1856
,,	1	John C. Warne	26th Feb.,	1856
,,	1	George Scott	8th July,	1857
,,	1	Rob. P. Fox (Adjutant)	27th Nov.,	1857
,,	2	Ed. Trevor Dunn	31st Oct.,	1856
,,	1	John M. G. Tongue (Instructor of Musketry)	16th April,	1858
,,	1	J. C. Thomas	16th April,	1858
,,	2	A. C. Hallowes	10th Sept.,	1858
,,	2	R. N. Surplice	10th Sept.,	1858
,,	1	G. C. Ross	10th Sept.,	1858
,,	1	Hugh B. Church	24th Sept.,	1858
,,	2	R. S. Brydges Leech (Instructor of Musketry)	29th Oct.,	1858
,,	1	Thos. P. Butler	7th Dec.,	1858

APPENDIX.

List of Officers for 1862—(continued).

Rank		Name	Date	Year
Lieutenant	2	Chas. F. Lloyd	23rd July,	1858
,,	1	Redmond O. Mahoney	3rd Jan.,	1859
,,	2	E. H. B. Sawbridge	5th August,	1859
,,	2	W. R. B. Chamberlin	21st Oct.,	1859
,,	1	W. A. H. Plasket	18th Jan.,	1856
,,	2	John Cusack	14th June,	1855
,,	2	Cha. A. Hewett	14th Feb.,	1860
,,	1	R. P. O. P., Lord Louth	17th June,	1859
,,	2	Geo. Vaughan Wardell	23rd July,	1861
,,	2	Henry Dewé	15th Nov.,	1861
,,	1	John F. Caldwell	15th Nov.,	1861
,,	2	R. H. B. Airey	7th Jan.,	1862
,,	1	Wm. Magill	27th Jan.,	1862
,,	2	R. C. T. Atthill	23rd April,	1861
,,	2	Chas. Wm. Story	24th Feb.,	1862
,,	1	Wm. M. Brander	16th May,	1862
Ensign	1	Hen. F. Brouncker	28th Jan.,	1859
,,	1	H. A. Harrison	1st April,	1859
,,	2	Wm. Hitchcock	31st May,	1859
,,	2	Geo. Paton	23rd August,	1859
,,	2	Chas. J. Bromhead	30th August,	1859
,,	1	Harry R. Farquhar	30th Dec.,	1859
,,	2	Wm. de R. Barclay	31st Dec.,	1859
,,	1	Wm. Dinwiddie	4th July,	1860
,,	2	T. C. Dempster	29th March,	1861
,,	1	Oscar H. Blount	28th May,	1858
,,	2	Geo. Jas. Gordon	23rd July,	1861
,,	1	Albert J. Godfrey	15th Oct.,	1861
,,	2	Albert F. Adams	22nd Oct.,	1861
,,	2	Thos. J. Baynes	15th Nov.,	1861
,,	2	Rich. S. Pritchard	7th Jan.,	1862
,,	1	Percival T. Fortescue	8th Jan.,	1862
,,	2	Wm. Thos. Much	11th Feb.,	1862
,,	1	Thos. Rainforth	6th May,	1862
,,	1	Geo. Art. Lee	16th May,	1862
,,	1	Sam. Gun Raymond	15th Oct.,	1861
Paymaster	1	Fra. F. White (Hon. Capt. 11th July, 1861)	11th July,	1856
,,	2	John H. Chads	28th Jan.,	1862
,,	2	,, (Lieutenant)	29th May,	1857
,,	2	,, (Captain)	15th Jan.,	1856
Inst. of M.	2	R. S. B. Leech (Lieutenant)	17th Jan.,	1862
,,	1	J. M. G. Tongue (Lieutenant)	15th Feb.	1862
Adjutant	1	R. P. Fox (Lieutenant)	16th July,	1858
,,	2	John Cusack (Lieutenant)	3rd Feb.,	1860
Qr.-Mr.	1	Thos. Airey	28th May,	1852
,,	1	,, (Lieutenant)	15th Jan.,	1849
,,	2	Jas. Hawkins	21st Feb.,	1860
Surgeon	1	R. Gamble, M.D.	12th March,	1852
,,	1	,, (Surgeon-Major)	8th June,	1861
,,	2	Jas. L. Holloway	2nd Oct.,	1857
Asst. Surg.	1	Rob. Sutherland	19th Oct.,	1857
,,	2	John Colahan, M.D.	25th May,	1858

OFFICERS OF 24TH REGIMENT, DECEMBER, 1872.

Rank		Name	Date	
Colonel		Pringle Taylor, K.H. (General)	26th Nov.,	1861
Lieut.-Colonel	2	Thos. Ross (Colonel)	5th April,	1864
,,	1	Rich. T. Glyn (Colonel)	13th Feb.,	1867
Major	2	F. C. D'Epinay Barclay (Depôt)	29th Oct.,	1866
,,	1	H. Jas. Hitchcock	2nd Dec.,	1868
,,	2	W. J. M. Crawford	1st Oct.,	1870
,,	1	H. B. Pulleine	4th Feb.,	1871
Captain	1	Wm. Mathew Dunbar	2nd Sept.,	1862
,,	2	Walter B. Logan	16th April,	1864
,,	2	E. H. B. Sawbridge	14th March,	1865
,,	2	W. R. B. Chamberlin	16th May,	1865
,,	2	R. N. Surplice (Depôt)	23rd March,	1866
,,	1	John Moore Gurnell Tongue (Staff)	29th August,	1866
,,	2	John F. Caldwell	30th Oct.,	1866
,,	1	W. Maxwell Brander (Depôt)	13th Feb.,	1867
,,	1	Henry A. Harrisson	8th March,	1867
,,	2	Hugh B. Church	3rd Nov.,	1867
,,	1	Jas. J. N. Buchanan (P.S.C., Staff)	14th March,	1865
,,	1	Wm. Hitchcock	2nd Dec.,	1868
,,	1	Geo. Paton (Staff)	30th Oct.,	1869
,,	1	Harry Rich. Farquhar	22nd Dec.,	1869
,,	1	G. A. Lee	25th March,	1871
,,	2	Ellis Lee	31st Oct.,	1871
,,	1	Wm. Eccles Mostyn	31st Oct.,	1871
,,		Russell Upcher	31st Oct.,	1871
,,	1	Geo. Vaughan Wardell	10th Feb.,	1872
,,	2	Robt. Hy. B. Airey	3rd August,	1872
Lieutenant	2	Chas. Jas. Bromhead	20th Feb.,	1863
,,	2	Thos. Carroll Dempster (Adjutant)	16th April,	1864
,,	2	Wm. Thos. Much (Depôt)	14th March,	1865
,,	2	Thos. Rainforth	16th May,	1865
,,		Thos. John Baynes (Prob.)	30th Jan.,	1866
,,	2	Reg. Younghusband (Instr. of Musketry)	29th August,	1866
,,	2	Wm. Penn Symons	30th Oct.,	1866
,,	2	Edmund H. Randolph (Depôt)	2nd Nov.,	1866
,,	2	Chas. Erskine	16th Nov.,	1866
,,	1	Fred. Carrington (Instr. of Musketry)	13th Feb.,	1867
,,	1	Herbert B. Moffat (P.S.C.)	26th Feb.,	1867
,,	1	Reg. Rye Corcor (Adjutant)	8th March,	1867
,,	2	John J. Harvey	30th Sept.,	1868

APPENDIX.

List of Officers for 1872—(continued).

Rank		Name	Date	
Lieutenant	2	Herbert M. Williams	28th Oct.,	1868
	1	Teignmouth Melvill	2nd Dec.,	1868
,,	2	Levett Holt Bennett	12th May,	1869
,	1	Archer A. Morshead (S.C.)	30th Oct.,	1869
	1	Fra. Pender Porteous	22nd Dec.,	1869
	1	Wm. Carson Allen (Depôt)	27th April,	1870
,,	2	Wm. Sugden	1st Oct.,	1870
	1	John D. Dickinson	24th Dec.,	1870
,	1	Chas. St. L. Wilkinson	25th Jan.,	1871
	2	Chas. D'A Pope	4th Feb.,	1871
,,	1	Hy. Vernon Boothby	25th March,	1871
,		H. G. Going	24th March,	1869
	1	Chas. Winn Ealand	27th Oct.,	1871
,,	1	F. R. B. Liebenrood	27th Oct.,	1871
,,		Chas. Warren Walker (Prob.)	28th Oct.,	1871
,,	2	Gonville Bromhead (Depôt)	28th Oct.,	1871
,,	2	Josh. Hy. Banks	28th Oct.,	1871
,,	2	G. Stanhope Banister	28th Oct.,	1871
,,		Douglas D. Pryce (Prob.)	28th Oct.,	1871
,,	2	John Hoskyns	28th Oct.,	1871
,,	1	Fra. Tollemache Halliday	28th Oct.,	1871
,,	1	G. J. S. Toler	28th Oct.,	1871
,,	1	Ed. S. Browne	28th Oct.,	1871
,,	1	Ed. Wm. Curteis	28th Oct.,	1871
Ensign	1	John Haughton	28th Oct.,	1871
Sub-Lieutenant	1	Chas. Walter Cavaye	30th Dec.,	1871
,,	1	Edgar Oliphant Anstey	9th March,	1872
,,	1	Hy. Germain Mainwaring	21st Sept.,	1872
Paymaster	1	F. F. White (Major)	11th July,	1856
,,		,, (Lieutenant)	5th May,	1854
,,	2	Alex. S. G. Jauncey	1st Feb.,	1868
Instr. of Mus.	1	F. Carrington (Lieutenant)	17th August,	1870
,,	2	R. Younghusband (Lieutenant)	1st Oct.,	1870
Adjutant	2	T. C. Dempster (Lieutenant)	20th Dec.,	1869
,,	1	R. R. Corcor (Lieutenant)	22nd Dec.,	1869
Quarter-Master	2	Jas. Hawkins	21st Feb.,	1860
,,	1	Wm. Charters	18th July,	1862
Surgeon	2	W. F. Cullen	26th June,	1867
Surgeon-Major	1	J. Coates, M.D.	25th Jan.,	1856
Asst. Surg.	2	V. Mac Swiney, M.D.	31st March,	1868
,,	1	R. C. C. Hickson	31st March,	1864
,,	2	W. Tobin	1st April,	1871

A A

OFFICERS OF 24TH REGIMENT, JANUARY, 1879.

Rank		Name	Date	
Colonel		Pringle Taylor, K.H. (General)	26th Nov.	1861
Lieut.-Colonel	1	Richd. T. Glyn, C.B. (Colonel)	13th Feb.,	1867
	2	Hy. Jas. Degacher, C.B.	9th June,	1877
Major	1	Hy. B. B. Pulleine (Lieutenant-Colonel)	4th Feb.,	1871
,,	2	Wm. M. Dunbar	14th Nov.,	1874
,,	2	Wilsone Black (P.S.C.)	1st Dec.,	1875
	1	Walter B. Logan	9th June,	1877
Captain	2	W. R. B. Chamberlin	16th May,	1865
,,	2	J. M. G. Tongue	29th August,	1865
,,	2	John F. Caldwell	30th Oct.,	1866
,,	1	W. Maxwell Brander	13th Feb.,	1867
,,	1	Henry A. Harrison	8th March,	1867
,,	2	Hugh B. Church	3rd Nov.,	1867
,,	1	Wm. Degacher	2nd Dec.,	1868
,,	1	Geo. Paton	30th Oct.,	1869
,,		Harry Rich. Farquhar	22nd Dec.,	1869
,,	1	Wm. Eccles Mostyn	31st Oct.,	1871
,,	1	Russell Upcher	31st Oct.,	1871
,,	1	Geo. Vaughan Wardell	10th Feb..	1872
,,	2	Chas. Jas. Bromhead	19th Oct.,	1872
,,	2	Farquhar Glennie	26th March,	1873
,,	1	Wm. Thos. Much	14th Nov.,	1874
,,	1	Thos. Rainforth	1st April,	1875
,,	2	A. G. Godwin-Austen	15th Feb.,	1874
,,	1	Reg. Younghusband	14th March,	1876
,,	2	Wm. Penn Symons	16th Feb.,	1878
,,	2	Fred. Carrington	16th Feb.,	1878
,,	2	Herbert B. Moffat (P.S.C.)	4th May,	1878
,,	2	John Jas. Harvey	24th July,	1878
Lieutenant	2	Herbert M. Williams (Instr. of Musketry)	28th Oct.,	1868
,,		Teignmouth Melvill (Adjutant)	2nd Dec.	1868
,,	2	Lovett Holt Bennett	12th May,	1869
,,	1	Archer A. Morshead (P.S.C.)	30th Oct.,	1869
,,	1	Fra. Pender Porteus (Instr. of Musketry)	22nd Dec.	1869
,,	2	Wm. Sugden	1st Oct.,	1870
,,	2	Chas. D. A. Pope	4th Feb.,	1871
,,	2	Gonville Bromhead	28th Oct.,	1871
,,	2	G. S. Banister	28th Oct.,	1871

APPENDIX.

List of Officers for 1879—(continued).

Rank		Name	Date	Year
Lieutenant	1	F. Tollemache Halliday	28th Oct.,	1871
,,	1	Edwd. S. Browne	28th Oct.,	1871
,,	1	Edwd. W. Curteis	28th Oct.,	1871
,,	1	Chas. Walter Cavaye	30th Dec.	1872
,,	1	Nevill J. A. Coghill	26th Feb.	1873
,,	1	Edgar Oliphant Anstey	9th March,	1873
,,	2	Hy. Germain Mainwaring	21st Sept.	1873
,,	1	Jas. Patrick Daly	28th Feb,	1874
,,	1	Geo. Fred. J. Hodson	28th Feb.,	1874
,,	1	Wilfred Heaton	28th Feb.,	1874
,,	1	Ralph A. P. Clements	2nd Dec.,	1874
,,	1	Chas. John Atkinson	28th Feb.,	1875
,,	1	Wm. Edwd. Day Spring	30th April,	1875
,,	2	Quintan M. K. Logan	28th April,	1876
,,	1	Hon. Ulick de R. B. Roche	6th Sept.,	1876
,,	2	Heny. Julian Dyer	10th Oct.,	1876
,,	2	Courtney Vor Trower	17th May,	1877
,,	1	George Champney Palmes	10th Sept.,	1877
,,	2	Fred. Godwin-Austen	28th Feb.,	1875
Sub-Lieutenant	2	Thos. Ll. G. Griffith	11th Sept.,	1876
2nd Lieutenant	1	Edw. H. Dyson	1st May,	1878
,,	2	Reg. W. Franklin	11th May,	1878
,,	2	Wm. Weallens	11th May,	1878
,,	1	Wm. Whitelock Lloyd	12th June,	1878
,,	2	Lionel G. L. Dobree	29th June,	1878
,,	2	Arthur B. Phipps	14th Sept.,	1878
,,	2	Chas. E. Curll	14th Sept.,	1878
,,		Hy. Dolben	25th Sept.,	1878
,,		John D. A. T. Lloyd	4th Dec.,	1878
Paymaster	1	Fra. F. White, Hon. Major (Staff Paymaster, A.P.D.)		
,,	2	J. Mahoney, Hon. Major (Payr., A.P.D.)		
Instr. of Mus.	2	H. M. Williams (Lieutenant)	4th May,	1876
,,	1	E. P. Porteous (Lieutenant)	16th Feb.,	1878
Adjutant	1	T. Melvill (Lieutenant)	7th March,	1873
,,	2	H. J. Dyer (Lieutenant)		
Qr.-Mr.	2	Edwd. Bloomfield	24th Sept.,	1873
,,	1	Jas. Pullen	21st July,	1877

APPENDIX.

OFFICERS OF 24th REGIMENT, JANUARY, 1880.

Rank		Name	Date	
Colonel		Pringle Taylor, K.H. (General)	26th Nov.,	1861
Lieut.-Colonel	1	Richd. T. Glyn, C B. (Colonel)	13th Feb.,	1867
,,	2	Hy. J. Degacher, C.B.	9th June,	1877
Major	2	Wm. M. Dunbar (Lieutenant-Colonel)	14th Nov.,	1874
,,	2	Wilsone Black, C.B. (Lieut.-Col., P.S.C.)	1st Dec.,	1875
,,	1	J. M. G. Tongue	23rd Jan.,	1879
,,	1	John F. Caldwell	23rd Jan.,	1879
Captain	1	W. M. Brander	13th Feb.,	1867
,,	1	H. A. Harrison	8th March,	1867
,,	2	Hugh B. Church	3rd Nov.,	1867
,,	2	Geo. Paton, C.M.G.	30th Oct.,	1869
,,		Harry Rich. Farquhar	22nd Dec.,	1869
,,	1	Russell Upcher (Major)	31st Oct.,	1871
,,	2	Chas. Jas. Bromhead (Major)	19th Oct.,	1872
,,	2	Farquhar Glennie	26th March,	1873
,,	1	Wm. Thos. Much (Major)	14th Nov.,	1874
,,	1	Thos. Rainforth	1st April,	1875
,,	2	A. G. Godwin-Austen	15th Feb.,	1874
,,	2	W. Penn Symons	16th Feb.,	1878
,,		Fred. Carrington (Lieutenant-Colonel)	16th Feb.,	1878
,,	1	Herbert B. Moffat (P.S.C.)	4th May,	1878
,,	2	John Jas. Harvey	24th July,	1878
,,	2	Herbert M. Williams	23rd Jan.,	1879
,,	1	Levett Holt Bennett	23rd Jan.,	1879
,,	1	Archer A. Morshead (P.S.C.)	23rd Jan.,	1879
,,	1	Wm. Sugden	23rd Jan.,	1879
,,	2	(V.C.) Gonville Bromhead (Major)	23rd Jan.,	1879
,,	2	G. Stanhope Banister	5th Feb.,	1879
,,	1	F. F. Halliday	12th April,	1879
Lieutenant	1	(V.C.) Edwd. S. Browne	28th Oct.,	1871
,,	1	Edwd. Curteis	28th Oct.,	1871
,,	2	Hy. Germain Mainwaring	21st Sept.,	1873
,,	1	Wilfred Heaton	28th Feb.,	1874
,,	1	Ralph A. P. Clements	2nd Dec.,	1874
,,	1	Wm. Edwd. Day Spring	30th April,	1875
,,	2	Quintin Mc. K. Logan	28th April,	1876
,,	1	Hon. Ulick de R. B. Roche	6th Sept.,	1876
,,	2	Courtney Vor Trower (Adjutant)	17th May,	1877

List of Officers for 1880—(continued).

Rank			Name		Date	
Lieutenant	-	1	Geo. Champney Palmes	- - -	10th Sept.,	1877
,,		1	Wm. Weallens	- - -	23rd Jan.,	1879
,,		1	Wm. Whitelock Lloyd	- - -	23rd Jan.,	1879
,,		1	Arthur B. Phipps	- - -	23rd Jan.,	1879
,,		2	Chas. E. Curll	- - -	23rd Jan.,	1879
,,		2	Henry Dolben	- - -	23rd Jan.,	1879
,,		2	John D. A. T. Lloyd	- - -	23rd Jan.,	1879
,,		2	Fred P. Smyly	- - -	12th April,	1879
,,		1	Jas. Hy. Connolly	- - -	12th April,	1879
,,		1	G. K. Moore	- - -	12th April,	1879
,,		2	Hugh O'Donnell	- - -	12th April,	1879
,,		2	Arnold W. Birch	- - -	17th May,	1879
,,		2	Alf. C. Worlledge	- - -	7th June,	1879
2nd Lieutenant		1	John D. M. Williams	- - -	21st August,	1878
,,		1	Wm. Cecil Godfrey	- - -	5th Oct.,	1878
,,		2	Percy T. Armitage	- - -	19th Oct.,	1878
,,		2	Thos. Leigh Hare	- - -	26th March,	1879
,,		1	Morden E. Carthew Yorstoun	-	26th March,	1879
,,		1	Reginald Campbell	- - -	26th March,	1879
,,		1	Percy K. H. Coke	- - -	26th March,	1879
,,		2	Anderson L. Kelly	- - -	26th March,	1879
,,		2	Art. Neill Gordon	- - -	25th May,	1878
,,		2	Chas. Sugrue	- - -	17th May,	1879
,,		1	Reg. Williams	- - -	21st June,	1879
,,		1	Francis C. K. Hunter	- - -	2nd July,	1879
,,		2	Arthur T. D. Neave	- - -	2nd July,	1879
,,		2	Joseph J. Burnett	- - -	2nd July,	1879
Paymaster	-	2	J.Mahoney,C.M.G.(Hon.Maj.,Payr.A.P.D.)			
,,		1	T.S.Coppinger,(Hon.Capt.,Payr.A.P.D.)			
Adjutant	-	2	C. V. Trower (Lieutenant)	- -	25th May,	1879
Quarter-Master		2	John Tigar	- - -	30th April,	1879
,,		1	John T. Tompkins	- - -	26th Nov.,	1879

OFFICERS OF LINE BATTALIONS, SOUTH WALES BORDERERS, (LATE 24TH REGIMENT), AUGUST, 1881.

Rank	Bn	Name	Date	Year
Colonel		Pringle Taylor, K.H. (General)	26th Nov.,	1861
Lieut.-Col.	2	Hy. Jas. Degacher, C.B.	9th June,	1877
,,	1	Wilsone Black, C.B. (P.S.C.)	4th Sept.,	1880
Major	1	J. M G. Tongue (Lieutenant-Colonel)	23rd Jan.,	1879
,,	2	John F. Caldwell	23rd Jan.,	1879
,,	2	George Paton, C.M.G.	19th May,	1880
,,	1	Russell Upcher	4th Sept.	1880
Captain	1	Farquhar Glennie	26th March,	1873
,,		W. Thos. Much (Major)	14th Nov.,	1874
,,	1	Thos. Rainford	1st April,	1875
,,	1	A. G. Godwin-Austen	15th Feb.,	1874
,,	2	Wm. Penn Symons	16th Feb.,	1878
,,		Fred. Carrington, C.M.G. (Lieut.-Colonel)	16th Feb.,	1878
,,	1	Herbert B. Moffat	4th May,	1878
,,	2	John Jas. Harvey	24th July,	1878
,,	2	Herbert M. Williams	23rd Jan.	1879
,,	1	A. A. Morshead, (P.S.C.)	23rd Jan.,	1879
,,	1	William Sugden	23rd Jan..	1879
,,	2	(V.C.) Gonville Bromhead (Major)	23rd Jan.,	1879
,,	2	G. Stanhope Banister	5th Feb.,	1879
,,	1	Edwd. Lethbridge	31st August,	1877
,,	1	(V.C.) Edwd. S. Browne	19th May,	1880
,,	1	Edwd. W. Curteis	7th July,	1880
,,	2	Henry G. Mainwaring	7th July,	1880
,,	2	Wilfred Heaton	4th Sept.,	1880
,,	1	Ralph A. P. Clements	4th Dec.	1880
,,	2	W. E. D. Spring	1st Jan.,	1881
,,	2	Quentin Mc K. Logan	2nd Feb.,	1881
,,		Hon. U. de R. B. Roche	18th June,	1881
Lieutenant	2	Courtney Vor Trower (Adjutant)	17th May,	1877
,,	1	Geo. C. Palmes	10th Sept.,	1877
,,	1	Wm. Weallens	23rd Jan.	1879
,,	1	Wm. Whitelocke Lloyd	23rd Jan.,	1879
,,	2	Arthur B. Phipps	23rd Jan.,	1879
,,	2	Charles E. Curll	23rd Jan.,	1879
,,	1	Henry Dolben	23rd Jan.,	1879
,,	1	John D. A. T. Lloyd	23rd Jan.,	1879
,,	2	Fred. Smyly	12th April,	1879

APPENDIX. 359

List of Officers for 1881—(continued).

Lieutenant	1	G. K. Moore (Adjutant)	12th April,	1879
,,		Hugh O'Donnell (Prob.)	12th April,	1879
,,	1	Arnold W. Birch	17th May,	1879
,,	2	Alf. C. Worlledge	7th June,	1879
,,	1	Wm. Cecil Godfrey	19th May,	1880
,,	2	Percy C. Armitage	7th July,	1880
,,	1	Reginald Campbell	7th July,	1880
,,	2	Anderson L. Kelly	16th August,	1880
,,	2	Wm. Stewart	30th Nov.	1877
,,	1	Reg. Williams	16th Oct.,	1880
,,	2	Francis C. K. Hunter	4th Dec.	1880
,,	1	Arthur T. D. Neave	1st Jan.,	1881
,,	2	Joseph J. Burnett	1st Jan.,	1881
,,		Henry M. Graham	18th June,	1881
,,	2	Arthur M. Sugden	11th August,	1880
,,	2	Edmd. Thwaytes	11th August,	1880
,,	2	Francis C. Grant	11th August,	1880
,,	1	Henry E. Every	23rd Oct.,	1880
,,	2	Rob. M. Rainey	22nd Jan.,	1881
,,	2	L. C. H. Stainforth	22nd Jan.,	1881
,,	2	John H. du C. Travers	22nd Jan.,	1881
,,	1	Wyndham Honywood	19th Feb.,	1881
,,	1	Douglas J. Gainsford	19th Feb.,	1881
,,	2	Gordon N. Caulfield	22nd Jan.,	1881
,,	2	John Beresford	8th June,	1881
Paymaster	1	T. S. Coppinger (Hon. Capt.) Pymstr., A.P.D.		
Adjutant	2	C. V. Trower (Lieutenant)	25th May,	1879
,,	1	G. K. Moore (Lieutenant)	28th Dec.,	1880
Qr.-Mr.	2	John Tigar	30th April,	1879
,,	1	John. J. Tompkins	26th Nov.,	1879

OFFICERS OF SOUTH WALES BORDERERS, JULY, 1892.

FIRST AND SECOND BATTALIONS.

Rank	Bn	Name	Date	Year
Colonel		Lieut.-Gen. Wodehouse (Hon. Gen.)	13th Nov.,	1888

Commanding 24th Regimental District:

Rank	Bn	Name	Date	Year
,,		C. J. Bromhead	13th Feb.,	1892
,,		,, (Colonel)	31st Jan.,	1889

First and Second Battalions:

Rank	Bn	Name	Date	Year
Lieut.-Col.	2	W. P. Symons, C.B.	31st Jan.,	1891
,,		,, (Brevet Colonel)	1st July,	1887
Major	1	G. S. Banister	15th Aug.,	1885
,,	2	(V.C.) E. S. Browne	2nd Nov.,	1885
,,	1	H. G. Mainwaring	2nd Nov.,	1885
,,	2	W. Heaton	28th Nov.,	1885
,,	2	R. A. P. Clements (D.S.O.)	24th Feb.,	1886
,,		,, (Brevet Lieut.-Col.)	1st July,	1887
,,	1	Q. Mc K. Logan	9th June,	1886
,,		Hon. U. de R. B. Roche	10th Feb.,	1891
,,	2	C. V. Trower	4th March,	1891
Captain		G. C. Palmes	9th June,	1882
,,	2	W. Weallens (Adjutant)	30th Sept.,	1882
,,	1	C. E. Curll	5th Jan.,	1884
,,	2	J. D. A. T. Lloyd	15th April,	1885
,,		F. P. Smyly	15th August,	1885
,,	2	A. W. Birch	15th August,	1885
,,		P. T. Armitage	28th Nov.,	1885
,,		R. Campbell	9th June,	1886
,,	1	F. C. K. Hunter	14th June,	1886
,,		A. M. Sugden	20th Sept.,	1886
,,	1	H. E. Every	28th Sept.,	1886
,,	1	E. S. Gillman	20th Jan.,	1887
,,		,,	25th Oct.,	1884
,,		J. H. du B. Travers	25th Feb.,	1889
,,		D. J. Gaisford	1st June,	1890
,,	2	H. M. Graham	25th Oct.,	1890
,,	1	G. Turner	31st Jan.,	1891
,,	2	W. B. Watts	10th Feb.,	1891
,,	1	B. W. S. Van Straubenzee	1st Oct.,	1891
,,	2	G. H. Grant	3rd Nov.,	1891
,,	2	G. F. Whitehead	30th Dec.,	1891
,,	1	H. F. Woodgate	4th March,	1892
Lieutenant	1	A. C. Way	10th Jan.,	1883
,,		,,	29th July,	1882
,,	1	C. A. R. Scott	29th April,	1885
,,		,,	28th Feb.,	1885

APPENDIX. 361

List of Officers for 1892—(continued).

Lieutenant	1	H. A. Moore	6th May,	1885
„	1	A. H. M. Hamilton-Jones	29th August,	1885
„	1	H. G. Casson (Adjutant)	25th August,	1886
„	1	F. St. J. Hughes	25th August,	1886
„	2	C. G. Beauchamp	25th August,	1886
„	1	C. Fitz W. Cooke	10th Nov.,	1886
„	2	J. Going	31st July,	1889
„	1	C. E. Fitz G. Walker	31st July,	1889
„	2	S. S. Bradford	26th March,	1890
„	1	V. Ferguson	1st June,	1890
„		T. S. Marquis	25th Oct.,	1890
„	1	H. P. Pulleine	10th Feb.,	1891
„	2	A. Canning	6th March,	1891
„	1	W. E. B. Smith	1st Oct.,	1891
„	2	W. H. F. Basevi	3rd Nov.,	1891
„		E. G. Jones (Prob.)	18th Nov.,	1891
„	2	M. J. B. de la Poer Beresford	18th Nov.,	1891
„	2	E. E. Bousfield	13th Jan.,	1892
„	2	A. S. Cobbe	4th March,	1892
2nd Lieutenant	2	E. G. Pennefather	16th July,	1890
„	2	N. B. Dunscombe	8th Oct.,	1890
„	2	T. E. Madden	20th Oct.,	1890
„	2	E. W. Jones	18th Feb.,	1891
„		„	4th Feb.,	1891
„	2	F. M. Gillespie	25th July,	1891
„	2	E. W. McK. Ballantyne	25th July,	1891
„	2	F. G. A. Wimberley	9th Sept.,	1891
„	2	A. B. Lindsay	7th Nov.,	1891
„	2	E. C. Margetson	5th Dec.,	1891
„	1	H. W. E. Parker	27th Jan.,	1892
„	1	F. G. C. M. Morgan	12th March,	1892
„	1	H. Cleeve	9th April,	1892
Paymaster	2	S. B. Astley (Hon. Captain)		
Adjutant	1	H. G. Casson (Lieutenant)	31st July,	1819
„	2	W. Weallens (Captain)	25th March,	1890
uarter-Master		J. Tigar	30th April,	1879
„		„ (Hon. Captain)	30th April,	1889
„	1	J. J. Tompkins	26th Nov.,	1879
„		„ (Hon. Captain)	26th Nov.,	1889
„	2	F. Bourne (Hon. Lieutenant)	21st May,	1890

THIRD BATTALION.

Hon. Colonel	Lord A. Ormathwaite	30th Dec.,	1876
Lieut.-Colonel	W. J. Thomas (Colonel, A.D.C.)	4th Oct.,	1876
Major	J. James (Hon. Lieut.-Colonel)	22nd March,	1884
„	J. A. F. Snead (Hon. Lieut.-Colonel)	May,	1878
Captain	H. A. Franklin	28th Feb.,	1885

APPENDIX.

List of Officers for 1892—(continued).

Rank	Name	Date	Year
Captain	(P.S.) J. A. Norton (H.)	25th Sept.,	1886
,,	C. Healey	25th Sept.,	1886
,,	T. W. Jones	10th Sept.,	1887
,,	C. S. D. O. Oldham, Capt., retired pay (H.)	3rd April,	1889
,,	Thomas W. M. Morgan (Inst. of Musketry)	16th August,	1890
,,	S. W. Morgan	1st August,	1890
,,	B. St. J. St. George (Captain, retired pay)	4th July,	1891
Lieutenant	H. J. V. Phillips	27th Nov.,	1886
,,	C. B. Holland	6th July,	1889
,,	H. H. Bromfield	6th Sept.,	1890
,,	H. S. S. Harden	6th Sept.,	1890
,,	H. de B. Hogarth	6th Sept.,	1890
,,	F. H. Walker	11th April,	1891
,,	W. H. Jeffreys	11th April,	1891
,,	C. H. Armitage	11th April,	1891
,,	D. C. S. Gwynne	11th April,	1891
,,	A. S. James	11th April,	1891
2nd Lieutenant	W. H. Kelsall	18th Feb.,	1891
,,	R. D. Stevens	28th Feb.,	1891
,,	G. Maxwell-Heron	19th May,	1891
,,	D. H. Morgan	8th July,	1891
,,	W. R. C. Ralston	24th Oct.,	1891
Inst. of Musketry	Thomas W. M. Morgan (Captain)	19th March,	1892
Adjutant	A. M. Sugden (2/ S.W.B. ; Captain)	4th Sept.,	1890
,,	,, (Captain in Army)	20th Sept.,	1886
Quarter-Master	J. Tigar	15th Sept.,	1883
,,	,, (Hon. Captain)	3rd April,	1889

FOURTH BATTALION.

Rank	Name	Date	Year
Hon. Colonel	J. H. Heyward	25th June,	1879
Lieut.-Colonel	R. J. Harrison (Hon. Colonel)	16th April	1887
Major	A. H. Gardner (Hon. Lieut.-Colonel)	21st May,	1887
Captain	R. T. Anwyl Passingham (H) Hon. Major	2nd March,	1878
,,	W. C. Hunter (Hon. Major)	30th June,	1881
,,	(P.S.) C. E. Isherwood Ramsbottom (Hon M)	18th Oct.,	1883
,,	E. H. A. Tolcher (H, Inst. Musketry)	9th July,	1887
,,	J. Lomax	25th May,	1891
Lieutenant	E. S. St. B. Sladen	21st March,	1891
,,	A. H. P. Harrison	15th July,	1891
,,	F. M. Colvile	15th July,	1891
2nd Lieutenant	W. C. N. Hastings	6th Feb.,	1892
,,	A. E. L. James	9th April,	1892
Inst. of Musketry	E. H. A. Tolcher (Captain)	4th Nov.,	1891
Adjutant	D. J. Gaisford (Captain, 1/ S.W.B.)	1st Feb.,	1892
,,	,, (Captain in Army)	1st June,	1890
Quarter-Master	J. Dovaston (temp. Qr.-Master in Army)	8th Jan.,	1879
,,	,, (Hon. Captain)	8th Jan.,	1889

C.

NOTES ON THE COLOURS.

The regiment would doubtless receive colours very soon after it was raised in 1689, and, moreover, in accordance with custom, every company would be provided with one.

It is understood that none of the early colours are in existence, and—in the absence of evidence—it is quite impossible to say what devices were inscribed on them.

It is well known, from the evidences in existence regarding the colours of the older regiments of James II.'s time, that, generally, the colonel's device or crest occupied a prominent place on, at least, the colonel's or first colour. This latter was almost invariably of some perfectly plain hue throughout, and in the case of the 24th (or Dering's Regiment, as it would then be designated,) "*may*" have been of green silk, with the crest or some device from the coat of arms of Sir Edward Dering (its first colonel) in the centre.

The other colours, viz., those of the lieutenant-colonel, the major, and the various captains, probably had, as a principal feature, the red cross of St. George; anything more, in the absence of information, must be conjectural. This state of uncertainty lasted until well nigh the middle of the last century.

The royal warrant of 1743 directed that "no Colonel should put "his Arms, Crest, Device or Livery on any part of the appointments "of the Regiment," and the fuller warrants of 1747 and 1751 gave very complete details of the colours.

In the case of the 24th Regiment, the King's colour was the "Union," consisting of the crosses of St. George and St. Andrew; in the centre $\frac{XXIV}{REGT.}$ surrounded by a wreath of roses and thistles. The regimental colour was green, the "Union" in the upper canton, the central device as in the King's colour; size, six feet six inches flying, and six feet deep on the pole; length of the pike (spear and ferrule included) to be nine feet ten inches. These dimensions remained in force until 1857.

APPENDIX.

The inspection returns, preserved at the War and Public Record Offices, often throw a good deal of light on the colours of the army. The earliest return of the 24th Regiment to be found is dated Carlisle, May 15th, 1750; with regard to the colours, the inspecting officer, General Onslow, simply states that "they are in good condition."

A close study of these documents reveals the fact that new colours were presented to the regiment in 1763, consequently it may be reasonably supposed that those mentioned by General Onslow as being in good condition in 1750 were, at that date, nearly new, and, therefore, of the pattern ordered and described in the warrant of 1747.

The device upon the new stand of 1763, in accordance with the pattern adopted on other colours of the same period (still fortunately preserved to us), would consist of the "Union" wreath of roses and thistles, rather spread about (covering, in fact, about one-third of the space); in the centre $^{REGT.}_{XXIV}$ worked in gold embroidery on the green silk of the regimental flag, within an oval border, of yellow silk, of fantastic and very free design.

As far as can be made out, another stand of very similar pattern was given in 1774, shortly before the regiment embarked for North America.

The history of these colours is somewhat obscure. The regiment itself was included in the surrender at Saratoga in 1777, but the colours did not fall into the hands of the enemy.* The inspection returns do not throw much light on the matter, but it may be gathered from that source that the stand carried in 1787 was reported as being in "good condition," which certainly leans towards the view that new ones must have been given out after the American War. At all events, the reliable evidence of the "returns" for 1810 informs us that a new set was given out about 1795; following the fashion, the central device consisted of a rather plain "heart"-shaped shield of red silk, thereon $^{XXIV}_{REGT.}$ the whole surrounded by a thinner, and much neater, wreath of roses and thistles.

The history of these 1795 colours was very eventful. They were

---

* See Lieutenant Digby's Journal.

carried through the Egyptian campaign of 1801 ; and upon the occasion of the Union with Ireland, the same year, orders were issued that the cross of St. Patrick should be introduced into the "Union" flag, and the shamrock into the wreath. As a consequence of this, many regiments received new colours from their colonels ; but those of the 24th Regiment, being apparently in good condition, were altered—that is, the "Union" taken to pieces and the cross of St. Patrick inserted, the shamrock also introduced into the wreath in such places where space could be found for it.

The Sphinx and " Egypt," having been authorised to be borne upon the colours and appointments, were at the same time added. This device consisted of a white silk Sphinx, with " Egypt " over, embroidered on a circular piece of red silk, encircled by two laurel branches, the whole about nine inches in diameter. Two were placed on a flag, one on each side, immediately under the central wreath. A sketch of these colours exists at the office of the Inspector of Regimental Colours, as sent from the head-quarters of the regiment in response to a circular dated 1807.

At the inspection, Cape Town, May 15th, 1810, these colours are reported upon as "entirely worn out, having been in use fifteen years." The end of their career was, however, nigh. Their further history may be gathered from the "returns."—" 24th Regiment, 1st " battalion, Bengal, 1812. The battalion are wanting their colours, " which were destroyed on the regiment coming from the Cape to " Bengal "—presumably to prevent them from sharing the fate of the greater part of the battalion, which was captured by a French naval squadron at the entrance to the Mozambique Channel.

By the time of the second inspection of 1813, the battalion had received new colours, pattern much the same as those destroyed, but the Sphinx and " Egypt " embroidered directly upon the silk of the flag, under the wreath, exactly the same on both colours.

The 2nd battalion, raised soon after the rupture of the treaty of Amiens, would receive new colours soon after its embodiment, probably quite similar to the 1812 colours of the 1st battalion, excepting that " 2nd Batt." would be placed in the heart-shaped central shield, immediately under the regimental number. These colours were carried by the 2nd battalion in the Peninsula, at Talavera, Fuentes d'Onor, Salamanca, and the siege of Burgos, then taken home with the staff of six companies. The remaining four, with all the serviceable rank and file and a due proportion of officers, formed a provisional battalion with the 2nd battalion of the 58th Regiment, and served on to the end of the war, most likely—as was the case with the other provisional battalions—without any colours at all.

By the year 1824, the colours of the regiment (given out, as we have seen, in 1812) had become worn out; the "returns" for that year state them to be "very old, and have not the honorary badges "and devices granted to the regiment," evidently referring to nine battle honours which were conferred upon the regiment, by Royal authority, between 1817 and 1825; all excepting one, viz., Cape of Good Hope, having been won by the late second battalion in the course of its distinguished career in the Peninsula and South of France.

A new stand of colours was presented March 21st, 1825; a careful drawing of them has fortunately been preserved by the maker, so we are perfectly able to realize their appearance when new. It will be noticed that the county title makes its appearance for the first time, though its nominal connection with Warwickshire dates from the end of the previous century.

In the centre of the green regimental colour $\frac{24}{REGT.}$ in gold embroidery on red silk, surrounded by a red silk girdle, thereon "Warwickshire" in yellow and gold; the girdle surrounded by a finely embroidered "Union" wreath, completely encircling it, and entwined at the top; below this wreath, the Sphinx and "Egypt," embroidered on the green silk of the flag; over the central wreath a scroll, bearing the words "Cape of Good Hope;" the other eight battle honours arranged on similar scrolls, four on each side of the wreath. The King's colour having precisely similar badges and ornaments.

Without any indication of the event in the inspection returns, or orderly room records, a new stand of colours must have been taken into use at some period between 1842 and 1847, replacing those presented in 1825.

The regimental colour of this set (the Chillianwallah colour) is deposited in St. Mary's, Warwick; a close examination proves that from the design of the embroidery, and other important details, it must belong to a period quite twenty years after the 1825 set was made.

In the centre is the regimental number XXIV alone, worked in Roman characters on the green silk of the flag, surrounded by a red girdle, thereon II Warwickshire.

On the 1825 colours the word is simply "Warwickshire;" the regiment received its county title in 1782, and up to about 1790 was distinguished in the *Official Army Lists* as the "Second Warwickshire." After, or about that date, it is described as the "Warwickshire Regiment," and so continued up to about the year 1838, when it reverted to its older name.

A Union wreath, much fuller in design than that of 1825, crossed at the top and tied at the bottom with large bows of ribbon, surrounded the girdle, the whole surmounted with a crown; the battle honours, nine in number, and the Sphinx, placed probably in the same order as in 1825. A scroll, or label, bearing the word "Goojerat" still hangs by almost a thread to the tattered fragments, it having been probably added, with other Punjaub honours, as soon as convenient after they were authorized.

The history of these colours at Chillianwallah and the disappearance of the Queen's colour is fully set forth in these records, and during the subsequent campaign, indeed for a considerable time afterwards, the regiment had only one colour on parade. A new one was, however, at once prepared, but not taken into use until towards the end of 1850; on the occasion of the inspection at Wuzeerabad, April 10th of that year, the inspecting officer—Brigadier-General Hearsey, C.B.—reports: "'The new Queen's Colour, which arrived "at Calcutta in October, has not yet reached the head-quarters of the "regiment."

This colour now hangs by the side of the regimental one of Chillianwallah fame; it will be noticed that its only device is XXIV in the centre surmounted with the crown, in accordance with the royal warrant of 1843—which directed that henceforth no battle honours or badges of any kind should appear on the Queen's colour, simply the number and crown.

A slight alteration in the size of the colours was made in 1857, which did not, however, affect the regiment, as it carried the so-called Chillianwallah colours until 1866, when they were deposited over the regimental monument in St. Mary's, Warwick.

The large colours, with the gilt spear-headed poles, were ordered to be discontinued in May, 1858, and very much smaller ones authorized, the pole itself to be surmounted by the crest of England—the lion and crown. This change affected the newly-raised second battalion, which received new colours made in accordance with this warrant; size: four feet flying, and three feet six inches on the pole. The central design of the regimental colour was XXIV on red silk inside a red girdle, thereon the word "Warwickshire." A new regulation wreath* (for the future strictly adhered to in all cases) was introduced, having three roses instead of two on each side, a crown over.

No battle honours were now permitted over the crown; consequently the twelve (" Punjaub," "Chillianwallah," and "Goojerat" having been authorized in 1853) were arranged six on a side upon the green silk of the flag, the Sphinx and Egypt at the base under the wreath; the whole surrounded by a silk and gold fringe. The Queen's colour, of similar size and fringed, had simply XXIV surmounted by the crown.

Under what circumstances these colours were lost at Isandhlwana is fully detailed in the records.

A second stand, to replace them, was made in 1880, very similar to those above described, but in accordance with the warrant of 1868, still smaller in size, being only three feet nine inches by three feet on the pole.

As the Chillianwallah colours of the regiment (now the 1st battalion) were retired in 1866, a new set was presented on 21st July, very much the same in design as that adopted by the 2nd battalion in 1858—above described; these colours were taken to South Africa, the deeply interesting history of the Queen's colour and the heroic efforts of Lieutenants Melvill and Coghill to rescue it are very fully

---

* The pattern of this wreath may be seen in the frontispiece.

detailed in this work. The regimental facings being changed from time-honoured green to universal white about 1881, the next regimental colour required by the "South Wales Borderers" will be in accordance with the new regulations—white, displaying the red cross of St. George. Long may the regiment, however, carry its cherished green flag, under which all its honours from the time of William III. have been won.

S. M. MILNE.

APPENDIX.

REGIMENTAL CALL.
24th REGIMENT (2nd WARWICKSHIRE).

REGIMENTAL MARCH.
24th REGIMENT (2nd WARWICKSHIRE).
"The Warwickshire Lads."

ADDENDA.

THE DRUM-MAJOR'S STAFF.—Since the earlier pages of this work went to press, it has been discovered that the authenticity of the foot-note given on page 137 is very doubtful. Another (and more probable) story describes the staff as presented to the regiment in India.

NOTE BY LIEUT.-GENERAL R. T. GLYN, G.B., C.M.G., ON THE OPERATIONS IN BONVANALAND IN MAY, 1878.—After having driven Kreli and his Galekas out of their country, I found they had taken refuge in Bonvanaland. I therefore demanded of "Moni"—the chief of the Bonvanas, a friendly tribe, and brother of Kreli—to give them up. As he failed to do so, I decided to occupy his country, and sent Harrison's company to occupy a strong position near Moni's kraal, where I formed a supply depôt. I ordered Moni to meet me there. The remainder of my force, with the exception of the mounted men, I ordered to move towards the Cwebe Forest, where I heard Kreli was hiding, and with my mounted men visited Harrison's post. There I found Moni's two sons, who said their father was blind, and too old to come and see me, but he had sent them. They promised to find out where Kreli was and to conduct me to the spot, which they did. In the evening they joined me, and reported that Kreli was in the Cwebe Forest. I then pressed on with my mounted men, accompanied by Moni's sons as guides, and surrounded the forest, which was a very large one, as well as I could with the small force with me; and, on arriving at the kraal where Kreli was supposed to be, found it had just been deserted. We followed the spoor for, I think, five days, to the Umtata river, which they had crossed into Pondoland, and there I had to leave them; but we had effectually stopped their returning.

www.ingramcontent.com/pod-product-compliance
Lightning Source LLC
Chambersburg PA
CBHW052054300426
44117CB00013B/2128